TWO BRAZILIAN CAPITALS

ARCHITECTURE AND URBANISM IN RIO DE JANEIRO AND BRASÍLIA

TWO BRAZILIAN CAPITALS

ARCHITECTURE AND URBANISM IN RIO DE JANEIRO AND BRASÍLIA

NORMA EVENSON

NEW HAVEN AND LONDON, YALE UNIVERSITY PRESS, 1973

Published under a grant from the Graham
Foundation for Advanced Studies in the Fine Arts.

Library of Congress catalog card number: 72-91293
International standard book number: 0-300-01540-2

Designed by Sally Sullivan
and set in Baskerville type.
Printed in the United States of America by
Connecticut Printers, Inc., Hartford, Conn.

Published in Great Britain, Europe, and Africa by
Yale University Press, Ltd., London.
Distributed in Canada by McGill-Queen's University
Press Montreal; in Latin America by Kaiman & Polon,
Inc., New York City; in Australasia and Southeast
Asia by John Wiley & Sons Australasia Pty. Ltd.,
Sydney; in India by UBS Publishers' Distributors Pvt.,
Ltd., Delhi; in Japan by John Weatherhill, Inc., Tokyo.

CONTENTS

LIST OF ILLUSTRATIONS

Unless otherwise indicated, all photographs are by the author. Agache refers to Alfred Agache, *Cidade do Rio de Janeiro: Remodelaçao, extensão, e embelezamento* (Paris, 1930). PDF refers to Prefecture of the Federal District, photographic section. *OC* refers to Le Corbusier's *Oeuvre complète.*

Copacabana

Favelas

Public Housing

Public Works in Rio

The Architectural Heritage of Rio

The Ministry of Education and Health Building

The Winning Plan by Lúcio Costa

The Satellites

Residential Districts

Central Business District and Banking Center

The Monumental Axis

PREFACE

The study contained in this book was partly inspired by previous research on the planning of Chandigarh in India. Through that work I developed an interest in the design of new towns, in problems of urbanization in developing countries, and in the nature and symbolic function of capital cities. The scope of the present work involves a consideration of modern architecture and urban design in Brazil seen in terms of the old capital of Rio de Janeiro and the new capital of Brasília. The ramifications of urbanism are wide, and any study involving cities will inevitably touch on matters relating to economics, sociology, and politics. The focus of this investigation, however, is on physical design, and it deals primarily with those aspects of the man-made environment which are still considered, for lack of a better definition, art.

Major research was pursued in Brazil during 1966–67, supported in part by grants from the Social Science Research Council and the American Philosophical Society. Assistance from the University of California was provided by the Center for Latin American Studies, the Professional Schools Research Program, and the Humanities Institute. Released time from teaching for the completion of the manuscript was provided by a University of California Humanities Research Fellowship.

This book is based on material obtained from a variety of published and unpublished sources, from discussions with architects, planners, and government officials, and also from personal observation. Needless to say, the work would not have been possible without the kindness and assistance of many Brazilians.

For facilitating my research in Rio de Janeiro, I owe my greatest thanks to Oswaldo Sampaio of the Secretariat of Public Works of the Guanabara Prefecture. He was not only a continuous source of information and encouragement, but was instrumental in obtaining entrée to other government agencies. Also of great service in furnishing information regarding the planning of Rio was Maria Teresa Camargo da Motta of COHAB, Stelio Roxo of SURSAN, Aecio Sampaio of the Secretariat of Public Works, Helio Modesto of CEDUG, Harry Cole of SERFHAU, and Josephina

Albano of CENPHA. Athanasios Hadjapolous of Doxiadis Associates provided extensive discussion of the Doxiadis plan for Rio, while information on the USAID program was supplied by David Fogle, B. J. Williams, and Layton MacNichol. Visits to Rio *favelas* were facilitated by Peace Corps volunteers James Wygand and Robert Jones.

In my consideration of Brazilian architecture, unusually generous assistance was given by Henrique Mindlin, whose experience, wisdom, and candor were of immeasurable value. Kindness and help were also provided by Wit-Olaf Prochnik, Roberto Burle-Marx, and Lourencio Diegues. I am particularly indebted to Susy Pimenta de Mello of the Federal University of Minas Gerais for her enlightening commentary and also for acquainting me with the national survey of architecture conducted by the University.

My initial study of the planning of Brasília began in 1961 when Lúcio Costa, then visiting the United States, provided a lengthy discussion of his master plan for the new capital. In continuing my investigations, I received considerable assistance from Hollister Kent whose doctoral dissertation, "Vera Cruz: Brazil's New Federal Capital," provides a detailed account of the process of site selection. Study of the Brasília competition was facilitated through original drawings and documents provided by João Villanova Artigas, Henrique Mindlin, Marcelo and Mauricio Roberto, João Henrique Rocha, and the firm of Rino Levi. My particular gratitude goes to Ernesto Silva, former director of NOVACAP and president of the Historical and Geographic Institute of Brasília, who provided extensive information regarding all phases of the Brasília project as well as documents relating to the competition. Research in Brasília was additionally aided by the cooperation of Nauro Esteves of the Department of Coordination of Architecture and Urbanism of the Brasília Prefecture, Italo Campofiorito of the Council of Architecture and Urbanism, Leo David of NOVACAP, and General Gomez Alcedes de Abreu of CODEBRAS. My thanks go also to Paulo Magalões for a detailed presentation of his proposals for Planaltina. Finally, I am deeply appreciative of Oscar Niemeyer's kindness in providing both interviews and access to material in his office.

Cities are dynamic and long-lived, and do not hold still while their portraits are painted. Inevitably, as this book has been in preparation, the rich and varied growth of Rio has continued, and Brasília has entered new phases of development. Perhaps some of the fascination of studying cities lies in the circumstance that one can glimpse only facets of a complex whole, and record only limited aspects of an almost illimitable subject. Whatever facts may be presented and generalizations made, there are truly no conclusions to be drawn. For nothing is concluded.

NORMA EVENSON

Paris, 1973

1. GOD IS BRAZILIAN

Brazil was first an imaginary place, a legendary island akin to Atlantis, lying somewhere west of Europe. Eventually the name was bestowed on part of a continent, real, but even more remote, a land more fantastic than legend, and more filled with promise. Even today, a quality of romantic unreality clings to Brazil. The vastness of its area still largely unsettled, the assumption of wealth untapped, the beauty and lushness of tropical landscapes juxtaposed with the sleekness of modern cities, and a people ranging from primitive simplicity to the most urbane sophistication, all contribute to the contemporary legend and stimulate the modern imagination as much as any Atlantis of the past. Even on Brazilian soil, reality is often difficult to distinguish from myth. The vast body of information, the subsoil of verifiable data which nourishes decision in industrialized societies, does not exist. Truth is elusive, and even the simplest facts are difficult to run to ground. No one, least of all the Brazilians, really knows Brazil except as a mixture of dream and reality. The dream is grandiose and seductive, the reality often harsh and disillusioning. The world's oldest land of the future has promised much, but the fulfillment of the promise is yet to be seen. Brazil is still a land of mystery.

The foreigner of Anglo-Saxon temperament approaches Brazil with reserve, ready to resist seduction, determined not to be charmed by spurious delights or blinded by beauty, convinced in advance that coexisting with the luxuriant landscape and the ease of life for some is a cruel poverty for many. He anticipates a stagnant society, medieval in its stratification, indifferent at the top and apathetic at the bottom. He prepares himself to encounter, together with a people renowned for their warmth and gaiety, a land of economic chaos, technically backward and controlled by an unstable government whose tyranny is sometimes modified only by its inefficiency. Although residence in Brazil inevitably alters many preconceptions, some of the ambivalence remains, and many of the clichés about Brazil are true, more or less. But everything about Brazil seems to be modified by *mais ou menos* (more or less), and this expression is employed more or less continually to describe the rather fluid nature of things.

Nothing is absolute; nothing is certain. All things are affected by other things, and two plus two usually makes four, more or less.

The immediate impact of Brazil is that of nature, not nature in the raw, but nature alluring, abundant, and shamelessly beautiful. The Portuguese settlers in Brazil found no stern and rockbound coast, but a paradise of beaches, mountains, and lush vegetation. One tries to imagine the Puritans landing in Salvador instead of New England, but one cannot conceive of Cotton Mather preaching a sermon in such surroundings, or of anyone listening to it.

The Brazilian landscape does not arouse pious thoughts; there are no sermons in stones, and flowers are not similies for timidity and chastity. The image of a tropical paradise is deceptive, however, since the savage natural force which nourishes and sustains this luxuriance seems to defy human efforts at subjection. Nature in Brazil is not a benign servant of man, but a power still dominant. One is reminded of this when, in Rio de Janeiro, brief heavy rains produce fatally destructive floods and landslides, rendering impassable important highways and streets, demolishing buildings, and disrupting services. Throughout vast areas of Brazil nature still rules uncontested, for, in spite of her potential wealth, Brazil remains in some ways not much changed since the days of colonialism. Communications and transport are bad, health and educational standards abysmal, land often remains in large feudal tracts, industry is undeveloped, and urban settlement has not moved far beyond the coast. In terms of national development, something has gone wrong, and it is difficult to decide if Brazil is to blame for the Brazilians or the Brazilians for Brazil.

Brazilians can provide a number of reasons for the sluggish development of their country: the long overdependence of the Portuguese colony on external rule with concurrent failure to develop self-sufficient local institutions, the attitude of the early settlers as temporary sojourners rather than permanent citizens, failure to attract sufficient immigration, difficulties of topography and climate, and even the racial composition of the country.

No one is more aware of the problems of Brazil than the Brazilians themselves, and recent political administrations, however divergent, have frequently recognized in terms of government policies the pressing need for the development of Brazil's resources. Included in governmental efforts have been programs to foster local urban planning, providing federal aid for the integration of such planning with a coordinated program of national economic development. But even the best laid plans need implementation, and at the moment the ability of Brazil to realize effectively many of her ambitious schemes seems questionable. The most admirable programs may fail to survive the cumbersome bureaucratic machine, may be hampered for political reasons, or lag for lack of technical personnel. The gap between intention and achievement is sometimes great.

However, there is a saying, "God is Brazilian," which, while said in jest, seems to be believed by many Brazilians. There appears a conviction that somehow, no matter what befalls, God will look after Brazil, more or less at any rate. For there is a pervasive sense of magic in Brazil, and miracles sometimes happen.

There are many ways of trying to understand people. The best indication of what people are is what they do, and one of the things they do is build cities. This book is concerned with architecture and planning in two cities in Brazil, the former capital, Rio de Janeiro, and the present capital, Brasília. Both are famous; each forms part of the image of Brazil, yet each is viewed with a somewhat distorted vision. Rio is known to the world primarily as a dream city, a confection of sea and mountains noted for mosaic sidewalks, a pleasure-loving populace and a world-famous curve of beach fringed by modern buildings. Everyone loves Rio, especially people who have never lived there. Brasília, the controversial new capital, begun in 1956 and forced into existence like a hothouse bloom, appears as both dream and nightmare, a stage set of mechanized classicism, lunar in its frigidity, and a triumphant symbol of hope. Both cities are typically and completely Brazilian. In each can be seen some of the best and the worst in modern Brazil. Both provide focal points for contemporary attitudes and efforts in Brazilian architecture and planning, and in each can be read those qualities of Brazil which both repel and attract, which inspire admiration for achievement and regret for promises unfulfilled.

2. RIO DE JANEIRO

Among the cities of the world there are a few whose names convey an immediate visual image, even to those who may never have set foot within their confines. The image may be compounded of historic landmarks, a famous street, a monument, a square, a lofty skyline, and often the visitor does not feel that he has really arrived until he has experienced at firsthand the things which make up his preconception of the city. Rio de Janeiro is unique among famous cities in that its most noted landmarks are natural rather than man-made. Sugarloaf mountain, Corcovado, Copacabana beach, the ring of mountains which surround the bay, are all accidents of nature. Rio is not primarily a city of bricks and mortar, but rather an interweaving of man and nature, perhaps the most successful in the world, a tribute less to an obsessive concern for natural preservation than to the strength of a landscape which, even in modern times, defies obliteration. Although Rio was long the capital of Brazil, it is not a monumental city and has no ceremonial focus. Rio is a city without shrines, except, of course, the beach, and the importance of the beach in the life of the city cannot be overestimated.

In addition to having an identifiable physical image, most great cities embody a collective identity, a mythical personality which, by an unconscious collaboration, is maintained by its citizens and accepted by outsiders. Some of the attraction of such cities is perhaps the personal aggrandizement of participating in and identifying oneself with this collective character. The validity of such urban stereotypes is questionable, of course, and taken individually almost no one is a typical New Yorker, Roman, or Parisian. Yet the force of the myth may be such that one way or another everyone finds himself living up to it, and in terms of the total city, the image may have relevance.

Carioca (the white man's house) is an Indian word which was given to the first settlement of Rio and which subsequently came to refer to the inhabitants of the city and to the legendary personality of Rio. The Carioca, according to the myth, is pleasure-loving, indolent, undemanding, impulsive, and tolerant. This image is customarily contrasted with that of the Paulista, legendary citizen of the rival city of São Paulo, who is energetic, hard driving, efficient, and acquisitive. Whatever the truth of these clichés, it is undeniable that they bear a logical relation to the characteristics of the two cities. Rio, with its beauty and beaches seems a natural setting for the Carioca, while São Paulo, with its prosperous and intensive economic activity, appears a fitting product of the Paulista temperament.

The city of Rio de Janeiro is politically the small state of Guanabara, formerly the Federal Capital District, an area of 538 square miles containing, in 1970, a population of 4,252,000 (fig. 1).[1] On the landward side Guanabara is backed by a range of mountains, the Serra do Mar, and on the seaward side, it lies between two bays, Sepetiba to the west and Guanabara to the east.

The first European to enter Rio harbor was the Portuguese navigator Gonçalo Coelho who discovered the port in January 1504 and, believing himself to be at the mouth of a river, named the site Rio de Janeiro (River of January).[2] During the subsequent period of contest between the French and Portuguese,[3] a fortress community was founded by Estácio de Sá on the Urca beach near the outcropping of Sugarloaf. This village was named, in honor of the king, São Sebastião de Rio de Janeiro, and this remains the official name of the city. Following the defeat of the French and the death of Estácio de Sá, the Portuguese governor-general of Brazil, Mem de Sá, moved the settlement to a fortified hill, the Morro do Castello, within what is now the central business district of Rio, and by the end of the sixteenth century the city had begun to occupy the flatland provided between the then existing hills of Morro do Castello, São Bento, Conceição, and Santo Antônio. From this center, expansion continued and continues westward (fig. 2).

Although in the growth of the city, swamps were filled, hills were leveled, and areas

1. *Sinopse preliminar do censo demográfico* (Rio de Janeiro, Instituto Brasileiro de Geografia e Estatística, July 1971), p. 189. This report is the most recent source of population figures available to the author.

2. Although some Portuguese writers attribute the discovery of Rio to Andre Gonçalves and Amerigo Vespucci in 1502, most historians credit the discovery to Coelho. Another Portuguese navigator, Martin Affonso de Souza, visited the site in 1531 but continued on to São Vicente, near Santos, founding a colony. Rio de Janeiro first appeared on maps in 1515.

3. Although Rio was discovered by the Portuguese, the first settlement on the site was established by a group of French Huguenots led by Nicolas Durand de Villegaignon. The name of the colony was La France Anarctique. In 1560 the French fort was captured and destroyed by Mem da Sá, and in 1565 a second Portuguese expedition arrived under the command of his nephew Estácio de Sá, securing the site for Portugal. In 1578, during the governorship of Salvador Corrêa de Sá, French ships entered the harbor in an attempt to seize the city and establish as king of Brazil Prior do Crato, a son of the Duque de Beja. Although the governor was in the interior with most of his military forces, it is reported that his wife, Dona Ignez de Souza, organized the townspeople to light fires along the shore at night and beat upon boxes in an attempt to create the illusion of a large fighting force. After ten days, the French weighed anchor and left. Two more French invasions were attempted in the eighteenth century, as a result of Portugal's opposition to Louis XIV in the War of the Spanish Succession. In 1710 a French expedition under the command of Jean François Duclerc attacked the city but, after several engagements, surrendered with 650 men. Duclerc was executed. To avenge this defeat, the following year a large French force under Duguay-Trouin arrived with 18 ships, over 700 cannon and more than 6,000 men, successfully occupying the city, freeing French prisoners, and extracting a heavy ransom before withdrawing.

of shoreline expanded, the pattern of settlement has always been dictated by topography, channeling growth along the valleys and shoreline. The distinctive natural formations of the site have prevented Rio from evolving into the amorphous sprawling mass characteristic of many large cities (figs. 3–8). Rio is a city of places distinguished by natural setting, each physically separate, each with its own identity. Many large cities have, during expansion, incorporated smaller communities whose former existence may remain only as a name. In Rio, however, these clearly defined localities, even within the modern city, frequently retain a sense of place, an individual architectural character, and a sense of community. One usually identifies one's place of residence in Rio in terms of such areas as Botafogo, Copacabana, Tijuca, or Ipanema, and one becomes familiar with the city in terms of its constituent communities.

Throughout Rio one is conscious of the physical setting; the mountains are always visible and usually close at hand. But by and large there has been little effort to build on the hills. Although a few hill areas in Gloria and Catete, together with the long ridge of Santa Teresa and mountainous parts of Tijuca, contain houses, most Cariocas prefer living on flatland (figs. 9–14). Reasons for the general reluctance to occupy the elevated sites of the city include unstable ground conditions with consequent danger of landslides, poor transportation facilities, and, in recent times, the desire for easy access to the beach. This has left the hills free for squatters, and many of the most spectacular building sites in Rio are occupied by favela shacks.

The development of Rio into one of the great cities of Brazil was given impetus by a number of factors. In the early days of settlement, it provided military advantages with its safe port, defensible hills, and abundant water supply. Administratively, it functioned as the capital of the southern part of Brazil, Salvador serving as political center of the North until 1763 when Rio became capital of all Brazil. Although the northern colony had prospered during the early days of settlement as a center of sugar production, a sugar slump in the middle of the seventeenth century brought depression to the North which has been a problem area ever since, rallying only during a brief rubber boom early in the twentieth century.[4] The discovery of gold in the South gave early impetus to immigration and development, and as mining declined, the production of coffee helped maintain southern prosperity. The excellent harbor

4. The rubber boom was responsible for a remarkable architectural efflorescence in the Amazon city of Manaus. With the development of the vulcanizing process in the nineteenth century, the demand for the product of the wild rubber tree which was native to the Brazilian forests caused a sudden growth and prosperity in what had been a relatively small town. By 1910 Manaus was exporting more than 75 percent of the world's rubber. Favoring an opulent Second Empire style, the city adorned itself with lavish private villas and government buildings of Italian marble, its most spectacular monument being an ornate 1,200-seat opera house in which world-renowned artists performed. The decline both of the city and of the wealth of the region resulted from the increasing dominance of Asian rubber in the world market. In 1876 an Englishman, Henry Wickham, smuggled rubber seedlings to England, whence they were transplanted to begin the plantations of Malaya, Ceylon, and Sumatra. A heavier yield from the Asian trees combined with the efficiency of the plantation system defeated Brazilian competition, and by 1924, Asia was providing 93 percent of the world's rubber.

of Guanabara Bay gave Rio preeminence as a center for southern trade and export.

Rio's position as an administrative center was dramatically augmented when, in 1808, the royal court of Portugal, fleeing the occupation of Napoleon's armies, established itself in Rio de Janeiro, and the city remained the center of the Portuguese monarchy until 1821 when João VI returned to Portugal, leaving his son Dom Pedro I as regent. During this period the city received a number of institutions befitting its capital status—the Royal Printing Press, Library, Museum, Medical School, and Academy of Arts, the Royal Theater of São João, the School of Beaux Arts—together with appropriately monumental building. Following independence, Rio retained its political position, continuing as capital until the official transfer to Brasília in 1960. Even since the foundation of the new capital, a major part of the national government operation has remained in Rio, and although it may be assumed that eventually all federal agencies will move to the interior capital, it is difficult to predict the speed of exodus.

As the political importance of Rio must inevitably decline as a result of the removal of the capital function, so its economic importance appears to have been usurped by São Paulo. In recent years, Rio's share in the Brazilian economy has declined, while that of São Paulo has increased in the same proportion, and the activity of its port is now surpassed in tonnage by the port of Santos serving São Paulo. In 1950–60, the gross domestic product of Guanabara increased at 4 percent per annum, while that of São Paulo grew at 5 percent, and, at present, industrial development in the Rio area is hampered by a shortage of adequately improved industrial sites. It is difficult to say, however, whether Rio is entering a state of decline. Although the city's economy seems sluggish compared with the dramatic boom of São Paulo, Rio, like all large cities, is growing, and current problems are those of expansion.

Like most major cities of the western world, Rio de Janeiro exhibited rapid and dramatic change during the nineteenth century. For the first two hundred years of its existence, the city had expanded gradually in a relatively compact area on the western shore of Guanabara Bay. The increasing political and economic importance of the city, however, produced a sudden impetus to growth, and the population increased from 60,000 to 500,000 toward the end of the century. The introduction of railways and tramlines permitted a pattern of fingerlike extensions from the center, spreading south toward the entrance of the bay, building up the areas of Flamengo, Botafogo, and Laranjeiras, and moving into the heights of Santa Teresa. To the north along the bay, São Cristavo flowered briefly as a fashionable area centering on the Imperial Palace, while, to the west, a reclamation project of the Mangue canal had stimulated settlement in Catumbi and Rio Comprido.

A ridge of mountains divides the city into two zones, North and South. The major direction for expansion was provided in the North Zone, where an area of relatively level land stretched westward along already established routes of transport, and settlement was encouraged by the creation of rail lines leading north and west (fig. 16). The ocean frontage in the South Zone had long been relatively inaccessible because of the intervening mountains, but as tunnels were cut through, beginning around the turn of the century, the South Zone leapt into importance as the most desirable and densely developed residential area. Recent years have increased pressures on available space in all zones, with more intensive land use in terms of high-rise building and continued extension of the city farther from the center. The whole state of Guanabara is becoming more or less urbanized, with a linear pattern of settlement stretching westward from the industrial suburb of Bangú, through Campo Grande, to Santa Cruz. Lying east across the bay from Rio de Janeiro, and linked functionally, although separated administratively, are Niteroi with a population of 324,367 and São Gonçalo with 430,349. Both of these municipalities lie within the State of Rio de Janeiro which surrounds Guanabara on the landward side. Also outside the boundaries of Guanabara, but contiguous to the city of Rio, are a number of communities to the north: Nilópolis (128,948), São João de Meriti (303,108), Duque de Caxais (431,345), and Nova Iguaçu (727,674). Together with Guanabara these communities form a single metropolitan area which could be considered greater Rio, and which had a population of over 7 million in 1970.[5] Because of the small size of Guanabara and its close urban linkage with the surrounding state of Rio, it would appear logical that when Guanabara ceased to be the Federal District it could have been absorbed by the State of Rio. (The city of Rio had, moreover, been part of the state of Rio de Janeiro until, in 1834, it was made an autonomous municipality and declared capital of the empire.) In 1960, however, officials of both the State of Rio and the city apparently were opposed to a merger. The State of Rio administration felt that the large city would become overly dominant in the affairs of the state, while the city leaders feared losing the cherished independence of the city.

What is Rio really like? Beneath the image of the dream city is a city like all cities, and along with most contemporary cities Rio is proclaimed too big, too crowded, and too expensive. Housing is in short supply, transportation is inadequate, and there are too many cars. Rio, like all cities, is "impossible" and getting worse, and people continue to move there.

5. Population figures from the *Sinopse preliminar do censo demográfico,* pp. 189–90. A comprehensive synthesis of economic and population projections for the Rio area may be found in the report produced by the firm of Constantine Doxiadis to accompany a master plan produced in 1965: Comissão Executiva para o Desenvolvimento Urbano (CEDUG)–Doxiadis Associates, *Guanabara—A Plan for Urban Development* (Rio de Janeiro, 20 November 1965) (hereafter cited as CEDUG–Doxiadis). The report predicted that the annual growth rate for Guanabara would decline from 3.3 percent in 1960 to 1.5 percent by the year 2000. The population of Guanabara for this time was projected at 8.4 million with a density of 96 persons per hectare of built-up area. This was considered equivalent to a saturation point based on constraints of topography and levels of desired population density. It was assumed that further population growth would be absorbed by the greater Rio area which, in 1960, had a growth rate of 4.2 percent. It was predicted that greater Rio would increase at a rate of 4 percent up to the year 2000, reaching a population of 18.2 million. For the same period, it was assumed that greater São Paulo would increase at a rate of 7.5 percent to reach a population of 33.7 million. CEDUG–Doxiadis, pp. 196–97.

The enchantment of Rio lies primarily in its larger aspects, in an unsurpassed meeting of mountains and sea and in the relation of city to site. It has been opined, in fact, that Rio is seen at its best from the air, and that closer examination brings increasing disillusionment. A city is more than scenery, and, although the God-made aspects of Rio may distract attention temporarily from many man-made defects, eventually one's gaze will focus on the more intimate texture of the city. It is in terms of bricks and mortar, asphalt and concrete, and men and machines that Rio becomes an imperfect city in a world of imperfect cities.

The initial impression of Rio is that of a "modern" city. Rio began to attract international attention during the 1930s as an innovative center for modern architecture, and the present-day city exhibits a continuing volume of new high-rise construction. The image of modernity is more apparent than real, however, and the urban façade of glass, concrete, metal, and asphalt often masks a primitive level of services and maintenance. Population increasingly outdistances the ability of the city to provide urban utilities, and it is by no means an unusual experience to be marooned without elevator service on the twelfth floor of a modern-looking apartment house, eating by candlelight a meal prepared on an alcohol stove, and eagerly awaiting the hour when rationed water may be available. Services of electricity and gas in Rio are periodically interrupted; water, especially in fashionable Copacabana, is often in short supply, and telephone equipment and service are possibly the worst in the world.[6]

All of Rio seems in bad repair. Buildings are poorly maintained, streets and sidewalks are neglected, and mechanical equipment is in hazardous condition. Everything seems to be breaking down, and the things that work just barely work. There is no margin of safety, and one often feels the whole city is resting on very thin ice. The fantasy arises that one day the final and irreparable breakdown will occur; there will be no water, no elevators, no lights, no gas, no telephones, no paving and side-

6. The increase in telephone service in recent years has been small compared to population growth, and the proportion of telephones (10 per 100 inhabitants in 1962) was actually decreasing during the 1960s. So scarce is telephone equipment that in 1963 the number of pending applications for telephones was reported as 192,820 in the central area of Rio, and 17,050 in the rural area. Because of the shortage of equipment, telephones are seldom disconnected or transferred, and the telephone in a residence often bears the name of a long-gone inhabitant. Telephone directories must carry listings according to address as well as name, and it is not uncommon, in attempting to reach someone, to contact the nearest address that has a telephone in order to convey the desired message. Communications in general are bad. Mailing a letter usually entails a lengthy wait in a post office, for no system of mailbox pickup operates. (It is true Rio possesses a small number of highly decorative cast-iron Art Nouveau street mailboxes, but anyone sufficiently foolhardy to deposit a letter in one of them reportedly risks a six-month delay in having the letter picked up.)

The average quantity of water supplied to the state has been estimated at 318 litres per person per day, of which 30 percent is lost due to defects in the supply system, making an actual real supply of 222 litres per person per day. Large areas of Guanabara are not connected to a sanitary sewer system, and about half the built-up area of the city has no connection to the gas system. Existing sources of electricity are inadequate, and expanding the supply will necessitate modifying the current frequency in the existing system of Guanabara State. All statistics included above are from CEDUG—Doxiadis, pp. 111–19.

walks, and the whole urban façade will disintegrate just as the hills themselves now crumble and slide to the destruction of the city below. No one will mind very much, and everyone will go to the beach.

Brazil is typical of many developing countries in possessing a relatively small educated elite and a great uneducated mass.[7] Conspicuously lacking is the stratum of society which produces technicians and skilled workers, the people who fabricate, maintain, and repair the equipment and products of industrial society and keep the physical mechanism of a modern city in operation. Without such people, much of the talent at the top is wasted.

In spite of the Carioca legend of ease, the visible pace of Rio is frenzied. Street traffic, unregulated and undisciplined, moves with the speed and abandon of a racing competition, while horns blare continually. By and large, Rio drivers are savage, recognizing no law save a pecking order of size and horsepower. Buses tear through the streets, weaving and lurching with total disregard for the vehicles and pedestrians without or the safety of passengers within. In the struggle for survival, such small conveyances as scooters or motorcycles have been eliminated from competition. From observation of Rio traffic one would assume that it is required by law to operate all vehicles at maximum speed at all times, regardless of traffic volume, width and nature of street, or proximity to pedestrians (who seem to be regarded primarily as targets).

Driving appears to be considered in Rio as primarily a blood sport, and to the excitement and hazards of the moving traffic are added the challenges of unmarked open manholes, paving breaks, and sudden roadblocks. Streets are poorly marked and, maddeningly, direction signs at intersections are frequently placed after, rather than before, the crossing, enabling the confused motorist to ascertain, when it is too

7. Support for popular education in Brazil was almost nonexistent until an attempt was made at organizing a modern educational system in 1945. By 1950, national literacy had risen to 49.3 percent, with a wide disparity between urban and rural areas; Guanabara's literacy rate was 85 percent.

Until recently, the Brazilian educational system was organized to provide a program of elementary education taking from four to six years depending on the ability of the child, with secondary education divided into a four-year course (the *ginásio*) and a three-year course (the *colégio*). Elementary education may also be followed by commercial and industrial apprenticeships or agricultural and teacher-training programs. In 1971, the Federal Education Council initiated a new organizational pattern for education, combined with a system of decentralized control, which gives increased responsibility to individual municipalities for developing schools. Under the new system, the primary grades and the ginásio will be combined into a First Degree School (Primeiro Grau) providing eight years of schooling for children seven to fourteen years old. A Second Degree School (Segundo Grau) will provide two to five years of schooling, and the university will serve as the third level. Although in theory the government provides free compulsory education for all children between seven and fourteen, school attendance laws have not been strongly enforced, and both the inaccessibility and the low quality of many schools have hindered educational attainment. Among Brazilian cities, Guanabara ranks high in education, exceeding even affluent São Paulo in school attendance. Even in Rio, however, the rate of attrition among pupils is high. It was found that during 1958–68, of the children beginning primary education, only 46.5 percent completed four years. Of students entering the ginásio, only 22.7 percent completed four years, and of those entering the colégio, only 16.1 percent finished the three-year program. Arnaldo Niskier, *A nova escola* (Rio de Janeiro: Bruguera, 1972), p. 63. Middle- and upper-class families tend to favor private schooling over public education, and a 1964 school survey indicated that in Botafogo and Copacabana the percentage of children in public schools was as low as 54 percent and 49 percent respectively. CEDUG–Doxiadis, p. 54.

late, the direction in which he should have gone. In general, the condition of streets deteriorates sharply in the suburbs, where many residential streets are still unpaved, dusty and rutted in dry weather, and impassable morasses when it rains (figs. 19, 20). Rio driving is hard on cars, maintenance is poor, and there is no automobile inspection.[8]

On the credit side, motoring is still an adventure in Rio, and the honeymoon of man and machine is still in force. Automobiles are still luxuries, highly prized and expensive, and behind the steering wheel, it has been observed, the Brazilian thinks he has a god in his stomach.

Although one of the best-known elements of Rio's townscape is the ubiquitous pattern of mosaic sidewalks, Rio is not a city of leisurely strollers. The famous sidewalks, continually eroded by street-widening, are a good idea crudely executed (fig. 17). The black-and-white patterns are composed of stones about one inch in diameter rather roughly laid on a carelessly prepared ground. Well fabricated and maintained, these sidewalks would be a delight, but undulating surfaces slimy with spit, rough joints, and frequent breaks, make them hazardous terrain for walking. Street crossing requires both patience and agility; traffic lights are few, and pedestrians have no recognized rights of way. The only concessions made to foot traffic within the city are to be found in the network of narrow streets in the central business district which are restricted to pedestrians, and also in the periodic open-air markets for which some streets are temporarily closed off (fig. 18).

While in large aspects still a beautiful city, Rio at small scale is not always a gracious city, and it lacks many of the expected attributes of a major metropolis. Long considered the cultural center of Brazil, it provides only a limited array of cultural activities and will disappoint any visitor expecting an active and distinguished legitimate theater, opera, ballet, or symphony. Public art collections are meager, and libraries and educational institutions inadequate. By international standards, it lacks even a first-class restaurant. Rio is not a major tourist city, and, beyond the beach, a few scenic views, and the annual spectacle of the carnival, there is little to attract outsiders. The city belongs primarily to its own inhabitants; it is essentially a place to live, and, in spite of its high-rise urbanity, the social focus of the city is domestic. Rio is a family-centered town.

Although sharing with most modern cities problems of expansion and congestion combined with increasingly brutal incursions of the motor, Rio retains many agreeable physical facets. Perhaps the most reassuring aspect of Rio as a whole is its essen-

8. In 1964 the proportion of automobile ownership in Guanabara was 37.2 per 1000 inhabitants. However, the proportion was higher in central areas of the city: 125 per 1000 in Copacabana, 90 in Botafogo, 85 in Tijuca, and 84 in Lagôa. The rate of automobile ownership is, of course, low compared with the United States and Europe. Parking facilities in Rio are relatively haphazard. The central district has no public parking garages, and existing lots are inadequate. Throughout the city, parking on the sidewalk is commonplace, leaving the street clear for moving traffic but considerably inconveniencing pedestrians.

tial old-fashionedness. Except for the rapid and intensive building within the South Zone and the central business district, Rio is evolving at a relatively slow pace and has yet been spared the orgy of self-destruction which characterizes many North American cities. Although the Second Empire aspects of Avenida Rio Branco have been almost entirely obliterated, many other areas retain a nineteenth-century quality, and, on the whole, Rio may be the best-preserved Art Nouveau city in existence. Both the Second Empire and Art Nouveau flowered late in Rio, and one can date some of the most exuberant examples as late as the 1920s. The old-fashioned open-sided trolley which until recently wound through the heights of Santa Teresa afforded a tour of turn-of-the-century villas, some of which are marvels of fantasy, including imaginative works of Gothic Revival, Swiss Cottage Style, Second Empire, and Art Nouveau. To one whose taste includes picturesque form, bravura decoration, and uninhibited use of color, Rio is a source of constant delight. Even many slum neighborhoods contain small gems of building.

In spite of the relative poverty of the city, Rio is remarkable in terms of total environment and has somehow managed to avoid the seemingly endless areas of physical blight which inundate many more prosperous cities. For it seems one of the paradoxes of our time that the richest societies frequently produce the most repellent physical surroundings. A low general standard of living is not always outwardly manifested in the urban ambient. Even Rio slums, however unsatisfactory in terms of hygiene and density, are seldom eyesores, and the more prosperous squatter settlements, such as Jacarezinho, often exhibit a sensitive adaptation of building to site, as well as an agreeably human pedestrian scale.

One of the most noticeable aspects of Rio, and perhaps one of the most important, is that it is loved by its inhabitants. Whatever the inconveniences and failings of the city, Cariocas seem convinced that Rio affords them as good a life as may be found in an imperfect world. In perhaps no other city do people seem in better accord with their environment. What seem major flaws to outsiders frequently seem minor disadvantages to Cariocas, and traffic hazards, natural disasters, poor services, and governmental inefficiency are met with consistent good nature. If one's house and life are in periodic danger from landslides, if urban utilities are consistently interrupted, if rents are high and accommodations congested and noisy, this is considered a small price to pay for living in Rio.

3. COPACABANA

The word Copacabana originated with the Quechy Indians of Bolivia, who thus designated a sacred site in the Titicaca where they worshipped first their local gods and later the Virgin Mary. An image of the Virgin of Copacabana is reported to have been brought from Bolivia to Rio by a Portuguese adventurer in 1628, and it was installed in a chapel on the coast. One of the earliest books published in Rio (1747) contains an account of a Portuguese bishop who warded off shipwreck by praying to Our Lady of Copacabana, and in gratitude rebuilt the neglected chapel which housed her image. As the legend grew, the name Copacabana was applied to the whole beach area in which the chapel stood.[1]

The beach is still a site for prayer, but not to the Virgin Mary. Popular religion in Brazil has evolved a loose framework of ritual, embracing elements of Christianity, African voodoo, and spiritualism, but recently the fastest growing cult has been that of the goddess of the sea. As part of her worship, prayers and offerings are bequeathed to the outgoing tide, and candles are burned along the beach. When represented in popular art, the goddess appears as a remarkably toothsome young woman rising from the waves, her long dark hair floating about her shoulders, and her spectacular body asserting an emphatic corporeality beneath clinging and diaphanous draperies. She is obviously a goddess to whom one may bring problems, the nature of which one might hesitate to broach to the Blessed Virgin.

Copacabana comes to mind almost immediately when one thinks of Rio, and many people have as their only image of the city its often-photographed crescent of beach bordered by an unbroken façade of high-rise building. Although Copacabana has been urbanized only since the turn of the century, its fashionable cachet has been sufficient to make it virtually a symbol of Rio. To most Cariocas, Copacabana appears to rank as one of the world's finest urban achievements, failure to live there being regarded as a major eccentricity requiring apologetic explanation. From a small, isolated, and

1. This legend is cited by Charles Anderson Gould in Adalberto Szilard and J. O. de Oliveira Reis, *Urbanismo no Rio de Janeiro* (Rio de Janeiro, 1950), p. 14.

largely inaccessible stretch of sand, Copacabana has evolved into the major focus of Rio, the place from which all distances seem to be measured. It is difficult to call to mind a residential area in any other city which possesses an equivalent aura and attraction, or which is as important symbolically.

Physically, Copacabana consists of a narrow strip of land in the South Zone of Rio, lying between the ocean and a band of mountains (fig. 21). The beach is approximately 2.5 miles long, and the land varies in depth from a tenth to three-quarters of a mile. Although a tiny settlement existed on the site as early as 1800, the hills separating it from the rest of the city prevented easy occupation. Even had the area been readily accessible, however, it would have required the twentieth-century cult of sun and sea bathing to provide the overwhelming attraction which the area now possesses. It is reported that "as late as 1872 a rash resident was warmly ridiculed in Rio newspapers for urging opening of a mule-powered tram line to Copacabana. Pedro II's ministers of government lived miles away and cared naught for swimming."[2] The first tunnel through the mountains, the Alaôr Prata, was built in 1892, giving access by horsedrawn streetcar from adjacent Botafogo, and providing the initial impetus for the development of Copacabana as a residential area of single-family houses. Additional access was provided when the Leme tunnel was completed in 1904, and at the same time the oceanfront street, Avenida Atlantica, was established. This avenue marked the limits to which private property could encroach on the beach. As the century advanced, pressures of urban expansion combined with the magnets of sea and sun to produce a building boom which has yet to abate. During the 1930s the area was still dominated by low-rise housing, with a few high-rise buildings beginning to appear along the shore. Although during the 1940s the Second World War halted most new construction in Europe and the United States, the building spree in Copacabana accelerated until the oceanfront carried a virtually unbroken wall of high-rise apartments, and the initial pattern of single-family dwelling was on the way to obliteration throughout the area (figs. 22–27). In the decade 1940–1950, Copacabana increased in population from 74,000 to 129,000, and by 1960 had grown to 185,650. According to the 1970 census, Copacabana had by then achieved a population of 237,559 living in an area of 2.8 square miles. From end to end, and from beach to mountains, Copacabana has become a mass of tightly packed masonry embodying one of the densest concentrations of population to be found in any modern city. Under present regulations, there is still room for increase, and it has been estimated that if Copacabana were to continue to build according to current building regulations, the population could reach 635,000.[3]

2. Ibid.

3. This prediction was made in CEDUG–Doxiadis, p. 301 (see chap. 1, n. 5). That Copacabana may be reaching a saturation point in population, however, is indicated by an apparent decline in rate of growth. The Doxiadis plan was based largely on 1960 census figures and current growth trends. According to these, Doxiadis estimated a population of 242,000 in Copacabana in 1965, a figure exceeding that reported in the census of 1970.

In many respects, Copacabana fits within Patrick Geddes's definition of a "superslum," that is, an area which, although fashionable and expensive, exhibits building congestion equivalent to that of many poorer districts. Copacabana thus provides yet another argument against judging the desirability of housing solely in terms of density. The term superslum, however, is not altogether inappropriate if by the word slum one means an intensely built and densely occupied urban area with a variety of residential and commercial uses, with noisy dirty streets through which pounds a constant stream of heavy traffic, where drainage is bad and water is scarce, where there is little open space and greenery, and where buildings, streets, and sidewalks are often dilapidated. Copacabana may be considered an amiable, well-heeled slum whose inhabitants live there by choice. No Carioca dreams of a house in the suburbs; he longs for an apartment in Copacabana. In Rio, suburbs are for poor people, people who have to live in houses because they cannot afford apartments. Perhaps in no other city are the burdens of modern urban living accepted with such willingness as in Rio, and what are elsewhere considered drawbacks of city life seem to be regarded as positive joys. Cariocas seem to like noise. They like crowds and traffic. Said one Copacabana enthusiast of its teeming streets, "It's exciting just to go out and buy a newspaper." Copacabana exhibits all of the characteristic slum pleasures. Children play on the sidewalks and in the streets, dodging automobiles. Day and night the ill-kept sidewalks are crowded with people making the rounds of small shops or just standing and talking, while other people lean out of windows to watch what's happening in the street. Grocery shopping takes place in the animated villagelike atmosphere of outdoor street fairs. Such fairs occur throughout Rio, consisting of stalls and pushcarts set up once or twice a week either in available open space or streets from which motor traffic has been temporarily excluded (fig. 28).

Although its population is predominantly middle and upper class, Copacabana embodies a social mixture through its large resident servant class and through the juxtaposition on the nearby hills of large favelas, Rio's characteristic squatter slums. The lively attractions of Copacabana make it easier to get and keep a servant there than in any other part of Rio, and the presence of a large service class saves Copacabana from the socially antiseptic air of many middle-class districts.

Although Copacabana is primarily a residential area, it has become increasingly important as a commercial, business, and entertainment center. Copacabana contains one of the most important shopping areas in Rio, most of the best hotels, restaurants, and theaters, and a growing number of offices. By 1956, 10.8 percent of the block area of Copacabana was given over to commercial use.

The urban functions present in Copacabana are, of course, not unique, and mixtures of high-rise housing, shopping, and entertainment facilities exist in many other cities. Copacabana is perhaps unique, however, in combining these elements with the easygoing atmosphere of a beach resort. Convenient access to the beach represents Copacabana's greatest attraction, and to be able to don bathing attire at home and stroll easily to the shore is considered ample compensation for high rents, congested space, and a view extending no farther than the building across the street. Because of the proximity to the beach, dress in Copacabana is informal, and correct street attire frequently consists of little more than a suntan. Copacabana beach draws people from other parts of Rio, but it is keyed to the use of local residents. There are no bathhouses or lockers, and much of the beauty of the beach lies in the circumstance that it is completely uncluttered.

Although the building pattern of Copacabana is dense, with only 1.4 percent of the built-up area given over to parks and squares, the presence of strong natural elements prevents the congestion from becoming oppressive. On one side the ocean beach creates a limitless vista, while on the other the mountains thrust up, dwarfing the masses of building below and forming a great natural wall defining the site. So assertive are the configurations of the setting, that one never feels imprisoned in a totally man-made world.

With increasing pressures of urban expansion in Rio, and with the near exhaustion of available ground area in Copacabana, it was inevitable that similarly intensive urbanization would overtake adjacent beach areas. Comparable to Copacabana in fashion and undergoing rapid new construction are Ipanema and Leblon, adjoining portions of a narrow strip of land between the lake, Lagôa Rodrigo de Freitas, and the ocean. As did Copacabana, Ipanema-Leblon appears to be undergoing a cycle of development from single-family houses to apartments and commercial building (figs. 29, 30). In order to maintain a relatively low-rise character along the oceanfront, apartment buildings were initially limited to four stories, but there is a present trend toward higher blocks.

The increased development of the areas beyond Copacabana has added a disastrous burden of traffic to its own already congested streets. Copacabana has provided a narrow corridor linking the central part of Rio with districts lying still farther out, and the two major arteries, Avenida Copacabana and Barata Ribeiro, although relatively narrow for the purpose, have come to function as expressways carrying a constant roaring stream of buses, cars, and trucks.

Avenida Atlantica bordering the ocean, although free of buses, has been similarly encumbered with automobiles. Because of the prohibitive difficulty of widening other streets in Copacabana, it was perhaps inevitable that this lovely and justly famed waterfront would be renovated to provide for the constantly increasing needs of the automobile. By 1969, work was under way in an effort to widen Avenida Atlantica, a project which necessitated extending the street into what was previously beach area, and augmenting the beach through fill. The new street provides three traffic lanes plus a parking lane on either side of a center strip. In common with other new waterfront roadways in Rio, the expanded avenue tends to diminish the intimate relationship of the city and the sea.

Copacabana is experiencing a fate common to many urban districts in being compelled continually to adjust its own fabric for the convenience of traffic moving to areas farther from the center of the city. By the same token, Copacabana has contributed to the decline of older districts lying between it and the center of Rio, for in order to facilitate a rapid traffic flow from the business district to Copacabana, the intervening area has sacrificed the beauty of its waterfront esplanade to a new motor freeway built on land fill. The motor-dominated waterfront of Copacabana maintains a pattern of development characteristic of modern Rio.

In an effort to relieve traffic pressures in the South Zone, the Rebouças tunnel was opened in 1968 to connect the Lagôa-Leblon district with the North Zone and central business district. This was combined with the creation of a new motorway surrounding the lakefront, a project involving the removal of a large favela settlement. Beyond Leblon, the mountains drop precipitously to the sea, blocking all but a negligible amount of oceanfront construction until one reaches the town of Barra da Tijuca. At this point, the hills lie sufficiently inland to provide a wide low-lying area (fig. 31). Initially serving as a beach resort, this district is now being urbanized according to a general plan developed by Lúcio Costa. Population projections for the new area are ambitious, and burgeoning high-rise apartment projects have prompted journalistic predictions that "in this spacious and sparsely inhabited area a new city is to spring up that will look like a science fiction writer's dream come true."[4] To make Barra da Tijuca more accessible to central Rio, it has been necessary to drive three new tunnels through the coastline mountain barrier, the Tunel do Pepino, the Tunel do Joa, and the lengthy Tunel Dois Irmãos.

Additional pressure for oceanfront development may manifest itself soon across the bay in the state of Rio de Janeiro. Here the topography is similar to that of Guanabara, and with the completion of a bridge connection between Rio and Niteroi, a previously little-developed beachfront area will become conveniently accessible to Rio (fig. 32).

Copacabana, in its physical development, exemplifies not only uncontrolled operation of the profit motive, but also the law of supply and demand, and it is only one of many urban areas in which the collective preference of the inhabitants seems at variance with many generally accepted ideas of "good" urban living environments. Although Copacabana has largely escaped the blessings of comprehensive planning, as much of Copacabana begins to age and buildings deteriorate, it is possible to conceive of the area as a site of massive urban renewal, of demolition and rebuilding in accordance with more orthodox residential standards. Recent land-use laws have attempted to modify the unlimited occupancy of land, restricting the depth to which lots may be built, and thus attempting to insure the interior of the block some meas-

4. *Manchete*, special edition subtitled *The New Brazil* (Rio de Janeiro, 1971), p. 26.

ure of open space. This applies to new building and to rebuilding but does not affect existing construction. On the most desirable blocks, those facing the ocean, land coverage approaches 90 percent.

In 1950, an architectural engineer, Adalberto Szilard, and a civil engineer, José de Oliveira Reis, published a study of Rio in which was included an "ideal plan of Copacabana designed in accordance with the precepts of modern urbanism."[5] The grid of Copacabana would be modified into a configuration of superblocks, and the entire oceanfront would become a green park in which would be set widely spaced ten-story apartment houses. Commercial activities would be confined to sharply delineated areas, and most of the district away from the beach would consist of two-story residences, provided with abundant parks, athletic fields, and schools.

Attempting to counteract the already advanced pattern of closely spaced apartment building in Copacabana, the plan embodied a partial restoration of the previous pattern of low-density occupation. Such rigidly zoned schemes, in which the city is viewed primarily as a unified architectural complex, have been familiar in urban design since the 1920s. Recently, however, planning theory has favored a more flexible conception of urban environment, in which mixtures of activity—commerce, housing, and institutions—are regarded as necessary to insure urban vitality and visual interest.

Evidence of a more adaptable planning philosophy and realistic approach, necessitated by an actual, rather than an ideal, design situation, may be seen in a scheme proposed for Copacabana by the Doxiadis firm fifteen years after the Szilard and Reis plan. Having been engaged to prepare a master plan for Guanabara, the Doxiadis group included in its work a detailed study of Copacabana, together with suggestions for redevelopment.

After considering the problems of traffic, population density, and land use, the report stated, "in seeking a solution to the problems of any community by means of a plan, one tries to estimate the existing and future needs of the community in terms of the land areas that have to be set aside for the various main functions that make up its life. In Copacabana such a traditional approach to land planning is not possible, since the available land is not enough to serve the existing population, let alone substantially more numbers of people that will in the future reside in this area. . . . An untraditional approach will have to be used."[6]

The proposals made by the Doxiadis report involved an attempt to provide increased circulation and parking space for vehicles, together with safer and more adequate areas for pedestrian use. To accomplish this, the total ground area would be given over to streets and parking, while separate pedestrian circulation would be provided by raised decks paralleling the streets, with all shopping and commercial

5. Szilard and Reis, *Urbanismo no Rio de Janeiro,* pp. 107–15.
6. CEDUG–Doxiadis, p. 302.

facilities on this upper level (fig. 33). The pattern of high-rise housing would be maintained, but, within the blocks, raised pedestrian plazas would be created to provide play spaces for schools, additional siting for shops and cafes, and areas of greenery. The space beneath the plazas would provide parking. It was suggested that such a system of pedestrian decks could be constructed in stages, "allowing the gradual relocation of shops and business activities from their existing location on the ground floor."[7] Along the oceanfront, the pedestrian deck would extend over the Avenida Atlantica creating an elevated promenade the entire length of the beach, containing restaurants and sidewalk cafes. The advantage of such a scheme would be that it would retain the existing character of Copacabana, eliminating the need for massive demolitions. According to the report: "The basic elements of the plan can be achieved without tearing down existing buildings, but rather by hollowing out the first floor of buildings and moving shops up one floor; arrangements must be worked out with the State so that schools can be located within apartment buildings; regulations must be enacted permitting the joint use of structures for parking garages, shops and residents combined; the means of constructing the second floor pedestrian platform must be determined to the benefit of all."[8] Such systems of vertical separation for pedestrians and motors are already in use on a limited scale and can be seen in the Stockholm city center and the Barbican development in London.

Rio has many more pressing problems, however, than the amelioration of living conditions in its most fashionable neighborhood, and there is thus little immediate prospect of Copacabana falling victim to a superslum-clearance or civic-improvement project. Copacabana as a living environment has substantial drawbacks, and dwelling there involves many compromises with ideal conditions. But Cariocas are not searching for the ideal; they have a talent for the enjoyment of reality and are not seduced by drawings. For most of the inhabitants of Copacabana, the compensations appear worth the price.

7. Ibid., p. 305.
8. Ibid., p. 308.

4. THE FAVELAS

Rio, like many other cities in Latin America, contains a sizable population of squatters, slum dwellers who have illegally erected shacks on private or public land, and who, because of the chronic inability of these cities to provide more adequate housing, have become a permanent part of the urban scene. In Brazil, squatter settlements are called *favelas* and their inhabitants *favelados*. The precise origin of these communities in Rio is not known, but some of the early squatters were apparently ex-slaves who began settling hill sites after they were freed in 1888.

Favela was the name of a hill in Rio which was occupied in 1897 by a group of soldiers who, returning from service in the North, found that the government could not pay them. The term favela subsequently came to be applied to all squatter housing. Rapid growth of the favelas was given impetus during the 1930s when widespread agricultural depression combined with the lure of industrial employment to promote a sudden influx of low-income people into urban centers. In succeeding years the failure of the local housing market to provide enough cheap dwellings made large agglomerations of self-built housing one of the characteristic features of the Rio landscape as well as a source of continuous governmental concern.

Statistical information regarding the favela population varies widely, with the 1960 census reporting 337,000 and a COHAB (Companhia de Habitaçao Popular) survey in 1962 claiming 1,069,000. During 1964, for example, two government organizations attempting population surveys produced the totals of 350,000 and 927,000, respectively. In 1965, the Doxiadis organization attempted a survey of favelas based on interpretation of aerial photographs, which produced a total estimated population of 430,000. The population of favelas is thought to have doubled between 1950 and 1960, and, although in 1950 approximately one Rio inhabitant in fourteen was a favelado, by 1965 the proportion was estimated at one in nine, or 11.3 percent of the total population. The rate of growth for the favela population was then estimated at 7 percent per year as compared with 3.3 percent for the total population in Guanabara.[1]

1. CEDUG–Doxiadis, p. 137 (see chap. 1, n. 5). Of the increase in favelados during 1950–60, 39 percent were accommodated by expansion of existing favelas and 61 percent by the creation of 89 new favelas de-

Rio includes about 191 favelas, ranging in size from such small settlements as Ilha das Dragas which contains about 1300 people in an area of about 6.25 acres (approximately 208 persons per acre), up to Jacarezinho which contains as many as 29,760 in an area of 92.5 acres (a density of about 312 persons per acre).[2]

Favelas may be found in all parts of Rio, on swampy low-lying ground near the bay, on flatland, and, most conspicuously, on the precipitous hill slopes which occur throughout the city (figs. 34–36). The favelas are thought to have been formed largely by migrants to the city, people in many ways still rural in habits and outlook, who were thrust into urban living by the prevailing poverty of the countryside. The growing shanty slums of Rio are the visible manifestation of problems which are otherwise easy to ignore while lying on Copacabana beach. The ubiquitous favelas, intruding into even the most fashionable areas and crowning the hills of Copacabana, form a constant reminder of the economic difficulties, not only of Rio, but of Brazil as a whole.

In Rio, favela clearance has generally involved not a systematic and thoroughgoing effort, but a series of piecemeal operations. Some removal projects, such as those involving the more conspicuous hill slopes in Copacabana, may have functioned primarily as a species of urban cosmetic. Others, like the demolition of the shoreline settlement of Lagôa, provide land which is desired for other purposes. (In the case of the Rocinha favela near Lagôa the cleared site was used for a new motor freeway.)

Among Rio planners, there has been no lack of concern about the favelas, but there is frequent disagreement about how to treat a problem which is as complex as the problem of poverty itself. Even if Rio were able to rehouse every present favelado, the economic pressures which produce migration from depressed rural areas would continue to operate, and new favelas would likely spring up. Generally speaking, although favelas have provided a focus for limited rehabilitation and rehousing activities, there has long been a lack of thorough and coordinated study involving social, economic, and physical aspects of these settlements. Information has been fragmentary, like the reports that the legendary blind men produced regarding the elephant of which each had experienced a part. A socioeconomic survey of favelas was recommended in the Doxiadis report of 1965 but produced no governmental action. In 1967, however, as part of a projected program of favela rehabilitation, government surveys relating to health standards and housing conditions were instituted in three favelas.

---

veloped in Rio during this period. A notable increase in favela population was seen in the northern part of Guanabara, reaching as high as 214 percent in Zona de Madureira, which is close to an area of industrial employment.

2. This estimate was achieved by the Doxiadis firm through the use of aerial photographs. In the preparation of the master plan for Guanabara, a series of photographic studies of favelas was made from the air, and population estimates were based on the number of houses counted in selected areas of the photographs. In general, favela densities were estimated as ranging from 200 to 400 persons per acre. Available information indicated that occupancy in favelas averaged 4.8 persons per dwelling, only slightly higher than the 4.47 occupancy average for the State of Guanabara. However, since many favela houses consist of only one room, a much greater degree of congestion would be implied. CEDUG–Doxiadis, p. 137.

It would appear that within the favela population there is considerable variety. Although many favelados are recent immigrants, favelas often contain long-term stable populations, sometimes having housed several generations of the same family. Some favelas are regarded as hideouts for criminals and the most irresponsible elements of the city, while others appear to contain basically law-abiding and economically productive citizens, highly organized in terms of community and family. Although there is some range in the economic level of favelados, generally they represent the poorest people of the city, with a high rate of unemployment and underemployment, and it is reported that more than 50 percent of the people receiving public assistance are favelados.

Racially, the favelas contain a high proportion of blacks. Although Brazil has long had a reputation for racial democracy, the presumed result of a history of tolerant miscegenation, from all visible evidence Brazil's social stratification is strongly marked along racial lines.

Generally the Brazilian census includes a racial classification of black, white, and mixed, although popularly a much more complex pattern of color terminology may be employed.[3] Guanabara as a whole contains approximately the same percentage of blacks (11 percent) as all of Brazil, a smaller mixed population (18 percent as opposed to 27 percent in Brazil) and a larger percentage of whites (71 percent compared to 62 percent). Within the favelas, however, the population is nearly 40 percent black and about 30 percent mixed. Although all favelados are not black, nor all blacks favelados, in comparison with the rest of Rio, the favelas appear characteristically as colored neighborhoods.

By and large, a favela functions as a complete neighborhood unit, containing small shops, sometimes schools and community buildings, and it frequently exhibits a high

3. The terminology of the census employs the word *côr* (color) rather than race as a means of classification. The terms used are *branca* (white), *parda* (mixed), *preta* (black), and *amarela* (yellow, i.e., oriental). This may be contrasted with United States usage whereby a person with any amount of black ancestry is classified black regardless of his skin color. The percentage of blacks in the United States is about 11 percent as compared with 38 percent in Brazil (11 percent black and 27 percent mixed). Although it is risky to compare Brazil and the United States in terms of racial attitudes, one is tempted to equate the apparent racial harmony of Brazil with what reportedly existed in Mississippi before the advent of outside agitators. Racial tension in the United States has focused on political issues of civil rights and ideals of social equality. Brazil, with its more firmly established class distinctions and limited concept of political democracy, lacks some of the pressure points of racial conflict seen in North America. It has been hypothesized, in fact, that "the Brazilian white has never at any time felt that the black or the mixed blood offered any serious threat to his own status." Donald Pierson, *Negroes in Brazil: A Study of Race Contact at Bahia* (Carbondale: Southern Illinois University Press, 1967), p. 347. Although Brazilians have been notably free of the North American neurosis with regard to miscegenation, it would appear that if one is white and middle class, one's hypothetical sister is no more likely to marry a black in Brazil than in the United States. Additional discussion of some of the complexities of racial attitudes in Brazil may be found in the following: Roger Bastide and Floristan Fernandes, *Relaçõis raciais entre negros e brancos em São Paulo* (São Paulo: Editora Anhembi, 1955); Florestan Fernandes, *The Negro in Brazilian Society* (New York, 1969); Gilberto Freyre, *The Masters and the Slaves* (New York, 1956), and *The Mansions and the Shanties* (New York, 1966); Marvin Harris, *Town and Country in Brazil* (New York, 1956), and *Patterns of Race in the Americas* (New York, Walker, 1964). A moving account of daily life in a São Paulo favela may be found in *Child of the Dark: The Diary of Carolina María de Jesus* (New York, Dutton, 1962).

degree of community identity and organization. One of the greatest concentrations of effort which the favelados put forth is in preparation for the annual carnival in which rival samba groups from different favelas compete in elaborately costumed street performances. To participate in these spectacles, a favelado will invest not only prodigious time and energy, but also, in his costume, a large amount of money. Beyond this brief moment of glory, however, the favelado participates but frugally in Rio society.

As the social and economic conditions of the favelados vary, so the physical aspects of favelas show noticeable variation in terms of site, housing, and services. Generally, the poorest favelas appear to be those on low-lying areas near the water, while the best are on the hills. Approximately 65 percent of all favelas are located on hilly sites, frequently in districts where the sought-after flatland is occupied by middle- and upper-class building. As favelas develop accretively, the layout is generally irregular, and circulation frequently takes the form of narrow winding paths, usually unpaved, or crude steps. The small houses are densely packed, but on hilly sites the topography permits a vertical separation of buildings, giving a measure of light, air, and vista to almost every house. Although visually the hillside favelas are not always unattractive, at least from a distance, they perpetuate the primitive rural living conditions to which many of their inhabitants were accustomed. Sanitation is rudimentary, and the human population is frequently augmented by pigs, goats, and chickens (figs. 37–41).

Construction methods in favela houses include a type of building resembling wattle-and-daub, consisting of a loose wooden framework with mud infilling, wood-frame buildings with board siding and, in the best houses, commercially made hollow bricks. Dwellings may range from mean and primitive one-room hovels to relatively substantial two-story houses. Although the favelados are illegal occupants of the land, the investment of work and money which some have made in their houses indicates not only a degree of prosperity and self-respect, but also a sense of security in terms of land tenure. The houses of the more well-to-do favelados are often plastered and painted on the exterior and sometimes exhibit verandas and fenced-in yards. Interiors may have several rooms and comfortable furnishings, including refrigerators and television sets. Within favelas, houses may be bought and sold, although without transfer of land title. Many of the houses are undeniably crude and would provide totally inadequate shelter in a demanding climate. Fortunately for the favelados, Rio is warm all year, and although rain may come through the roof, no one will freeze. Moreover, the fact that it is possible to spend much time outdoors makes the small and crowded interiors of the favela houses more tolerable than they would be otherwise.

Services of electricity, water, and sewerage vary. Although the favelas are illegal, electricity is provided in some by concessions granted by the local electrical company. Within a given favela, the company will construct initial installations and lease a concession to a favela entrepreneur. The concessionaire will maintain the installations while providing current to the favela inhabitants at a markup. Water must frequently be brought into the favelas, most typically in cans carried on the heads of the women. Occasionally a favela will have its own springs and wells, and in some instances water may be supplied by the government. Favelados may also illegally tap a municipal supply. Usually a well-established favela will have an elaborate system of water rights enforced by long custom and agreement. Sewers exist in some favelas, but most rely simply on open ditches and the natural drainage of the hill slope.

As the favelados are illegal occupants of the land, they could theoretically be subject to eviction at any time. For political reasons, however, no government has attempted or is likely to attempt mass abolition of the favelas, and no one is more aware of this than the favelados themselves. The policy of the government toward the favelas has essentially been one of compromise. From a legalistic point of view, a government committed to the protection of property and the maintenance of law should not allow illegal seizure of land. Once the seizure is a fait accompli, however, and a favela comprises a large population, the practical and moral difficulties of destruction often become prohibitive. The favelados constitute a political force which is often exploited, but never ignored, and even if a government were willing to risk the opprobium of a forcible elimination of the favelas, it would probably involve a large-scale military operation. Moreover, it would be pointless to destroy the favelas unless replacement housing could be provided, and this is far beyond the immediate ability of the state. The favelas continue to survive and grow, because at present no practical alternative exists.

Government and private action with regard to favelas has involved attempts to improve community structure and physical facilities within the favelas, together with some efforts at relocation. Public agencies concerned with favelas have included the Leo XIII Foundation, operating under the Social Welfare Secretariat; the Department of the Rehabilitation of Favelas (Departamento de Recuperação de Favelas), a small agency under the Leo XIII Foundation; and BEMDOC, an AID-sponsored agency attached to the Leo XIII Foundation to conduct favela community-development research. In addition to the government agencies, a Catholic organization called the Cruzada São Sebastião has also been active in favela improvement. At present, major responsibility for directing both favela removal and rehabilitation has been assumed by CHISAM (Comissão de Habitacão de Interêsse Social da Área Metropolitana da Guanabara), founded in 1968 and affiliated with the national Ministry of the Interior. Within two years of operation, CHISAM reportedly directed the removal of more than 20,000 favela dwellings from central Rio, and the relocation of their inhabitants in the North Zone.

The work of government agencies within the favelas has been subject to political vagaries and has often been fragmentary and inadequately considered. An attempt by the Leo XIII Foundation to install a water-supply system, electricity, roads, walks, and steps in a favela called Vila da Penha (an attempt initiated without any comprehensive plan or effort to organize community support) was curtailed for lack of funds when about 60 percent completed. Only after the project was under way—and without connection to it—was a socioeconomic survey initiated by BEMDOC. Similar physical improvements in Jacarezinho were begun without any social groundwork, and were discontinued for lack of funds.

In 1966, a team of three Americans investigating favela problems commented regarding previous efforts at rehabilitation:

> The first problem has apparently been an incomplete understanding of the people in the favelas, their problems, community organizations and their felt needs. Secondly, improvement programs have often been planned and started without the knowledge, participation and support of the community. The improvements planned were not necessarily those wanted or needed by the community. Thirdly, the improvement plans generally did not require community contributions of labor or money, and the work planned did not have guaranteed financing to completion. The community apparently had no real interest and when projects were stopped, what little faith and support that existed was undoubtedly lost. Lastly, the improvement programs were often too limited in scope and were not aimed at the ultimate goal of providing the security of home ownership, land tenure, and the integration of the favela as a legal and permanent part of the larger community.[4]

Whether or not all the favelados would prefer to have legal ownership of their houses and land is open to question. One of the advantages of favela living may in fact be freedom from property regulations and taxation coupled with what is sometimes a relative security in occupancy.[5]

Opinion has been divided regarding the desirability of rehabilitating existing favelas as opposed to relocating the inhabitants. Justification for rehabilitation has been based on the circumstance that favelas frequently embody a complex and well-organized internal community structure, together with established economic ties with adjoining parts of the city. The locations of many favelas are convenient to employment, and thus, commuting costs for inhabitants may be reduced or eliminated. Furthermore, within the favela itself, there is opportunity for small unregulated busi-

4. Bernard Wagner, David McVoy, and Gordon Edwards, *Guanabara Housing and Urban Development Program* (Report and Recommendations by AID Housing and Urban Development Team, 1 July 1966). This report was used in formulating USAID programs and strongly influenced the decision to support a favela rehabilitation program.

5. A Peace Corps volunteer assigned to the Jacarezinho favela reported that he once tried to instigate a movement among the inhabitants to obtain land titles, only to learn from the favelados that they had no desire to obtain ownership of their house plots. Many had resided in the favela as long as twenty years and were convinced that the government would make no attempt to remove them.

ness enterprise. It was suggested by the American observers, moreover, that the present financial investment in favelas is too great to be ignored.

> Generally speaking, the cost of upgrading favelas will be less than the cost of relocation of favelados in new housing construction. Furthermore, a good part of the necessary investment in the case of the favela is already there in the form of land, building materials for dwellings, and also certain community facilities. Many favelas have schools, meeting houses, churches, stores and small shops; they also have self-help constructed water and electricity distribution systems and, in some instances, sewer systems. Here and there the favelados got together and built sidewalks and steps or widened a road and paved it. Small industries are scattered throughout most favelas and are operated by individual owners or as family enterprises. Favelas have all kinds and types of structures and a good many houses are of perfectly sound construction with fairly generous space standards.[6]

It was estimated that upgrading the favelas in their existing locations might be achieved at half the cost of new construction. However, from available evidence, not all of them would be suitable subjects for massive rehabilitation. Many hillside favelas are unsafe and subject to landslides, while others, on pilings over water, tidal flats, and swamps, can be said to have virtually no land at all. Densities and building patterns in many favelas would probably have to be altered to effect much physical improvement, and would thus involve some dislocation unless additional land could be added to the favela.

During 1967, assisted by some American financing, the first attempt at a coordinated survey of favelas with a view toward rehabilitation was begun. Three favelas were selected as presenting likely areas for renovation: Braz de Pina, a settlement on low-lying swampy ground near the main highway in the industrial North Zone; Mata Machado, located on a small elevation near the Tijuca forest; and Morro da União, situated in an outlying suburban district near the town of Iraja. The cooperation of the inhabitants was obtained for the surveys, which included an analysis of physical conditions, a socioeconomic study, and a medical survey of health conditions.

The program of physical rehabilitation, as initially outlined, was to provide land titles for plots and improvements in circulation, sanitation, utilities, and building construction. Water mains were to be established following street lines, but each house would be required to make its own connection. The state Electrical Energy Commission would make basic installations, and inhabitants would pay the prevailing city rates for electricity. For acquisition of land title and for rehabilitation costs, favelados with sufficient resources were to pay 5 percent of the minimum wage for

6. Wagner, McVoy, and Edwards, p. 15.

approximately three to four years. Housing cooperatives, financed by the National Housing Bank of Brazil, were to be formed to provide building materials on credit and instruction for house improvement. The rehabilitation of Braz de Pina began in 1968, with work commencing in Mata Machado shortly after.

As the favela rehabilitation program has had only limited application, its long range success cannot yet be evaluated. There are some, however, who deem it suitable for only a small number of settlements, and in the opinion of a government housing official, "Less than ten percent of the favelas in Rio possess the conditions for urban rehabilitation, or for the integration of their area and population into the neighborhood in which they are located."[7]

In addition to attempts to rehabilitate favelas, there have been increasing government efforts at relocation of slum dwellers through the construction of minimal-cost houses designed for purchase by favelados. In 1963 the Leo XIII Foundation had begun construction of two low-cost housing groups, Vila Aliança, consisting of 2,183 houses, and Vila Esperança, with 464 houses. The direction of these projects, however, was soon absorbed by a new government organization, COHAB (Companhia de Habitaçao Popular). The program of COHAB at one time received American assistance through USAID.

Vila Aliança, which received its first occupants in December 1962, was constructed in the North Zone about twenty-seven miles outside Rio, near the town of Bangú. On the ill-founded assumption that the community would integrate with Bangú, no commercial facilities were provided, with the result that many of the houses were subsequently adapted as shops. Vila Esperança, a considerably smaller settlement, was composed of the relocated inhabitants of a single favela. Sited in a bayfront industrial area about fifteen miles from Rio, the community was much more conveniently located with regard to transportation and employment.

In its first three years of operation, COHAB was reported to have constructed approximately 10,341 houses accommodating about 50,000 people. Its policy has been not to retain government ownership of housing, but rather to sell low-cost houses outright through a series of monthly payments. COHAB housing developments are designed by government architects but built by private contractors, the basic building material being hollow clay bricks. Each house has water, electricity, gas, and sewage disposal. In order to keep costs down, the houses are minimal, but each of the five basic plans is designed to be enlarged by either the owner or professionals. House expansion takes the form of additional rooms or a second story, and for this purpose building materials are sold at cost with instruction and supervision provided.

According to the regulations of COHAB, the prospective purchaser of a house must be investigated by the Guanabara Department of Social Service. He must be

7. Mauro Ribeiro Viegas, president of COHAB, quoted in "O Rio sem favelas," *Manchete*, Summer 1967, p. 100.

able to prove the need for a house, must have lived in a favela during the previous year, be able to establish financial responsibility, and make a down payment of up to 10 percent of the cost of the house and lot.[8]

Because of the currency inflation in Brazil, houses are not sold at fixed prices. Rather, the price is based on the purchaser's ability to pay, each payment ranging from 15 to 25 percent of the monthly minimum wage for a set number of payments. The price of a 220-square-foot house is the equivalent of about $960, and for the family of a working husband, with a wife and two small children, the monthly payment might be less than $3.00.

The two largest housing projects constructed by COHAB near Rio in the 1960s are Vila Kennedy, initially designed with 4700 houses for a population of 23,000–25,000, and Cidade de Deus (City of God), planned with 4800 houses for a population of 25,000. As with other COHAB projects, the need for cheap land necessitated the use of outlying sites. Vila Kennedy, originally conceived as an extension of Vila Aliança, is located in the area of Bangú about twenty miles from Rio, while Cidade de Deus is in an outlying district of the South Zone near the town of Jacarepaguá.

Much of the criticism leveled at the work of COHAB concerns the location of its projects. It is frequently pointed out that organized relocation of population should be attempted only when integrated with an overall plan for the economic and urban development of Guanabara. Many feel that the siting of COHAB settlements in isolated areas far from existing employment centers, where the inhabitants must depend on inconvenient and expensive transport, creates more problems for the inhabitants than do the favelas. In defense of COHAB, however, it must be borne in mind that a viable and thoroughgoing master plan for Guanabara may be long in coming and, even if developed, would not necessarily be effectively augmented. It would not be feasible in the meantime to halt all decision and action affecting the development of the state. COHAB projects are located in what is assumed to be the general direction of population spread and industrial development and may ultimately offer reasonable proximity to employment.

Profiting from the experience of Vila Aliança, COHAB planners designed later projects to include a range of community facilities, including shops, schools, and buildings for small factories and workshops. The most publicized COHAB project of the 1960s is Vila Kennedy, which occupies a wide valley bisected by one of the major suburban highways. In 1963, following the death of President John Kennedy, the settlement acquired its present name, together with a twenty-foot replica of the Statue of Liberty which stands in the center of the small town square (figs. 46–50).

Although the direction of Vila Kennedy was Brazilian, the name and the commemorative statue tended to emphasize American involvement, and the project has

8. Financial responsibility includes a written record of employment and evidence of ability to pay for the house and support a family of 5.2. In addition, the purchaser must have no police record.

been cited as typifying the failings of many American-assisted programs. A characteristic American reaction to Vila Kennedy may be found in an article that appeared in the *Wall Street Journal* in 1967 under the headline, "Foreign Aid Flop. 'Showcase' Community in Brazil Deteriorates Due to Poor Planning." Beginning with a comment by foreign aid mission director, Harlan Harrison, "It's a stinker," the article proceeded in a tone of high dudgeon to catalog the more obvious defects of Vila Kennedy.

The inconvenient location and high cost of commuting were cited as contributing to an unemployment rate for which minimum estimates were given as 40–50 percent. The bus journey to Rio was reported as taking two hours each way, and the fare, even though subsidized, was considered prohibitive for many residents. (Because of the time and money involved in travel, women working as maids in Rio usually saw their families in Vila Kennedy only on weekends.) Attempts to provide employment within the community itself were reported largely unsuccessful. A bakery, sponsored by the Food for Peace program, was considered to be so badly managed that, "The flour became mildewed and the profits from the bread, which were supposed to be used to finance vocational training and other such programs, weren't being put to any use at all." A sewing center was languishing because "Brazilian officials haven't followed through as promised. The center has 24 machines, but only 12 of them work. The others arrived in such poor condition they could not be used."

As to the physical condition of the settlement, the writer reported that "streets falling into serious disrepair make many parts of town impossible for automobile traffic and even difficult for pedestrians. Seven or eight persons live in many of the small houses—most of them have only two rooms—yet only very occasionally can a visitor detect any effort to build on an additional room or two." An AID worker was quoted as stating, "In projects like this we darned well should impose conditions on the local government, and then make them stick to their part of the bargain," and he added, "Five years from now, this place will be a shambles. It is already turning into a slum." Mr. Harrison of AID was quoted in conclusion: "We certainly have no more Vila Kennedys on tne books. We've found there can be a big gap between the theory of a project and carrying the project through. We want the Brazilians to help themselves more. The question is how hard do you want to pound the table to get them to do it."[9]

In addition to other failings, Vila Kennedy exhibits a thoroughgoing banality of design, and, with its seemingly endless rows of tiny houses, each on a postage-stamp plot, it appears to have carried the ideal of the single-family house to a ludicrous ex-

9. Alfred L. Malabre, Jr., "Foreign Aid Flop," *Wall Street Journal,* 20 March 1967, p. 1. The statements quoted are indicative of the impatience felt by some American officials when working in an unaccustomed environment and confronted with an unfamiliar pace of achievement. Although Vila Kennedy did not reflect the most optimistic expectations surrounding its foundation, the project was by no means a total failure.

treme. The dominant visual aspect of the town is that of an enclave of 1930s tourist cabins grown to monstrous proportions and given a basic layout of nineteenth-century English bylaw streets. The flatness of the site does not provide the changes in level which frequently give visual interest to equally small favela houses, and, before owners begin to make alterations, the prevailing monotony is relieved only by variations in the color of the paint applied to the plaster finish of the exteriors.

As might be expected, the treatment which owners give their houses varies considerably. Some are permitted to deteriorate into hovels, the ground around them untended, while others are lovingly cared for, exhibiting well-constructed additions and surrounded by fenced-in gardens. Although most of the houses are freestanding, some, including those designed for the addition of a second story, are in rows.

Cidade de Deus, begun during 1966, is similar to Vila Kennedy but exhibits some changes in general layout (figs. 51, 52). The street pattern is modified to provide shorter streets, and the grouping of houses around small open spaces provides an improvement in visual cohesion together with economies in the construction of utility lines. The location of the project, however, is far from centers of employment, and commuting time to Rio is estimated at from two to three hours.

The task which COHAB set for itself was deliberately circumscribed, that of building low-cost dwellings. The bulk of the COHAB program has centered on single-family houses, although some effort has been devoted recently to the construction of apartment units. While many planners and architects favor apartment housing for its economy of land use and urbanity of appearance, such building may not be wholly suitable for the purposes of COHAB. Apartment housing is relatively expensive, and, in terms of the present building economy, small brick houses constructed on cheap land, using a familiar local material adapted to existing manual skills and designed for tenant renovation may be the best housing solution for low-income groups. Small houses represent the type of housing which former favelados are used to, and they are perhaps best adapted to large numbers of children and semirural habits.

COHAB officials are well aware of criticisms of their work, but they point out that it is easier to talk of ideals than to achieve something under prevailing conditions. As one staff designer observed: "We know that we aren't making life sublime for these people. It isn't within our power to do that. They are poor, and we can't change it. Their lives will always be hard. All we are doing is building them a house that is cheap. And we're not giving it to them; they have to buy it. To make it cheap, we have to go outside the city. They have to want a house enough to make some sacrifices for it."

The price of a COHAB house, combined with commuting costs, doubtless puts such housing beyond the reach of many people. By being removed from physical juxtaposition with middle-class neighborhoods, the former favelados lose many opportunities for convenient and casual employment—the domestic and laundry work, customarily done by favela women, and the odd jobs which children could obtain. Thus a family moving to a COHAB project may find that its cost of living becomes higher at the same time its income is reduced. Shopping facilities are limited in COHAB communities to those merchants affluent enough to be able to buy the regulation two-story shops. Thus many favela peddlers and shopkeepers are excluded from the new communities, and the only services and goods available are likely to be higher priced than in the city. A family moving to Vila Kennedy has to want a house enough to be willing not only to bear the expense, but also to endure the dullness of an isolated semirural lower-class ghetto.

The work of COHAB, like most human enterprises, is neither a total failure nor a total success, and in spite of the shortcomings of such projects as Vila Kennedy and Cidade Deus, the inadequacies of Rio housing have been such that in 1967 ten applicants were reported for every house available. But at best, such developments can only partially relieve the housing problem. Even if COHAB projects were more conveniently located, even if physical design were improved and administration made more effective, the problem of squatter settlements would remain. Obviously, neither favela rehabilitation programs nor low-cost housing projects touch the causes of favelas, which are bound ultimately to the economic progress of Brazil.

5. THE PLANNERS OF RIO

A city is a place within the natural world consecrated to human life. It consists of an interweaving of human works, human institutions, and individual human lives. The name of a city symbolizes, therefore, an entity which is partly physical, partly intangible. To the extent that a city is physical and measurable, it can be described in terms of miles of pavement, square footage of floor space, automobiles per capita, gallons of water, acres of park, kilowatts of electricity, or tons of sewage. Its human contents may be considered in terms of literacy, average income, incidence of tuberculosis, and murders per month. Yet, there are other aspects of a city which cannot be so easily quantified; these concern the quality of life. It is easy enough to recite homilies paraphrasing Aristotle's dictum that "Men come together in cities in order to live; they remain together in order to live the 'good life'," but what is a good life, and who decides if it is good?

Assuming, as we are frequently told, that cities are for people, city planning must have as its primary goal the enhancement of the quality of urban life. But life is complex, and the good does not always appear as a clear-cut option. Frequently people ignore an obvious good for a more subtle and less apparent good, and this is seen frequently in the heavily compromised urban environment.

Rio de Janeiro developed not from a single, long-range plan, but from an accumulation of decisions, from conscious design effort, and accretive growth. Like most major cities, Rio embodies a complex collaboration of people who may be unaware that they are collaborating, but who, through their collective attitudes, habits, and institutions, are unconsciously designing their city.

Although the Portuguese, unlike the Spanish, did not develop a prescribed geometric plan for their colonial settlements, the sixteenth-century city of Rio exhibited a more or less regular grid. Expanding from the initial settlement on the Morro do Castello, the town occupied an area between the four hills of Castello, São Bento, Conceição, and Santo Antônio. The principal street was the Rua Direita (now called the Rua Primeiro de Março) which extended along the coast from Morro do Castello to the hill of São Bento. The western boundary of the city was marked by the Rua dos Ourives (now called Rua Miguel Couto) stretching from Morro do Castello to the hill of Conceição. From this relatively compact settlement, the city began expanding westward in the seventeenth century, with the direction of growth partially determined by the development of gold mines in the state of Minas Gerais. Gold ore was initially transported from the plateau of Minas as far as Parati in the Baía da Ilha Grande and then by water to Sepetiba. The ore was then taken overland to Rio along an old Indian road, and the present-day suburban settlements of Santa Crüz, Campo Grande, and Bangú originated as small stations along this route. In order to avoid the difficulties of trans-shipment, a road establishing a direct connection with the mine fields was constructed across the Serra do Mar early in the eighteenth century, and Rio became the main point of export for the area of Minas Gerais. This road created the main line of expansion for the city, and during the eighteenth century Rio grew westward almost to the foot of the mountain of Tijuca. Four penetration roads were established which have continued to be the main axes of urban development. The first road, Rua dos Barbonos (now called Evaristo da Veiga) extended southward from the Morro do Castello, dividing at Lapa to provide access to both the south and west. The other roads provided penetration westward, with one passing between the hills of Providencia and Conceiçao to what is the present port, thus opening the way for the growth of the city along the bay to the north.

The rapid expansion of the nineteenth-century city was encouraged by the development of railroads and tramlines. The railways, first established in 1858, followed the old commercial route westward through the North Zone, fostering the growth of a string of suburban settlements, and the commuter trains remain a heavily used means of working-class travel.[1] Trolley lines provided access throughout the city, aiding especially in the development of the fashionable South Zone. The first horse-drawn streetcars were introduced by an American, Charles B. Greenough, in 1868, with electrification following under the direction of a Canadian company in 1892.[2]

In terms of transportation, much present-day difficulty stems from the intense concentration of residential population in the South Zone which is separated by a band of mountains from the commercial and industrial centers of the North Zone. Increasing pressures of traffic between these two areas have resulted in heavy expenses for tunnel construction, together with extravagant use of waterfront fill to provide addi-

1. The pattern of commuting in Rio may be contrasted with that in the United States where, beginning in the nineteenth century, an essentially upper- and middle-class suburban movement developed. In the United States, commuting by rail characterized the more prosperous elements of the city, with the lower classes concentrated in the central areas. In Rio this pattern was reversed. The central city contained the most expensive and desirable residential land, while the suburbs with their cheaper land and poorer services absorbed the lower classes.

2. Greenough had been manager of the Bleecker Street Horse Car Company of New York. The electrified system developed by the Canadian Light and Power Company provided the city with five groups of trolley lines: Jardim Botanico, Santa Teresa, São Cristavo, Villa Isabel, and Carris Urbanos.

tional road connection. Obviously some of this problem might be alleviated if the North Zone could be upgraded residentially. Although it is now predominantly industrial and lower class, the North Zone once flourished as a center for fashionable residence, having been established as the site of the Royal Palace under Dom João.

The arrival of the Portuguese royal family in Rio in 1808 had a generally stimulating effect on what had previously been only a remote and backward colonial port. Describing the changes wrought by the royal refugees, the wife of an English naval officer recorded:

> The first sensible effect of the arrival of the royal family in Brazil was the opening of its numerous ports; and in the very first year ninety foreign ships entered the single harbor of Rio. . . . The effect of the residence of the court was soon felt in the city of Rio de Janeiro. It was before 1808 confined to little more than the ground it occupied when attacked by Duguay-Trouin in 1712; and the beautiful bays above and below it, formed by the harbor, were unoccupied, except by a few fishermen, while the swamps and morasses which surrounded it rendered it filthy in the extreme. A spot near the Church of San Francisco de Paulo had been cleared for a square, but scarcely a dozen houses had risen around it and a muddy pond filled up the center, into which the Negroes were in the habit of throwing all the impurities from the neighborhood. This was now filled up. On one side of the square a theater was begun, not inferior to those of Europe in size and accommodation, and placed under the patronage of St. John; several magnificent houses rose in the immediate neighborhood, the square was finished, and another and much larger laid out beyond it on one side of the city, while on the other, between the foot of the mountain of the Corcovado, with its surrounding hills, and the sea, every station was occupied by delightful country houses, and the beautiful bay of Boto Fogo, where there were before only fishermen and gipsies, soon became a populous and wealthy suburb.[3]

A wealthy Portuguese merchant presented the regent Dom João with a tract of land situated in São Cristavo, on the site of what had once been a Jesuit seminary. This land lay in the North Zone and west of the old city amid open fields between the mountains and the bay, and it contained a gentle hill which Dom João named Boa-Vista, making it the site of his new palace. Seeking to provide easier access between his palace, called the Quinta da Boa-Vista, and the city, the regent had a swampy area between the hills of Paulo Caieiro and S. Diogo do Mangal filled in to make a new road. In order to avoid the dangers of a carriage accidentally driving off the right-of-way into the water, the road was lined with regularly spaced stone posts carrying oil lamps, and the new street was given the name, Caminho das Lanteranas (Way of Lanterns). This name was soon changed, however, to Caminho do Aterrado,

3. Maria (Dundes) Graham Callcott, *Journal of a Voyage to Brazil* . . . (London, 1824). Quoted in Hugh Gibson, *Rio* (Garden City, 1937), pp. 241–42.

the term *aterrado* meaning landfill, and the entire district came to be called the Aterrado. As an encouragement to settlement in the new area, a royal decree of 1811 exempted from taxes for ten years houses having two stories or containing five or more doors and windows. Landfill of the area continued, with drainage provided by canals paralleling some of the streets, and the fashionable district which eventually extended from the palace to the older part of Rio came to be called the New City.

Later, as the North Zone began to develop a predominantly industrial character, its desirability as a place of upper-class residence inevitably declined, and many of the large mansions of São Cristavo have survived only because their size made them adaptable for commercial use.

The establishment of the court in Rio attracted not only increased Portuguese immigration, but it also encouraged an influx of foreigners. The city was thrown open to foreign commerce, and foreign mercantile houses were permitted to settle there, thereby adding to the diplomatic colony a sizable foreign business community. Generally, the foreigners have been credited with promoting an awareness of the natural beauties of the Rio site and with taking the lead in establishing fashionable extensions of the city in the South Zone. The English, in particular, were associated with the areas of Gloria, Flamengo, and Botafogo (which had previously been a fishing village) and with the heights of Cosme Velho and Laranjeiras where the predominant Anglo-Saxon presence gave the name Morro do Ingles (Hill of the English) to an elevated site. It was the foreign community which first established residential areas in the hills of Rio, the French and English in the heights of Gloria and Catete, and the Germans in Santa Teresa. Still farther from the center of the city, the French established residences in the forest of Tijuca mountain, while the English founded the town of Alto da Boa-Vista in the same mountainous area. In addition to the aesthetic attractions, the hill sites were sought as a refuge from the yellow-fever mosquito which haunted the lowlands of the city.[4] The court and diplomatic corps eventually established a summer capital in the mountains of Petropolis, but those whose commercial interests necessitated frequent access to the center of the city found relative safety in visiting the business center during daylight and returning to the nearby hills at sunset. Eventually the long high ridge of Santa Teresa was made conveniently accessible to the central part of Rio through the adaptation of an eighteenth-century aqueduct to carry trolley cars (fig. 15).

In its early days of development, and especially during the eighteenth century, the planning of Rio consisted of a series of piecemeal public works directed by military engineers. Such works included drainage and filling operations, the construction of the Carioca aqueduct carrying water from Santa Teresa to the hill of Santo Antonio, and the Passeio Publico, a major public park facing the harbor entrance.

4. Yellow fever was first recorded in Rio in 1849, and recurred annually; bubonic plague and malaria were also common. Eventual improvements in hygiene and medicine as well as the filling in of marshes and swamps assisted in the control of these diseases.

With the advent of the nineteenth century and the new status of the city as a royal capital, Rio received the embellishments of imported French classical design. Although almost all of Europe had united against the political and military hegemony of Napoleon's France, the cultural prestige of the French maintained its dominance, and in 1816, Napoleon having been vanquished, a mission of French sculptors, painters, and architects was brought to Rio to direct artistic life and further the Europeanization of the city.

Included in the mission was the architect Auguste Victor Grandjean de Montigny who was responsible for the design of a number of major public buildings reflective of the prevailing French classicism. His work also involved larger aspects of Rio, and he has been termed, "the first urbanist, in the present sense, which the city had."[5] His many projects involved the remodeling of squares, the enlarging and straightening of streets, and the improvement of communications throughout the city. He was a pioneer in efforts to improve household sanitation and to establish favorable standards of building orientation with regard to sun and wind. Grandjean de Montigny did not return to France, but remained the rest of his life in Rio, meeting a good Carioca death through pneumonia contracted at the carnival of 1850.

Much of the landscaping of mid- and late-nineteenth-century Rio represented the work of another Frenchman, Auguste Glaziou, who was invited to Brazil by the emperor Dom Pedro II. He traveled extensively in the Brazilian interior, studying local flora, and returned to Rio to establish the famous Botanical Garden and to redesign the major parks of the city, including the gardens of the Imperial Palace and the Tijuca Forest.

As France provided the dominant cultural influence in nineteenth-century Brazil, it is natural that the renovations of Paris, directed by Baron Georges-Eugène Haussmann, should have inspired a Brazilian counterpart.[6] In 1871 the counselor of state, João Alfredo Correia de Oliveira, initiated a study having as its aim a thoroughgoing redevelopment in which the lingering colonial aspects of Rio would be effaced, and the city would emerge a completely modern capital worthy of an empire. The commission formed to make the planning study consisted of three engineers, Jorais Jardim, Marcelino Ramos, and Francisco Pereira Passos. The work of this commission had little effect, however, until thirty years later when Francisco Pereira Passos, then sixty-six, was made municipal prefect of Rio and was able to initiate a program of massive urban renovation.

5. Fernando Nascimento Silva, ed., *Rio de Janeiro em seus quattrocentos anos*, 1965, p. 122.

6. Georges-Eugène Haussman was made prefect of the Seine in 1853 by Emperor Napoleon III, receiving almost dictatorial power to direct Parisian planning. Through his determined efforts the French capital underwent the most comprehensive program of urban redevelopment yet seen in a modern city. Haussmann has been both praised for his long-range vision and bold concepts, and condemned for his insensitivity and high-handedness. A highly controversial figure in his own time, Haussmann was dismissed from office in 1870, shortly before the collapse of the Empire.

Embelezamento e Saneamento

Passos outlined his intentions in his prefect's message of September 1, 1903, in which he put forth a thoroughgoing scheme for the "*Embelezamento e Saneamento da Cidade*."[7] Although more ambitious and comprehensive plans would, in later years, be devised for Rio, the prefecture of Pereira Passos may mark the period of most intensive actual accomplishment in urban development.

The planning of the Passos administration was, like much planning of the period, reflective of the influence of Haussmann's work in Paris. Although Haussmann's achievement included technical improvements and modernization, the most conspicuous product of his effort was a series of broad tree-lined boulevards constructed through massive demolition and rebuilding. These new and spacious arteries reinforced the image of Paris as the world's most beautiful city, and were soon imitated in many other countries. Brussels, Rome, Stockholm, Madrid, and Barcelona all showed evidence of Parisian remodeling, while in Mexico the Emperor Maximilian had given the new world its first copies of French boulevards.

In the United States, the monumental embellishments of French design were influential in the creation of the famed 1893 Chicago Fair which inspired in its turn the City Beautiful Movement. The turn of the century was marked by an enthusiastic interest in urban design manifested both in comprehensive planning and the creation of new civic complexes and boulevards.

Although the work of Passos included a general urban renovation, its greatest visual impact, like that of Haussmann, lay in the creation of new monumental avenues. The most famous of these was the Avenida Central, known since 1912 as the Avenida Rio Branco. This new street was designed to lead north and south diagonally across the peninsula of the central business district, terminating at the waterfront at each end. Connecting with the avenue were two new streets bordering the water; at the north end, the Avenida Rodrigues Alves serving the docks and warehouses of the port, and at the south end, the Avenida Beira-Mar, a landscaped boulevard extending to the beach of Botafogo (fig. 53). The Avenida Beira-Mar, which was considered for many years one of the most beautiful streets in the world, was constructed on fill and provided a dual carriage way separated by a central strip of planting. A stone embankment along the water created a wide pedestrian promenade with a view toward the hills of Niteroi. The Avenida Central thus served as a link between the North and South Zones of Rio and facilitated circulation through the oldest and most congested part of the city.

Visiting Rio many years later, Le Corbusier regarded the work of Passos with unreserved admiration:

7. *Embelezamento* means to beautify and embellish, while *saneamento* means to make wholesome, habitable, and agreeable.

> The Prefect Passos, out of a simple sea path, developed a system of avenues of dazzling beauty. They skirt the calm waters of the bay and then once past the Pão de Açúcar (Sugarloaf), they come face to face with the great waves of the sea. The mosaic pavements, black and white marble, make lovely walks. Of a colonial city, charming and hidden in the trees, this other Haussmann has made the most dazzling township in the world. It is a port of call for big ships; the little bays stand out with their famous border. The city used to be timid, hidden in the hinterland; she has suddenly come to life. She has made a start; she will go from strength to strength. The traveler thinks he sees here the world's most beautiful city. And all from a simple mirage created by the road.[8]

Just as in the creation of the Parisian boulevards, extensive demolition of existing structures was required. In constructing the Avenida Central, seven hundred buildings were reportedly razed, with demolitions lasting from 28 February 1903 until 8 March 1904.[9] The street was inaugurated by President Rodrigues Alves on 15 November 1905, as part of the festivities celebrating the anniversary of the proclamation of the republic. As completed, Avenida Central was 1,820 meters long and 33 meters wide, with treelined sidewalks on either side and, down the center, a line of ornamental lampposts carrying the first comprehensive electric street lighting in Rio.

Avenida Central became the site of the most important business and commercial buildings as well as various government offices in the city. In keeping with the inspiration of Haussmann's Paris, the prevailing architectural style was a reincarnation of the most flamboyant French Second Empire mode. Housed in elaborate masonry piles along the street were the National Academy of Fine Arts, the National Library, and the Supreme Court. The eastern terminus of the street was punctuated by the Monroe Palace containing the National Senate in an exuberantly ornamented dome-crowned marble replica of the pavilion which Brazil had erected at the St. Louis Fair of 1904.

The most impressive of the new monuments, however, was the Municipal Theater completed in 1909. Consistent with the spirit, although shy of the scale of its Parisian prototype, the theater embodied an elaborate confection of marble, gilt, and statuary. With its lateral façade bordering the Avenida Central, its columned entrance

8. Le Corbusier, *The Four Routes* (London: Dennis Dobson, 1947), p. 36. First published in France as *Sur les quatre routes* (Paris: Gallimard, 1941). Le Corbusier admired not only Passos's work, but also his strongminded personality. He informed his readers: "In the early days the Prefect, who was considered a madman, used sometimes to go at night with a demolition squad to the house of some owner who refused to evacuate. He would raze it to the ground. Next morning the site was vacant; routine and selfish private interests had been vanquished. Methods pursued in the interests of the community must always be daring."

9. José Alipio Goulart in *Favelas do Distrito Federal* (Rio de Janeiro, 1957) claims that during the construction of the Avenida Central between 2,000 and 3,000 buildings were destroyed. Because many of these were low-priced lodging houses, he maintains that thousands of people were evicted and, unable to obtain suitable housing elsewhere, were forced to move into favelas.

terminated an elongated plaza, the Largo da Mae do Bispo (now the Praça Floriano) and provided a monumental focus for the fan-shaped intersection of Avenida Central and Avenida 13 de Mayo.

As the twentieth century advanced, the initial low-rise character of Avenida Central (renamed Avenida Rio Branco) began to give way to new high-rise construction until, today, only an occasional building of the old scale can be found, a deteriorating remnant wedged between skyscrapers. The major monuments remain, however, overshadowed, but through their massive plasticity successfully asserting their presence against the bland façades of the surrounding office blocks (figs. 54–60). The plaza in front of the Municipal Theater is bordered on one side by the dignified classicism of the National Library, and on the other by the garish lights of a row of movie theaters which have given the name Cinélandia to the district.

Avenida Rio Branco, whatever its transformations, remains the center of Rio, and is, in this sense, a place as much as an artery. José de Oliveira Reis has described the street as "the heart of the city, her palpitations formed by generations of Brazilians. In our moments of national or civic glory, of great emotions, in pleasure and in suffering, in the Avenida Rio Branco a city meets its heros, and its heros are received by the city. In carnival, for four joyous nights, in which the multitudes have their moments of greatest and most spontaneous pleasure, in mad dances, clubs, processions of societies, or simply being present, always the avenue is the favored place."[10]

In addition to the construction of a number of new avenues within Rio, including the now famous Avenida Atlantica along the shore of Copacabana, the administration of Pereira Passos established and improved a number of scenic roads through the spectacular mountains surrounding the city, especially in the Tijuca area. Additional access was given to Copacabana at this time through construction of the Leme tunnel inaugurated in 1904.

The general renovation of the city included numerous works of sanitation, especially directed toward mosquito control and the elimination of yellow fever. The new building program included the construction of markets, schools, and hospitals, and the creation of additional parks. In fact, it is of interest to note a series of laws enacted at this time directed toward improving hygiene and liberating the city from the vestiges of colonial provincialism. Among this legislation were the repeal of a law prohibiting elaborate carnival costumes, the establishment of a law banning the herding of milk cows through the streets, prohibition of the keeping of pigs within the city limits, prohibition of the sale of meat exposed in the doorways of butchers' shops under unhygienic conditions, prohibitions against street begging and the sale of lottery tickets in the streets, establishment of a service to apprehend stray dogs,

10. "As administrações municipais e o desenvolvimento urbano," in Nascimento Silva, ed., *Rio de Janeiro em seus quattrocentos anos*, p. 129.

and a law requiring painting of those portions of buildings visible from the space in front.[11]

In the years following the administration of Pereira Passos, similar public works continued but at a more modest pace. Avenida Niemeyer was constructed along the edge of the mountainous coast leading south of the city, creating a scenic experience similar to that of the Cote d'Azur. This was begun in 1916.

In the central business district, the part of Rio which had long been subject to the greatest pressures on land, the Morro do Castello, the hill on which Mem de Sá established his first settlement in 1567, was demolished beginning in 1920 to provide waterfront fill. Castello had contained a picturesque maze of narrow lanes embodying some of the oldest buildings in the city, together with a monastery and orphanage, and, in the demolition, which was accomplished largely by washing away the hill with high-pressure hoses, 470 buildings were destroyed. The new land was used initially as the site for an international exposition in 1922 commemorating the first centennial of Brazilian independence, and it subsequently provided space for government offices, some of which were housed in former exhibition buildings. The removal of Castello hill was accomplished during the prefecture of Carlos Sampaio, an administrator whose energetic attentions to Rio almost rivaled those of Pereira Passos. When asked why he did not demolish Santo Antônio hill instead of Castello, since it would be easier, he replied that "any prefect could take down Santo Antônio."[12]

The Agache Plan

Rio's first comprehensive plan appeared during the prefecture of Antônio Prado Júnior, whose administration lasted from 1926 to 1930. Although not put into effect, the scheme provided a thoroughgoing study of the city and was partially used as a guideline for future development. The plan was the creation of a Frenchman, Alfred Agache, who was invited to Brazil in 1927 to participate in a series of meetings on urban development, and who remained until 1930, publishing his recommendations as *Cidade do Rio de Janeiro: Remodelação, extensão, e embellezamento.*[13] Agache, who was described in his report as an "architect-urbaniste," held the title, Architect to the French Government, and was also secretary general of the French Society of Urbanists.[14] Working with him were two other French architects, E. de Gröer, and W. Palanchon, together with a French sanitary engineer, A. Duffieux.

11. Ibid., p. 135.

12. Ibid., p. 143.

13. Alfred Agache, *Cidade do Rio de Janeiro: Remodelaçao, extensão, e embellezamento* (Paris, 1930).

14. The French Society of Urbanists (Société Française des Architectes Urbanistes) had been formed in 1912 by a group of specialists involved in city planning activities. They also formed the Committee for Urban and Rural Hygiene, which had its base of operations in the Musée Social in Paris. Anticipating the need for trained urban specialists after the First World War, this group was instrumental in establishing the Institute of Urbanism at the University of Paris, subtitled the National School for Advanced Study in

That a Brazilian official, seeking assistance in formulating a city plan, would turn to France is not altogether surprising. In Brazil the cultural prestige of France remained in many ways undiminished since the first delegation of French artists had arrived more than a hundred years previously to direct artistic life. French was a second language for many educated Brazilians, and some felt themselves as closely identified with French as with Iberian civilization. In terms of technical development, Brazil was still a backwater, and a progressive-minded prefect, wanting advanced ideas, would tend to look abroad for them.

Agache began his report by outlining his principles of city planning. "Urbanism," he claimed, "is a science and at the same time an art—but before all it is a social philosophy."[15] Attempting to define the problem of the master plan, he cited the difficulty of separating the social and economic aspects of the city from its physical form, concluding, "its form expresses its nature." He stressed that an urban plan must be designed to be "adaptable to the purposes of the city, to its functions, and to its future possibilities."[16] Agache chose to define the city in terms of "anatomy" and "function." "Anatomy" pertained to the physical aspects of the city, the topography, the physical plan, the neighborhoods, open space, and buildings. He described "function" in physiological terms, employing a vocabulary similar to that which Le Corbusier sometimes employed. The functions of the city were cited as circulation, respiration, control, and coordination (activities embodying the function of a nervous system), and digestion (the system of services for water, sewerage, drainage, etc.).[17]

In his conception of urban design, Agache was a conservative classicist of the Beaux-Arts tradition, envisioning civic embellishment in terms of wide monumental avenues, imposing classically ordered architectural ensembles, formal landscaping, and baroque axes. In 1912, Agache had been awarded third place in the international competition for the new capital of Australia, Canberra, a competition which reflected the persistence of the classical conception of a government city. The Agache plan for Canberra—similar in spirit to that of the second-prize winner, Eliel Saarinen, and the winner, Walter Burley Griffin—conceived the Australian capital as a traditionally monumental city, embodying long axial avenues, ceremonial plazas, and symmetrically disposed ensembles of classicized government building. Although denied the opportunity to create a major capital in entirety, Agache would emphasize in his planning of Rio the transformation of the city into a monumental government center.

Urbanism and Municipal Administration. Its areas of study included the evolution, social organization, economic organization, administrative organization, and artistic and technical construction of the city. It was from the concepts of Agache that the term *urbanismo* was adopted in Brazil to describe city planning activities. "O termo urbanismo, na sua definição moderna, foi criado pelo arquiteto francês Alfred Agache em 1912, e desde entao universalmente adotado." Cláudio Bardy, "O Século XIX," in Nascimento Silva, ed., *Rio de Janeiro em seus quattrocentos anos,* p. 121.

15. Agache, p. 8.

16. Ibid., p. 119.

17. Ibid., p. 6.

In introducing his report, Agache discussed the background of modern city planning, indicating his respect for the work of Patrick Geddes, and his familiarity with the principles of Garden City planning. Agache expressed particular admiration for the urban design of Daniel Burnham, prefacing his own scheme with Burnham's famous exhortation to "make no little plans." Although an obvious precedent for the sort of overall plan which Agache produced for Rio lay in the work of Haussmann in nineteenth-century Paris, a more immediate parallel could be found in Burnham's civic schemes, the most notable of which was a plan for Chicago published in 1908.[18] Both Burnham and Agache attempted to renovate realistically the existing fabric of a large and complex city, projecting overall improvements in transportation systems and street layout, and augmenting recreational facilities. Most importantly, each sought to create within the city previously lacking elements of monumentality. Burnham, seeking aesthetic stimulants to enjoyment and civic pride, attempted to infuse a utilitarian prairie city with Beaux-Arts civic complexes of overwhelming grandeur; Agache sought to give what was already one of the most beautiful cities of the world the visual attributes of a major national capital.

Included in the Agache report was a historical survey of the development of Rio, providing a statistical analysis of the existing city. It was noted that the population had increased from 811,443 inhabitants at the time of the planning renovations in 1906 to 1,157,873 at the time of the 1920 census, with the estimated population for 1928 at about 1,900,000. Rio had achieved a population ten times that of a century earlier, a rate of growth matched by few other cities. (London and Paris had merely quadrupled in the same period, although Chicago, New York, and Berlin had comparable rates of increase.) In terms of urbanized land, Rio occupied an area of about 98.4 square miles, roughly comparable to the size of Washington, D. C. (93 square miles), Rome (94.2 square miles), or Buenos Aires (111 square miles). It seemed apparent that the city would continue to grow, increasing in commercial and governmental activity and expanding outward toward the suburbs.

The study directed by Agache encompassed many aspects of the city, and included proposals for improvements in sanitation, expansion of the port facilities, redevelopment of the central area, establishment of new streets, and reorganization of the transportation system. The transportation proposal, which was directed toward the improvement of both local circulation and links with the outside, contained the suggestion that existing rail lines in the North Zone be realigned and consolidated at a new central station. This rail terminus would serve as a transportation hub for the

18. Burnham's design typified the Beaux-Arts classicism of the City Beautiful Movement. His work included service on the Senate Park Commission of 1901 which replanned Washington, D. C., according to the classical principles of the L'Enfant plan. He also devised a development plan for San Francisco in 1904–06, and in 1905 he planned for the Philippines the development of Manila and a new summer capital at Baguio. Burnham greatly admired the work of Haussmann, stating, "The task which Haussmann accomplished for Paris corresponds with the work which must be done for Chicago." *Plan for Chicago* (Chicago: The Commercial Club, 1909), p. 18.

whole city, with the major street arteries of Rio extending from its radial plaza, thus creating direct routes inward toward the commercial center and outward toward São Paulo. A cross-axial route would provide access to the South Zone by means of tunnels and lead toward Petropolis in the opposite direction, while diagonal connection would be established with the waterfront, and new circular avenues would provide additional circulation within the city (fig. 61).

Although in the 1920s the automobile had yet to become the curse of Rio, the streets were cluttered with streetcars which Agache thought should be replaced by a faster means of transport. A rapid transit system was proposed which would run underground in the central areas and extend outward to provide a transportation loop encompassing the whole Federal District. This metro system would include a tunnel connection with Niteroi. Although the transportation proposals were made intuitively, without extensive feasibility studies, the suggestions embodied in the Agache plan remained as a guide for Rio, and have been generally incorporated into subsequent plans.

Along the bay frontage of the North Zone, it was proposed to extend the commercial and industrial port through fill and to construct new dock facilities. Adjacent to the docks, near the approach to Ilha do Governador, an airport would be established. In the 1920s, few could anticipate the space-devouring potential of aviation, and the allotted airport space was minimal in terms of future needs. The general siting, however, was prophetic of future land use, for Rio's international airport was subsequently created on the island itself.

Although Agache attempted to deal with the overall utilitarian functions of Rio, his plan was dominated by an effort to develop the city as a monumental national capital. He may have been aware that in 1891 a federal commission had established an inland district in the state of Goiás as the site of a new Brazilian capital, but, since few at the time took this project seriously, he evidently assumed that Rio would continue to house the national government indefinitely.

While endowed with phenomenal natural beauty, Rio was deficient in the symbolic attributes of a great capital. Government buildings tended to be scattered and intermixed with commercial structures; thus, visual consciousness of the city as a government center was vitiated through lack of a ceremonial focus. Realizing this, Agache sought to create within Rio a series of monumental civic complexes—symbolic focal points in which the authority of the state could be embodied in appropriate architectural dignity.

In a statement dealing with the aesthetic aspects of the future city, Agache observed that, in the modern city, the multistoried commercial building had achieved visual dominance, just as the church had dominated in the Middle Ages. The cathedral had expressed the life spirit of medieval times, providing a focus for art and music, and epitomizing the prevailing social and economic forces, and he felt that the modern city needed an equivalent expression of the forces of urban life. Agache thought that such a monumental focus could no longer be found in a single great building, but rather through the establishment of great building complexes embodying an interworking of architecture and open space.

Although Agache was essentially a traditionalist, he had absorbed some of the ideals of athleticism and hygiene permeating much of the design orientation of the Modern Movement in the 1920s. Agache described modern life in terms of a physical culture which "exhibits a liberation of the living forces of our bodies—elements indispensable in our daily lives." The modern city, therefore, in addition to administrative palaces, exposition halls, workshops, libraries, museums, and schools, needed sport grounds, swimming pools, gardens, and large parks. Agache considered whether, instead of letting these

> elemental characteristics of our modern life be dispersed to the four winds, and losing all of their symbolic expression through their dispersal, could we not, by bringing them together, not in a single building, but in an organic complex where buildings and open spaces balance in value, arrive at the creation of great monumental cities—compositions in which one could see the profiles of commercial buildings, expressing economic forces, associated with symbols of the social ideals of our epoch?
>
> We appear here to encounter the true artistic problem of the great city—of which the solution depends much more on the organization of good complexes than on the erection of monuments or single buildings imperfectly conceived and badly realized. For a long time cities have been embellished in the latter manner; today we understand that our true aesthetic will result, above all, in the logical and regular satisfaction of our economic and social exigencies.[19]

In his verbal emphasis on physical culture and the inclusion of sport grounds and parks in large urban complexes, Agache seemed to suggest an open-textured ambient similar to that favored by certain modern visionaries, most notably, Le Corbusier. His designs, however, were relatively conventional, and although the Agache plan involved the creation of a number of new monumental complexes serving to embellish focal points within the central city, they embodied essentially single-purpose traditional government, commercial, or educational functions.

Agache made no attempt to counteract the existing urban fabric of Rio, and adhered in his designs to the prevailing street and block pattern. Although new avenues were created, no effort was made to alter the system of traffic or to reorganize land use. Compared with many of the schematic urban conceptions being developed by modern architects in the 1920s, the Agache plan appears as essentially a nineteenth-

19. Agache, pp. 129–30.

century vision of the city. The plan incorporated both newly created and proposed areas of waterfront fill land, and although such districts provided ample freedom for experiment, they were projected in terms of Beaux-Arts design. Within these tracts, a series of monumental government complexes were to be linked by means of boulevards and landscaped malls.

At the time Agache began his scheme, the hill of Castello had been razed to provide a fill area of 700,000 square meters along the bay adjacent to the business district. This land was largely vacant, containing only a few buildings left over from the 1922 exposition. Agache highly approved of the demolition, feeling that the presence of hills within the central district not only hampered ventilation, but forced an excessive burden of traffic on a single major artery, Avenida Rio Branco. He also approved the long-standing project to remove Santo Antônio hill, indicating in his plan the creation of approximately 650,000 square meters of resulting fill along the shoreline. This new land would extend from the central business district southward to the hill of Glória.

The fill area established by the destruction of Castello would be developed, according to the plan, as a district of ministries, an area in which all major government agencies would be located. This would not only have practical advantages, but it also would provide the opportunity to achieve an aesthetically unified entrance to the city adjacent to the port.

The new land derived from the demolition of Santo Antônio would provide a reclaimed area on the east side of central Rio extending from the business district across the residential areas of Catete and Flamengo to the base of the hill on which is sited Glória church, one of the oldest and most conspicuous landmarks of Rio. The new landfill would replace a deeply curving shoreline with a virtually straight line of frontage, and change the Avenida Beira-Mar, the beautiful waterfront boulevard, to a landlocked street. This part of Rio provides the most spectacular view of the bay, with the mound of Sugarloaf guarding the ocean entrance to the south, and the hills of Niteroi visible across the water. It is this shoreline which greets passengers arriving by ship, before the vessels round the peninsula to the wharves.

Because of the importance of this location, Agache determined to develop the reclaimed area as the dominant monumental complex of the city—a symbolic gateway to Rio. As he phrased his intention, "Of all our land conquered from the sea this in front of the bay is a place of honor, where will be located a federal government complex which will give to the work of men a grandiose aspect which is presently lacking in the city. Rio de Janeiro will offer to the visitor arriving by sea, a monumental entrance corresponding in importance to the destinies of the capital."[20]

A great plaza 350 by 250 meters would take the form of a hemicycle opening to-

20. Ibid., p. 161.

ward the bay (figs. 62, 63). This plaza would serve as a site for military parades, civic demonstrations, and as a ceremonial place of welcome where officials could receive eminent visitors disembarking from their ships by means of launches which would carry them to a waterfront stairway of honor flanked by ceremonial columns. Five civic buildings would face the sweeping plaza. Next to the water on either side would be a palace of fine arts and a palace of commerce and industry, the latter intended to house periodic expositions. The inner side of the square would contain the Senate and the Hall of Deputies on either side of a great auditorium designed to accommodate congresses, celebrations, and concerts. The architectural style of the proposed buildings was a ponderous stripped classicism of the type which in the succeeding decade would be particularly favored in Nazi Germany and Fascist Italy. As presented in the Agache plan, the proposed new civic center seemed to embody a megalomaniacally scaled vision of an imaginary superstate. Within the vast reaches of the plaza, antlike formations of troops would echo in their geometric formations the rigid massing of the buildings, while at night, searchlights would illuminate and unify the assemblage. Attempting to remedy Rio's lack of monumentality, Agache projected a complex where a disciplined nationalism could be expressed through military pomp and ceremony.[21]

Extending from the plaza on either side of the central auditorium were two major avenues, creating a fanlike penetration into the city, one leading into the North Zone and the other providing an axial link with a new commercial plaza within the demolition area of Castello hill. This street was designed so that its directional axis extended outward toward Sugarloaf. The other avenue would intersect Rio Branco at the point where this street previously encountered the shoreline, the intersection, being marked by a circular plaza called the Plaza of Paris, to contain a water basin and fountain. From this plaza, Avenida Rio Branco would continue with a boulevard connection to the new shoreline, at which point the avenue was to be separated from the monumental waterfront complex by a park (fig. 64).

Between the new monumental bayfront development and the area containing the district of ministries Agache's plan proposed a peninsular extension designed to accommodate a formal garden. Within this landscaped area and terminating an axial palm-fringed water basin would be a monumental structure termed by Agache a "basilica" or "pantheon consecrated to national glories." According to the planner:

21. Although the civic plaza of the Agache plan seems prophetic of the civic design of Nazi Germany, a common inspiration for both may lie in the visionary schemes produced by Claude-Nicolas Ledoux and Etienne-Louis Boullée in the late eighteenth century. The austere geometry of Agache's monumental building seems closely allied generally to nineteenth-century romantic classicism. It might be noted, also, that there were several monumental urban schemes developing contemporaneously with the Agache plan. During the 1920s, the monumental conceptions developed by the 1901 McMillan Commission for Washington, D. C., were largely realized, and the American capital began to materialize as a white classical city. Within the British Empire, two new classically ordered cities had been planned in 1912: Canberra in Australia and New Delhi in India. Although progress in Canberra languished, the Indian capital designed by Sir Edwin Lutyens was already evidencing one of the most grandly scaled Beaux-Arts government complexes yet conceived.

"The location clearly defines this monument in the general composition, as it expresses an inherent symbol of national life to the citizenry. Between the palace of government, the palace of expositions, and various ministries—a place which forms a synthesis of all the activities of the country—a temple elevated in memory of the citizens who have contributed to the prosperity of the capital."[22] Foreign embassies would be sited on lots near the "pantheon."

The reclaimed land in the vicinity of the Plaza of Paris would be developed as a district of high-class housing, a highly desirable area because of its convenient access to both the governmental and commercial centers of the city. Zoning regulations would prohibit high-rise construction and restrict the area to low-rise, widely spaced buildings.

The new boulevard leading from the monumental waterfront plaza to the old site of Castello hill was to have been 50 meters wide, embodying three carriage ways separated by strips of planting. At the site of the old hill, the street would widen into a trapezoidal plaza, beyond which it would continue somewhat narrowed in width. The plaza, comprising an area of 3¾ acres would have, in its center, a monument to the foundation of the city. Surrounding the plaza would be a complex of architecturally unified commercial buildings, the ensemble designed to accommodate a planned hierarchy of building heights (fig. 65). Building blocks directly bordering the street would be restricted to 25 meters in height, other blocks would reach 60 meters, while the high-rise towers of the ensemble would reach 100 meters. At street level, ground floor façades would be recessed to provide for sheltered pedestrian promenades 6 meters wide. The architectural treatment of this complex endows a contemporary building type with an essentially classical and conservative, yet sober and simplified, envelope. The material of construction appears to be concrete, with the framing elements emphasized, and the overall ordering of repetitive building forms appears somewhat prophetic of the more austerely modern, but equally disciplined, rebuilding scheme designed by Perret for Le Havre after World War II.

Although, obviously, a complete rebuilding of the banking and commercial district would not be feasible, Agache outlined a proposal for the gradual renovation of this area. He considered the existing pattern of long narrow building lots impractical for buildings over three stories and felt that, to improve the design and functioning of the central area, each city block should be organized as a unit (figs. 66, 67). In his opinion, "an understanding among the owners for a reconstruction of the block would permit application of new regulations for safeguarding hygiene and organizing circulation without the obligation of extensive expropriations."[23] Each block would have an underground parking garage serving all occupants, and the ground floor of each block would be given over to shopping arcades creating passages through

22. Agache, p. 162.

23. Ibid., p. 170.

the blocks. Although the established building pattern which permits structures to be built to the outer limit of the plot would be maintained, some effort would be made to control overbuilding and congestion through height limits, setbacks, and courtyards. As the central business district occupied the oldest part of Rio, many streets were too narrow to be appropriate for motor traffic, and Agache suggested that they be given over completely to pedestrians.

In addition to the government and commercial complexes, another opportunity for monumental composition lay in the development of the university. The site of the existing university was a narrow stretch of land near the foot of Sugarloaf and the bay of Botafogo; most of the university buildings were constructed in the nineteenth century along the Avenida Pasteur. Although the site was somewhat constricted and hemmed in by mountains and water, it was easily accessible from the major residential district of Rio as well as from the business and government centers. The location, moreover, had considerable natural beauty.

Agache proposed to extend the university along two axes. The pattern of growth along the Avenida Pasteur would be extended to the beach lying between Sugarloaf and the hill of Babylonia (the Praia Vermelha). This oceanfront area would be developed with a symmetrically balanced building ensemble focusing on a landscaped park which would open toward the sea. A similarly formal building composition would be created along a landscaped mall extending at a right angle from the Avenida Pasteur. University facilities, at the time Agache began his work, had become somewhat scattered throughout the city, and it was part of his scheme to bring them all together in a single place, creating a "cité universitaire."

When the Agache plan was formulated, Copacabana was fashionable but still an area of low density, while Ipanema and Leblon were even more sparsely settled. Agache, however, foresaw the increased development of these areas and stressed the need for transportation links with the rest of the city. He was of the opinion that the Avenida Atlantica established the permissible building line dangerously close to the ocean, and that it should have been designed to be twice its existing width. He was also concerned about the existence of hazardous currents, and for the safety of bathers advocated the creation of periodic breakwaters.

Around the borders of Lagõa, Agache projected a new avenue and laid out additional residential streets. Although by and large he maintained a conventional street pattern in his planning, he felt Leblon and Ipanema should be zoned for single-family housing, for which he projected a new scheme of residential building. Here, a district would be laid out in superblocks, each containing a central park, and house lots would front either on the peripheral streets or on the interior parks and access lanes. Although a rigid cul-de-sac street system was not attempted, the design of slow traffic lanes provided ample separation of through and local traffic. The plan contained some of the elements of the contemporary Radburn scheme, although the communal park area was both smaller and discontinuous, and greater space was provided in individual house plots. Since the proposed district would lie between two natural recreation areas, the lake and the ocean beach, there probably would be little need for extensive parks within the residential complex. No attempt was made to provide the complete community facilities of a neighborhood unit.[24]

In contrast to later planning efforts in Rio, the Agache proposal devoted relatively little attention to the problem of favelas. In discussing these settlements, Agache acknowledged the social cohesion and community life of many favelas together with the degree of personal freedom which squatter life offered. He felt, however, that these advantages were offset by the physical squalor and the dangers of infectious disease and fire, and he was convinced that the favelas could not be rehabilitated. He stressed, however, that no attempt be made to remove favelas until replacement housing was available. Ultimately, he hoped that sufficient low-cost housing for favelados would be included in a proposed pattern of working-class suburbs.

The completion in 1930 of the Agache plan for Rio coincided with a change in political administration, and no attempt was made to effect comprehensively its proposals. The report embodied a generally well-conceived set of recommendations for Rio, however, and still serves in some ways as a general guide for planning. Those aspects of the Agache plan which had least subsequent effect on the city were the attempts at monumental design, while the most influential were the more utilitarian proposals regarding transportation, circulation, and sanitation.

In the years that followed, Rio continued to expand and change in the piecemeal fashion common to most cities. The site previously occupied by the old hill of Castello, where Agache had wanted to establish a monumental and unified commercial complex surrounding a commemorative plaza, was simply absorbed into the existing pattern of the business district.

The area of fill resulting from the demolition of Castello, where Agache had wished to establish a monumental district of ministries, received no comprehensive planning, and forty years later exhibited a mixture of government offices haphazardly erected, leftover exhibition buildings from the 1922 centennial, and parking lots. Bordering the bay itself is an elevated freeway, the Avenida Kubitschek, completed in 1960.

The waterfront extension, in which Agache had sought to establish the ceremonial "pantheon" set amid formal landscaping, became in the 1930s the municipal airport, perhaps the only airport serving a major city which is a five minute stroll from the

24. The residential scheme that Agache produced for Leblon relates to trends in residential design having their origins in the Garden City tradition. The Garden City Movement, in addition to advocating the decentralization of the city, focused attention on the planning of the domestic environment, and was characterized by schemes in which street area could be reduced and greater amounts of park space provided. The residential complex was increasingly regarded as a pedestrian-oriented area which would provide within its confines schools, shopping, and communal facilities. The Radburn plan produced for New Jersey in 1929 emphasized the cul-de-sac street and oriented houses toward large interior parkbands containing pedestrian circulation.

business district. Only in the early visionary schemes of Sant'Elia and Le Corbusier, in which planes are shown landing directly in the commercial center, is there a more convenient relation between air transport and the city than exists in downtown Rio.

Highly approving of this practical use of the site, Le Corbusier once observed that "old-fashioned planning of a type which, it seems to us, offers no solution of modern problems, had intended this spot for the erection of a Capitol. The Capitol had not been built since the Brazilians had little notion what to do with a Capitol if they got one. . . . a triumph of wings is well worth the loss of a Capitol."[25]

The demolition of Santo Antônio hill got under way in the 1950s, but the use to which the resulting waterfront fill was eventually put was far different from the monumental gateway which Agache had envisioned. Instead of limiting the filling operation to the bayfront between the central district and Gloria hill, the present fill extends all the way to Botafogo, providing space for a motor freeway linking the business district with Copacabana. At the water's edge, a new beach has been created, and the ceremonial aspects of the area are limited to a memorial to Brazilian World War II soldiers.

Although Agache doubtlessly considered his monumental center necessary to convey Rio's image of a capital, the projected ensemble embodied a spirit at variance with both the Carioca temperament and the local predilection in building. While in certain parts of Europe, government complexes similar in style and scale would echo to the thud of boots, impassioned shouts of allegiance, and the frenzied exhortations of political demagogues, the inhabitants of Rio de Janeiro would be building apartment houses in Copacabana.

The completion of the Agache plan coincided with the Pan American Architectural Congress which met in Rio in 1930, an occasion which generated considerable discussion of the proposal. An American observer noted at the time that "opinion on the whole is flatteringly favorable to the plan." Among the criticism, however, was the claim that the plan was

> foreign to local conditions. It is said to be an illogical attempt to graft French city planning . . . onto Rio. As an example of the unsuitability of the plans submitted, the new gardens and parkways are cited. Formal gardens of the Le Nôtre School, favored by the plan, owing to their lack of shade, have come in for severe criticism. It is further claimed that a city such as Rio, cut up and spread inevitably by the mountains which perforce separate district from district, does not lend itself to the French system of a "place centrale," and radiating avenues.[26]

Although Agache's master plan was officially suspended in 1934, in 1938 a succeeding prefecture created a city plan commission headed by José de Oliveira Reis, which

25. Le Corbusier, *Four Routes*, p. 106.
26. "Rio and Its Skyscrapers," *The Brazilian American*, 12 July 1930, p. 5.

was charged with adapting the Agache plan to changing conditions in Rio. The work of this commission concentrated primarily on the pressing needs of road communication within the city. The increasing development of the South Zone made improved access necessary, and, to achieve this, a greater number of tunnels through the intervening mountains was considered essential. The commission envisaged the eventual employment throughout Rio of a total of eleven tunnels. The first tunnels constructed in Rio had been through relatively narrow mountain barriers, such as those connecting with Copacabana. To open up more direct routes between the North and South Zones, however, more lengthy tunnels were proposed, including a passage between Lagoa and Rio Comprido, as well as a still longer tunnel between outlying Gavea and the North Zone. Also proposed were a number of new streets, seven radial and nine perimetal thoroughfares.

Among the new streets subsequently established were the Avenida Brasil serving the industrial suburban reaches of the North Zone, the Avenida Niemayer circling the central waterfront, and the Avenida Presidente Vargas which intersects Avenida Rio Branco and provides the major traffic link between the business district and the North Zone.

Agache had proposed, as part of his master plan, that a major avenue be created in the central part of the city, intersecting Avenida Rio Branco at the site of the church of Candalária and leading westward to connect with the railroad station. Continuing from the station, the avenue would serve to channel circulation through the North Zone. This new street, christened the Avenida Presidente Vargas, was eventually begun in 1940 (figs. 68–70). It continued the existing line of the Mangue canal, and Agache had originally named the street Avenida do Mangue. During the nineteenth century, proposals had been considered to extend this canal all the way to the bay, but they were abandoned because of the many obstacles in its way. Similar obstructions lay in the path of the new avenue, and its creation required demolitions on a scale similar to those undertaken in the construction of Avenida Rio Branco. Because of the extensive destruction involved, the street was opposed by some federal authorities, banking establishments, and church officials.

Three major churches, Bom Jesus do Calvario, S. Domingos, and S. Pedro were destroyed to make way for Avenida Presidente Vargas. However, the great church of Candalaria, one of the historic monuments of Rio which stood directly on axis with the street, was not only spared, but was intended to provide a dramatic terminal focus. Upon reaching the church the avenue divides, passing on either side of it.

Although Avenida Presidente Vargas was to be two blocks in width, the city expropriated a strip of land four blocks wide. The blocks bordering the new street were then redimensioned and sold at auction, bringing profits to the city far exceeding the expropriation costs. The avenue was designed for high-rise commercial use, and, although the building line was set close to the curb, a covered pedestrian promenade was created by requiring a setback of the first two floors. Although the initial height regulations restricted buildings to twelve stories, real-estate interests altered the ruling to permit twenty-two stories, except for those buildings directly surrounding the church of Candalária.

The initial conception of the avenue was that of a monumental landscaped boulevard wider than the Champs Elysées which would carry a treelined parkband down the center. During construction, however, the demands of the motor took precedence over aesthetics, and the entire surface was paved so that the center could serve as a parking lot. Punctuating the intersection with Avenida Rio Branco, the ancient church of Candalária, initially projected as the dignified focal point of a gracious avenue, now forms a small island in a sea of parked cars. The street itself presents an intimidating expanse of pavement bordered by a lengthening wall of high-rise building uniformly lacking in architectural distinction.

Le Corbusier in Rio

A century after Grandjean de Montigny arrived in Rio to direct artistic life in accordance with prevailing French canons, another Frenchman appeared to inspire a generation of Brazilian architects with the concepts of the Modern Movement as it had been developing in Europe. While the conservative and classically oriented Agache had been plotting monumental avenues and classical civic complexes within the established framework of Rio, Le Corbusier had achieved fame through the creation of a new urban image.[27]

Through a series of visionary schemes Le Corbusier had urged the dissolution of the prevailing urban fabric, and the project for a City for Three Million People, which he had exhibited at the Salon d'Automne in Paris in 1922, embodied concepts which would be seen repeatedly in his work. Le Corbusier conceived civic design in terms of four basic principles: the decongestion of the centers of cities, increase of density, enlargement of the means of circulation, and enlargement of the landscaped areas.

The conventional city block would be replaced by large expanses of greenery in which standardized apartment housing would provide high densities without sacrifice of open space. For office accommodation Le Corbusier developed first a cruciform glass-walled skyscraper and later what he termed the "chicken-claw" skyscraper, in which a dominant concave façade is oriented toward the sun. Within the business district, as in other parts of the city, space would be opened up, with high-rise office buildings geometrically disposed amid expansive plazas. Le Corbusier sought the end of the "corridor-street" in which motor traffic funneled between walls of buildings,

27. For an analysis and critical discussion of Le Corbusier's urban design see Norma Evenson, *Le Corbusier: The Machine and the Grand Design* (New York, 1969). See also bibliography.

favoring the creation of motor freeways separated from building lines. By raising buildings on pilotis and elevating streets, Le Corbusier claimed to have achieved an almost total liberation of the ground area for pedestrian use.

Le Corbusier's schemes fused a Garden City emphasis on greenery and open space with a Futurist romanticism of modernity and mechanization, and he once stated, "having absorbed the romanticism of the past, I felt able to give myself up to that of our own age, which I love."[28] Le Corbusier was one of the first to grasp the excitement inherent in the motor road and to conceive of the limited-access freeway as an integral part of urban design.

In 1929 Le Corbusier arrived in South America to lecture in Buenos Aires, and he included a visit to Brazil in his tour. As one of the leaders of the Modern Movement in design, he was generally well-received, and while in São Paulo he was officially welcomed in the Municipal Chamber and was even seated on the President's rostrum, a courtesy reserved for only the most distinguished visitors. The President-elect, Júlio Prestes, took advantage of Le Corbusier's presence to discuss with him current proposals in Brazilian city planning. According to Le Corbusier: "I had excluded Rio from my architectural mission in South America, because my colleague from Paris, Agache, was at that moment establishing the master plan of the city, and it wouldn't do to disturb someone at work. But the architects of Rio ferreted me out in Buenos Aires, and upon my arrival in São Paulo, disinterested parties persuaded me to come to speak in Rio. I then agreed to speak of my ideals about architecture, and of my plan for the amelioration of Paris."[29]

Like most visitors, Le Corbusier was rhapsodic about the beauty of Rio.

> The sea, the bay opening toward the sea filled with islands and promontories; the mountains which lift themselves toward the sky tempestuously, carving out innumerable shifting vistas—a sort of tumultuous green flame above the city, always, everywhere, changing aspect with each step. The tourist never ceases his praises, his enthusiasm is renewed at each crossing; the city seems to him to have been made for his diversion. One is clothed in light, the people are welcoming, I am welcomed with open arms, I am happy, . . . I swore to myself not to open my mouth about Rio. And here I find myself with an irresistible need to speak.
>
> Here in Rio de Janeiro, a city which seems radiantly to defy all human col-

28. Le Corbusier, *City of Tomorrow* (London: Architectural Press, 1947), p. xxv.

29. Le Corbusier, *Précisions sur un état présent de l'architecture et de l'urbanisme* (reprint, Paris, 1960), p. 236. Le Corbusier later published an illustration from the Agache plan together with the disapproving caption, "Here a city planner of the classical school has once again proposed courtyards and corridor-streets." *The Radiant City* (New York, 1967). During Le Corbusier's visit, however, the conservative Agache appears to have expressed no hostility toward his radical compatriot. Le Corbusier reported that upon arrival in Rio he was taken by the prefect to visit Agache in his office, and that on this occasion Agache referred to Le Corbusier's iconoclasm, telling the prefect, "Le Corbusier is a man who shatters windows, a man who makes the wind blow, and we others, we follow after him. . . ." *Précisions*, p. 237. Agache was present in the audience when Le Corbusier addressed the Association of Architects on 8 December 1929.

laboration in its universally proclaimed beauty, I have the strong desire, a bit mad, perhaps, to attempt here a human adventure—the desire to set up a duality, to create "the affirmation of man" against or with "the presence of nature."[30]

This affirmation would take the form of an immense motor freeway 100 meters high which would stretch through the city linking major points and containing apartments within the structure below the roadway (fig. 71). The giant wall would abut on Sugarloaf and follow the line of the hills toward the central district where it would bifurcate with one arm reaching into the North Zone and the other leading across a bridge toward Niteroi. At the point of projection toward Niteroi, the business center would be rebuilt to provide for three massive high-rise slabs extending at right angles to the roadway, with the rooftops incorporated into the roadway.

Le Corbusier claimed that the whole freeway structure could be built without interfering in any way with the city below. Only the concrete supports would require ground space, and the apartments would begin 30 meters above the ground, presumably clearing all existing rooftops. Between this 30-meter level and the 100-meter level of the roadway, ten double stories of apartments could be provided, with descent for vehicles from the rooftop freeway to the streets below to be made by elevator.

The romantic aspects of the scheme prompted Le Corbusier to lyricize that he had created in his elevated apartments "almost the nest of a bird planner. . . . The airplane will become jealous of such liberties which seemed to be reserved for him." He proclaimed that the tumultuous peaks of Rio would be exalted by contrast with the great horizontal band of building. "The steamers which pass, magnificent and moving structures of modern times, will find there, suspended in the space above the city, a response, an echo, an answer. The entire site begins to speak, of the water, of the land, of the air: it speaks architecture. This discourse is a poem of human geometry and an immense fantasy of nature. The eye sees two things: nature and the product of human labor. The city announces itself by a line which, alone, is capable of harmonizing with the violent caprice of the mountains: the horizontal."[31]

Le Corbusier's second visit to Rio occurred in 1936 at the invitation of the minister of Education and Health, Gustavo Capanema, who requested that he advise in the development of the new Ministry of Education and Health building and in the creation of a new university complex in Rio. During this period, in addition to working directly with the group of architects involved in the Ministry project, Le Corbusier

30. Ibid., pp. 234–36.

31. Ibid., pp. 244–45. For the city of São Paulo, Le Corbusier projected a similar elevated apartment building creating a great cross axis focusing on the center of the city. A variation of the scheme was also produced during 1930–34 as part of a plan for the development of Algiers. Two outlying suburbs, St. Eugène and Hussein-Dey, were to be linked to a new central business district by means of an elevated vehicular express route following the mountainous outline of the coast and containing apartments for an estimated 180,000 people within its framework. Similar apartment buildings housing 200,000 people would be constructed on an elevated site above the city called Fort l'Emperor and linked to the new civic center by an elevated freeway.

gave a series of six public lectures on urbanism and architecture, with the result that, "the new works of European architecture . . . suddenly, with the words of Le Corbusier, took on body and soul. His stay in Rio de Janeiro was thus of immeasurable value and an unforgettable and lasting influence."[32]

At this time, Le Corbusier developed further the project he had envisioned in 1929, in which the extended districts of the city would be linked by a continuous apartment slab carrying a motorway on the roof. Although in its initial form this scheme had been designed to leave the ground level of the city untouched, Le Corbusier produced a sketch in 1936 in which the entire urban fabric had been drastically renovated (fig. 72). The ground area from Leblon to the central district and into the North Zone was shown clear of buildings except for widely spaced giant skyscrapers. Through this, wound the snakelike form of the apartment-freeway, extending inward through the North Zone to the central district, and forming a loop through the South Zone, with the smooth continuous geometry of the man-made wall threading through but contrasting with the rugged and jutting mountains of the site.

Le Corbusier's visionary schemes were generalized conceptions of an ideal environment, rather than specific attempts to focus on the detailed workings of real cities. His view was Olympian and formalist, encompassing a matchless sense of great scale, and his schemes presented not cities, but ideas about cities. They outlined possibilities, but did not bridge the gap between actuality and image, and, with an artist's poetic license, they simplified the complex reality of urban function for dramatic effect.

Confronted with a specific problem, however, Le Corbusier was well able to fuse practical possibilities with imaginative design solutions. The university project involved the development of a new area as the site of a university city (figs. 73, 74). Feeling that the old location near the Praia Vermelha was too constricted, and because of the insistence of the military in reserving the beach for their own institutions, Capanema proposed reestablishing the whole university on a site near the mountains in the North Zone. The new complex would be in the vicinity of Tijuca, lying in a valley between the long mountain ridge of the Serra do Mar and a hill, Mangueira, the site of a well-known favela.

As the site lay astride major rail and motor routes through the North Zone, the scheme produced by Le Corbusier embodied the creation of a great platform providing a concourse for rail and motor circulation through and into the site. On one side of the platform would be the faculties of art, architecture, and engineering, and on the other the faculties of law, letters, philosophy, and science. The configuration of the buildings would be linear, following the line of the transportation platform.

The building type embodied a series of parallel slabs united at ground level by

32. Quoted by Henrique Mindlin, *Modern Architecture in Brazil* (New York, 1956), p. 1.

lower buildings. Separated from this complex would be a parallel grouping containing the medical school and hospital. Included centrally in the complex was a favored building type of the architect, a museum, developed on a square plan with a series of concentric galleries. Although Le Corbusier's scheme was admired, it was never used, and the university site was subsequently shifted to an island near the Ilha do Governador.

Le Corbusier's design sense may be seen reflected in a number of later design projects for Rio. One example, the scheme which Affonso Reidy produced in 1948 for the development of the demolition area of Santo Antônio hill, appears in many ways to be a pastiche of Le Corbusier devices, duplicating even his drawing style. In contrast to the Castello area, which had been developed as a continuation of the surrounding street and block pattern, Reidy's scheme attempted to develop the new area as a unified complex crossed by two major streets, one of them an elevated freeway. Within the redeveloped district was projected a row of high-rise office slabs, parallel and widely spaced, separated at ground level by grass and paved plazas. On one side of the complex was placed an apartment house of the linear setback type seen in many of Le Corbusier's schemes. Included also were the fan-shaped auditoriums and the concentric museum form favored by Le Corbusier.

Also in harmony with Le Corbusier's urban conceptions was a project designed in 1946 by Paul Lester Wiener and Jose Luis Sert for a new industrial community, Cidade dos Motores, about 20 miles from Rio. Sponsored by Brigadier General Antonio Guedes Muniz, chief of the Brazilian Airplane Engine Factory Commission, this projected new town of 25,000 was to provide an alternative to the haphazard development characterizing the Duque du Caixas area. The unbuilt project, which related a planned industrial district to a residential settlement, incorporated many of the prevailing tenets of modern urban design. It would have included four neighborhood units containing apartment housing, community and recreation facilities, together with a common civic center.

The overall conception of a planned industrial settlement had much in common with Le Corbusier's linear-industrial schemes of the 1940s, and Le Corbusier himself was enthusiastic in praise of the scheme. He once commented: "I have examined these plans with deep joy and I have studied them with extreme pleasure. It is a work well done; landscape, climate, geography, topography, science of the engineer and of the architect combined result here in a harmonious and precise whole, inspiring confidence. Mastership radiates from these plans. It is stimulating to see these liberating principles of a sound doctrine being applied (especially when one has had some part in its genesis)."[33]

33. Le Corbusier, "Architecture and Urbanism," *Progressive Architecture* 28 (February 1947): 67.

The Doxiadis Report

In 1960 Rio ceased officially to be the capital of Brazil, and the former Federal District became the State of Guanabara. Although no longer the political focus of the country, and second to São Paulo in economic importance, Rio continued to expand, and exhibited, in company with most major cities, an intensification of urban problems. In 1964 the governor of Guanabara, Carlos Lacerda, following the Rio tradition of consulting foreign specialists, negotiated a contract with the Greek planning firm, Doxiadis Associates, to prepare within the following year a "physical long-term Urban Development Program and Plan for the State of Guanabara." The contract was authorized through COHAB, and, to aid in the coordination of necessary information surveys, a new agency was formed called CEDUG (the Executive Commission for the Urban Development of the State of Guanabara).[34]

The report submitted by the Doxiadis firm in 1965 appears to be the most comprehensive study of Rio yet attempted, and embodies the first land-use map ever made of Guanabara, together with a thorough compilation of statistical information about the city. The report attempted first to examine the "Ekistic" conditions of the city, defining the term as used "to designate existing conditions related to all the demographic, social, economic and physical aspects of Human Settlements. These concern the natural setting, their population, their economy, their social and community structure, their land-use pattern, the distribution of community buildings and facilities, the transportation network, the existing networks of public utilities, etc. EKISTICS is the science of Human Settlements as developed by Dr. C. A. Doxiadis."[35]

The aim of the study was to outline the problems of the city and to establish policies for long- and short-term solutions. Included would be a physical plan for the year 2000, indicating various phases of development, and considering the growth of Guanabara within its metropolitan and regional setting. A thirty-five year program for the urban development of Guanabara would be determined in relation to both needs and financial resources, and within this program a series of specific projects for the first five years would be developed. Finally, a program of implementation would be formulated in terms of administrative organization, training of technical personnel, and legislation.

The problems of Rio as outlined by the report included a failure of civic facilities to keep pace with the increase of population. Housing was considered inadequate, and squatter favelas were growing. Utilities throughout the city were found insuffi-

34. The administrative head of CEDUG was Colonel Americo Fontenelle who was also appointed traffic director for the State of Guanabara in 1964. The architect, Helio Modesto, was put in charge of technical and planning services, while the team of Greek consultants was headed by A. Hadjopoulos.

35. CEDUG–Doxiadis, p. 5 (see chap. 1, n. 5).

cient, and community facilities in education, health, recreation, and commerce were badly distributed. Throughout the city were areas of blight and obsolescence. The system of mass transit was criticized as uncoordinated: services ran independently of one another, there was no standard gauge, and suburban trains operated on the same tracks as long-distance traffic. Automobile traffic was heavy and complicated by problems of topography. In terms of industrial development, there was a shortage of industrial sites within the city, while the port facilities were congested and unable to expand because of their close proximity to the equally congested central business district.

Because of the intense pressures on the central part of Rio, and its limited capacities for absorbing additional population or commercial functions, long-range emphasis in the plan was placed on the urbanization of the greater Rio area, with the assumption that by the year 2000 the entire habitable area of Guanabara would be completely urbanized. The direction of projected expansion was assumed to be that already established along lines of transport in the North Zone. The outlying towns of Campo Grande and Santa Cruz were considered as nuclei for urban growth, while central Rio would extend to absorb Bangú and Jacarepaguá. In order to ease pressures in Rio and create incentives for the development of outer Guanabara, it was proposed that the bay of Sepetiba lying along the coast west of Rio, be developed as an alternate port and industrial center. This would create two major commercial-industrial nuclei for the state.

As an overall scheme for development, the entire greater Rio area—including Niteroi across the bay and adjacent parts of the State of Rio to the north—was conceived in terms of a large highway grid through which would be threaded a linear pattern of urbanized settlement (fig. 75). The strips of settlement would not be along the highway lines, but would cut through the centers of the blocklike divisions made by the grid. Within the center of each block would be a civic, commercial, and business nucleus, and connecting these nuclei, running primarily north and south, would be bands containing educational facilities, institutions, and special residential uses.

The purpose of the master plan was "to create a framework for the infrastructure that will permit the future balanced growth of the city, and will help solve the problems of the present city, without unduly destroying its charm and character. . . . The central area functions of the city should be permitted to expand along axes that will provide the spines for the structuring of communities around them."[36] At the metropolitan scale, it was envisaged that urban expansion would extend northward along a zone to the east of the Avenida Brasil, while, within Guanabara itself, growth would continue westward along an axis leading to Sepetiba Bay. It was estimated that by

36. Ibid., p. vii.

the year 2000, the state would contain two major urban communities; one, the old city of Rio in the eastern part, the other, the new urban complex in the west. Linking these two centers would be a "Central Zone or spine of internal development of the State, and a number of other smaller urban communities will be structured around and alongside this central spine of the State."[37]

The central spine would be designed to follow a line of transport consisting of a proposed new rapid transit line using the existing right-of-way of the Central do Brasil railroad and a new motor freeway. In order to offset expropriation costs in establishing the transport line, it was proposed that air rights over the transit line and highway be given over to continuous multistoried commercial building (fig. 76). This conception of linear urban development employing a transport line combined with a continuous structure has appeared in a number of theoretical permutations since Edgar Chambless created his Roadtown scheme in 1910, a design which projected a multistoried building over underground railroad tracks.[38] With relation to Rio, the immediate prototype would be Le Corbusier's project involving a continuous apartment house carrying motor traffic on the roof, which he first sketched in 1929. The Doxiadis scheme was not meant as visionary, however, but as a practical solution to the problem of financing urban growth. It proposed that rapid transit lines be underground, and the motor freeway be either underground running on each side of the transit line, or, at grade. The type of overhead building suggested in the Doxiadis report would use the first two floors for parking garages, with pedestrian access placed at the third level. The complex would be bordered by service roads at ground level, with pedestrian bridges above.

By and large the Doxiadis report was not concerned with details of physical design; it was primarily devoted to outlining major planning needs and directions of future metropolitan growth. In attempting this, it was observed that "the need for a systematic transportation survey and plan was identified by the consultants at a very early stage of the study."[39] The study began by the establishment of a main road network based on proposed land use and expected population distribution for the year 2000, which was then tested using a mathematical model. From this, a modified road network was produced and cost estimates prepared. The proposed new road system would consist of 242 miles of freeways, with full control of access, and 310 miles of high-standard expressways or major arteries. In addition, 48 miles of rapid transit line were proposed along the two most heavily traveled corridors of the state, the east–west axis of the North Zone and the South Zone connection with the central district. Within the central city an underground system would extend from Ipanema

37. Ibid., p. viii.
38. For a description of this scheme see Edgar Chambless, *Roadtown* (New York: Roadtown Press, 1910).
39. CEDUG–Doxiadis, pp. iv–v.

through Copacabana and along the bay to the central district which would be served by a loop system. In the North Zone, lines would run partly underground and partly aboveground.

In terms of immediate action, the report outlined eight projects to be undertaken within the first five years of the plan. First, a tract of 1,155 acres of land in the North Zone—extending from the central business district along the shore of the bay to the state boundaries—was to be developed as a "Zone of higher order central functions of regional and national importance." This would involve a general upgrading of the area, which was essentially run down, poorly served by roads, and, when in residential use, occupied by slums and favelas. Redevelopment here would incorporate into what was primarily a port, warehousing, and industrial area new commercial and business functions as well as state and federal administrative buildings and institutions. The shoreline would be improved for recreational use with additional parks and recreational areas set up. High-density housing would be built, including housing for low-income groups employed in the central zone and the port.

The second project suggested was the development of the central spine of settlement leading through the North Zone, in which a strip of commercial building would employ air rights over newly created transport lines. Next proposed was the development of 525 acres of industrial land along the northern boundaries of Guanabara and 425 acres in the Sepetiba region. Transportation projects were outlined involving improvements in existing streets together with the establishment of traffic signs, signals, and warnings. There were projects for favela housing, with proposed construction of 17,000 new dwelling units, and a full-scale socioeconomic survey of favelas was suggested.

Educational facilities would be improved through construction of 500 new primary and 136 new secondary schools, while the recreational development of 1,600 acres of parkland, four playfields, and twelve playgrounds was included in the program. Central to the recreational proposal was the improvement of the shore of Guanabara Bay in order to provide much needed waterfront parkland in the North Zone, while similar development of shoreline along the coast of Jacarapaguá was also suggested. Finally, the five-year program was to embody improvements and expansion of all public utilities.

Although the Doxiadis report dealt primarily with large-scale aspects of Rio, two areas of the city were selected for detailed analysis: Copacabana and Mangue. Copacabana was selected because it, "with its dense pattern of urban living, has accumulated serious problems, as a result of the pressure upon all its urban networks and the lack of adequate community buildings and facilities."[40] A summary of the Doxiadis proposals for Copacabana is included in chapter 2. Mangue was chosen for con-

40. Ibid., p. 299.

sideration because it was "on the fringe of the present Central Business District of the City of Rio de Janeiro and in the area where blight has manifested itself and where corrective measures setting the pattern for its renewal should be taken. This community falls in the direct line of expansion of the present center of the city and should be so planned as to accommodate some of the major objectives of the Master Plan for the central area."[41] Mangue, a deteriorating area of mixed industrial, commercial, and residential use, had for some time been considered by Rio planners as the logical site for urban renewal, and the Doxiadis report reinforced prevailing opinions (figs. 77, 78). In addition to lying in the path of natural expansion westward from the central district, Mangue also comprised the area through which traffic from the North Zone would pass to reach the new Santa Barbara tunnel leading to Botafogo in the south.

For both Copacabana and Mangue, detailed study was made of land use, population densities, traffic patterns, utilities, condition of buildings, etc. In the case of Copacabana, suggestions were made regarding future alterations in building form to achieve improved use of the congested site. For Mangue a general redevelopment was suggested. No specific plan for this was made; rather, the report attempted to outline the major considerations necessary in attempting redevelopment. It was suggested that corrective measures include preservation of some properties, rehabilitation of others, and demolition of those structures beyond economic repair. The plan stressed that "the tools for achieving the aims of the plan should be a combination of techniques of clearance, rehabilitation or conservation which will integrate planning of the area with the future of the area surrounding it and make possible an orderly and planned pattern of growth." The report predicted: "It is very probable that the plan for Mangue will propose a different internal street system and larger size blocks more compatible with the function and design of large scale central area building complexes, to permit the erection of modern office, commercial or residential buildings. Therefore it would seem necessary for reparcellation of the land to take place by blocks for the various parts of Mangue where plots are too small to permit economic assembly and construction by private individuals."[42]

Although the Doxiadis proposals were not adopted in detail, the Guanabara government began a program of demolition and renewal in Mangue in 1967. The district was subsequently rebuilt in a pattern that included high-rise commercial building and apartment housing.

In approaching the favela problem, the Doxiadis firm first attempted to obtain a foundation of reasonably accurate information regarding favela population. As existing sources of data provided widely varying figures, they decided to approach the problem by employing aerial photographs in which, following a random-sampling

41. Ibid.

42. Ibid., p. 312.

process, the number of favela houses, or *barracos,* were counted stereoscopically. Population estimates were based on the number of houses, and the resulting figure was 500,000 projected for 1964. To obtain additional information, a socioeconomic survey was proposed and sample questionnaires developed.

It was felt that the favela problem could only be met in terms of a long-range, fifteen-year program. Within the first five years the foundations of the program would have to be established, surveys taken, experimentation and demonstration undertaken, legislation prepared, and basic housing projects carried out. As experimental guidelines for physical planning, the report included sample site plans for new communities and basic schemes for adapting community layouts to different types of topography. Minimum standards for plot sizes and housing types were suggested, together with indications of utilities and circulation patterns, with emphasis placed on the development of housing nuclei which could be expanded by occupants. Sample house types were developed and projections made regarding construction techniques. It was considered that there was "no single method of construction or type of material which could solve the favela problem in its entirety,"[43] and a variety of methods and materials would have to be used, together with optimum solutions for varying site conditions. Although, for immediate projects, conventional construction would be more economical, increasing use of prefabrication would characterize the long-term program.[44]

Among the recommendations of the Doxiadis report was the outline for an improved governmental organization for planning. To coordinate planning activities among the large number of governmental bodies involved in urban development in Guanabara, a new Secretariat of Urban Development was proposed which would oversee the implementation of the master plan. This organization would be responsible for master planning, top policy formulation on urban development, coordinating state planning activities, and reviewing and controlling the implementation of urban-development programs prepared by other governmental, semigovernmental, or private organizations. Within the existing Secretariat of Public Works, detailed project planning would be done by the Department of Urban Engineering, and execution of redevelopment projects by SURSAN (Superintendência de Urbanizaçao e Saneamento), while enforcement of development programs would be assigned to the Department of Urban Engineering and the Department of Buildings.

The Doxiadis investigators were well aware that the greatest impediment to effective planning in Rio would lie in the disorganization of government agencies in-

43. Ibid., p. 79.

44. For purposes of immediate action and experimentation, a pilot project for favela resettlement was proposed for a specific site selected for its range of topography as well as its good connections with existing employment centers. The purposes of the project would have been to experiment and produce optimum methods of construction, and to determine ideal plot size and orientation for flat, gently sloping, and steeply sloping sites, together with a planned community layout. Although the site was approved by the government, this project, like other proposals in the Doxiadis report, was shelved when the administration changed.

volved in urban planning. Lack of coordination, redundancy of effort, failure to provide communication of information, combined with the frequent inefficiency of Brazilian bureaucracy has made long-range urban planning in Rio almost impossible.[45]

The Doxiadis report, like the Agache plan, was shelved as the political administration of the city changed. The Agache plan had been written in French and translated into Portuguese when published. The Doxiadis report, however, remained in its original English, and few copies ever found their way into government planning offices.

Among those planners familiar with the Doxiadis recommendations, opinion was somewhat divided as to its applicability. Some had reservations regarding the development of the Sepetiba Bay area, and it was felt that the large-scale grid pattern suggested for the urbanization of Guanabara was somewhat arbitrary and insufficiently related to topography and existing patterns of settlement. It was also pointed out that some of the suggestions, such as the redevelopment of Mangue, had already been under consideration by local planning officials. Not everyone was in agreement regarding the desirability of the multi-level scheme for Copacabana or the development of the North Zone transportation line.

For effective realization, both the Agache and Doxiadis plans had presupposed the willingness and ability of the municipal government to administer long-range coordinated planning. In Rio, however, because of the multitude of government agencies involved in planning activities, and the frequent reluctance of political administrations to continue projects of predecessors, the realities of life may be better adapted to short-range efforts achievable within a single administration.

Both of the plans for Rio, however, although not adopted in totality, provide sources of reference for planners. As a Guanabara official phrased it, "Both of these plans have been locked away in a drawer, but sometimes we peek into the drawer."

Planning in Modern Rio: Aims and Realization

The planning efforts of modern Rio embody a summation of varied approaches to civic development. Prefectural leadership has manifested itself in a series of specific public works and redevelopment efforts, the most comprehensive of which were the achievements of the Pereira Passos administration. With the creation of the Agache plan in the 1920s, an attempt was made to provide an overall scheme for urban development and to create within Rio new aspects of monumentality. A still more com-

45. In their attempts to obtain information upon which to base their planning efforts, the Doxiadis organization was frequently hampered by a lack of cooperation on the part of Guanabara government agencies. This in part may have resulted from the prevailing disorganization and uncommunicativeness of Brazilian government offices. However, other factors may have included a resentment of foreigners engaged in work which many felt Brazilians could do for themselves, and political opposition to Carlos Lacerda.

prehensive vision was embodied in the Doxiadis plan which established outlines for the future urbanization of the State of Guanabara and the greater Rio area. Whatever guidance these plans may have provided, the development of Rio has been based, not on an authoritative master plan, but on a series of decisions governed by the most pressing needs of the moment. In the view of some, changing conditions in the contemporary city require constant flexibility, and a Rio planner recently observed, "What must exist is a process of planning, with the addition of various plans, which need always to be reformulated."[46]

By and large, the planning of Rio rests in the hands of several local government agencies, but it is influenced also by national planning policies. The government policy of President Costa y Silva attempted to foster the development of city planning throughout Brazil, and legislation was created to facilitate federal financial assistance to municipalities developing master plans in harmony with an overall national plan of economic and urban development.[47] The intentions of this program were admirable, although perhaps overambitious, for added to the difficulties of establishing a viable plan for national economic development was a lack of technical personnel at the municipal level. The effects of the program may be assumed to be gradual, rather than immediate. Included in the new program was a federal planning agency with the power to declare certain politically separated areas unified for purposes of planning. In the case of Rio de Janeiro, this could involve the establishment of a metropolitan area including Guanabara and adjacent urbanized portions of the State of Rio. Some attempts at voluntary collaboration have been made through the Greater Rio Commission, which includes representatives of both federal agencies and local municipalities.

At one time, Brazilian building, especially in the field of housing, was handicapped by a lack of financing institutions. This situation was remedied through the creation of the National Housing Bank (BNH), established in 1964 with American assistance.[48] Receiving federal tax money, and with the authority to borrow abroad, the

46. Francisco de Melo Franco, head of the Secretaria de Planejamento e Coordenação Geral, quoted in *Jornal do Brasil*, 19 January 1972.

47. Provision for this federal assistance was included in the 1967 Brazilian constitution. As the new program was initially proposed, municipalities were to submit master plans to a new federal planning agency which would give approval before granting financial support. Also included in the new legislation was a program to assure minimum standards for the development of subdivisions and an attempt to insure adherence to regulations on the part of local municipal authorities.

48. In general, American involvement in Brazilian city planning has been connected with USAID programs of financial and technical assistance. In order to expand such programs, a HUD (Housing and Urban Development) office was set up in Rio in November 1966, under the auspices of USAID. When it was initiated, the office described its goals as "to assist in the creation of new housing institutions, especially in the financial field, and strengthen the BNH and other institutions; to encourage new ideas and approaches to solve the housing problem; and to strengthen urban and metropolitan planning agencies." *Sector Goal Statement: Housing and Urban Development*, unpublished USAID document, 1966. The HUD office was staffed and organized in terms of four fields: finance, urban planning, housing, and community development. Assistance programs focused not on clearly identifiable American achievements but on collaborative projects administered by Brazilian agencies, in which the American contribution remained in the background largely in the form of money and technical advice. The HUD office in Rio ceased operation in 1969.

BNH was empowered to create private and public housing finance systems, and to plan urban growth and development. Initially the National Housing Bank centered its efforts on six key programs: low-cost public housing; labor cooperatives; savings and loan associations; real-estate credit societies; "impact" programs; and company housing.[49] This bank is the agency through which federal support for local planning is administered, and thus serves as a general coordinating center for housing and urban development. To provide technical assistance in the formulation of policies, the BNH created SERFHAU, the Federal Service for Housing and Urban Development. SERFHAU was intended to serve as a centralized information bank, assembling, coordinating, and making available for decision-making all relevant data regarding Brazilian urbanization. In conjunction with SERFHAU and the Catholic University in Rio, the bank established the National Center for Housing Research (CENPHA), a private organization designed to promote research and professional training in the housing field.

Within Guanabara itself, planning activity has continued to embody the efforts of a variety of public agencies, including the Secretariat of Public Works, under the authority of which is the Department of Urban Engineering and the Highway Department. SURSAN has continued to play an important role in redevelopment, while efforts relating to economic improvement have been directed by COPEG (Companhia Progressodo Estado da Guanabara). For the execution of specific planning projects, the state government frequently creates a separate agency called a CEPE (Comissão Executiva de Projetos Específicos). Such an agency has been involved in the redevelopment of Mangue.

The scope of each government agency is not always clearly defined, and the power of a particular organization may depend somewhat on the political influence of its director. The problem of multiplicity has continued, frequently producing duplication of effort and confusion of information. Often a new agency will be established to perform a specific task, and will remain in existence, even though its work has been absorbed by another organization. The need for increased coordination of govern-

49. The program of low-cost public housing centered primarily on the large projects directed by COHAB, of which Vila Kennedy and Cidade de Deus were the most noted examples in Rio. The cooperative housing scheme was designed to promote the establishment of housing cooperatives among labor unions and was sponsored by the American Institute for Free Labor Development. The first stages of this program were financed principally by half of a $20 million loan from the Inter-American Development Bank (BID) in 1966, with the balance of the loan going into BNH public housing support.

The savings and loan program was designed to parallel American savings and loan operations by organizing private savings for use by private enterprise in low-to-middle-cost housing. This scheme operated through the Brazilian federal and state Caixa banking system, with AID having provided a $20-million seed capital loan to the BNH to assist in the development of the project.

"Impact" programs were established to provide emergency funds for the completion of buildings already begun, but stalled for lack of money. (A frequent sight in many parts of Latin America is ambitious structures which stand for years half-finished and deteriorating because the owners either began without adequate financing, or because delays in construction combined with currency inflation to make the initial funds inadequate.) The company housing programs were formulated to assist in employee housing sponsored by industrial concerns, the national housing act providing a write-off of a compulsory one percent payroll deduction, provided that the one-half percent was used for company housing.

ment agencies and for a more centralized authority for directing overall planning has long been recognized among Rio officials, and as the planning needs of the city become increasingly complex some reorganization may be put into effect.

In general, the urban problems of Rio are similar to those of most large cities, deriving from rapid and uncontrolled expansion. They include a shortage of housing, utilities, and community services, together with inadequate transportation. Solutions to such problems are made difficult by the relative poverty of the city, the lack of technical resources, and the organizational ineffectiveness of the government. In addition, the topography, which gives the city its scenic beauty, creates many problems not found elsewhere. The hills, which provide dramatic outcroppings throughout the city, are frequently unstable and subject to slides, especially during the winter rains. The exact amount and location of damage is unpredictable, and to clear all the dangerous sites of the city would involve taking out of settlement some of the most desirable real estate in Rio. In 1966 the mountainous area of Santa Teresa received considerable damage through slides, with loss of life and destruction to buildings and roads. The following year, a sudden landslide completely obliterated a large high-rise apartment building, together with several houses, in a fashionable part of Laranjeiras. Part of the civic maintenance of Rio involves continuous effort at shoring up portions of the hills and repairing the damage done by slides. During the annual rainy season, the already shaky system of utilities often gives way. Power, water, and gas lines may be destroyed; during 1967 a major electric power station was totally inundated with mud.

Because of the mountain barrier between North and South zones, continuous civic effort and expense has been devoted to the creation of tunnel connections. The early turn-of-the-century tunnels were relatively short, but more recent examples, such as the Rebouças tunnel leading from Lagôa to the North Zone, and the Dois Irmãos tunnel piercing the massive coastline barrier to connect Rio with Barra da Tijuca, involve both technical challenge and a serious drain on the financial resources of the city (fig. 79).

As residential population rises in the South Zone, problems of communication will become increasingly demanding, giving rise to the opinion that, if Rio is to develop successfully, it may be necessary to upgrade the North Zone in terms of residence. As the cities of Brazil themselves cling to the coastline, so within Rio the populace clings to the waterfront. The congested appearance of such districts as Copacabana gives the impression of an acute shortage of land, yet, in fact, the available area of Rio is extensive, and except for the coastline, the pattern of building is low rise. If a more substantial part of the population could be persuaded to live in the North Zone where communication with the central area is relatively easy, the continuing cost of tunnel construction could be avoided, and a greater economic balance of population could be achieved throughout the city. The North Zone which was, during the time of Dom João, a fashionable residential area, but which is now primarily commercial and industrial, has been permitted to deteriorate unnecessarily to the point where it is now inhabited only by those who cannot afford to live elsewhere. No attempt is made to control the smoke and smell of the industrial area, the bay becomes increasingly polluted, and no effort is made to develop its shoreline for recreational use. Maintenance of roads and services and the distribution of civic amenities clearly favor the more fashionable parts of the city.

One decision in terms of institutional placement, however, did establish a nucleus for some improvement of the North Zone. This was the decision to create a new site for the university on an island created partly by fill close to the bayshore. This filling operation executed between 1949 and 1952 joined several small islands into a single landmass near the larger island of Governador. Although the new site provided ample land for university expansion, its location seems in many ways impractical; it is far from the middle-class residential districts from which most of its students come, and transportation facilities to the site are poor.

The selection of the site could, however, be justified as part of an effort to upgrade the North Zone. The presence of a prestigious cultural institution with a large resident population of students could serve as a stimulus to the development of local facilities such as restaurants, theaters, and shops, and might also be influential in improving residential development on nearby Governor's Island. As presently envisioned, however, the university will remain primarily a commuter school, with students and faculty arriving largely by automobile from distant parts of the city along already overburdened transportation routes. Surrounded by squatter slums and low-grade industry, the university seems likely to remain a social as well as a physical island.

Although the planning of modern Rio reflects an energetic effort to cope with contemporary pressures, large-scale urban design projects have not always been distinguished by sensitivity of detail. This may be seen in one of the most conspicuous redevelopment areas, the portion of the central business district previously occupied by Santo Antônio hill (fig. 80).

The plan of Alfred Agache had provided for the development of Santo Antônio in a manner that would have related closely to the surrounding urban pattern. Near the center of the new district a focal point was to be created in the form of a rectangular plaza surrounded by a complex of architecturally unified building consisting of high-rise towers connected by lower structures. Although Agache's proposals for redevelopment sites in Rio incorporated new and sometimes monumentally scaled architectural ensembles, he generally sought to harmonize the street and block pattern of the new extensions with the prevailing urban texture.

Later plans for Santo Antônio have reflected the preference of many modern architects for a re-ordering of the city wherein frequent streets and small city blocks are replaced by larger land parcels containing widely separated buildings. This new sensibility may be seen in the plan which Affonso Reidy produced for Santo Antônio in 1948, a scheme which incorporated many of the concepts popularized by Le Corbusier. As it is presently being developed, the Santo Antonio district embodies modifications of a plan devised by the Office of Urban Engineering during the 1960s, in which the site is organized into superblock quadrants separated by two broad streets. The most dramatic building on the site is the new cathedral rising from a circular base into a beehive shape. Intended as an architectural focal point, the church is surrounded by open space providing an expansive entrance plaza and abundant parking lots. The remainder of the new district is being developed with large, widely spaced, high-rise commercial offices. No effort seems to have been made at effecting a graceful transition between the new district and its surroundings, and, like many other modern renewal schemes, Santo Antônio creates an abrupt and rather coarsely scaled break in the civic fabric.

The land removed from the Santo Antônio site was used to create a strip of waterfront fill extending from the central district adjacent to the airport along the bayfront to Botafogo (fig. 81). This work had been initiated in 1952 during the prefecture of João Carlos Vital, and continued during the administration of Dulcidio Cardoso who systematized demolition and filling operations under the Superintendent of Works for Santo Antonio (SOST). Development of the area continued into the 1960s. Although the demolition of Santo Antonio and its use as bayfront fill had long been contemplated, the eventual development of the project was conditioned by the specific traffic problems of the 1950s. By this time, because of the building boom and intense concentration of population in the South Zone, a need was felt to facilitate rapid movement of motor traffic between Copacabana and the central district, and it was perhaps inevitable that the new landfill would find use as a freeway site. The width of the fill, however, was sufficient to accommodate more than a roadway, and has been developed to provide a linear park with beach frontage along the bay. The planning of this new park, called Glória-Flamengo after the adjacent neighborhoods, was planned by a group of designers, headed by Maria Carłota de Macedo Soares and included the noted landscape architect Roberto Burle-Marx.[50]

In its realization, the park exhibits a certain confusion of aim, and it appears to be more a landscaped freeway than a recreation area. The roadway is designed in such a way that it absorbs an extravagant amount of land, incorporating useless grass plots between the roadways, and in some areas it completely bisects the park. Far from being a sheltered retreat from the noise and mechanization of the city, the park throughout subordinates human use to the demands of the machine. Pedestrian access to the park

50. The design group for the Glória-Flamengo Park also included architects Jorge Machado Moreira, Affonso Reidy, and Helio Mamede, the engineer Berta Leitchic, and botanist Luiz Emygdio de Mello Filho.

is difficult, with the few elevated walkways and underpasses so widely spaced that most visitors attempt the dangerous passage across the traffic wherever they can.

Although the ground contains planting, trees are relatively undeveloped, and the open expanses are largely lacking in shelter from the intense sun. At night, the park is rendered equally uninviting through a system of lighting developed by Richard Kelly of New York. The park is illuminated by high-powered lamps set on posts 150 feet tall, bathing the ground in a cold and eerie glow. These giant standards appear to have no virtue beyond whatever prestige derives from the world's tallest lampposts and a possible contribution to park safety in making it so disagreeable that no one would be tempted to enter its confines after dark. The extravagant height of these lamps will become even more absurd when vegetation in the park develops. Only the treetops will be illuminated, and the ground will be thrown into shadow.

The facilities of the park, besides the beach, include playgrounds, soccer fields; a memorial to World War II military dead (figs. 82, 83), and a new Museum of Modern Art by Affonso Reidy. Planned additions will include a number of restaurants and a swimming pool. In providing additional beach and recreation areas for the city, the Glória-Flamengo park has removed some of the pressure of intensive use from the ocean beaches of the South Zone. In terms of urban aesthetics, however, the city has suffered the loss of one of its most beautiful waterfront areas. Before construction of the fill area, the bayfront was marked by a row of buildings and a treelined boulevard and embankment. This dramatic meeting of city and bay, with its urbane and scenic promenade has been vitiated by a roaring freeway and a sunbaked strip of grass. One of the loveliest urban aspects of Rio has been sacrificed for the convenience of traffic from Copacabana, just as Copacabana itself has been renovated to accommodate traffic from still more outlying areas.

Regarding the development of greater Rio, perhaps the most important recent action has been the commencement of a bridge connection between Rio and Niteroi. Such a direct link across the bay was long considered, a tunnel having been suggested as early as 1875.[51] As presently projected, this bridge will extend from the port area in the North Zone near the university across the bay to the port district of Niteroi. The resulting ease of communication between the two sides of the bay could encourage more intensive urbanization of Niteroi, with increasing development of its oceanfront area as a residential district. It could also give further impetus to the unification of the metropolitan area of Rio in terms of planning. Improved bay transport, and the

51. The initial tunnel proposal, made in 1875 by an English engineer, Lindsay Bachnal, was abandoned in the face of bureaucratic opposition. Proposals for bridges were made in 1932 and 1943 but were opposed by military interests who preferred a tunnel, and in 1953 a French firm, Etudes et Entreprises, was engaged to establish the location of the proposed underwater connection. Although studies for the anticipated tunnel continued during the 1950s, administrative opinion began to favor the substitution of a bridge, and in 1963 the decision was made to abandon the tunnel project.

possible addition of future bridges, could inspire an increased awareness of Rio-Niteroi as a single bay-centered metropolis.

In Rio, where the hand of God achieved a masterpiece of scenic splendor, the hand of man has not always been similarly inspired. Rio, like all cities, is a mixture of success and failure, but the unmatched beauty of the site sets a standard of visual perfection which one inevitably wishes to see embodied in the development of the city. Few settlements have been so generously endowed, and it is perhaps this generosity of nature which renders the citizens of Rio somewhat cavalier in their attentions to the city they love. The beauty of Rio is not regarded as a hothouse bloom to be tenderly nurtured and pruned; the majesty of the site expands the vision. One thinks big. Le Corbusier's desire to counter the tumultuous landscape with a compelling human presence is inherent in many planning decisions. To demolish hills, to create new land, to penetrate the mountains with tunnels, to bridge the bay—all seem assertive human acts responsive to the grand gesture of nature.

Thus, while Rio often seems deficient at the level of routine urban management, the most ambitious public works may be achieved with surprising dispatch. One tends to find fault less with the expansiveness of conception than with the coarseness of execution, for small-scale design is sometimes slovenly. Rio is not a city of little niceties, and, although many quarters still present visual links to a more gracious past, the vision of her planners seems firmly fixed on the vaster scale of the modern age.

A city can seldom be defined by formula, as is evidenced by an effort that *Life* magazine made in 1948 to arrive at the ideal urban community. It was claimed here: "If a group of Americans were asked to define the kind of city they would like to live in, they might mention good job opportunities, a wide variety of healthful recreation near at hand, first rate schools, good hospitals and plenty of cultural activities. Recently some of *Life*'s editors set out to determine what American city comes closest to this ideal. After considering many candidates they came up, somewhat brashly, with an answer: Madison, Wisconsin."[52] Obviously, Rio, in company with Paris, Rome, New York, and Tokyo is not an ideal city like Madison. Yet it might be remembered that the cities which are loved most are often those which are not ideal environments, which are not smoothly running mechanisms in which the traffic flows, the flowers bloom, and the elevators always work. Some cities have magic; others don't, and people often cling to cities where life has rough edges. The life of a city, like a human life, comprises a complex interweaving of events rather than a succession of problems successfully solved. The planners of Rio have been part of its life, but they have never controlled its destiny.

52. "The Good Life in Madison, Wisconsin," *Life*, 6 September 1948, p. 51.

6. THE BRAZILIAN ARCHITECT

A Cultural Colony

At sunrise one October morning in 1930, a steamer docked in Rio carrying on deck two architects of international repute, Eliel Saarinen and Frank Lloyd Wright, both of whom had been invited to Rio to participate in judging a competition for a memorial to Columbus. As the two stood surveying the harbor scene, they found themselves suddenly surrounded by excited young men, a delegation representing the more than seven hundred striking students of the National School of Fine Arts, which then included the School of Architecture.

The strike had come about as a protest against the dismissal of Lúcio Costa from his post as director of the School. Costa had been attempting to renovate the traditional Beaux-Arts architecture curriculum to bring it into accord with more modern theories, and had invited the modern architects Gregori Warchavchik and A. S. Buddeus to join the faculty.[1] Within less than a year, conservative opposition had brought about Costa's removal, and the subsequent student strike, which was to last six months, involved not only personalities, but also the issues of the Modern Movement itself. Learning of the arrival in Rio of two notable modern designers, the students sought help in obtaining their demands for new professors and a revision of architectural training.

According to Wright, Saarinen had strong reservations, warning his companion, "Look out. This is a revolutionary country—first thing you know SSSKKK (he drew his finger across his throat)—and it will be all over with you."[2] Wright, however, was eager to join the fray and threw himself enthusiastically into a round of meetings and speechmaking.

1. The Instituto Paulista de Arquitetos, a conservative professional body, made a formal protest against the appointment of what they termed "futurist" professors. Both Warchavchik and Buddeus were removed on grounds that they had not been appointed through open competition.
2. Frank Lloyd Wright, *An Autobiography* (New York: Duell, Sloan and Pearce, 1943), p. 517.

As Wright described his first speech, he told his interpreter, "in a sentence or two what I wanted to say. He would put it over to the young rebels with such effect that they would go wild. The Latins love to go wild. I gave them all I could—pleaded their cause as the future of Brazil. If Brazil was to have a future, how could she deny her youth the advanced thought of the world whether or not her elders disagreed with that thought." Moved to an apparent frenzy of admiration, "the masses of youngsters charged the judges' bench, pushed their dignitaries aside . . . and picked me up and carried me down to the street, called a taxi, and sent me off to the Copacabana with all on board who could stick."[3]

Clearly having the time of his life and greatly fancying his revolutionary role, Wright claimed: "The authorities were very negligent or else indulgent because they didn't arrest me, but finally they did arrest one of the coveted professors who spoke alongside me—Araujo. Saarinen said my turn was next."[4] Undaunted, Wright accepted a medal from the National Academy only "on condition that the society help the boys in their struggle for freedom." Similarly, he appeared at a dinner given by the Architects' Society of Brazil, where "I pleaded the cause of the boys until I brought tears to their eyes to go with the seven different kinds of wine."[5]

Like many another visitor, Wright readily succumbed to the charm of Rio, rhapsodizing, "Ah—the Rio de Janeirians are a fiery, gallant folk. I never thought I would ever like the Latins so much. Olgivanna and I hardly touched the ground during our stay."[6]

Although Wright was doubtlessly respected by the Brazilians, his work seems to have had little direct effect on the course of Brazilian design. The tide of major influence came rather from Europe, bringing with it the formal qualities of the International Style, and the greatest single inspirational force would be not Wright's romantic agrarianism but Le Corbusier's message of mechanization, rationalism, and uncompromising urbanity.

Whatever the nature of his influence there, Wright exemplified what Brazil had yet to produce, a truly innovative modern architect whose roots lay deep in his native soil. Wright had always been intensely conscious of his American origins, and the poetic imagery of his work embodied some of the most profound and enduring American passions. At the time of Wright's visit, Brazil could claim no native architect of comparable stature, nor had the previous century in Brazil produced any body of contemporary design which might be considered truly reflective of local traditions.

Although the architecture of both the United States and Brazil had been based on a European heritage, and had continued to reflect outside influence, compared with the United States, Brazilian building had been more consistently dependent on foreign sources. In Brazil, imported architects and craftsmen were frequently more

3. Ibid.
4. Ibid., p. 518.
5. Ibid.
6. Ibid., p. 519.

highly esteemed than local designers, and there had been little conscious divergence from prevailing European styles. Brazilian architecture had introduced no structural innovations comparable to the American balloon frame or steel skyscraper construction, and no new developments in building services. The contribution of the United States to modern commercial building, and the inventiveness in materials and spatial conception seen in American residential design, had no Brazilian counterparts. Brazil had known no native builder comparable to Richardson, no articulate iconoclast like Sullivan, and could exhibit no architectural achievement embodying genuinely original concepts. Although politically independent, Brazil had remained in many ways a cultural colony.

In comparing the cultural evolution of Brazil and the United States, the two ex-colonies may be seen to have exhibited a number of similarities, but also significant divergence of circumstance. In both cases a colonial society transplanted a cultural tradition from its homeland to an alien setting. In each case, this society eventually became ethnically differentiated and politically separated from the founding nation, and each new nation became immersed in the process of formulating, both consciously and unconsciously, its own cultural identity.

In the case of the United States, a measure of cultural independence seems to have been achieved almost from the beginning, while in Brazil a combination of circumstances seem to have encouraged a longer period of cultural dependence. The North American English colonies included large numbers of ideological dissenters, deeply conscious of the intellectual and religious differences separating them from many of their fellow countrymen. They arrived in the new world in family groups, bringing with them a tightly organized society intent on permanent settlement. Political independence, when achieved, was accompanied by the trauma of war and a conscious formulation of national ideals. The political base of the new republic rested on a codified and presumably permanent set of principles which have been regarded ever since as a fixed orientation for American society.

Brazil, by contrast, was settled by men with no ideological quarrel with the old world, no set of new ideals or principles to separate them from their countrymen in Portugal. Brazil tended to attract, not families seeking a permanent residence, but single men intending a temporary sojourn before returning to Europe. In Brazil, the transition to political independence was made without the extended and violent crisis which might have compelled a conscious examination of national identity and purpose. The issue of slavery, which in the United States had provoked a major civil war, was similarly resolved gradually and without bloodshed.

While national identity in the United States was inextricably involved with a conscious formulation of political and social principles, such a verbal formulation was lacking in Brazil, where national identity was essentially unconscious, resulting from the evolution of a given cultural tradition and ethnic intermixture conditioned by life in a vast tropical landmass. The American identity has tended to be defined in terms of abstract ideals, "truths" which are "self-evident." The Brazilian identity, by contrast, is not embodied in a set of semisacred documents or verbalized political concepts.

Unrelated to specific political premises or social ideals, Brazilian culture often eludes clear-cut definition. Brazilians tend to define themselves in terms of human qualities, with a vocabulary of personality type and temperament, rather than a terminology of intellectual abstractions. Confronted with a complex cultural and racial mixture, fragmented socially, yet united by common circumstances of life and family-like traits of character, Brazilians have often found self-analysis difficult. Observing what seemed a pervasive lack of self-confidence among his countrymen, a Brazilian scholar once commented that the "theme of racial and national doubt constitutes a leitmotif that from beginning to end will be found running through the symphony of the best Brazilian writing."[7]

A long failure of Brazil to develop a clear social identity resulted in what the sociologist Clodimir Vianna Moog once termed "*mazombismo.*" The *mazombo,* the colonial Portuguese born in Brazil, often felt himself inferior to the *reinol,* the citizen of the home kingdom, exhibiting an attitude described as "the absence of any desire to be or satisfaction with being a Brazilian, or as the lack of a collective ideal and, more especially, as the total lack of any feeling of belonging to the place or community in which one lives." The long-range result was "the incapacity to create a community that is conscious of its destiny and able to give birth to new cultural forms inspired by the new land."[8] Pronounced class distinctions and widespread illiteracy tended to enhance cultural fragmentation, leading Moog to describe Brazil as not a continent, but an archipelago with seven islands, each with its peculiar intellectual climate and landscape. Lacking a culturally unified audience, Brazilian intellectuals long tended to orient themselves toward Europe, and France in particular.

Thus while the new republic to the north embarked on a lively and independent intellectual and artistic life, Brazil remained relatively stagnant, seemingly unable to put down cultural roots, and continually dependent on European models. As the architect Henrique Mindlin noted: "With few exceptions, a derivative culture was all that had been achieved from the Declaration of Independence in 1822 to the end of World War I."[9]

With regard to architecture, in contrast to North America, where harsh climatic

7. Afrânio Peixoto quoted in Samuel Putnam, *Marvelous Journey: A Survey of Four Centuries of Brazilian Writing* (New York, 1931), p. 16.

8. Clodimir Vianna Moog, quoted in J. O. de Meira Penna, *Brazil Builds Brasilia* (Rio de Janeiro, 1960), p. 7. The quotation is taken in part from Clodimir Vianna Moog, *Bandierantes and Pioneers* (New York, 1964). In this book the author compares Brazilian and North American culture, explaining national character by distinguishing the concept of the *bandierante* (the early settler of Brazil) from that of the true pioneer (the settler of North America).

9. Henrique Mindlin, *Brazilian Architecture* (Rome, 1961), p. 28.

conditions necessitated immediate departures from European architectural usages, the climate of Brazil created circumstances in many ways similar to those of the mother country, presenting no incentive for rapid innovation. The settlers of Brazil, unlike those of Peru and Mexico, encountered no highly developed indigenous building forms which could have stimulated an interaction of cultures. Having no reason to do otherwise, Brazilian colonial builders, employing traditional masonry construction, created adaptations of the Portuguese baroque together with a relatively sober and functional vernacular building which has been highly regarded for its suitability to the Brazilian climate, landscape, and way of life.

Although initially based on Portuguese precedents, Brazilian architecture was subject to strong French domination in the nineteenth century (figs. 84–87), and it was this incursion which, in the opinion of some, discouraged a genuinely creative local architecture from evolving. As Henrique Mindlin expressed it: "This new and alien movement, completely rootless, boasting a history and a culture very different from the Portuguese, could not help but be a disintegrating force. The art of building in Brazil was split in two. On one side, building of Portuguese origin, but bearing a genuinely 'native' stamp, went on; and on the other, under the regulating and rationalizing French influence, a more erudite and sophisticated architecture appeared."[10]

As the nineteenth century progressed, Brazilian building reflected most prevailing European trends, including all varieties of picturesque eclecticism together with French Second Empire and Art Nouveau (figs. 88–101). In spite of the disciplining doctrine of Beaux-Arts classicism, Brazilian builders seem to have retained a baroque sense of plasticity, and a predilection for color and ornate decoration. One of the most successful of the nineteenth-century importations was the Art Nouveau which, with its sinuous curvilinear and foliate forms, accorded well with the lush tropical landscape and with the sensuous, emotional temperament of the people.

Nineteenth-century architecture was subject to heavy criticism during the early doctrinaire phases of the Modern Movement, receiving frequent condemnation on moral, technical, social, and aesthetic grounds. Finding much of their own justification in a dissociation from the past, many modern architects exaggeratedly disavowed any immediate antecedents, claiming to have freed themselves from the corruption of historic precedent. This was particularly true in Brazil, where the introduction of the Modern Movement coincided with the sudden emergence of an internationally recognized group of gifted and creative local architects. Modern architecture became a source of national pride, and it was not unnatural to view the building of the preceding century—which, with its stylistic variety and imitative forms, had frequently been designed and executed by foreigners—as marking a period of artistic decadence.

To a more tolerant eye, however, it appears that, although nineteenth-century Bra-

10. Henrique Mindlin, *Modern Architecture in Brazil* (New York, 1956), pp. 2–3.

zil may not have produced a markedly original effort in architecture, such cities as Rio generally fared well in terms of man-made environment. The surviving older buildings have proved not altogether unworthy companions for the more famed modern additions, as may be seen in central Rio, where the dignified ochre classicism of the National Library provides a grandly scaled foil for the austere and pristine geometry of the ABI (Brazilian Press Association) building. The architectural richness of Rio, as of many other cities, consists of a graceful and harmonic interplay of past and present (figs. 109–11, 113).

The association of much nineteenth-century building with foreign dominance influenced a relatively short-lived neocolonial revival related to the Brazilian Regionalist Movement of the 1920s (fig. 102).[11] This style, which attempted to resurrect a local heritage through the use of old Iberian forms rich in tile decoration, had contemporary counterparts in North America, where a New England "colonial" revival flourished together with Spanish colonial styles. In the United States, Spanish colonial building had received impetus through the 1916 San Diego Exposition, while the neocolonial building of Brazil is considered to have reached its climax in Rio at the centennial exhibition of 1922.

The Modern Movement

The Modern Movement, as it was introduced into Brazil, represented the mainstream of theory and form as it had been evolving in the 1920s and 1930s. Like previous artistic movements in Brazil, the Modern Movement in architecture was initially an importation from Europe. In contrast to other artistic imports, however, it stimulated an unprecedented burst of original creativity, inspiring what was soon to be recognized as a uniquely Brazilian achievement.

The roots of the Modern Movement lay in the dramatic upheavals of the nineteenth century, embodying both response to and reaction against the realities of the industrial age. In the century which saw drastic change in almost every aspect of life, architecture seemed to retain a fundamental contradiction. Building technology had been subject to sweeping technical innovation, including the introduction of metal framing and reinforced concrete, together with increasingly sophisticated building services. Standardization and prefabrication gave evidence of the increasing applicability of new industrial methods to building construction. At the same time, architectural design, freed from the lingering restraints of Renaissance discipline, exhibited a formal permissiveness dominated by a variety of styles largely drawn from architecture of the past.

11. The Regionalist Movement had its center in Recife in northern Brazil, and was strongly influenced by the sociologist Gilberto Freyre, who formulated the manifesto of the movement in 1926. Essentially the Regionalist Movement involved a reaction against alien influences and an effort to return to grass-roots Brazilian traditions, not only in the fine arts, but in all the ordinary aspects of living.

Although this seeming inconsistency of form and technical potential was later to be regarded as reprehensible escapism and as a fundamental failing of nineteenth-century architecture, the persistence of revival styles may be seen as a not unnatural accompaniment to a period of unprecedented change. Many people had justifiably ambivalent feelings regarding the blessings of the industrial age, and, in view of the overwhelming and frequently disastrous alteration of the physical environment which it produced, it is not altogether surprising that artistic taste might sometimes cling to the outward forms of an earlier era. Reflecting the prevailing confusion and disunity, architects seemed unsure of the implications for their work of the rapid social and technical changes taking place around them.

The philosophy of the Modern Movement, as it began to evolve early in the twentieth century, concerned, first of all, a new state of mind on the part of designers regarding the conditions of the modern age. Rejecting revivalism and historic styles, repudiating all nostalgia for the past, modern architects enthusiastically embraced what they conceived as the essence of the industrial era. It was the mission of the architect to attune himself to the contemporary world and to create in his work forms appropriate to the new age—to its technical possibilities, its social concepts, and its urban scale. Modern man, a somewhat mythical being, was idealized as a creature wholly reborn, transformed by his new way of life—as rational, disciplined, and efficient as were the industrial processes he superintended.

Attempting to describe the new rationalist spirit, one of the movement's major theorists, Le Corbusier, once wrote, "The modern sentiment is a spirit of geometry, . . . Exactitude and order are its essential condition. . . . This is the passion of the age. With what astonishment do we regard the disordered and spasmodic impulses of Romanticism! . . . No longer do we get these eruptions of overcharged personality. . . . In place of individualism and its fevered products, we prefer the commonplace, . . . A general beauty draws us in, and the heroically beautiful seems merely theatrical. We prefer Bach to Wagner."[12]

Increasing urbanization led to an emphasis on building for mass society, inspiring many architects to produce theoretical designs embodying a total renovation of the urban fabric. The existence of industrialized production encouraged a desire to mechanize building, to employ new materials and methods for mass-produced, standardized construction. A prevailing philosophy of democratic humanitarianism could be seen manifested in Walter Gropius' conception of the modern architect as no longer the individualistic artist using design as a means of self-expression, but as an efficient and disciplined teamworker serving the needs of society. The rhetoric of the Modern Movement involved many inconsistencies and frequent illogic, yet taken as a whole it represented a set of common acceptances and attitudes among designers.

12. Le Corbusier, *City of Tomorrow* (London, 1947), p. 38.

Although modern architects frequently felt themselves to be embattled revolutionaries, struggling heroically against overwhelming reactionary forces, the prevailing mood was optimistic. The brave new world was near at hand, and by means of modern organization and technology, mankind was achieving an unprecedented control over destiny. In the words of Le Corbusier: "One thing I am certain of: the vast and agonized labor of the 19th century and the dramatic explosions that have begun the 20th are the heralds of a new age of harmony and joy. Just as the premonitory gleams of dawn in the east, as night dies, leave no doubt about the imminent appearance of the sun, so a thousand signs and concrete events are now affirming the imminent birth of a new era."[13]

In terms of their own work, the architects of the Modern Movement were often much less revolutionary than their ideals. Conceiving themselves as organizers of large-scale environments, their commissions were frequently small buildings for individual clients. Although they spoke enthusiastically of advanced technology, their work generally employed neither technical innovations nor new materials. In spite of the rationalist rhetoric of functional design, modern building was often fully as formalist as traditional work, and, although the engineer was admired for his presumably unbiased approach to design, the role of the architect as artist seemed perpetuated. So intensely did many modern architects believe in their ideals, however, they appear to have been virtually unconscious of the discrepancy between theory and reality.

During the 1920s the most advanced European design had begun to reveal a unity of appearance which, through its universality, would come to be called the International Style. Associated with the mainstream of modern design through the 1930s and 1940s, the formal attributes of this style would characterize most architecture recognized as modern.[14] The unity of modern design seems to have been a self-imposed discipline, in part a reaction against the florid and chaotic variety of nineteenth-century building. The International Style was characterized by a clear rectilinear frame, light external curtain walls, generous use of glass, and a preference for smooth, finely finished surfaces. The term "machine aesthetic" came into use to describe the precise "machined" finishes common to the style, as well as to imply a relation between architecture and the much-admired forms of industrialism.

The frame of mind dominating the Modern Movement was puritanical, as though reflecting the cold and cloudy Northern European climate which nurtured its lead-

13. Le Corbusier, *The Radiant City* (New York, 1967), p. 343.

14. Critics and historians have recently begun to differentiate between the International Style and a variant of modern design characterizing the 1930s, which has been called the Moderne (sometimes the Art Deco). In the United States this style provided a popularization of the modern idiom and influenced a wide variety of design. Although it is possible to see some reflection of the Moderne in Brazil, it does not appear to have been a dominant element in Brazilian design. It seems reasonable to consider the modern architecture which Brazil began to produce during the 1930s as an original interpretation of the International Style. There are, however, certain parallels between Brazilian design and the Moderne. Both employed curves and decoration, and both embodied a sensual appeal which the more austere International Style had eschewed.

ing practitioners, many of whom were Dutch, German, or Swiss. The self-denying asceticism and strong moral tone of the movement could be seen in the famous essay by Adolf Loos, "Ornament and Crime," which equated ornamentation of surfaces with primitiveness and moral depravity. The frivolity and decorativeness of Art Nouveau was disowned, and the plasticity and emotionalism of expressionist work were replaced by an austere and impersonal geometry. The critical vocabulary maintained strong moral overtones. Exposed interior columns were "honest," geometric forms were "pure," and undecorated surfaces were "clean."

For the young, the rhetoric of the Modern Movement was hard to resist. It promised freedom from the failures of the past—a chance to wipe the slate clean and begin again. It spoke enthusiastically of a new life in which modern technology would be instrumental in solving the major problems of mankind—a message which would be all the more appealing in an unindustrialized country like Brazil. In a poverty-ridden and backward land, with an ill-nourished and largely illiterate population, the new architecture—associated with urbanism and industrial advancement—seemed an aspect of the future which could be grasped at once.

In Brazil, the effects of the Modern Movement began to be felt during the 1920s, and in São Paulo, in 1922, a seminal event called Modern Art Week served to acquaint large numbers of people with recent trends in painting and sculpture, literature and poetry, philosophy, modern criticism, and music. Progressive-minded architects in Brazil had been attentively observing the work of European modernists, and São Paulo architects Gregori Warchavchik and Flavio de Carvalho produced some of Brazil's earliest examples of the International Style. Warchavchik was instrumental also in promoting modern theory in Brazil, publishing on 1 November 1925 in the *Correio de Manhá*, an article, "About Modern Architecture," which summarized modern principles of design.

Although such European practitioners as Mies van der Rohe and Walter Gropius were admired, the most influential contemporary architect was Le Corbusier, whose theoretical doctrines came to be revered, according to Lúcio Costa, "not as one example among several others, but as the Holy Scripture of Architecture."[15] He observed that "their socio-economic, technical and artistic aspects were painstakingly analyzed by our architects. They welcomed the dogmatic discipline of Le Corbusier's theories and conceived an ascetic passion for his high social principles."[16]

When Le Corbusier first arrived in Brazil in 1929, he had already achieved an enthusiastic group of followers. The architect Henrique Mindlin was of the opinion that Brazilian architecture, in spite of stylistic importations, had embodied a traditional awareness of peculiarly Brazilian needs and that, "this tradition, or rather, the

15. Lúcio Costa, "Arquitetura contemporânea," in Fernando Nascimento Silva, ed., *Rio em seus quattrocentos anos* (Rio de Janeiro and São Paulo, 1965), p. 253.
16. Lúcio Costa, "Testimony of a Carioca Architect," *Atlantic Monthly* 197 (February 1956): 138.

spiritual attitude it reflected, brought to self-awareness by the ideas advanced by Le Corbusier, whose work focuses all contemporary achievements, was the one which served as the foundation for the modern architecture movement in Brazil. Le Corbusier's ideas . . . produced a stimulating trauma that gave it vigor and direction."[17]

The Modern Movement in Brazil coincided with the political revolution imposed by Getúlio Vargas in 1930 and partook of the political enthusiasm stimulated by his new regime. Surrounding himself with energetic young administrators, both military and civilian, Vargas promoted what has been termed the "Movement of '30," a species of New Deal designed to promote modernization of the country together with economic and social progress. The optimism of the Modern Movement, and its rhetorical associations with technical and social advancement, seemed a perfect reflection of the Brazilian mood. During a visit to the United States in 1944, Henrique Mindlin reported himself "sometimes getting so excited about the enormous potentialities of his country's rich and only partly developed resources that he can't sleep nights."[18] A building boom abetted by inflation and a shortage of industrial investment possibilities promoted intensive construction activity in Brazilian cities, augmented by an energetic government program of works. "The job to be done is so big," Mindlin observed, "that there is plenty of room for everybody."[19]

Suddenly Brazilian architecture, previously unknown to the world, experienced an astonishing efflorescence of creativity, attracting international notice. Lúcio Costa commented: "Never before has architecture passed through such a transformation in such a short period of time."[20] Virtually without a period of transition, Brazil became the center of a mature modern architecture. While modern architects elsewhere felt themselves frequently frustrated in the struggle for commissions and recognition, hampered by a sometimes hostile public and a conservative profession, Brazilian modernists seemed to have achieved almost instant popular acceptance and generous and indulgent patronage. Oscar Niemeyer once observed that "the success of modern architecture in Brazil has been such, that in a very short time it has become the normal and popular taste, with everyone, from government officials to private citizens, wanting modern buildings because of the attention paid to them both here and abroad."[21] The initial progress of modern architecture in Brazil seemed all the more impressive when viewed from Europe and the United States, where, following the slowdown of the depression, building activity was sharply curtailed by the Second World War.

Perhaps the most famous landmark of Brazilian architecture in the 1930s was the Ministry of Education and Health in Rio, sponsored by the progressive-minded min-

17. Mindlin, *Modern Architecture in Brazil,* p. 3.
18. Henrique Mindlin, "Brazilian Yardstick," *Architectural Forum* 80 (March 1944): 64.
19. Ibid.
20. Quoted by Mindlin in *Modern Architecture in Brazil,* p. 1.
21. Oscar Niemeyer, "Considerações sôbre a arquitetura Brasileira," *Módulo* 7 (February 1957): 5–10. Quotation from English supplement.

ister of education, Gustavo Capanema. In 1935, a competition for a new ministry building was held, in which a cautious jury awarded prizes to projects of academic conservatism, while disqualifying modern entries. Capanema, however, felt that the new ministry ought to embody a departure from traditional design, and, although he awarded the prizes as the jury directed, he asked Lúcio Costa, one of those rejected, to submit a new design. Having requested that the other disqualified architects be included in the project, Costa became the director of a team including Carlos Leao, Jorge Moreira, Affonso Eduardo Reidy, Oscar Niemeyer, and Ernani Vasconcellos. A project was developed by May 1936, at which time Costa suggested that Le Corbusier be invited to comment on it. During Le Corbusier's subsequent visit to Rio, he worked for about a month directly with the ministry architects.

The site selected for the Ministry of Education and Health building was in the central district on land formerly occupied by Castello hill. Although Agache had urged unified planning of the area, it had been developed in a continuation of the prevailing pattern of the surrounding commercial district. The building site, therefore, was on a city block surrounded by relatively narrow streets and high-rise offices. Dissatisfied with this location which he declared inappropriate for a grandly conceived building, Le Corbusier suggested placing the ministry on fill land along the bay. The site he selected was near the airport, roughly the same area which Agache had sought to develop for the "pantheon." Le Corbusier's projected building would have been a horizontal slab set amid landscaped grounds and oriented toward the bay view (fig. 103).[22]

Unable to promote a change in site selection, Le Corbusier then produced a schematic design for the development of the ministry in its existing location. He felt it essential that the building avoid the conventional Rio ground coverage in which structures were built to the edge of the lot line, leaving only interior courts to provide light and air. The scheme eventually built provided for a high-rise office slab lifted on pilotis, intersected at ground level by a low building containing an auditorium and exhibition area. The ground area of the block was left open to be developed as a landscaped plaza and circulation space. According to Le Corbusier, "The project actually in execution constitutes a great urban innovation; it permits the breaking up of the pattern of streets and blocks, and the introduction of a new urban space, as well as providing more efficient circulation."[23] The lifting of the building on pilotis created a long vista through the columns, but the quality of the surrounding buildings was such that the architect urged the readers of *Oeuvre complète* to "try not to see the neighboring buildings which appear at the end spoiling the perspective between the poles, the result of shabby narrow minded town planning."[24]

22. The site Le Corbusier wished for the Ministry of Education and Health building appears to have been approximately that now occupied by the Museum of Modern Art.

23. Le Corbusier, *Oeuvre complète 1934–1938* (Zurich, 1939), p. 78.

24. Le Corbusier, *Oeuvre complète, 1938–1946* (Zurich, 1946), p. 82.

The extent to which the Ministry of Education and Health building may be considered Le Corbusier's design appears to be a matter of some discussion. Lúcio Costa has stated unequivocally that "the design as well as the construction of the existing building, from the first sketch to the definitive completion, was accomplished without the slightest assistance from the French master, a spontaneous local contribution to the public realization of the principles he had always fought for."[25] According to Costa, Le Corbusier's participation was not only, "emphasized, but also exaggerated in honor of his creative and theoretical work, and the commemorative inscription intentionally lets one presume the master's participation in the original outline of the constructed building, when it refers to a different design destined for another place, but which effectively served as a guide for the definitive design."[26] Costa seems to imply that Le Corbusier contributed only the scheme for the waterfront site.

Le Corbusier did, however, produce a second design, which was for the existing site, although there seems to be some disagreement as to the nature of this scheme. Henrique Mindlin, in *Modern Architecture in Brazil,* includes a series of evolutionary sketches for the Ministry. In the first of these, the initial Brazilian design is shown as a U-shaped building bisected by a low lobby and auditorium block. Two designs by Le Corbusier are shown, the waterfront project and a scheme for the actual site, in which the office building appears as a long slab built close to the street line, while the auditorium and lobby block follows the intersecting street to create an L-shaped ensemble. The final scheme, in which the office block, increased in height, has been shifted from the street line to a central part of the site, is credited solely to the Brazilian designers. A similar presentation may be found in Stamo Papadaki's *Work of Oscar Niemeyer,* which also indicates that the final site plan and development of building form was the work of the Brazilian team.

Le Corbusier, however, in his own published work, includes a drawing which he labels his second project, showing the building in its definitive form (fig. 104). No mention of the intermediate L-shaped scheme is made, and the reader is led to assume that the final scheme was developed by Le Corbusier. In addition, Le Corbusier credits himself with having made a number of decisions regarding the detailing of the Ministry. "He wondered why the official buildings in Rio were constructed of stone from Burgundy (imported on cargo ships), while the countryside of Rio is studded with gray and rose-colored granite. He specified this granite both for the end walls and the immense paved area covering the terrain occupied by the Ministry: he did more, he recommended the use of blue and white faience from Lisbon, . . . thus provoking a harmonious contrast with the rude granite and shiny glass surfaces."[27]

While Le Corbusier's participation in the design process of the Ministry of Education and Health may have been essentially advisory, there is no doubt that the build-

25. Costa, "Arquitetura contemporânea," p. 254.
26. Ibid., p. 255.
27. Le Corbusier, *Le Corbusier 1910–1960* (Zurich: Girsberger, 1960), p. 134.

ing embodied a number of concepts which he had long been promoting. The freeing of building lines from the street pattern, the use of pilotis to free the ground level, and the simplicity of building form in the high-rise slab all have precedents in his work. The use of the sunbreaker to shield the glass of the exposed northern façade may also be seen as relating to experiments which Le Corbusier had made previously with sun-shading devices.

Although a number of designers claim to have "invented" the architectural sunbreaker, its early and consistent advocacy tends to be associated with Le Corbusier, who included this device in projects designed for Algiers in 1933, as well as in a housing scheme projected for Barcelona in the same year.[28] In the Ministry of Education and Health building, the sunbreakers (*brise-soleil* or *quebra-sol*) took the form of horizontal blue asbestos louvers set outside the glass wall and maneuverable by means of interior cranks.

The construction of the Ministry was slow, lasting from 1937 to 1943 (figs. 105–07). Even before the building was finished, however, it had begun attracting international praise, deemed not only "the most beautiful government building in the Western Hemisphere,"[29] but "one of the finest buildings to be found in the world."[30] Philip Goodwin, comparing Rio with her contemporary counterparts, observed: "Other capital cities of the world lag far behind Rio de Janeiro in architectural design. While Federal classic in Washington, Royal Academy archaeology in London, Nazi classic in Munich, and neo-imperial in Moscow are still triumphant, Brazil has had the courage to break away from safe and easy conservatism. . . . The capitals of the world that will need rebuilding after the war can look to no finer models than the modern buildings of the capital city of Brazil."[31]

By the time the Ministry of Education was complete, Rio could boast a number of

28. Le Corbusier's sunbreaker schemes for Barcelona and Algiers are published in *Oeuvre complète 1929–1934* (Zurich, 1935), pp. 168–69, 170–71, 195–99. Stamo Papadaki in his book *Oscar Niemeyer* (New York, 1960), claims: "The first contemporary building with a permanent and continuous device for protection against the sun was, to the best knowledge of the author, designed by Georges Ovide Leclerc and the author. This 'sunbreak'—the term had not been coined then—consisted of a series of cantilevered, horizontal, permanent concrete slabs projecting about ten feet from the glass wall and supported by the structural columns of the building." The building was a memorial to Christopher Columbus to be erected in the city of San Domingo, and the concrete louvers were to shield the chapel. The project was published first in the Spanish magazine *Arquitetura* (no. 6, 1929), but the international competition for the design took place in 1928. Papadaki, *Oscar Niemeyer*, p. 114. Lúcio Costa once claimed that "the first *brise-soleil* (a system of exterior sunshades or louvers—sometimes movable—to offset the tropical glare while permitting free circulation of air) was the work of Alexandre Baldassini." "Testimony of a Carioca Architect," p. 138. In the same article he stated that, in Brazil, "the first building constructed on *pilotis* (columns raising the building mass above the ground) was designed in 1931 by Stelio Alves de Souza." A degree of precedent for the sunbreaker may also be found in the traditional building of colonial Brazil in which window openings frequently carried heavy wooden lattices serving to provide internal privacy as well as sun protection.

29. Philip Goodwin, "Brazil Builds for the New World," *California Arts and Architecture* 60 (February 1943): 22.

30. G. E. Kidder Smith, "The Architects and the Modern Scene," *Architectural Review* 95 (March 1944): 84.

31. Philip Goodwin, quoted in "Brazil's Leadership," *Carnegie Magazine* 17 (May 1943): 52.

distinguished modern structures, including the Santos Dumont airport terminal by Marcelo and Milton Roberto, with its seaplane station by Atilio Corrêa Lima. Within the central business district, not far from the Ministry of Education, the Roberto brothers had built the headquarters of the Brazilian Press Association (the ABI building) (fig. 112). Widely photographed upon its completion in 1940, this building took the form of a pristine block sheathed in granite and travertine, the exterior modeled by a sunbreaker of fixed vertical panels. It became clear that the sunbreaker, in addition to its function in controlling glare, could be an important element in architectural aesthetics, adding sculptural drama to the building façade. The use of the sunbreaker in varying forms, together with pilotis, became one of the hallmarks of Brazilian design.

Rio and São Paulo provided headquarters for Brazil's major architectural practices as well as the setting for much modern building. It was in Rio, however, that the most famous designers established their studios, and the city's status as cultural center was augmented by the active presence of Lúcio Costa, Oscar Niemeyer, the Roberto brothers, and Affonso Reidy, as well as the landscape designer Roberto Burle Marx. To the outsider, Brazilian architecture became cloaked in an aura of glamour; its practitioners appeared as pampered celebrities with status comparable to movie stars or soccer players. The *Architectural Review* commented in 1954:

> From Europe our view of the new architecture of Brazil is almost as misty and romantic as was our forefathers' of Hy Brazil, that vast and legendary glass tower off the coast of Galway, inhabited by fabulous creatures. To the European architect few creatures could appear as fabulous as his Brazilian counterpart as he appears in the stories which filter back from Rio—of men with Cadillacs, supercharged hydroplanes, collections of modern art to make the galleries blush, bikini-clad receptionists and no visible assistants—nor could any glass towers of medieval imagination appear as improbable as the skyscrapers which are reported to have been returned to the vertical by hydraulic jacks resting on refrigerated quicksands. . . . Our trouble is the lack of authoritative eye-witnesses, for Brazil is a boom-province of the Modern Movement which the Movement's masters have hardly visited since Le Corbusier lent his authority and support to the pioneer efforts of Costa and Warchavchik in the 'thirties.[32]

For some observers, a close examination of Brazilian architecture served to dispel much of the glamour of the distant view. Modern Brazilian building, initially praised because it had succeeded in looking modern at a time when architects in other countries were still battling against Doric columns, was subsequently subject to sweeping criticism for its failure to accord with many of the basic precepts of the Modern Movement.

32. "Report on Brazil," *Architectural Review* 116 (October 1954): 235.

The theory of the Modern Movement presupposed a highly industrialized, urbanized society and took for granted precision of workmanship within a technically advanced building industry. The promulgators of modern doctrine were imbued with a philosophy of social democracy, believing the function of architecture to be the fulfillment of the needs of the masses. The ideal project for a modern architect would be a large-scale housing development, a factory, hospital, or school, in which construction should be mechanized and standardized. Even in Europe, architects frequently found actual conditions of work somewhat at variance with their ideals. In Brazil, the discrepancy between ideal and reality was far greater. Brazil, at the time the Modern Movement was introduced, was still a socially stratified, unindustrialized country, with an unmechanized building industry and untrained workers. Power and patronage was vested in a small ruling class, and architects themselves were drawn from an educated elite. In spite of programs of public works and limited efforts at low-cost housing, it could not be claimed that Brazilian architecture had a broad social base.

Lúcio Costa once observed that the Brazilian architectural achievement was "unexpected, because Brazil of all countries would seem to be one of the least predisposed to modern architecture, in the face of the proverbial inefficiency of its workmen, the absence of an apprenticeship system, the relative backwardness of industry, and the general dislike of 'collective living.' "[33]

The rapidity with which Brazil adopted modern architecture was surprising only if one believed all of its theoretical tenets. Brazilian building underlined the essentially formal quality of much modern design. It was the very artificiality of the modern style which made it so easy to adopt, and, with what was apparently an unconscious grasp of the distinction between design and theory, Brazilian architects were able to produce a clearly modern style free of European technological and social underpinnings.

Although the International Style had tended to present a façade of "rational" uniformity free of national and personal idiosyncracy, Brazilian building soon departed from this mainstream to embody an open and unashamed expression of the Latin temperament. An English critic once credited the Brazilians with having created the first national style of modern architecture, a style "which has been the envy of the world . . . and has kept the smooth surfaces—sometimes—and the simple geometry—when it feels like it—but it has carried them all to a degree of freedom so marked and so personal that the Italian critic Grillo Dorfles has, with some justification, termed it Neo-Baroque" (figs. 115–18).[34]

Brazilian architecture evidenced modernity without puritanism, relating in its forms not only to the sensuous baroque tradition, but also to the more recent Art Nouveau and expressionist styles. While some Brazilian work retained an austere discipline of form, that which seemed to characterize the Brazilian achievement em-

33. Costa, "Testimony of a Carioca Architect," p. 137.
34. Reyner Banham, *Guide to Modern Architecture* (London: Architectural Press, 1962), p. 63.

bodied free-form planning, emotional lyricism, and decorative surface treatment. Clearly unconvinced that ornament was crime, Brazilian designers became noted for an imaginative fusion of art and architecture. The Ministry of Education and Health building had made notable use of tile decoration, a practice relating to older Brazilian tradition and enthusiastically adopted in many modern buildings. Landscaping also flourished as a newly rejuvenated art form, seen frequently in conjunction with the new architecture in the work of the talented Roberto Burle-Marx.

Building Technique

The principal structural material for all large building in Brazil was reinforced concrete. At the inception of the Modern Movement, Brazil produced no structural steel, and even now this material remains highly expensive there. Most high-rise building tends to employ a concrete frame, with infilling panels of hollow bricks. The building trade remains unmechanized; a British architect working in Brazil once observed that the contractor and architect "must work without the assistance of quantity surveyors or of specifications as we know them . . . Specifications would present some difficulties in a country where the manufacture of fittings and components is in its infancy, where the range of materials is limited, their performance uncertain, and standard catalogued sections almost unknown." He went on to note that "a number of excellent buildings have been spoiled by the failure of facing materials—or by the failure of owners, including public authorities, to keep up repairs and maintenance after they have taken over the building."[35] Poor maintenance has been cited with regard to many Brazilian buildings, including the Ministry of Education, where a Japanese visitor noted in 1954, "poor upkeep and bad plastering have almost wrecked the architectural effect."[36]

Opinions about Brazilian workmanship vary somewhat. Traditionally, the most skilled workmen have been foreign immigrants—often Portuguese and Italians. Brazil still suffers from an incomplete transition from an agricultural to an industrial society; training in building skills seems inadequate, and work-site supervision is often faulty. One observer noted: "They build wonderful walls with poor bricks, and I don't think I've ever seen such good plaster work. But otherwise, the Brazilian architects are lost indoors. They lack all inside technicians, joiners, window fitters and such."[37] Another observer, after complaining that lumber in Brazil was often insufficiently cured, resulting in warping, noted that "tile layers and stucco pourers are generally sloppy . . . and lack of thoroughness is one of the great building problems in the country. It is not uncommon to see a structure several years old with holes in the plaster near the ground."[38]

35. Peter Craymer, "Report on Brazil," p. 236. 36. Hiroshi Ohye, ibid., p. 237.
37. Donald Newton, letter in *Architectural Forum* 84 (February 1946): 62.
38. Carleton Sprague Smith, "Architecture of Brazil," *Architectural Record* 119 (April 1956): 194.

To some outsiders, building codes may seem lax and safety standards careless, although the lack of arbitrarily hampering regulations has permitted much of the design freedom in Brazilian building. The circular spiral stairways without guardrails seen in some of Niemeyer's buildings, for example, would not be permissible in many places. One visitor claimed that "Niemeyer can only be understood if one knows Rio. There one can do the craziest things unpunished. Everything flourishes and grows, everybody seems to live on air and nobody ever presents an account. . . . One can criticize the construction; but mistakes are not very deadly here, as they would be in our climate, and it is not justifiable to measure them with a Swiss yardstick."[39]

An American engineer making a study of Brazilian building codes and practice in 1945 noted that to a North American the most striking feature of Brazilian concrete building was the slenderness of construction. "The concrete columns appear almost as rods; the beams and girders narrow to the point of wood-joist construction."[40] Observing that "the Brazilian code is less restrictive than those under which North American engineers practice," he found Brazilian standards far from inadequate, and similar to those currently employed in Europe, especially in Germany. Brazilian building was based on "the broad concepts of reinforced concrete design as garnered from all European countries and incorporated with modifications into a bolder building code. Our South American neighbors have included provisions for design on an ultimate strength basis such as have been used in the Soviet Union for many years."[41] Considering the existing United States code overconservative, he pointed out: "There are buildings in the United States constructed at about the beginning of this century that are almost as slender as are now being erected in South American countries today. . . . They were designed before we had building codes, and most of the work was done by engineers who had come from Europe." In response to queries about failures in Brazilian construction, the American claimed that he had found no evidence of such mishaps.[42]

In addition to the general lightness of construction, it was observed that the low wage scale in Brazil encouraged the construction of complicated designs needing elaborate formwork—hence the prevalence of circular staircases. No opportunity to save on the amount of steel was overlooked, however, and it was noted that, "you fully appreciate the high cost of steel when you see unreinforced footings carrying 24-story buildings."[43]

One of the prevailing inadequacies of Brazilian building has been in the provision of building services, and it is here that one becomes aware that much architectural modernity goes no deeper than the façade. A common sight throughout the business

39. Mrs. Walter Gropius, "Report on Brazil," p. 237.
40. Arthur J. Boase, "Building Codes Explain the Slenderness of South American Structures," *Engineering News–Record* 564 (19 April 1945): 68.
41. Arthur J. Boase, "Brazilian Concrete Building Design Compared with United States Practice," *Engineering News–Record* 902 (28 June 1945): 80.
42. Ibid., p. 88.
43. Boase, "Building Codes," p. 72.

district of Rio are the long queues of people waiting for elevators, and it is not unusual for such a line to extend out of a building and halfway up the block. In some cases, the designer has failed to calculate the number of elevators necessary for the building, while in other instances poor maintenance will have put necessary elevators out of commission.

Air conditioning is rare and ventilation often faulty in Brazilian buildings, and the sunbreakers, when used, by no means solve the problem of solar heat. Mechanical equipment is generally badly maintained, and the unreliability of electrical services adds to the difficulty. In Rio, the rainy season always brings an annual disruption of services, and modern buildings must occasionally function without lights or elevators.

Since the inception of the Modern Movement, architects in many countries have voiced complaints about the backward methods of the building industry, urging, albeit somewhat ineffectually, increasing mechanization and prefabrication. The theoretical advantage of mechanization lies in increased speed of construction and reduced costs through the elimination of hand labor. For various reasons, in spite of optimistic expectations surrounding new building methods, they have not generally succeeded in producing either a dramatic drop in building costs or a revolution in construction time. The introduction of new techniques tends to be initially costly, necessitating a heavy investment in equipment and factory installations, and requiring a large volume of construction to be economically feasible.

In Brazil, where wages are low and unemployment high, there has been no overwhelming incentive to reduce the labor component in construction, nor is the local temperament necessarily obsessed with ideals of speed and efficiency. There have, however, been some limited attempts to modernize building methods. In Rio, the first Brazilian efforts at prefabricated concrete panel construction have been undertaken by the engineering construction firm, Engefusa, which employs an adaptation of a French system. This method involves the use of standardized concrete wall panels containing window frames and utility ducts, made in temporary factories erected on the building sites. Although not yet noticeably cheaper than traditional practices, it is considerably faster, and has been used primarily for relatively low-cost cooperative housing in the suburbs of Rio.

The principal difference between the Brazilian method and its French prototype is the elimination of sound insulation and the employment of thinner slabs in Rio. While the French system employs double wall panels separated by a layer of insulation, the Rio housing has simple four-inch-thick concrete panels. French floor slabs are six inches, while those in Brazil are four inches.

Although Brazilian steel production has increased, the relatively high cost still makes large-scale steel construction unfeasible. Rio at present has only one steel-frame high-rise building, the Avenida Central building by Henrique Mindlin, completed in 1961.

The Profession

There has been a tendency, especially in the United States, to regard architecture as a complex group activity involving a number of specializations, its creation based ideally on an accumulation of data, with each design embodying, in theory at least, sophisticated social and psychological research, scientific methodology, and elaborate programming, as well as advanced technical expertise in structure and environmental controls. Although the hubristic image which some architects hold of themselves as "leaders of the environmental team" is not always realized in practice, architectural firms in Europe and the United States frequently include large and varied staffs capable of offering a wide range of architecture services. While the small individual practice is by no means dead, the ideal of the architect as an independent artist relying essentially on intuitive sensibility for his design decisions is generally far from fashionable.

In Brazil, however, this latter concept of the profession is still dominant, and a British architect working in Brazil once observed: "The architect is not the administrative head of a complicated team, but more like an artist working with a select band of personal assistants." This leads to a generally relaxed work relationship where "clients, friends and contractors meet around the drawing board in this informal atmosphere, and all the parties concerned in the project come to know one another intimately."[44]

In contrast to the type of practice in which the architect supervises the total development of the design and produces complete working drawings, a Brazilian architect will frequently farm out both working drawings and detailing. Because of the lack of standardized components, and variations in materials, many architects avoid exact specifications, leaving decisions in this area to the contractor. Brazilian designers, by and large, do not seem to mind if their designs undergo some modification in the process of construction, and the image of the architect frequently held in Brazil is that of an artist whose contribution to the building may be essentially a conceptual sketch which is then realized by others. Many architects do not concern themselves deeply with technical problems, preferring to rely on the talents of a construction engineer to put their design concepts into effect. The more unconventional designs of Oscar Niemeyer, for example, have been made possible through a long and singularly harmonious collaboration with the engineer Joaquin Cardoso.

Although some modern theorists consider architecture essentially a science in which all decisions can be rationally achieved, Brazilian architecture has continued as a vehicle for emotional expression. As Lúcio Costa phrased it:

Our architecture is important because it has succeeded in adding plastic lyricism

44. Craymer, "Report on Brazil," p. 236.

> and concern for human emotions to the structures in which we live and work. On these additions depends the survival of architecture when its mere functionalism will have outlived its usefulness—survival not only as a didactic example of an outmoded technique of construction, or as testimony of an out-dated civilization, but in the more profound and permanent sense of a work of art still valid because it will still be able to touch the heart.[45]

Walter Gropius, on a visit to Brazil in 1954, noted that "all the buildings are practically modern. But, of course, only some of them are well designed because the architects are not given sufficient time to do their working drawings well."[46] It is not difficult to find evidence of carelessness in some Brazilian buildings. One visitor visiting Niemeyer's famous Pampulha gambling casino in 1946 reported that:

> The mass, grouping and fenestration of the entrance to the Pampulha Casino is one of the finest things in the world today. And ten feet inside the Casino is a ghastly sight. Two ordinary pieces of gas pipe—flues for the kitchen stove—stick up into the room like an obscenity. I asked about the pipes, and found out an amazing thing. The building cost them $500,000 to build, but they forgot the kitchen. They installed it afterward, but didn't care about the looks of it. This seemed typical to me of all that we have seen of the new architecture.[47]

A visiting Japanese architect once commented that "conditions in Brazil make things easy for the architect and do not encourage restraint, or close study of building problems. . . . But for this reason the architects of Brazil have been able to contribute to the Modern Movement a wonderful quality of imaginative fantasy."[48]

Oscar Niemeyer

Within the galaxy of Brazilian architectural talent, the name of Oscar Niemeyer was the first to become well known internationally, not only because of the evident skill of his design, but also because his work seemed in many ways to epitomize what was most essentially Brazilian in the country's new architecture. The young Niemeyer had entered the National School of Fine Arts in 1930, and following graduation entered Lúcio Costa's office. According to Costa: "I tried to dissuade him from his intention of working with me in my office, because the turn-over of work was small and would not give him sufficient remuneration. He promptly turned the tables on me and suggested compensating me for the right to take any part, whatsoever that might be, in my professional activities."[49]

45. Costa, "Testimony of a Carioca Architect," p. 137.
46. Walter Gropius, "Report on Brazil," p. 237.
47. Newton, letter in *Architectural Forum*.
48. Ohye, "Report on Brazil," p. 237.
49. Quoted in Stamo Papadaki, *The Work of Oscar Niemeyer* (New York: Reinhold, 1950), pp. 1–2.

To Niemeyer, Costa ranked with Le Corbusier as a prime influence on Brazilian design. He considered Costa to be the founder and the leader of the Modern Movement in Brazil, and the honest and disinterested master of a generation of young designers. Studious and thoughtful by nature, Costa was not only a respected designer, but a theorist and philosopher whose writings showed deep concern for the relation of modern architecture to the native culture of Brazil. Joining the Serviço Patrimonio Historico e Artistico Nacional (SPHAN) when it was first formed in 1937, Costa combined an active career in modern design with a concern for the study and preservation of the monuments of the past. Like most practitioners of the Modern Movement, he saw modern technology as a liberating force, one which would assure the well-being of future generations. He spoke of "a burning faith in the emancipating virtues of *mass production* (this magical gift afforded to man by machinery), implying as it necessarily does *mass distribution;* . . . and the attainment at last, *for the masses,* of an *individual* standard of living worthy of human conditions." Social and material salvation could come only with "the introduction of the true machine age . . . that clear and distant mirage located far and away above the tragic turmoil in which we live, move and have our being. For whatever may be said and done to prevent it, the day will surely come when reason will come into its own."[50]

Although universally respected among Brazilian architects, Costa tended to avoid the limelight, preferring to work in a quiet and "almost hermetic seclusion."[51] He was generous, however, in promoting the reputation of his onetime assistant, Niemeyer, and it was observed, "Lúcio Costa, who after having been considered for many years as the Allah of Brazilian architects, decided (in a gesture of unheard-of and, perhaps, excessive modesty) to become Oscar's Mohammed, his most devout and generous prophet."[52]

Niemeyer's first opportunity to contribute to a major project came with the Ministry of Education and Health building. Up to this time, his contribution in Costa's office had not been particularly distinguished, and Costa had not originally included him in the collaborative design group. The young architect strenuously insisted, however, that he be allowed to contribute, and his addition to the staff proved a wise decision. Costa was later to state that it was Niemeyer's participation which assured "the integrated success of the undertaking. . . . Oscar Niemeyer, trained in Rio and with a thoroughly Carioca mentality, was the one who at the crucial moment saw the latent possibilities of the project and made them realities."[53]

From this moment, Niemeyer's reputation began to soar, receiving impetus from his 1939 World's Fair pavilion in New York, done in collaboration with Costa, and

50. Lúcio Costa, "In Search of a New Monumentality," *Architectural Review* 104 (September 1948): 127.
51. Kidder Smith, "Architects and the Modern Scene," p. 84.
52. Rogers, "Report on Brazil," p. 240.
53. Costa, "Testimony of a Carioca Architect," p. 138.

from a striking group of buildings created for the Belo Horizonte suburb of Pampúlha in 1942. This latter ensemble, which included a church, gambling casino, yacht club, and restaurant, epitomized many of the qualities for which Niemeyer would be known—mastery of the modern idiom combined with inventiveness and freedom of form. Niemeyer was a virtuoso designer, intuitive and quick, exhibiting a flamboyant improvisational skill which led Walter Gropius to characterize him as a "Paradiesvogel." Looking at some photographs of Niemeyer's work in 1947, Le Corbusier had remarked to him, "You're doing baroque with reinforced concrete," adding indulgently, "but you do it very well."[54]

In Niemeyer's work, architecture became a means of personal self-expression, highly plastic, sensuous, and lyrical, and decidedly not everyone's cup of tea. The editor of a noted Italian journal once complained: "I cannot overlook the many and often unforgivable faults in the work of this capricious artist, nor can I sympathize with this tendency to prefer works of brilliant fancy (designed after virtuoso sketches) to sound technical solutions to architectural problems (including social problems, which are almost completely neglected in his work): I do not object so much to the capriciousness of his themes as to the impossibility of fitting them into any organic system."[55]

Moralizing criticism could be found directed not only against Niemeyer, but against Brazilian building as a whole. A Swiss designer, Max Bill, visiting the 1954 São Paulo Bienal, took the occasion to scold his hosts vehemently. The formal emphasis of Brazilian architecture he considered a form of academicism, denouncing the ubiquitous free forms as purely decorative and thus divorced from serious architecture. He declared the use of the glass wall impractical in the absence of air conditioning, and considered the brise-soleil to be inappropriately employed as a cosmetic, frequently on all four sides of a building. The pilotis, inspired initially by Le Corbusier, seemed to be assuming baroque forms in Brazilian adaptations. To the staid and humorless Swiss sensibility, Brazilian building revealed "shocking things, modern architecture sunk to the depths, a riot of anti-social waste, . . . Here is utter anarchy in building, jungle growth in the worst sense. . . . For such works are born of a spirit devoid of all decency and all responsibility toward human needs. It is the spirit of decorativeness, something diametrically opposed to the spirit which animates architecture which is the art of building, the social art above all others." Reminding his auditors of "the true principles underlying modern architecture," Bill urged that the architect be "modest and clear," that architecture "must serve man."[56]

Well aware of the nature of the criticism directed toward his own architecture and that of other Brazilians, Niemeyer was articulate regarding the dilemma of the mod-

54. Quoted by Oscar Niemeyer in "contradição na arquitetura," *Módulo* 31 (December 1962): 20. Quotation from English supplement.

55. Rogers, "Report on Brazil," p. 240.

56. Ibid., pp. 238–39.

ern architect in Brazil. He introduced a collection of his work in 1950 with the observation: "Architecture must express the spirit of the technical and social forces that are predominant in a given epoch: but when such forces are not balanced, the resulting conflict is prejudicial to the content of the work and to the work as a whole. . . . I should have very much liked to be in a position to present a more realistic achievement: a kind of work which reflects not only refinements and comfort but also a positive collaboration between the architect and society."[57]

In a similar book published six years later, Niemeyer continued his analysis of the state of Brazilian building. He considered criticism from foreign architects unjustifiably harsh.

> It seems that they do not use the same measure—severe and objective—when they deal with their own projects as when they are examining ours. . . . Our modern architecture reflects the social contradictions in which we live and in which it has developed. . . . Presented to clients not interested in problems of a general building economy and to a government body that shies from plans of national dimensions and from large scale construction projects, our architecture is forced to make improvisation its basic element. . . . The great variety of forms that is seen in our architecture stems from the lack of an effective social and economic basis. The absence of a large building industry with prefabricated assemblies and parts further encourages the development of a wealth of individualistic architectural forms and solutions. Thus, what appears ludicrous to someone looking from the outside, to us is a necessity dictated by present day conditions. For this reason, we refuse to strive for a more rigid and impersonal architecture—the European tendency, the result of applying industrial techniques—as we refuse to pretend that there exists a basis for "social architecture." To do the contrary would mean to accept an architectural poverty, to deprive our architecture of what it has that is fresh and creative or to instill in our buildings political demagogery.[58]

Niemeyer's own political and social convictions, which had led him to membership in the Communist party, made him particularly self-conscious regarding his position as a successful practitioner supported by the economic and political establishment. "I believed, as I still do, that unless there is a just distribution of wealth—which can reach all sectors of the populace—the basic objective of architecture, that is its social ballast, would be sacrificed, and our role of architect relegated only to wait upon the whims of the wealthy."[59]

Considering the social imbalance of Brazilian society as prejudicial to serious architecture, Niemeyer had permitted himself during the early phases of his career, "to

57. Quoted in Papadaki, *Work of Oscar Niemeyer*, p. 5.
58. Quoted in Stamo Papadaki, *Oscar Niemeyer: Works in Progress* (New York, 1956), pp. 11–14.
59. Oscar Niemeyer, "Testimony," *Módulo* 9 (February 1958): 3.

believe that such as dedicated themselves to architecture body and soul must be very naive. . . . I looked upon architecture as the complement of more important things . . . as an exercise to be undertaken with a sportive spirit—nothing more. This allowed me a certain negligence, which pandered to my easy-going Bohemian nature, and accounted for the fact that I took on too many projects, executed them hurriedly, relying upon my ability and powers of improvisation which I was certain I possessed." The architect, moreover, found himself encouraged by numerous clients "desirous of giving their buildings something showy and spectacular to be talked about."[60]

Niemeyer was not alone among contemporary architects in feeling a conflict between his social conscience and his artistic instincts, once remarking that "it is strange how the power of beauty makes us forget so much injustice."[61] At the same time, unlike some of his colleagues, he remained undeluded by the myth of "social architecture," maintaining repeatedly that social problems should be solved in their own terms.

It may be noted that the criticisms which Niemeyer directed toward his work were intended not to deny its value but to illustrate an evolution in his own development. In general, he saw his works as "positive factors within the Brazilian architectural movement, to which, at a very opportune time, they contributed effectively, by their dashing creative spirit, which still characterizes this movement today."[62] By 1955, however, when he began developing the design for a new museum in Caracas, Niemeyer was attempting a series of self-imposed disciplinary measures. These were marked, according to the architect, by a deliberate reduction of work in his office and a refusal to assume projects of purely commercial interest. He hoped by this to dedicate himself more effectively to those projects which he did undertake. He also attempted to fix a set of rules for new projects, by which he would strive for formal simplicity and a greater balance of form with functional and technical problems.

It was with this new spirit that Niemeyer was to assume direction of his greatest project, the creation of a new monumental capital for Brazil.

Is That All?

It has been said that Brazil was discovered twice: first in 1500 by Pedro Alvares Cabral, the Portuguese Navigator, and again in 1942 by Philip Goodwin, when he arrived with G. E. Kidder Smith to organize an exhibition of Brazilian architecture for the Museum of Modern Art in New York. This exhibition, together with a book produced by its organizers, provided many people outside of Brazil with their first

60. Ibid., p. 4.
61. Oscar Niemeyer, "The Contemporary City," *Módulo* 11 (December 1958): 5. Text of address presented at the International Students' Congress in Leningrad.
62. Niemeyer, "Testimony," p. 4.

comprehensive view of the new Brazilian architecture. At that time, the freshness and originality of Brazilian work and the sudden emergence of a school of young innovative designers aroused worldwide interest. The Brazilians themselves were gratified by their sudden preeminence, and confident of achievements to come.

The next major presentation of Brazilian architecture to foreign view came with Henrique Mindlin's book *Modern Architecture in Brazil,* published in 1956. Although the Brazilian accomplishment in design was still worthy of note, it was clear that much of the euphoria and optimism, the sense of excitement and leadership which had accompanied earlier years, had dissipated. Mindlin noted that, "in the middle fifties, after twenty years of impressive output, there was a general feeling that perhaps the whole movement had reached a routine period, if not a downward phase, that the summits attained in the most famous buildings were not to be achieved any more."[63] Lúcio Costa, who had been helping Mindlin to make his final selection of examples, regarded the assembled work and asked somewhat despondently, "Is that all?"[64]

Reviewing the same book later, Costa noted that although the recent work shown revealed maturity and style, one retained the suspicion that it was the earlier achievements of Brazilian architecture—the Brazilian Press Association building, the Ministry of Education and Health, the Seaplane terminal, the Pavilion at the World's Fair in New York, and Pampúlha—which had marked its high point. Appearing to have reached its zenith at the outset, modern architecture in Brazil seemed unable to evolve further, increasing in output, but with no change in direction or demonstrable growth in quality. According to Costa: "the feeling of doubt and apprehension returns, because, in spite of the ingenious solutions and formal innovations, everything turns, in the last analysis, around the same well-known points and one comes to the sad conclusion that Brazilian architecture has already done its job."[65]

If Brazilian architecture no longer occupies the same position which it did during the 1930s and 1940s, the reason may lie less with Brazil than with architectural developments in the rest of the world. Viewed within the general evolution of postwar building, modern architecture in Brazil is neither as impressive in volume nor as stylistically unique as it once seemed. The initial contribution of modern Brazilian building lay in its departure from the puritanical austerities of the orthodox International Style, and in its embodiment of the ebullient Latin spirit in a lyrically expressive form. It opposed an ideal of discipline with freedom and self-expression.

It was this freedom, which initially seemed unique to Brazil, which came to dominate postwar architecture throughout the world. Le Corbusier led the way with his sculptural conceptions in exposed concrete, and although the work of some architects, most notably Mies van der Rohe, maintained an elegant restraint of form, many de-

63. Mindlin, *Brazilian Architecture,* p. 36.
64. Ibid., p. 37.
65. Ibid.

signers reveled in a climate of total permissiveness. Those foreign critics who condemned the extravagances of Brazilian building in the 1950s seem to have been ignoring similar trends elsewhere. With increasing affluence, simplicity and economy no longer seemed of high priority, and emotionally oriented formal experimentation became a legitimate architectural goal. To an era capable of absorbing into the man-made environment Wright's Guggenheim Museum, Saarinen's TWA Terminal, and Utzon's Sydney Opera House, the formal freedom of Brazilian building would cease to astound.

With rapid communication of ideas and images, architecture has become more truly international, with every designer drawing consciously and unconsciously on a vast store of visual experience. Brazilian designers have continued receptive to outside influences, and much of the building seen in recent decades has paralleled developments abroad. As elsewhere, the Brazilian architectural scene exhibits a variety of formal concepts. The lightness of form, the extensive use of glass together with varied sunshading devices, may still be seen in much Brazilian building. The use of exposed concrete and a more massive conception of sculptural form, influenced by Le Corbusier's postwar work, is also in evidence.

Within Rio, new high-rise building continues, with additional office structures in the central district, and apartment housing spreading through the oceanfront South Zone as far as Gavea. Two of the more notable additions to the central business district have been the work of Henrique Mindlin, who, unlike many Rio architects, maintained a large professional staff and a willingness to undertake complete supervision of large complex projects. His towering steel-frame Avenida Central building, occupying a dominant site on the avenue created by Perreira Passos, presents in its narrow slab a stripped-down, matter-of-fact expression of the vertical framing and glass infilling (fig. 114). Nearby rises Mindlin's Bank of Guanabara building, a more sculpturally conceived tower dramatizing the horizontal levels with unbroken strips of masonry and glass.

Like contemporary building elsewhere, Brazilian architecture embodies a wide range of quality, possessing a relatively small number of outstanding examples within a large body of routine commercial and government construction. In spite of the volume of modern building since the 1930s, the Ministry of Education and Health building easily maintains its position as the most distinguished modern monument in Rio. In apparent deference to the dominant qualities of this noted structure, Oscar Niemeyer, when developing the design of the Barão de Mauá building adjacent to the Ministry plaza, chose not to attempt a dramatic architectural statement which might compete with the older building, but to create as a foil and backdrop a bland and self-effacing slab sheathed in flat gray panels (fig. 108).

The Brazilian predilection for audacious form may be seen continued, however, in a number of Rio buildings. The new cathedral, taking the form of a beehivelike dome, provides the city with its major new monument, while the Museum of Modern Art by Affonso Reidy and the free-form residence of Oscar Niemeyer typify the currently visible stylistic range (figs. 120–21). Among the more daring additions to contemporary Rio is the Panorama Palace Hotel in Ipanema (fig. 119). Although hill sites have been generally avoided for major building, this project attempts the construction of a large concrete structure part way up a precipitous mountain slope, and accessible only by a freestanding outside elevator. The plan of this dramatically sited building curves to follow the form of the mountain, and embodies a massively projecting concrete terrace.

The Contemporary Architect—A Self Assessment

In 1961, the School of Architecture of Minas Gerais organized a survey in which a group of leading Brazilian architects was asked to comment on the status of the architectural profession in contemporary Brazil. Among those questioned were men who had pioneered in the Brazilian Modern Movement and were still actively practicing. As young men, many of these architects had been caught up in the enthusiasm and optimism surrounding the early development of modern Brazilian building, and they regarded their work as forming part of a new era of social and economic progress. Thirty years later, although many could look back on successful careers and distinguished achievement, the national environment in which they worked remained in many ways unchanged. Industrialization was still rudimentary, and the mechanization of building, which had been so confidently regarded as inherent in the Modern Movement, seemed as remote as ever. Affonso Reidy observed, "our country is only today able to begin thinking of industrial production on a large scale of prefabricated elements for building."[66]

Socially, Brazil remained essentially stratified, with a population largely poor and illiterate and the achievement of political democracy still far from realization. Although the architectural profession was still characterized by small private practice, when asked to comment on the role of the architect in the "present socio-economic moment of the country," many of the respondents chose to see themselves in an idealized role as leaders in large-scale planning directed toward national goals of social welfare.

Reidy typified the comments of his colleagues when he maintained that it was the duty of the architect "to intervene in planning, influencing decisively the solution to problems related to social well-being. The human element must be the center of all our preoccupations, and the standard to which we must relate all measures."[67] Sergio Bernardes expressed himself similarly, declaring: "The role of the Brazilian

66. Affonso Reidy, in *Inquérito Nacional de Arquitetura* (Belo Horizonte, 1963), p. 185.
67. Ibid., p. 47.

architect, first and foremost, is to plan for Brazil. To create an architecture which is bound within our economy, our way of life, our regions, our people. The architect is the analyst and legitimate coordinator of the progress of the country, for comfort and social well-being."[68]

Such sentiments are not unique to Brazil, but reflect the prevailing rhetoric of contemporary architects. In part a manifestation of simple ego and a desire to aggrandize the profession, these statements embody also a genuine desire to see architecture as a force for social betterment. Implied is a state of chronic dissatisfaction with the nature and function of architecture in contemporary society.

Many of the architects cited conditions of patronage which they judged inimical to a high level of architectural production. Henrique Mindlin considered architectural quality to be jeopardized by the large amount of building governed by "irresponsible speculation and short vision, and the absence of concern for its purpose." He complained that "a larger sense of architectural work, human, social and economic, is rarely considered, either in the field of private initiative or in the sector of government action. Because of this, the architect has almost no opportunity to contribute to a better Brazil. The little which has already been done gives testimony to the rare cases in which there is a client possessed of a certain idealism or an intelligent administrator sensitive to the eternal values of architecture."[69]

Marcelo and Mauricio Roberto pointed out that only about two percent of Brazilian building received the collaboration of an architect, and in urbanism the situation was even worse. All of the architect's effort did not

> go beyond projects which are scorned or mutilated at the time of realization (Brasília included), for it is exclusively the influence of profit, expediency and the lack of imagination of the unstable speculator which corrupts and dominates authority. Thus in this "socio-economic moment" the architect is little more than a marginal individual, a non-essential luxury, accommodating, even well-paid, sometimes, and working successfully; always, however, limited to isolated accomplishments of restricted interest—when his destiny should be an intense participation in the struggle for collective well-being.[70]

Contributing to the same discussion, Oscar Niemeyer repeated his often-expressed view that:

> Architecture is a reflection of the ambient in which it is realized. If social conditions and technical progress are just and correspond, there will be an equilibrium of a high level—if on the contrary, society presents differences of class and fortune, this will arrest the interests allied to collectivism; it can be beautiful,

68. Ibid., p. 59.
69. Ibid., p. 51.
70. Ibid., pp. 53–54.

but its contents will be prejudiced. The position of the architect in this socio-economic moment must be to support the progressive movements capable of giving society a better structure and to architecture corresponding social and human qualities.[71]

The area of architecture most closely related to social welfare is that which concerns mass housing. Almost no country in the world has a truly satisfactory housing situation, and the shortage of decent dwellings in a developing Brazil is strikingly acute. Most of the architects of the survey, when asked to suggest a direction for the solution of the housing problem, could only stress that it was essentially an economic, rather than an architectural problem. As Henrique Mindlin pointed out: "A real and total solution to the housing problem can only come through the economic development of the country and general elevation of the standard of living."[72]

Although some low-cost housing has been attempted in Brazil, it has been limited to occasional government-sponsored projects (figs. 42–44). One of the best-known and most highly regarded of such housing developments in Rio was the Pedregulho project built in the North Zone district of São Cristavo in 1950–52 (fig. 45). Projected as one of a series of neighborhood housing units, Pedregulho was intended for low-ranking municipal employees, and the 12.5-acre site was designed to include a number of community facilities, including a health center, school, playground facilities, a market, and laundry. The most dramatic feature of the ensemble was an 826-foot-long apartment building, its dramatically undulating form following the contours of an elevated site. At the time of its inception, the Pedregulho project was highly praised, not only for the aesthetic quality of its overall design by Affonso Reidy, but also for the enlightened social implications of its initial planning which involved the use of data provided by future tenants and city welfare workers. Well aware of the isolated nature of such housing efforts, however, Reidy observed that "Brazil is one of the countries negligent of the problem of housing. One could almost say, ignorant of its existence."[73]

In spite of a degree of disillusionment which may be felt, now that the honeymoon of the Modern Movement is over, architecture in Brazil maintains a high degree of cultural importance. At a time when Brazil was seeking artistic identity, it was the modern architects who gave the country an art form wholly its own. Brazil is the only modern nation in which architecture may be said to provide a major source of national pride.

When Costa suggested that Brazilian architecture had "already done its job,"[74] he was unaware that Brazilian architecture would soon play a crucial role in a momentous project—the creation of a new capital. Brazil had previously attracted worldwide

71. Ibid., pp. 58–59.
72. Ibid., p. 128.
73. Ibid., p. 121.
74. Mindlin, *Brazilian Architecture*, p. 36.

attention through an originality and freedom of architectural form. Now she was once again to become an international focus as the government body which Niemeyer once accused of shying from "plans of national dimensions and from large scale construction projects"[75] undertook a building enterprise so audacious as to be without contemporary parallel. Within a period of a few years, an isolated inland site would be transformed from wasteland into a new government headquarters.

Viewing with admiration the scope of the new city, André Malraux observed: "Modern architecture was up to now an architecture of buildings: it created houses. That some day such an epic individualism should be surpassed, none of its historians had any doubts. But nearly all of them thought that the greatest architecture, that which creates cities instead of buildings, would be born in the Soviet Union—and it is appearing right here."[76]

In the establishment of the new capital, Brazilian architects would be charged not only with the utilitarian task of giving the city physical existence, but also with providing the nation with a new set of symbols—monuments intended to exemplify the renewed aspiration, optimism, and sense of national purpose inherent in the creation of the city.

75. Papadaki, *Niemeyer: Works in Progress,* p. 12.
76. Quoted in Penna, *Brazil Builds Brasília,* p. 13.

7. BRASÍLIA

In the course of an expedition through South America in 1913, Theodore Roosevelt had occasion to cross the western edge of the Planalto, the high central plain of Brazil. Describing this "healthy land of dry air, of cool nights, of clear, running brooks," he stated:

> The air was wonderful; the vast open spaces gave a sense of abounding vigor and freedom. . . . the sky was brilliant; far and wide we looked over a landscape that seemed limitless; the breeze that blew in our faces might have come from our own northern plains. The midday sun was very hot; but it was hard to realize that we were in the torrid zone. . . . Surely in the future this region will be the home of a healthy, highly civilized population. . . . Any sound northern race could live here; and in such a land, with such a climate, there would be much joy of living.[1]

These interior uplands, which inspired such enthusiasm in the former president, had long been regarded by Brazilians not only as an area for potential settlement, but also as the site for a new national capital. This goal was finally achieved in 1960 when, during the administration of President Juscelino Kubitschek de Oliveira, the city of Brasília was dedicated.

Brasília sprang into existence during the 1950s with the same unexpectedness as Brazilian modern architecture of the 1930s, and was characterized by the same unorthodoxy of approach. In a world of common sense and caution, of feasibility studies, long-range economic analyses, demographic projections, sound fiscal policies, and well-reasoned programs and proposals, Brasília became an actuality as a result of political will and spontaneous enthusiasm. Just as no one had anticipated that an unindustrialized country noted for its long cultural dependence would suddenly as-

1. Theodore Roosevelt, *Through the Brazilian Wilderness* (New York: Scribner's, 1914), pp. 174–76. For this quotation the author is indebted to Hollister Kent, who employed it in "Vera Cruz: Brazil's New Federal Capital," Ph.D. diss., Cornell University, 1956).

sume an innovative role in modern design, few would have predicted that a nation notorious for its inefficiency and poor organization, its repeated failure to execute plans, its chronic inability to construct adequate urban housing or maintain rudimentary urban services, would, within the space of a few years, create a new capital city in an isolated wilderness.

The audacity of Brasília, the speed and bravura with which it was realized, reinforce the image of Brazil as a land of promise, where all the rules need not be obeyed, and where an ebullient human spirit has dominance over the pedestrian dictates of prudence. Although Brasília in its present stage may appear primarily a grand gesture and a symbolic monument, the foundation of the city was accompanied by the expectation that it would be instrumental in aiding the long-term development of the interior, serving as a magnet for population and economic enterprise. Brasília was also planned as the focal point of a new system of interior highways linking the north and south of Brazil, providing, for the first time, a ground transportation system uniting the country from within.

One of the peculiarities of Brazil is that in spite of a prevailing mythology of boundless resources and untapped wealth, Brazilians have yet to take full possession of their own land. The great spontaneous migration which populated the United States had no Brazilian counterpart, and for all the optimism which has surrounded Brazil, this vast territory long remained a string of coastal settlements, frequently more closely tied to the outside world than to each other. Communication and transport failed to develop effectively; the main railroads ran essentially east to west, serving to bring interior products to the coast, but unable to provide a coordinated system of inter-regional transportation. Even coastal shipping was so poorly developed that not long ago it was reported to take less time for a foreign ship to load merchandise in Salvador, carry it to Rotterdam or Liverpool, unload it, reload it, and ship it to Rio de Janeiro, than it would to ship it directly along the coast from Salvador to Rio.[2] In spite of many pioneering efforts at exploration and exploitation of the interior, viable and lasting settlement somehow failed to thrive.

Discussing the achievements of the early Brazilian pioneers or "Bandierantes," Israel Pinheiro, who administered the initial construction of Brasília, observed:

> Once the gold mines were exhausted, . . . and the alluvial soils used up, and the mineral soils abandoned as being unsuitable for agriculture and too distant from the population centers forming along the seaboard, we found ourselves back at the point of departure: we returned to the coast and never again left it. Between our cities and the distant outposts of those heroic standard bearers, there remained only a few sparse settlements, without sufficient means of subsistence and beyond aid of any kind. Along the coast, from which we could communicate

2. Kent, "Vera Cruz," p. 68.

east with the Mother country and maintain our close dependent relationship, we built an industrial civilization utterly unrelated to the Interior.[3]

Regarding the pronounced regional differences of his country, a Brazilian scholar once observed that within Brazil itself one could experience three distinct ages of cultural development: "the age of the motor in the modern coastal cities of Rio de Janeiro, São Paulo, Porto Alegre, Recife; the age of the mule, which is characteristic of the backlands, the *sertão,* with its semicolonial economy and conservative organization; and finally the stone age of the primitive Indian tribes of the jungle. From a XX-Century nation on the seacoast the westbound traveler goes back through feudal times until he reaches a prehistoric society beyond the great tributaries of the Amazon."[4]

The economic and social problems of Brazil are large and complex, and to many, considering the unstable and unbalanced economy, the depressed and feudal agricultural system, together with the general illiteracy, poor health standards and grinding poverty of much of the population, the establishment of a grandiose new capital seems a questionable enterprise. The Brasília project has attracted considerable criticism, and, in spite of the optimistic hopes that Brasília will contribute substantially to the settlement of the interior, few would consider the city a substitute for thorough regional and national planning.

In its short existence, the physical image of Brasília, with its wide motor roads, uniformly modern buildings, vast monumental axis, and dramatic government complex, has become a widely known symbol of Brazil, as familiar to outsiders as the beach of Copacabana and the statue of Christ on Corcovado. While Rio still provides an embodiment of romantic natural beauty, Brasília presents the vision of a totally manmade environment. Rio, in spite of recent renovations, retains many of the qualities of nineteenth-century urbanism in her wide treelined avenues and varied architecture. Brasília, by contrast, is entirely of the twentieth century, a standardized city scaled to the motor, in which the avenue has been replaced by the freeway.

Describing a visit which she and Jean Paul Sartre paid to Brazil, Simone de Beauvoir recalled that, in Rio, "we often wandered along the Avenida Rio-Branco: a sea of pedestrians on the sidewalks, the roadway packed with vehicles; stores, kiosks, posters, bars opening out onto the street with coffee machines glittering beside big jars of juices—pineapple, orange, *cajou,* passion fruit; then banners and slogans."[5] Confronted with Brasília, she observed: "What possible interest could there be in wandering about among the six- or eight-story *quadra* and *superquadra* . . . exuding the same air of elegant monotony?" She noted with regret that "the street, that meet-

3. Israel Pinheiro, "Uma realidade: Brasília," *Módulo* 8 (June 1957): 3–8. Quotation from English supplement, p. 12.

4. J. O. de Meira Penna, "Brazil Builds a New Capital," *Landscape,* 5 (Spring 1956): 18.

5. Simone de Beauvoir, *Force of Circumstance* (New York: Putnam's, 1964), p. 527. First published in France as *La force des choses* (Paris: Librairie Gallimard, 1963).

ing ground of riverside dwellers and passers-by, of stores and houses, of vehicles and pedestrians—thanks to the capricious, always unexpectedly changing mixture—the street, as fascinating in Chicago as in Rome, in London as in Peking, in Bahia as in Rio, . . . the street does not exist in Brasília and never will."[6]

To many, attracted by older urban forms, Brasília may appear sterile and regimented, epitomizing some of the most unimaginative and inhumane aspects of modern civic design. In the opinion of the Italian critic Bruno Zevi, "It is a city of Kafka."[7] Brasília is not a city lover's city and at present lacks many of the agreeable attributes of an established urban complex. Brasília appears in photographs almost like an architect's full-scale mockup—a bland and sketchy idea in need of greater detailing. If one thinks of a city as a human settlement imbued with the richness of history, with the patina of a long and varied human experience, with the physical complexity and architectural diversity resulting from a long series of adjustments, additions, and design decisions, Brasília is not yet a city at all.

Brasília, to be appreciated, must be taken on its own terms, as a bold gesture, and an act of faith in the future. A French visitor to Washington, D. C., in 1851 subsequently described the city as "striking proof of this truth that one cannot create a great city at will."[8] Just as Washington was long considered a "failure," so Brasília may stimulate doubts, and if the new capital is not a city lover's city, it is also not a city planner's city. As with many other human achievements, Brasília was done wrong, and in defiance of orthodox procedures.

Much of the present impact of Brasília is dependent on experiencing the city in its remote inland setting. As one approaches the new capital, flying over vast and formidable tracts of unsettled land, the first intimations of the city's existence—delicate lines of roadway cutting through the undergrowth—provide a thrilling glimpse of the human presence, like Friday's footprints in the sand. Reservations regarding the wisdom of the project and the quality of the plan tend to subside when Brasília, pristine and glittering, is first perceived (figs. 122–25). In context, Brasília appears as cities ought to appear—as a welcome sign of civilization—and one is reminded of that time in history when the works of man were regarded not as a threat to the natural environment, but as "improvements" in the landscape. Brasília is a human triumph, a source of legitimate pride for its creators, and a stimulus to continuing effort. Even Fidel Castro, who may well have felt little rapport with the government establishment promoting Brasília, upon first viewing the city, declared: "It's a joy to be young in Brazil."[9]

6. Ibid., p. 551.

7. "Opiniões sôbre Brasília," *Habitat* 58 (January–February 1960).

8. Jean-Jacques Ampère, quoted in Elizabeth Kite, *L'Enfant and Washington* (Baltimore: Johns Hopkins Press, 1929), p. 28.

9. "Fidel Castro visita Brasília," *Brasília* 40 (April 1960): 87. (*Brasília* is an official publication of NOVACAP.)

8. THE EVOLUTION OF AN IDEA

Juscelino Kubitschek once observed, "Brasília is not an improvisation: it is a maturation."[1] He wished to stress that the creation of the new capital was not an arbitrary or precipitous decision on his part, but the fruition of many years of preparation. Concurring, Israel Pinheiro pointed out, "No other national problem has been debated and analyzed over so long a period of our history—from colonial times up to the present day."[2]

The first recorded advocacy of a new capital appeared in 1789 in a statement by a group of political revolutionaries in the state of Minas Gerais, who called themselves the "inconfidentes Mineiros." Pioneers in the movement for independence from Portugal, they incorporated in their program the concept of a new governing center free of the symbolic associations of the colonial regime.

References to the need for an inland capital recurred frequently throughout subsequent Brazilian history. It may be recalled that in 1808 the Portuguese court sought refuge from Napoleon by settling in Rio de Janeiro, and although this event stimulated notable civic development in Rio, the regent, Dom João, evidently had little fondness for this beautiful city. It is recorded that, from the beginning of his stay, the refugee monarch voiced dissatisfaction with the climate and conditions of Rio, announcing his intention of seeking a more suitable capital farther south. For strategic reasons, however, an inland site was considered preferable. Reference to such an inland city was contained in a speech by William Pitt published in 1806 on the subject of the Portuguese colonies. Pitt described a city called "New Lisbon" to be founded in the central part of Brazil, "whence the royal roads would radiate like waters that flow down the upland slopes."[3] In 1810, Chancellor and Royal Crown Advisor Veloso

1. Quoted by Raul de Sá Barbosa, "Brasília, evolução, História de una ideia," *Módulo* 18 (June 1960): 29. Quotation from English supplement.

2. Israel Pinheiro, "Uma realidade: Brasília," *Módulo* 8 (June 1957): 3–8. Quotation from English supplement, p. 12.

3. Barbosa, "Brasília, evolução," p. 33. Quotation from English supplement.

de Oliveira urged that: "The Court should not settle in a seaport. . . . The capital should be in a healthy, agreeable location free from the confusion of the clamorous multitudes of people indiscriminately thrown together."[4]

In addition to receiving official support, the idea of the new capital was also promulgated through the popular press. An article in the daily newspaper, *Correio Brasilense,* declared in 1813:

> Rio de Janeiro possesses none of the qualities required of a city destined to be the capital of the Brazilian Empire. If the courtiers who came from Lisbon have sufficient patriotism and gratitude to the land which welcomed them in their time of trouble, they will generously sacrifice the comforts and luxuries which they enjoy in Rio de Janeiro and establish themselves in the interior lands near the headwaters of the great rivers. They must build there a new city, and begin to open up roads leading to all the sea ports, removing the natural obstacles to navigating the various rivers, and in this way spread the foundations for the most extensive, united, well defended and powerful empire which can exist on the surface of the globe.[5]

The idea of the inland capital seems to have been inextricably bound to a conception of Brazil's manifest destiny, and was embodied in much of the rhetoric of the independence movement. One of the principal figures of the republican revolution of 1817, Father João Ribeiro, urged that a central city be raised "at least 30 to 40 leagues away from the sea-coast, as a residence for the Congress and the Government. . . ."[6]

To the patriarch of Brazilian independence, José Bonifácio de Andrada e Silva, the foundation of a new capital seemed a natural accompaniment to the creation of a new nation, and in 1821, the instructions prepared for the Brazilian delegates to the Portuguese council included recommendations for such a city. Instructing the delegates, Bonifácio stated: "It seems to me highly desirable to construct a central city in the interior of Brazil . . . which will be in the latitude of approximately 15° . . . This central court will be the focus of roads leading to various provinces and seaports, by which means Government communications may circulate with promptness, and which will also favor the commercial development of the vast Empire of Brazil."[7] The name "Brasília" was first suggested in 1822, by a Brazilian delegate, who proposed, "In the center of Brazil, between the headwaters of the confluent rivers Paraguai and Amazonas, the capital of this kingdom will be founded, to be called Brasília, or by some other name."[8] The name reappeared the following year in a memorandum

4. Henrique Luttgardes Cardoso de Castro, *Brasília e o desenvolvimento nacional* (Rio de Janeiro, 1960), p. 11.

5. Ibid., p. 10.

6. Barbosa, "Brasília, evolução," p. 34.

7. Castro, *Brasília e o desenvolvimento nacional,* p. 11.

8. Ibid., p. 12.

addressed by José Bonifácio to the General Constituent and Legislative Assembly of Brazil, proposing the establishment of a new capital in northwestern Minas Gerais, and calling the city either Petrópole or Brasília.

Although the creation of a new governing center had seemed an appropriate expression of newly acquired independence, no direct action was taken to effect such a project. The idea remained alive, however, appearing in political pronouncements throughout the nineteenth century. The historian and diplomat Francisco Adolfo de Varnhagen did much to keep the proposal before the public, making frequent references to the new city in his writings. He favored a site in the province of Goiás, and suggested that the city be called Imperatória, a name "that explains its mission."[9] Other names suggested during this period for the proposed new capital were Pedrália and City of Tiradentes.

Although a bill in support of the new capital had been introduced in the legislature by Senator Holanda Cavalcanti in 1852, it was not until the proclamation of the Brazilian republic in 1889 that legislative groundwork for the city would actually be established. After considerable debate, specific provision for the new national capital was incorporated into the Constitution of 1891, in which Article 3 stated: "From now on, an area of 14,400 square kilometers will belong to the Government for the location of the new capital." To reinforce this provision, a bill was passed to "authorize the exploration and demarcation of the area intended for the new capital on the central plateau of the territory of the Republic."[10]

In specifying a location within the central plateau, the Brazilian legislators were adhering to the generally held view that this part of Brazil provided the most reasonable site for the new capital. Although the concept of centrality was important in siting the city, it had never been suggested that the capital be located in the geographic center of Brazil. To have done so would have placed this new urban center in the northeastern corner of the State of Mato Grosso, in an area of impenetrable wilderness, impossibly remote from any centers of population or directions of population growth. In 1890, the national population center was in the northern part of the State of Minas Gerais, with trends of movement toward the south. The placement of the new city was designed to combine a symbolic rather than literal centrality of siting with a realistic relation to actual patterns of settlement. In terms of climate, resources, and relative accessibility, the plains of the central highlands could be seen as a suitable area into which population movement might be deflected from existing centers.

The initial attempt to find a specific site for the new Brazilian capital was made by a government commission formed in 1891 under the leadership of Dr. Luiz Cruls, director of the Federal Observatory. The central plateau of Brazil, which had been

9. Barbosa, "Brasília, evolução," p. 37. Quotation from English supplement.
10. Ibid., p. 39. Quotation from English supplement.

designated as the locality of the capital, was a vast territory, including areas of the states of Mato Grosso, Goiás, Bahia, Minas Gerais, and São Paulo. As a detailed study of this terrain would have involved years of effort, Cruls simplified the initial problem by deciding to limit explorations to a district in Goiás.

On 29 June 1892, the twenty-two member expedition left the railhead of Uberaba and set out for Pirenópolis to begin field studies. Among the factors which the commission considered relevant in forming the basis for site selection were climate, soils, geology, topography, animal and plant life, and availability of potable and medicinal water, building materials, and water power. The result of their investigation was the delineation of a 160 by 90 kilometer rectilinear area, the so-called Rectangle of Cruls, which, in accordance with the requirements of the 1891 constitution, provided an area of 14,400 kilometers.

It is of interest that in the report which Dr. Cruls submitted, he quoted from a subreport by Dr. Glaziou, the botanist of the expedition, regarding a site for the actual construction of the city. Dr. Glaziou had felt that, because of the quality of the soil, the availability of water, the advantageous climate, and the beauty of the landscape, the site for the new capital should be in the valley formed by the rivers Torto, Gama, Vicente Pires, Riacho Fundo, and Bananal. The expedition had camped in this valley for several days, and Glaziou had found himself greatly attracted to the terrain which he felt was easily adaptable to the creation of boulevards and the siting of buildings. The falls of the Paranoa, moreover, could provide a suitable source of power.

Following the publication of the Cruls report in 1894, serious governmental support for moving the capital seemed to subside, and although henceforth the area selected by the commission would appear on many maps as "Future Federal District," there seemed no immediate inclination to develop it as a capital site.

Interest appeared to revive again early in the 1920s, and on 18 January 1922, the president of the republic, Epitácio Pessôa, approved a law providing for the transfer of the capital, giving instructions for the projection of appropriate railway connections from the future city to Rio and Santos. On 7 September 1922, in commemoration of the 100th anniversary of the founding of the republic, the president dedicated a monument on a hill just outside the small town of Planaltina within the Cruls Rectangle. Although this monument was a symbolic representation of the cornerstone of the new capital, it heralded no new developments and served primarily to honor the tiny municipality with the presence of the chief executive.

In 1934, Getúlio Vargas, having ruled as dictator since 1930, called an election which made him president. At this time he created a new constitution containing a provision that "the capital of the Republic will be transferred to a centrally located point in Brazil," and parliament must "without loss of time take the necessary steps for the transfer of the capital."[11] No money was ever appropriated to support these

11. Quoted in Frank Arnau, *Brasília: Phantasie und Wirklichkeit* (Munich, 1960), p. 115.

intentions, however, and the constitution was suspended when Vargas reestablished himself as dictator in 1937.

In spite of many who favored the project, further action with regard to the new capital was not taken until 1946, after Vargas had been deposed and Marechal Eurico Gaspar Dutra had been elected president. Vocal support for the project was provided by the politician Teixero de Freitas who claimed that the transfer of the government center was "not only unpostponable, but is also the imperative and first problem of Brazil . . . If necessary Belo Horizonte should serve as a provisional capital until the definite solution is found in the High Plateau."[12]

The new constitution created by Dutra not only repeated the intention to move the capital, but also stipulated that "the President of Brazil, within 60 days, shall select a Commission of reliable technicians who will be in charge of conducting the studies for the location of the New Capital."[13] This new commission consisted of twelve members headed by General Djalma Polli Coelho.

In beginning their work, the new commission disregarded the studies done by the Cruls Commission and attempted to begin selection of the general area of the capital all over again. They chose an area larger than 1,000,000 square kilometers for initial study and, within this, selected eight separate zones for more intensive examination. The selection was guided by three basic conditions: a central location in relation to the populated region of the country, a location permitting easy communication with different regions of the country, and proximity to an interstate border. As the commission expressed it, "the expedition is of the opinion that the principal functions of a Capital are not colonization and strategy, but administration and politics. In connection with the administrative function, the ideal location would be the demographic center. . . . The most important role of a Capital as a political center is to unify the country. To achieve this, its location should allow easy communication with the various regions of the country, especially with those which are most populated and developed."[14] The reasons for wishing to be near a state border, however, were never explained. It is possible that the commission had the precedent of Washington, D. C., in mind and felt it politically desirable to straddle a state boundary.

In 1947, two geographic expeditions were sent out by the Coelho Commission, the first, under Professor Francis Ruellan, studied each of the eight selected zones, and the second, directed by Professor Fábio de Macedo Soares Guimarães, and under the scientific leadership of Professor Leo Waibel, investigated the central plateau as a whole. Following the completion of the two expeditions, the members of the Coelho Commission discussed and voted on the results, making their recommendations to President Dutra in 1948. They could not come to an agreement regarding a specific site, however, and proposed two solutions for Congress to consider.[15]

12. Ibid.

13. Quoted in Hollister Kent, "Vera Cruz," p. 18.

14. Ibid., p. 22.

15. Seven of the twelve commissioners voted for an area of 78,000 square kilometers, of which the eastern

The matter was debated in Congress for almost five years, during which President Dutra's term of office ended, and Vargas was again elected. On 5 January 1953, a law was passed providing for a final demarcation of the Federal District. The area was defined through the collaborative effort of representatives from Goiás and Minas Gerais, who reconsidered the recommendations of both the Cruls and Coelho commissions. It was decided that the most suitable area for the new city should be selected within a rectangle of approximately 52,000 square kilometers located 15° 30′ to 17° South and 46° 30′ to 49° 30′ West of Greenwich. Within this area, which included land in both Minas Gerais and Goiás, the new Federal District of 5,000 square kilometers was to be located. The general area defined by the legislative group included almost all of the Cruls Rectangle and some of the areas suggested by the Coelho Commission.

The 1953 law provided that the president appoint a commission to select a specific site for the city, and that within two years the choice should be presented to Congress. Vargas named General Aguinaldo Caiado de Castro to head the commission, with Dr. Jerônimo Coimbra Bueno as technical director.[16]

As a prelude to the selection of a specific site for the new city, a Brazilian photogrammetic company, Aerofoto, a subsidiary of the airline, Cruzeiro do Sul, was asked to survey the study area through aerial photography. This was accomplished in August and September of 1953. At this point, Dr. Edson de Alencar Cabral, who had directed the Aerofoto survey, was asked to assume charge of the remaining technical work for the location of the new capital. He declined, however, proposing instead that foreign assistance be secured.

The question of employing foreign consultants involved considerable controversy. The project of the new capital was in itself a nationalistic symbol, and to some government officials, to ask outside help was a slur upon Brazilian abilities. Others, however, maintained that foreigners would be more likely than Brazilians to accomplish the work within the time limit specified and, moreover, would be less susceptible to local political pressures. This view won out, and in December 1953, Dr. Cabral

boundary would be the state border between Goiás, Bahia, and Minas Gerais, and the southern and western borders would coincide with the Cruls Rectangle. The northern boundary was extended to cover the Chapada dos Veadeiros. The district selected would be 910 kilometers from the coast. The remaining five commissioners voted for a smaller district of 6,000 square kilometers which contained a number of good sites. This area, which came to be called the "Triangulo Mineiro," lay about 630 kilometers from the coast and included land in the western part of Minas Gerais and the southern part of Goiás.

The site selected by the majority group would have placed the capital in a relatively unpopulated area, while that selected by the second group would have located the city farther south, in what was already the economic frontier of Brazil, a zone somewhat settled and near the demographic center of the country. As the Coelho Commission had made no definite decision, however, the problem of site selection was placed back in the hands of Congress, and it became clear that the members of the Special Committee of Federal Representatives were somewhat at a loss regarding how to proceed. Thus, by 1948, in spite of all efforts, no real progress had been made beyond the recommendations of the Cruls Commission.

16. Bueno had been a member of the Coelho Commission, and was the former governor of Goiás. He had been responsible for directing the design of a new planned capital for this state, Goiânia.

reached a tentative agreement with the firm of Donald J. Belcher & Associates of Ithaca, New York, for the final work of site selection. A contract was officially approved on 20 April 1954.

The task of the Belcher firm, as outlined in the contract, was to study the 53,500 square kilometer quadrangle established in 1953 and to select five alternate city sites, each of approximately 1,000 square kilometers and each with the capacity to support an urban population of 500,000. Within a period of ten months, an area larger than New Hampshire and Vermont combined was to be thoroughly surveyed. Once the five sites were selected, they were to be examined in detail, and reports were to be submitted to the government commission for a final choice. A Federal District comprising an additional 4,000 square kilometers surrounding the chosen site would then be delineated.

According to one member of the Belcher staff: "It was a miracle that the job was completed within the contract period and it was only because of the use of aerial photography in interpretation and photogrammetry . . . that the presentation was made within the specified ten months. With normal ground methods alone, ten years would not have been sufficient to accomplish the same work."[17]

Pressures of time would be an important factor in this and many subsequent phases of the evolution of Brasília. In the opinion of the American planner:

> It would have been very easy to get led astray by going into the sociological and economic aspects of such a move; how it would affect the present capital city and its population, what impact it would have upon the economy of the area surrounding the new site and how the country as a whole would be changed. Perhaps a complete population study should have been done. But to do this at all would have meant that a thorough job would have to be done. If a study of ethnic groups or the problems of movement from rural to urban centers had been made, the work for which we were responsible, the control of the Brazilian section involved in selecting five sites for a capital city of 500,000 persons, would never have been finished.
>
> This is not to belittle the part that sociology and economics play in the total planning picture, because they are quite definitely parts of the integrated whole which is called planning, but in this case, it had to be assumed that these factors were being taken care of by Brazilians. They were responsible for making population estimates and it was the job of the survey team to do the physical site selection.[18]

Within the team, however, some efforts were made at analyzing social aspects of the proposed city, and "the final choices were five sites which were a result of some hard-

17. Kent, "Vera Cruz," p. 88.

18. Ibid., pp. 88–89.

headed scientific recommendations concerning elevation, topography, soils, rock, water, climate and communication and a group of standards set up by philosophical discussion, placing the Brazilian as a person in this ideal capital city."[19]

Following the completion of the site studies, an expedition was organized to permit members of the government commission to visit the five locations selected. Because of difficult landing conditions, however, only two of the sites were actually seen from the ground. Major responsibility for the final decision appears to have rested with the head of the commission, Marechal José Pessôa, and although two members resigned from the group on grounds that the decision was achieved too hastily, a final official judgment was made in the second week in April 1955.

The site chosen was precisely the spot which had been so favorably described by Dr. Glaziou and recommended by the Cruls report sixty-one years previously. It lay 25 kilometers southeast of the town of Planaltina where, in 1922, President Epitácio Pessôa had dedicated a monument to the new capital.

The present Federal District of 5,814 square kilometers lies between the parallels of 15° 30′ and 16° 03′ and is bounded on the east and west by the rivers Descoberto and Prêto. The terrain is gently undulating, with a type of vegetation called *campo cerrado,* or tree savanna, characterized by large tracts of short grasses and occasional clumps of shrubs and low scrubby trees. The region is crossed by valleys set close together, subdividing the land into mesas locally called *chapadas.* The altitude ranges from 2,953 to 3,609 feet. The climate of the district is relatively mild, with the lowest recorded temperature 39.2° F, and the highest, 98.6° F. Relative humidity ranges between 55 percent and 86 percent, and the seasons consist of a dry winter lasting from April to September and a rainy summer extending from October to March.

Within the Federal District, the city itself occupies a roughly triangular site originally bounded by two rivers, the Bananal and Gamma, which converged to form the Paranoá. Subsequently, the Paranoá was dammed, creating a 15-square-mile artificial lake surrounding the site of the city. The water table of the site ranges from 164 to 328 feet, and the soil presents no obstacles to construction other than a hardness, which eventually necessitated a type of building supported by concrete stakes.

While efforts to establish a site for the new capital had been proceeding quietly, Brazilian political life had been exhibiting its characteristic complexity and theatricality. In 1954, following charges of corruption and pressures by some members of the military establishment for his resignation, Vargas committed suicide. A somewhat chaotic period ensued, with presidents João Café Filho, Coimbra da Luz, and Nereu Ramos rapidly succeeding. By 1955, a complicated four-sided contest for the presidency was under way, with the governor of Minas Gerais, Juscelino Kubitschek de Oliveira, appearing as a compromise candidate.

19. Ibid., p. 89.

Kubitschek won a narrow victory with approximately one-third of the vote. Some contended that his failure to achieve a majority made it unconstitutional for him to assume office, and it required considerable pressure from War Minister General Lott to enable Kubitschek to be inaugurated in 1956. Although he had arrived in office with a somewhat doubtful mandate, Kubitschek's administration was characterized by remarkable dynamism and self-confidence. With the slogan of providing "Fifty Years of Progress in Five Years," he made strenuous efforts to stimulate the economic development of the still backward country, including the introduction of the automobile industry. His methods were sometimes controversial, and he is often credited with promoting Brazil's disastrous monetary inflation. The most notable achievement of his administration, however, is the construction of the new capital.

Kubitschek's initial support for the city seems to have come about somewhat by accident. During a political rally in Goiás during the 1955 campaign, someone in the audience called out to Kubitschek, "What about Brasília?" The candidate impulsively shouted back, "I will implement the constitution." He later admitted, "I had hardly considered Brasília before then."[20]

From this moment onward, the new city became virtually a compulsion with the president, who placed behind the project all his political skill and personal enthusiasm. Although the groundwork of Brasília had been laid over a period of many years, the physical realization of the city was the achievement of a single political administration. Some felt the project was undertaken with undue haste, but speed was necessary under the circumstances. Once Kubitschek had determined to build Brasília, the task had to be accomplished within his single five-year term of office. By law he could not succeed himself, and he knew that Brazilian politicians are loathe to continue any project begun by a previous administration. In order for Brasília to endure, therefore, it would have to be sufficiently complete before Kubitschek left office so that the project could not with reason be abandoned.

In August 1956, as the initial step in developing the new capital, the Brazilian Congress authorized the creation of NOVACAP (Companhia Urbanizadora da Nova Capital), a government corporation charged with directing the construction of Brasília. Dr. Israel Pinheiro da Silva was made president of the organization, with Bernardo Sayao de Carvalho Araújo, Ernesto Silva, and Iris Meinberg serving as directors.

For Kubitschek, Brasília was a focus of intense pride, and it is inevitable that many would perceive the city as one man's monument to himself. The city has never been free of criticism. To Kubitschek's political enemies, the Brasília project was a waste

20. "Kubitschek's Brasília," *Time,* 25 April 1960, p. 38. During the time when the selection of the final site of Brasília was being made, Marechal Pessôa had attempted to bring the governors of Goiás and Minas Gerais together to discuss the question of securing land for the capital. Kubitschek is reported to have been both uninterested and uncooperative, and this influenced the decision to use a site in Goiás.

of labor, time, and money, ruinous to the Brazilian economy. As costs rose, a frequently hostile press dubbed the president a "Brazilian Pharoah." Rio's *Correio da Manhã* once termed the project "The limit of insanity! a dictatorship in the desert!" while *O Globo* pronounced the verdict of "Madness."[21]

In spite of the long evolution of the Brasília project, the sudden creation of the city seemed to many both surprising and precipitous. The concept of the inland capital had become part of Brazilian mythology, and the very longevity of the idea may, to some, have seemed reason enough to assume that the city would continue only as an idea.

The planning of Rio had proceeded without regard to the proposed new capital. Shortly after the demarcation of the Federal District by the Cruls Commission, Rio underwent, during the prefecture of Perreira Passos, an extensive renovation including the construction of a large number of government buildings. Alfred Agache had begun his monumental plan for Rio five years after President Epitácio Pessôa had laid the symbolic cornerstone of the new capital in Planaltina. A book on the planning of Rio published in 1950 had assured the reader that "Rio seems unworried by President Dutra's desire to sign his last decree in 'Brasília,' probable name of the proposed new federal capital in Goiás called for by the 1946 Constitution. Cariocas who give the current studies of the capital commission any attention generally oppose moving the federal government inland."[22] As late as March 1956 an architectural journal had published designs for a new Federal Senate to replace the existing building at the termination of Avenida Rio Branco. It was hard for many people to realize that, after so many years of studies, proposals, investigations, and legislation, the new capital would actually be built.

To the opponents of Brasília, the time was not yet ripe; Brazil had no need for a new capital, and lacked the resources to construct one. To the city's supporters, Brasília was long overdue. As Kubitschek phrased it, "I am not the founder of Brasília, but in my soul came the realization that the hour had come . . . to promote a new era for our land."[23]

In discussing the creation of Brasília, a Brazilian scholar pointed out that:

> The removal of a capital is by itself an essential element of a given historical picture. The choice of the site of a new capital is likewise a momentous decision which affects the destinies of a nation. The moment and the site are the two coordinates of the situation: the moment being its dynamic aspect, its symbolical projection in time: the site its static, fundamental geo-political proposition. The

21. Ibid., p. 39.
22. Adalberto Szilard and José de Oliveira Reis, *Urbanismo no Rio de Janeiro* (Rio de Janeiro, 1950), p. 14.
23. "A história da construção de Brasília," *Brasília* 40 (21 April, 1960): 47. The statement is contained in Kubitschek's New Year's message of 1957.

> moment during the reign of Peter the Great in XVIIIth century Russia, and the site of that "window opened towards Europe," are the two coordinates which place St. Petersburg on an historical map. The moment of Ataturk's revolution and the Anatolian centralizing concept explain the choice of Ankara as the capital of the new Turkey. Similarly, it is this particular moment of Brazil's historical development which seems to prompt, as a spatial corollary, the idea of moving inland the seat of the government. If strong and critical judgment might be levelled against the cold Castillian plateau that Phillip II chose when he raised Madrid to the status of the "only Court"; the sickly estuary of Peter the Great; the marshes of Washington; the lonely hills of the Australian Federalists who built Canberra, or the remote wastelands of our state of Goiás—nevertheless, in all these cases, the choice of the proper site has followed as an imperative the far-reaching political schemes of the ruler. This is the reason we so often find this inspired act in the decisive moments of a nation's history, at the turning-points of the life of its people; . . . Thus many Brazilians believe that the full process of national development will only take place with the relevant act of the removal of the Federal Government to the Central Plateau.[24]

Among the factors favoring the Brasília project was the increasing population pressure within Rio, where shortages of housing, inadequacies in services, and problems of transport and communication were becoming acute. The topography of the city made expansion difficult; building sites were at a premium, and the government establishment was scattered somewhat chaotically throughout the teeming commercial metropolis. By 1956 one could convincingly argue that the old crowded capital was inadequate to meet the future needs of government. Then too, Rio, with all its beauty and ease of living could be seen as symbolically inappropriate for an administrative capital center. A proponent of Brasília once condemned Rio as a

> place of luxury, pleasure and *dolce far niente*. . . . Rio breeds a parasitical bureaucracy, and there is neither the physical nor mental climate for a small and efficient civil service, capable of coping with the urgent problems of a growing colossus. A resort town, surrounded by all the seductions of nature and steeped in a luxurious atmosphere, a Cythera where one basks in the sun, swims in the cool waters, and enjoys the pleasures of life with nonchalance is not the proper site for a capital. . . . A large city, with its pressures, its passions, its economic interests, the exaggerations of a very vocal press, and the constant danger arising from an emotional populace, is not the proper seat for a federal government.[25]

The new capital could thus be justified as an effort to free the government from

24. J. O. de Meira Penna, *Brasília* (Rio de Janeiro, 1960).
25. J. O. de Meira Penna, "Brazil Builds a New Capital," *Landscape* 5 (Spring 1956): 21–22.

what had become a cumbersome and frequently corrupt bureaucracy and to bring a more efficient and dedicated administration in closer touch with the problems of Brazil as a whole. In place of the part-time multiple employment common in Rio, the civil servant of the new capital would presumably bring full-time concentration to his government job, and government offices, which in Rio generally operated only half-time, would work on a full schedule.

Also important in making Brasília possible was the circumstance that Brazilian technical capacity was, perhaps for the first time, equal to such a project. Of great importance in this respect was the development of the aviation industry. Before highway and rail links could be constructed, an efficient air service kept lines of communication open to the new capital, even assisting initially in the transport of building supplies.

In the long run, however, the most important factor in keeping Brasília alive may have been the popular support which the project eventually received. Brazilians are not a nation of patient plodders; they seek no petty successes, but, when inspired, they can bring about the most ambitious projects with astonishing speed and dedication. With what now seems shrewd political insight, Kubitschek sensed that the Brazilian people were ready for an adventure, and that popular imagination might respond to a grand gesture more readily than to pedestrian and practical enterprises. By 1960, Kubitschek was able to proclaim confidently: "The capital is moving, and anybody who tries to stop it will be lynched by the people."[26]

26. "Kubitschek's Brasília," p. 39.

9. THE COMPETITION

Having accomplished the first administrative steps for the construction of the new capital, Kubitschek approached an old friend, Oscar Niemeyer, for assistance in developing a plan for the city. It would not be the first collaboration between the two. It was Kubitschek who, as mayor of Belo Horizonte in 1942, had promoted the development of Pampulha where Niemeyer had distinguished himself as an innovative modern architect. In the intervening years both men had risen to national preeminence.

It was apparent from the beginning that Brasília was to be an architect's, rather than a planner's, city, a circumstance which has drawn repeated criticism. As currently conceived, the creation of a city involves numerous considerations other than physical design, and to many, the faults of Brasília may be traced to its initial conception as an architectural scheme, rather than the collaborative product of multidisciplinary urban specialists. Among those consistent in attacking the design of Brasília has been the Brazilian sociologist, Gilberto Freyre, who once demanded, "Doesn't Brazil also possess economists, ecologists, and social scientists ranking in the same category as her architects?"[1]

Considering the realities of the situation, however, Kubitschek may have been justified in placing the creation of the new capital directly in the hands of an architect. The Brazilian president did not want to plan a city; he wanted to build a city. Within a short period of time, it was necessary to give Brasília physical reality, and only the indisputable presence of a sufficient investment of asphalt, concrete, and steel on the Brasília site could assure the continuance of the project. Had Kubitschek sought to begin with a series of lengthy and probably inconclusive social and economic studies, it is unlikely that Brasília would ever have come into existence.

Although Niemeyer agreed to begin designing some buildings for Brasília, it was

1. Gilberto Freyre, *Brasis, Brasil, Brasília* (Lisbon: Edicão Livros do Brazil, 1960), p. 156.

decided, partly in response to urging by the Institute of Brazilian Architects, to determine the city plan through a competition.

Urbanism and the Modern Movement

Brasília provided the first opportunity for a comprehensive application of the principles of the Modern Movement to the design of a major city. Although for many years modern designers had seen their mission as that of shaping the large-scale environment, the Modern Movement had been known more for visionary projects than realized urban plans.

Modern concepts of urban design had, like modern architecture, taken form during a period of reaction to the effects of the nineteenth century. From the beginning of the industrial age, the cities of the Western world had been subject to unprecedented and uncontrolled expansion. As urban population grew and boundaries sprawled, unregulated land use produced a seemingly chaotic mixture of functions. Even the extensive program of urban improvement and beautification seen in nineteenth-century Paris appeared inadequate to cope with the scale of basic urban problems. In the view of many modern planners, urban centers could no longer be permitted the jungle growth of laissez-faire development; the scope of the modern city demanded comprehensive order and control.

A strong influence on ideas of city planning at the turn of the century was the Garden City Movement founded in England by Ebenezer Howard. The Garden City Movement sought to deflect the growth of urban population through a systematic program of decentralization based on the creation of self-sufficient new towns, each physically limited in size through the employment of a greenbelt. The concerns of Garden City planning tended to emphasize the residential environment, an interest which eventually inspired the neighborhood unit concept. The neighborhood provided for the design of housing coordinated with schools, shops, parks, and community facilities, with the aim that the needs of daily life might be within walking distance of each dwelling. Neighborhood planning usually involved the modification of the traditional urban street and block pattern into a larger system of superblocks. Such a system would likely include internal parkbands, separate pedestrian circulation systems, and segregation of local and through traffic.

Although the architects of the Modern Movement tended to place their faith in the large central city, rather than in the small-town ideals of the Garden City Movement, they shared the concept of hygienic environment based on abundant greenery, open space, and opportunity for outdoor recreation. The modernists also adopted the Garden City concept of satellite towns as a means for urban expansion, and the use of the greenbelt to define urban areas. While accepting some Garden City ideas, most modern designers remained convinced that the high-density metropolis was the natural habitat of modern man, and that by employing the resources of modern technology and the organizational skill of modern society, they could reorder and revitalize the urban environment. The city could theoretically combine the dynamism and excitement of contemporary society with wholesome and serene living. As most modern designers sought to accommodate large concentrations of population, apartment housing was usually favored over single-family houses. By employing a wide placement of buildings, however, adequate open space could be combined with efficient distribution of utilities, roads, and dwelling area. The most influential synthesizer of modern concepts of urban design was Le Corbusier, whose visionary schemes fused modern transport and standardized high-rise building with a comprehensively-ordered, open-textured urban fabric.

Eventually, most modern architects began to share a set of common concepts of urban design. Cities tended to be conceived in terms of functional zoning, with areas of industry, commerce, institutions, and residence, physically separated. Systems of traffic separation would be included, and the neighborhood superblock, generally incorporating apartment housing, would be the basis for residential schemes. The city was viewed as a unified work of design, and just as many people found modern architecture somewhat antiseptic, so many viewed modern urban projects as monotonous and regimented.

Although occasional opportunities for community design arose in large housing projects, the depression and then the Second World War prevented building on a truly urban scale. It was only after the war that the image of the perfected environment so long nurtured would find a degree of realization. By the 1950s, modern designers at last found themselves in a position to apply their principles to large urban schemes. Britain had begun an energetic program of new town building, while the rest of war-damaged Europe commenced major rebuilding projects. In the United States, although free of war destruction, cities exhibited self-generated programs of internal renewal as well as rapid suburban expansion. Within the wide range of postwar building, however, the scope of Brasília was unique. Nothing currently attempted in urban design could be considered comparable to the establishment by a major nation of a new national capital.

The designers of Brasília would have an opportunity unparalleled in the world to make their urban ideals a reality. They would be doing more than designing a new full-scale urban environment. They would be creating for the first time in the modern idiom a symbolic national capital. The program of the city provided opportunity for the full range of design—the creation of circulation and transport systems, housing, commercial facilities, and government buildings, ranging from the utilitarian to the monumental. Brasília remains the greatest single opportunity to be given to an architect in our time.

The competition for Brasília was announced by NOVACAP in September 1956—

a contest open to all architects, engineers, and urbanists licensed in Brazil. The program for the contest has been termed "perhaps the simplest ever issued for a competition of this size."[2] Entrants were requested to submit two essential documents, "(a) A basic layout of the city, indicating the position of the main items of the urban structure, the location and interconnection of the various sectors, centers, installations and services, the distribution of the open spaces and lines of communication, to the scale of 1:25,000, and (b) A supporting report."[3] The program also indicated additional areas of planning to which reference might be made, depending on the special capacities of the entrants. These included agricultural economics, land tenure, water and power supply, employment opportunities, and the planning and investment required at various stages of development.

It was stated that the projects would be judged initially on the functional elements, and then from the standpoint of architectural synthesis. The "functional elements" were cited as (1) consideration of topographical data; (2) size of the city projected in relation to population density (human scale); (3) integration of urban elements within the city; and (4) relation of the city and surrounding region. "Architectural synthesis" would include general composition and specific expression of the government site. The projected city was to accommodate a population of 500,000.

NOVACAP made available to the contestants detailed maps and aerophoto mosaics of the topography of the site, plus information on soil conditions and climate. The government also facilitated visits to the site for the competitors. The closing date of the competition was 11 March 1957, providing a period of six months for the entrants to complete their presentations.

The jury included Oscar Niemeyer, who had become director of the Department of Architecture of NOVACAP, Paulo Antunes Ribeiro, representing the Institute of Brazilian Architects, and Horta Barbosa of the Society of Engineers. Three foreigners were also invited, Stamo Papadaki from the United States, André Sive from France, and William Holford from England. The president of NOVACAP, Israel Pinheiro, served as nonvoting chairman.

Attracting twenty-six entrants, among them some of the most distinguished architects in Brazil, the competition provided a summation of generally prevailing principles of modern urban design.

The first meeting of the jury was held on 12 March 1957 in the Ministry of Education building in Rio. After an examination of all projects, a group of ten were selected for more detailed study, and from this group, the recipients of the five prizes were selected. The jurors' report, which was signed on 15 March 1957, awarded the

2. William Holford, "Brasília: A New Capital City for Brazil," *Architectural Review* 122 (December 1957): 397.

3. Ibid. The complete program of the competition may be found in Portuguese in "Edital de concurso para o plano pilôto da nova capital do Brasil," *Brasília* 3 (March 1957): 19–20.

first prize of Cr $1,000,000 to Lúcio Costa. The remaining awards were distributed as follows: second prize of Cr $500,000 was given to a collaborative design by Ney Fontes Gonçalves, Baruch Milman, and João Henrique Rocha; third and fourth prizes of Cr $400,000 and Cr $300,000 were combined and divided equally between the Rino Levi firm and the MMM Roberto partnership; and fifth place of Cr $200,000 was given to each of three collaborative projects, that of Henrique Mindlin and Giancarlo Palanti, a group headed by Carlos Cascaldi and João Vilanova Artigas, and the collaborative design of a group called Construtécnica

Dissenting from the jury's decision was the representative of the Institute of Brazilian Architects, Paulo Antunes Ribeiro, who refused to sign the verdict and submitted a separate report. Ribeiro contended that the judgment had been made in haste and without sufficient study of the entries. He also indicated in his report that the final distribution of prizes had been made not through the collaborative decision of the whole jury, but by the three foreign jurors meeting privately with Niemeyer. As William Holford explained the situation, "it was the foreign members of the jury who were being asked, presumably as the most disinterested and impartial judges, to tip the balance in favour of one scheme as against another."[4]

Ribeiro contended that the Costa scheme was too slight for serious consideration, proposing that all the prize money be divided among the ten projects initially selected for study (plus another project he favored), with the understanding that these architects form a group to produce a collaborative design for the city.[5]

The Gonçalves, Milman, and Rocha Plan

The plan devised by Ney Gonçalves, Baruch Milman, and João Henrique Rocha, which was awarded second prize in the Brasília competition, was perhaps most notable as an exercise in functional zoning (figs. 126–28).[6] Employing a strict geometric plan, the scheme conceived of the city in terms of three sharply defined and separated zones. Nearest the lakefront would be the government district, an elongated rectangle, with the complex of government offices at its center and superblocks housing government employees on either side. Lying beyond this sector, and separated by a greenbelt, would be the commercial center, while at the upper edge of the city, at the point farthest from the lake, would be the industrial district. Located between the commercial and industrial areas would be a district of housing for employees of

4. Holford, "Brasília: A New Capital City for Brazil," p. 397.

5. The complete text of the Ribeiro report was incorporated into the minutes of the committee for judging the pilot plan. These minutes are published as "Atas da Comissão Julgadora do Plano Pilôto de Brasília," *Módulo* 8 (July 1957): 17–21. Ribeiro's statement appears on pp. 19–20. An English supplement is included, in which the Ribeiro report appears on pp. 15–16.

6. In addition to the principal designers, the plan included the collaboration of Antonio José da Silva, Carlos Fonseca de Castro, Cerise Baeta Pinheiro, Elias Kaufman, José Luís Ribeiro, Milton de Barros, Renato Lima, and Yvanildo Silva Gusmão.

the commercial and industrial centers. Rather tenuously connecting these areas would be a system of major streets. A single axial artery would connect the industrial area with the government center, continuing across a bridge to connect with one of the peninsulas of the lake. One peninsula would be used for housing, the other for a university city. Separate areas would be provided for a sport center, a medical center, a transport center, and a military center and air base.

In beginning their report, this planning group stated that the organization of the plan "followed the methods of up-to-date architecture and urbanism, aiming at the doctrines and resolutions established by the International Congresses of Modern Architecture (CIAM), but always fitting them to the peculiarities and practices of this our country."[7]

The formulation of the plan had involved attempts to predict future population of the city based on the existing number of government officials as well as the general rate of increase in the Brazilian population. It was estimated that by 1960 Brasília would have a population of 204,000 inhabitants, by 1980, 270,000, and by 2050, a population of 673,000. Foreseeing the possibility of Brasília developing into a great urban center, a system of satellite expansion was proposed in which units similar to the residential center for commercial and industrial employees would be repeated at close intervals along the line of transport extending from the industrial area.

In developing housing for the city, the planners decided on three types: single-family houses, and apartments of either three or twelve stories. The three-story apartments were considered relatively cheap to construct and, because they would not need elevators, relatively easy to maintain. They would be more economical than houses in terms of land use, and, at the same time, because of their close relation to the ground, they would be reasonably suitable for families with children.

The twelve-story apartment blocks would have the advantage of possible standardization and industrialized methods. A high population density could be accommodated while freeing a large ground area, and an economic use of public services in terms of outside extensions of water, gas, and telephone lines as well as roadways would be effected. It was projected that 12 percent of the population would live in single-family houses, 57 percent in three-story apartments, and 31 percent in twelve-story buildings.

According to the planners, the proposed housing types had been determined largely by assumptions of the sort of buildings which were within the technical capacities of the Brazilian government to construct. "If it were not for this reason, we could have conceived a vertical city with all inhabitants lodged in buildings on the lake shore."[8]

7. The plan of the office of Gonçalves, Milman, and Rocha, unpublished competition report, 1956. Illustrations of the plan are published in "Plano pilôto n°2–2° Lugar," *Modulo* 8 (July 1957): 49–55.
8. Ibid.

The neighborhood units would be based on the primary school, giving each urban unit 8000 people. The block size was determined by establishing a maximum distance between house and school of one-quarter mile or a six-minute walk, producing blocks one-half mile by one-half mile square. Each superblock was designed for a variety of housing types, with single-family houses sited on cul-de-sac streets along one edge of the block, three-story apartments in the center, and twelve-story apartments together with commercial facilities on the side of the block opposite the single-family houses. Schools would be sited within parkland at the center. The superblocks were grouped in such a way that buildings of the same type would form continuous bands throughout the residential area. Residential density was calculated at fifty persons per acre, with open space of ten square meters per person. Dwelling area was based on a standard of seventeen square meters per inhabitant.

The government center was to be contained in a rectangular area one mile by one and one-half miles. A cultural center would be included in the district to take advantage of access, and because the designers considered the majority of cultural institutions to be related to the government. The desire was "to make the most of the urban composition which is necessary for monumental purposes."[9]

The main pattern of vehicular circulation within the district was based on an internal loop road, with cloverleaf intersections at the entrances into the area. Although the architecture of the proposed government center was not developed with any detail, the site planning involved an interrelated pattern of squares. Describing their intentions, the planners said:

> We looked for the virtues that gave charm to the ancient cities, according to Camillo Sitte's lessons in his classical work. Thus we placed the buildings in conformity with their volume, in positions of gratifying effect in the squares. In the largest, the horizontals predominate, and in the smallest, the verticals. Squares will intercommunicate. In these no definite geometrical centers will be found, but there will be the possibility of placing the various monuments in accordance with the effects of perspective desired.[10]

In creating the monumental center, visual primacy was to be given to the presidency of the republic, which would occupy the central place of the composition, "dominating a vast square"[11] and equidistant from subordinate organs of government. The legislature and supreme court were to be located at opposite ends of their own square.

The commercial district, consisting of twenty-two-story office buildings and two-story shops, would provide for the separation of vehicles and pedestrians by funneling motor traffic from the periphery into cul-de-sac parking areas. The description of

9. Ibid.
10. Ibid.
11. Ibid.

the pedestrian circulation system stated: "We created internal streets with the irregularity of the old public squares that serve to increase the perimeter of show windows of commercial stores."[12] Every shop would have guaranteed access to vehicular streets and to pedestrian ways. The business district was planned initially to take the form of a square one mile by one mile, with a central street axis and minor streets dividing the area into rectangles. Future expansion was foreseen in the form of added superblocks along the main motor axis.

The city was designed primarily for automobile circulation, with separate systems of pedestrian and motor traffic. The planners also advocated the use of bicycles, "so common in the countries of advanced civilization."[13]

In evaluating this scheme, to which they awarded second prize, the jurors cited a number of flaws. They objected to the isolation of the commercial district and to its somewhat mechanical composition of identically dimensioned superblocks. They felt that the satellite system might be difficult to extend indefinitely and that the designers should have utilized the more elevated sites of the city. They noted also that the extended road system had no plan for peripheral development, observing that, in view of the separation of urban sectors, utility services might be expensive. They praised the overall density of the scheme, however, and its "pleasant grouping of dwellings on the shore of the lake."[14]

The greatest weakness of the design appeared in the overall conception of the city as a collection of rigidly separated sectors. The idea of creating a central business district as a totally isolated area, surrounded on all sides by a greenbelt and having only one indirect street link with other parts of the city, seems to bear no relation to either urban function or aesthetics.

There also seemed to be no reason for separating the residential areas of the government employees from those which housed the commercial and industrial communities. The planners gave as their reason a desire to place residences near the place of work, but with regard to the employees of the commercial district this would not be valid. Parts of the government housing were just as close to the business district as was the housing planned for the commercial sector. Even if the design provided for notable physical convenience, however, this might not compensate for the questionable social planning inherent in a city with two such sharply differentiated residential communities.

This design of the city seemed to underline a decided hierarchy of occupation. The desirable land nearest the lake was devoted to the government enclave, while other parts of the city were given a physical subordination symbolic of their secondary function. Although this could be interpreted as suitably defining the role of the city as a capital, it would contain an implied social segregation of citizens which seems both unnecessary and undesirable. Brasília, as conceived in this plan, loses its sense of

12. Ibid.
13. Ibid.
14. "O julgamento do concurso de Brasília," *Habitat* 40–41 (March–April 1957): 2.

being one city, becoming rather a series of disjointed enclaves. The sense of fragmentation was emphasized, moreover, by the poor street connections between sectors of the city.

In terms of physical design there was a degree of awkwardness in the relation of the government area to the lake. The proximity of this portion of the city to the shoreline implied a degree of strong visual and functional rapport, yet the rigid and internally-focused geometry of the plan denied any relation to its physical setting. It was the intent of the planners that the lakeshore be left free for recreational use, but this seems insufficient justification for the total lack of integration between this area and the adjoining built-up districts.

One may question also the projected plan for satellites. There is no indication of the nature of these settlements or of their functional relation to the city. As outlined in the plan, they would be sited close together along the rail line, extending farther and farther from the city. If they were intended to represent self-sufficient communities, no economic justification was given for their placement. If they were foreseen as accommodating commuters to Brasília, then their suggested transportation connections seem inadequate.

In general, although the plan represented a rather painstaking effort, the scheme appears an overformalized, mechanically ordered diagram, rather than a convincing representation of a living city.

The Levi Plan

In entering a competition, a designer may assume an essentially practical approach, creating a scheme which he has reason to believe may actually be constructed. He may also use the competition for exhibition purposes—as a vehicle for displaying his most imaginative and daring concepts. At the time of the Brasília contest, there was still reason to doubt that the city would be successfully realized, and Rino Levi evidently chose to employ the competition for the creation of a visionary tour de force rather than a more pedestrian scheme within the existing capacities of the Brazilian government to construct (figs. 129–31).[15]

The most dramatic feature of the Levi plan was its conception of high-rise housing. Levi employed the device of the neighborhood unit but adapted it to large-scale apartments, with community facilities lodged partly within the buildings and partly at ground level. By concentrating population in tall buildings, Levi sought a relatively compact city in which most inhabitants would live no farther than a kilometer from the city center. A considerable amount of traffic might thus move on foot.

Levi claimed to have organized his neighborhood units "in accord with the physical, spiritual and social needs of the population, having in view the development of

15. Collaborating with Rino Levi on the design project were Roberto Cerqueira Cesar and L. R. Carvalho Franco. The structural aspects of the scheme were devised by Paulo Fragoso.

group consciousness, a sense of self determination and civic spirit."[16] In the center of the city was the "intensive housing area" consisting of six ensembles, each of which would accommodate 48,000 inhabitants and be provided with a district center. Housing for each ensemble would consist of three superblock buildings, each with 16,000 inhabitants. Occupying a low-rise complex adjacent to the apartment blocks, the district center would provide commercial facilities, a social and cultural center, two primary schools, a secondary school, a health center, a church, cinema, and playgrounds. The distance between superblock buildings would be one-half mile (800 meters) "in order to offer good panoramic views."[17]

Each superblock was to consist of a structurally connected grouping of eight high-rise towers, each tower composed of four twenty-story units rising one atop the other to a total height of 300 meters—the height of the Eiffel Tower. Although architecturally unified, each superblock would contain thirty-two separate buildings. Horizontally linking the twenty-story units at their bases would be massive supporting trusses. These trusses were to provide a site for internal streets, each containing community facilities for one "unité" of 4,000 people. Each unité would thus consist of a horizontal grouping of eight twenty-story towers and would provide, in its interior street, thirty stores, a nursery, a kindergarten, a health center, and recreational facilities. The population of each twenty-story unit would be 500 persons, with living area calculated on the basis of 25 square meters of space per person.

Vertical transportation was to include both express and local elevators. The express elevators would stop only at the internal streets every twenty stories. From these levels, local elevators would service the individual blocks. External transportation in the city was to be based on automobiles and buses, with garages provided at the basement level of each superblock and a bus terminal at ground level.

Although the presentation of the plan emphasized the intensive housing area, the urban scheme also included, in outlying areas, complexes of what were termed "extensive housing." In these districts, housing would consist of both single-family houses and low-density apartments, units being projected with populations of 15,000 subdivided into three unités of 5,000 each. Each neighborhood of 15,000 would have a commercial center, a social and cultural center, a health clinic, a church, and a cinema. Secondary schools, sport clubs, and hospitals would serve two or more neighborhoods. Each unité of 5,000 would be served by a nursery school, kindergarten, and primary school, together with a health center and playgrounds. Population density in these outlying residential districts was projected at forty to eighty persons per acre.

16. *Brasília—O Plano pilôto,* unpublished competition report, 1956. Portions of the plan, accompanied by an explanatory text in Portuguese, are published as "Plano pilôto para Brasília," *Habitat* 40–41 (March–April 1957). Illustrations of the plan are published as "Plano pilôto n°17–3° Lugar," *Módulo* 8 (July 1957): 56–59.

17. Ibid.

The urban center of the city was designed to occupy a site adjoining the lake and surrounded by the towering superblocks of the intensive housing area. This district was to include the offices of government ministries together with the business center and cultural and recreational facilities. Although some high-rise building was included in the area, the architectural scale was dwarfed by the surrounding apartment buildings. In contrast to the building pattern of most cities, in which business activities occupy high-rise construction, and housing is generally of lower density, Levi created a scheme in which the commercial center appeared as an open-patterned, low-density district overshadowed by the 300-meter superblock units.

Although the city center would contain government offices, the symbolic government center would not be located there. A complex of monumental buildings representing the major agencies of federal power, the executive, legislative, and judicial, was to occupy a somewhat isolated site, on a point of land jutting out into the lake, near the site which had already been selected for the president's palace.

An industrial area was included in the city, but designed to be minimal, providing only necessary service functions for the city. A separate site along the lake was set aside for a university complex.

The circulation system proposed for the city was simple and categorized according to four types of movement. The major arteries would be elevated expressways, including a north–south axis running tangent to the city center, and three east–west transversal streets serving the intensive housing districts. At ground level, a series of roads would link other housing districts with the elevated roads, connecting also with the railroad station and airport. Within the residential areas would be cul-de-sac access roads and, in addition, pedestrian ways separated from motor traffic.

Levi projected his plan for the prescribed 500,000 people. He felt that some expansion might be possible, however, through the addition of three more ensembles of intensive habitation and several more low-density residential districts. Although no satellite system was included in the plan, Levi stressed that the growth of the city should be legally restricted.

In evaluating the project, the jury noted the lack of a transport center and objected to the express roads passing close to the apartment buildings. They felt that the vertical superblocks were unnecessarily tall and might create problems of wind resistance. They also considered the necessity for inhabitants to change elevators inconvenient. By and large, the jury believed that the housing scheme created an excessive concentration of residential population.

On the credit side, however, they acknowledged a good use of site with regard to the lake view. The design was praised for its "high sculptural quality in harmony with great technical competence."[18]

Levi's conception of the neighborhood unit as a single structure had precedents in

18. "O julgamento do concurso de Brasília," p. 2.

the design of Le Corbusier. Attempting to reinforce the concept of the central city in opposition to the decentralists of the Garden City Movement, Le Corbusier established what he called "vertical garden cities" in which high-rise apartments would include a number of communal facilities. His visionary Radiant City project of 1930 had incorporated a neighborhood unit of 2,700 people—the number which would use the single entrance of an apartment block. Later, following the Second World War, Le Corbusier had created an apartment scheme which he called the Unité d'Habitation, first realized in an apartment block built in Marseilles which attempted to provide its 1600 inhabitants with many facilities for daily living. The concept of the internal commercial street was incorporated into this building, but with limited economic success.

The current population crisis and the phenomenal pressures of contemporary urban growth have led many designers to conceive of urban dwelling in terms of massive concentrations of people in high-rise structures and even in underwater colonies. Considered as a purely visionary design, the Levi plan reflects a widespread contemporary image of the future city. Within the context of Brasília, however, the design could have little applicability. Given the rapid construction of Brasília within an isolated wilderness area of Brazil, it would hardly be reasonable to complicate the task with extravagant feats of construction. Levi correctly claimed that his scheme was technically possible, but it would have been far beyond the existing resources of Brazil. The gigantic superblocks were designed for steel construction, a material notable for its scarcity and high cost in Brazil. When completed, moreover, the buildings would require elaborate and smoothly functioning technical services of a type difficult to achieve on even a small scale in Brazilian cities.

Visionary urban schemes with images of concentrated housing are usually proposed for situations in which a congested population creates an unusually heavy demand on land, a factor which has prompted many of the contemporary Japanese schemes. Levi's design for Brasília, however, seemed intent on solving problems unlikely to exist in the new capital. Even if the projected superblocks were technically possible, population pressures in Brasília would hardly necessitate such a dwelling type. Although the scheme embodied imagination and visual drama in its presentation, a realization of the plan might have revealed many weaknesses with regard to livability.

The MMM Roberto Plan

Sharing the joint third-fourth prize with Rino Levi was the firm of noted modern architects, MMM Roberto.[19] Although the program of the competition had requested

19. The initials MMM refer to three brothers, Marcelo, Milton, and Mauricio Roberto. Initially, this architectural firm consisted of a partnership of the two elder brothers, Marcelo and Milton, known profes-

only a physical plan for the future capital, the entry of the Roberto organization included detailed planning for the whole Federal District and was accompanied by an impressive body of statistical analysis. Much admired for the thoroughness of its presentation, the Roberto scheme also presented a highly original conception for the organization of the capital city (figs. 132–34).

The proposals for the Federal District included ecological studies and recommendations for overall land use and economic development. Detailed studies for the agricultural development of the district contained presentations of a model farm and plans for urban zones within the rural area. Projections of population composition and growth were included, together with suggestions for political and administrative organization. Justifying the scope of their report, the planners pointed out, "the Plan must take into account the proper integration of the Urbs with the surrounding region. That is why we took care to preserve the balance of the whole Federal District area. Unfortunately it is an arbitrary geometrical area, which does not correspond to a natural region. Within these limitations, an ideal solution was not possible."[20]

In introducing their design for the capital itself, the designers observed that:

> Most large capital cities of today, Paris, Moscow, Berlin, Buenos Aires, Madrid, Washington and even Rio de Janeiro, are the products of baroque ideals. Their architecture shows mainly a preoccupation with the exhibition of military and economic power. . . . We have tried to design a Capital for a Nation that places the true values of human life above foolish exhibitionism or reckless mechanical complication. It is, we hope, a city for citizens, not for slaves or robots. There is no preoccupation to imitate other Capitals, as it seems more appropriate to take account of our own realities, and look to the future, rather than just copy the past.[21]

While acknowledging that "a city must be an organic whole," the planners felt that in view of Brazil's rapidly expanding population, "it would be unwise to design with absolutely rigid limits. That is why we have adopted a structure that will enable an increase of about 100% over the plan without destruction of the urban system.

---

sionally as MM Roberto. Mauricio joined the office in 1945, prompting a change of name to MMM Roberto. Milton Roberto died in 1953, thus only two of the Roberto brothers participated in the Brasília competition. Associated with them on the development of the plan were the architects Antonio A. Dias and Ellida Engert, the engineer Paulo Novaes, and an agricultural consultant, Fernando Segadas Vianna. Other consultants included the architects Estephania A. Paixão, Marcello Campello, Marcello Fragelli, and Sergio A. Rocha. Engineering consultants were H. J. P. Linnemann, Ivo Magalhães, H. M. Azevedo Netto, J. R. Rego Monteiro, and N. A. Gaspar. Advice on statistical analysis was given by A. Teixeira de Freitas and J. Lyra Madeira.

20. The quotation is taken from an unpublished English-language competition report submitted by the Roberto office. The same report is published in Portuguese, "Plano pilôto da nova capital do Brasil," *Habitat* 42 (May–June 1957): 2–24. All subsequent quotations from the Roberto report will give the wording of the English report. For the reader's reference, however, page numbers for the same quotation will be provided from the published version in *Habitat*.

21. Ibid., p. 2.

"If all adequate precautions are taken, the design will be good for, at least, 50 years, and possibly a century. Beyond that, we have not ventured to speculate." During the period of growth, "the control of the city expansion and maintenance of its structural stability is fundamental."[22] Fearing that Brasília, like other major Brazilian cities, might become subject to excessive population pressures, the planners urged the creation of a national territorial and demographic policy to direct population surplus to new cities.

In the development of the Federal District, the Roberto plan recommended a population distribution in which Brasília would have 504,000 inhabitants and the rural districts 126,000, providing a total of 630,000 at an overall density of 126 inhabitants per square kilometer. This was considered the "optimum for the local ecological conditions." The plan considered the maximum acceptable population as 720,000 within the capital city and 180,000 in the rural areas, but it also considered a possible expansion to an upper limit in which the city would house 1,008,000 and the rural area 252,000, providing an overall density of 252 inhabitants per square kilometer.

The city was conceived as a "polynuclear metropolis" consisting of a series of Urban Units of 72,000 inhabitants each. Describing the process by which they developed this plan, the designers noted that:

> At first it seemed convenient to place all the federal employees in a concentrated area, in a monumental group of buildings. This solution would also increase the facilities for intercommunication between the different departments. It is readily apparent, however, that this plan would bring about all the usual evils of the Metropolis: central congestion, a long journey to work, traffic complications, etc. The advantages of easy communications between departments are quite deceptive beyond certain limits in the size of the organization. There is no real advantage in putting together all the government offices. We thought it would be more appropriate to limit the departments in the Federal Park to those bodies that have a direct participation in the guidance or in the policy-making decisions of Government, or else, those that have high symbolic value.[23]

The Federal Park was designed to house the presidential palace, together with the legislative, executive, and judicial buildings. Also to be sited within the federal enclave would be headquarters for the ministries concerned with defense, economics, labor, and foreign affairs. Included in addition would be cultural buildings, accommodations for official guests, and the barracks for the presidential guards. The federal complex would be located within a park area near the lakefront.

The other government activities would provide functional nuclei for the Urban

22. Ibid.

23. Ibid., p. 7.

Units of the city. The initial plan of the city would provide for seven Urban Units designated according to the following activities: Unit One would house the regional administration, including offices of the regional and metropolitan services administration, national statistical services, and schools and research institutions devoted to economics and administration.

Unit Two would contain activities related to communications, including the central organs of the national transport and communications systems, together with centers for technical education. Unit Three, the center of finance, would contain the metropolitan financial center and federal bureaus dealing with money, banking, taxes, and budget control. Large private investment firms would also be lodged here.

The arts would be concentrated in Unit Four, which would comprise the metropolitan art center, theaters, and concert halls, together with schools of art, music, dance, and handicrafts. Unit Five would focus on letters and science, providing headquarters for national agencies dealing with education and culture. University councils and administration as well as schools of philosophy, letters, and science would be located here.

Welfare activities would provide the theme for Unit Six, which would house medical and social research centers, national social welfare organizations, and labor organizations. And Unit Seven would contain agencies involved with production, including national departments supervising and assisting production activities, centers for economic planning, and agencies dealing with conservation of national resources.

It may be noted that the Roberto plan, in contrast with the other competition schemes, did not establish a separate and self-contained university city. Instead, university activities would be distributed throughout the Urban Units according to specialized areas of study. It was believed that "both teachers and students should participate in the life of the city, and not have one of their own."[24]

According to the plan report: "All the Urban Units have an equivalent status, there are no suburban areas, or satellites. All the Units are complete towns, with all the elements needed in a modern urban community."[25] It was believed that the division of the urban area into separated units would achieve an optimum use of land with a minimum waste of space in roads and empty areas, achieving the advantages of urban density without the evils of congestion.

In design all Units followed the same basic plan. Each had a polygonal plan encompassing an area of 5 million square meters. Radial arteries would extend from the center to the periphery, and within each would be a circular band of greenery.

The concentric geometry of the Urban Units appears similar in form to many of the diagrammatic ideal cities produced by Renaissance architects. Renaissance designs had embodied a concept of rational, ordered perfection, in contrast to the more

24. Ibid., p. 17.

25. Ibid., p. 12.

organic and irregular accretive patterns of existing cities. Explaining the design of the Units, the Roberto report stated that: "The almost flat nature of the terrain made possible a fully rational layout. There was no justifiable purpose in introducing romantic irregularities or useless complications."[26]

The center of each Unit was to be occupied by the Urban Core containing the office buildings, shopping and amusement facilities of the Unit. This area, covering approximately 500,000 square meters, would be designed with the office buildings in the outer perimeter and with a square in the center for shops and recreation. The square was conceived as a

> lively town center, where people will meet each other, window shop, and amuse themselves. The central square was designed as an inviting and attractive setting in which people will feel part of a collectivity without losing themselves in a crowd.
>
> While from the outside the Core displays a monumental appearance in harmony with its importance in the Urbs, from the inside, in the central square, the big buildings are out of view, and the eye will look upon pleasant and varied surroundings architecturally scaled in proportion to human beings. . . . We tried to provide an interesting arrangement of the big buildings in the Core, avoiding monotonous repetition, but, to emphasize the democratic ideals of the community, we avoided any symbolic and dominating structure. We feel that the city belongs to everybody; the poor should not feel humiliated by oppressive ostentation, nor the rich abased by senseless uniformity. In the Core of the City relations between different social groups must find a setting where everybody will be at ease.[27]

The Urban Units were to be divided into neighborhoods, each with an average population of 3,966 inhabitants in an area of 225,000 square meters. Within the neighborhood would be local shopping facilities designed so that the maximum distance from a dwelling to the shopping center would be 300 meters.

Each three neighborhoods would be grouped to form a Sector, creating a wedge-shaped district extending from the periphery of the Urban Unit to the Central Core. Included in the Sector would be businesses and services requiring a bigger market than that of the neighborhood. By and large, the neighborhoods adjacent to the Core would contain apartment housing only. Neighborhoods on the outer edge of the Unit, however, would include both single-family houses, sited on cul-de-sac streets, and apartments.

In creating a polynuclear scheme, the planners hoped to remedy the chronic problem of urban traffic. Pointing out that the average daily trip to work in Rio was fif-

26. Ibid., p. 16.

27. Ibid., p. 17.

teen kilometers, they sought to reduce this in the new capital to an average of one kilometer. This estimate would take into account people who would work outside their Units. Within the Units themselves, distances would be even shorter, with the average distance within the neighborhood calculated as 150 meters, within the Sector as 350 meters, and within the Unit as 600 meters.

By greatly reducing necessary travel within the city, it was assumed that the motor vehicles could be restricted largely to carrying goods and materials. For passenger travel, the automobile was to be used mainly for recreation and movement outside the Urban Unit. For circulation within the Unit, the development of moving sidewalks to be employed in 80-meter stretches was proposed. Large-scale collective transport between the Urban Units and the Federal Park was to employ a monorail rapid transit system operating mainly at ground level, but occasionally both under and above ground.

The growth of the city could, in the future, be accommodated by increasing the number of Urban Units to ten, or even fourteen. To the designers, one of the advantages of the plan was that it permitted the building of the city by means of fully completed self-sufficient units, avoiding the discomfort and awkwardness of living in a partially completed large city.

The question of appropriate urban size is one that has concerned city planners ever since the rapid expansion of industrial-age cities made growth itself a problem. Although there is no universal agreement as to what constitutes the ideal maximum dimension for an urban complex, it is often assumed that small urban units are preferable, in terms of living environment, not only for physical convenience, but also in providing a sense of community which many think can only be achieved within a relatively small group. The population group of 72,000 which the Roberto plan established for the Urban Unit was comparable to the goals initially created for some of the British new towns.

All of the competition designs for Brasília made some effort at subdividing the city through the use of neighborhood units. The Roberto plan differed dramatically from the other plans, however, in using this device to effect a total fragmentation of the city. It distributed throughout the urban fabric not only minor urban functions, but major functions as well.

By eliminating the major urban center—the "downtown"—the Roberto plan presented a tempting solution to many urban difficulties. It might prove in practice, however, that the large commercial and administrative center has a legitimate function in the city. Urban life derives much of its meaning from intangibles, and many city dwellers gain a sense of satisfaction and excitement from the daily awareness of being part of a great city. However convenient life within the Urban Units might be, the citizens of the future capital might feel themselves cheated of a truly urban experience.

In examining the unusually thorough report of the Roberto firm, the jury noted that the "land use study is the best and most complete in the whole competition," considering that the "farm and village types are excellent," and the program for finance and construction both "practical and realistic."[28] They were less favorably impressed, however, by the physical conception of Brasília. It was felt that the division of the city into sharply separated segments prevented the creation of a truly metropolitan entity. They noted that "the head (the Federal Park) remains the same; the seven bodies grow to ten or fourteen and have distinct lives of their own." To the jury, the self-containment of the Urban Units seemed repressive, and it was observed that, "Although this is a plan for a 'Welfare City,' it is inhuman in the degree to which all positions and all circulation is controlled and restricted."[29]

Commenting on the Roberto plan, the British member of the jury, William Holford, stated:

> I have never seen anywhere in the world a more comprehensive and thoroughgoing masterplan for a new capital city on a cleared site. We all realized, at the same time, that if the Development Corporation adopted this plan they would take on board more than a pilot. They would have purser and quartermaster and bo'sun, a complete ship's company from cabin boy to captain, and a Director of the Line as well. The principle of the plan is to break down the metropolis into self-contained *unités d'occupation*—seven to start with, each with a main government activity in its business district; then ten; ultimately perhaps fourteen. The Federal Government Centre, detached from these hexagonal model towns, remains the same. The "regional city" is established, as it were, by decree. After admiring this scheme for several days, my own feeling was that everything in it was worthy of admiration, except its main objective. It was not an Idea for a capital city.[30]

The Mindlin and Palanti Plan

Introducing their plan, the team of Henrique Mindlin and Giancarlo Palanti emphasized the long-term nature of urban development, observing that "this planning, meanwhile, can not be more than an outline for realization.[31] Between the planning of a city, and actually giving it life there is the same distance as between the theoretical preparation of a good program of education and culture, and the formation and

28. "Resumo das apreciações do júri," *Módulo* 8 (July 1957): 15.
29. Ibid.
30. Holford, "Brasília: A New Capital City for Brazil," p. 397.
31. Collaborating in this plan were Walmir Lima Amaral, Marc Demetre Foundoukas, Anny Sirakoff, Olga Verjovsry, Gilson Mendes Lages, and André Gonçalves.

maturization of a generation of men, educated and cultivated as a consequence of the application of this program."[32]

The future of Brasília would depend upon the general development of the country and the region surrounding the proposed city, upon events which could not be foreseen at the time of the competition. Convinced that information was not available which would permit them to make detailed projections for the development of the future city, the designers observed that "the present study" would of necessity be limited "to a satisfactory organization of the essential elements of a city in the chosen site."[33] Under the circumstances, the pilot plan could do no more than outline a direction for future development.

Although the plan was projected for a population of 500,000 as required by the program, the designers were convinced that the city would need to provide for internal growth beyond this figure, citing as an example the large metropolitan area centering on Washington, D. C.

The overall design of the city was conceived in terms of two main axes (figs. 135–38). The east–west axis started from the presidential palace on the lake and projected inward to culminate at a monumental government complex sited beyond the edge of the city. Flanking this axis as it extended from the lake would be the embassy buildings. The avenue would then pass through the commercial district and continue bordered on either side by complexes of government ministries. The north–south axis would mark the line of development for the residential zones which would extend on either side of the monumental axis. The two major axes would intersect at a point between the commercial district and the area of ministries.

An industrial center, containing workers' housing, was sited near the projected rail line. This area would have a direct road connection to the city center running parallel to the monumental street. The peninsulas would be used as sites for the university, a medical center, and sport centers. The projected transport within the city was to be based on automobiles and trolleybuses.

The general configuration of the Mindlin-Palanti plan bears some resemblance to Le Corbusier's Radiant City design of 1930, which also employed a central axis flanked by superblock housing, isolating a complex of office buildings as a symbolic head at the outer edge of the city. Similarity may also be noted between this plan for Brasília and the plan of Chandigarh, the capital of Punjab, India, which was designed by Le Corbusier in 1951. Chandigarh embodied a cross-axial scheme in which major avenues would cross at the commercial center. From this center a monumental street was designed to focus on the capitol complex, an isolated enclave of monumental

32. "Plano pilôto de Brasília," *Habitat* 45 (November–December 1957): 2. Illustrations of the plan are published in "Plano pilôto n° 24–5° premio," *Módulo* 8 (July 1957): 70–73.

33. Ibid.

government buildings sited at the outer edge of the city. There is also some schematic resemblance between this plan and Lúcio Costa's for Brasília. The city as constructed is based on a cross-axial partie, with a monumental east–west axis, and a north–south residential axis.

Because the plan houses the government function along an extended axis, rather than centering it in a single enclave, the Mindlin-Palanti scheme appears to place greater visual emphasis on the city as a monumental capital than did some of the others. It is also the only plan in which the embassy district is made to play a strong architectural role in the city. The ministry complexes were projected as a series of paved plazas opening toward the axial street, each containing a grouping of uniform-height, high-rise slabs. The monumental complex itself would be square in plan and penetrated halfway by the axial approach street. At this point a cross-axial street would block further vehicular penetration. Directly on axis with the approach road would be the executive office, with the legislative and judicial buildings on either side. The symbolic focus of the civic axis thus placed considerable emphasis on the power of the chief executive, beginning at the presidential residence and ending at the presidential office.

The commercial center of the city was sited in an area following the direction of the cross-axial street below the line of ministries. It was conceived as a district of mixed high- and low-rise building fronting often on paved plazas and divided by secondary streets into superblocks.

Residential districts were projected in the form of square superblocks directing a line of urban expansion from either side of the monumental axis. Housing for these neighborhood units was projected in terms of only two types, single-family houses either freestanding or double, and ten-story apartment blocks. Population density would vary according to the particular concentration of housing within given blocks. Four superblock types were projected: Type One, that of highest density, would house 7,200 inhabitants in thirty apartment blocks at a density of 230 per acre. Type Two would contain eighteen apartment houses and eighty-eight single-family houses, providing for a population of 5,200 at 165 persons per acre. The housing for industrial workers would constitute Type Three, employing twelve apartment blocks and 132 houses. Superblock population would be 4,200 and density 136 persons per acre. Type four would contain double houses only, achieving a population of 3,420 and a density of 137 per acre.

Each superblock would contain a T-shaped band of greenery extending along one side and down the center. In this area would be sited commerce, schools, and community facilities. Housing layouts within the superblocks were simple and somewhat mechanical, with apartment blocks in uniform parallel rows and houses sited on identical plots on straight cul-de-sac streets.

The jury considered that the plan was appropriate in size and density as well as economical in land use. They claimed, however, that "the housing units would be formless in practice and do not sit very well on the site; but the road system is quite simple and direct."[34] They also objected to the segregation of the workers' housing. The jury was somewhat critical of the detailed architectural layout shown for the ministries and government center. It was noted that "the embassies are grouped at one point on the spine road, and ministries on the other, and the business center is in between. There does not seem to be any logic in the development of the plan from east to west."[35]

The Cascaldi, Artigas, Vieira da Cunha, and Camargo e Almeida Plan

This collaborative scheme, submitted by Carlos Cascaldi, João Villanova Artigas, Mario Wagner Vieira da Cunha, and Paulo de Camargo e Almeida, was among those which attempted to provide projections for regional development and detailed studies for varied aspects of the new capital's long-range evolution.[36] The consultants for the plan included specialists in electrical energy, regional planning, history, agriculture, law, education, hygiene, sanitation, and health. The planning report contained elaborate population projections, detailed schemes for educational systems, health facilities, administration, and government in the city, as well as thorough presentation of technical factors. Economic aspects of both the city and region were considered.

The physical configuration of the city was rectilinear, extending away from the lake (fig. 139). The area adjacent to the lake itself was set aside for the university. Beyond this rather loosely planned area, the urbanized edge of the city provided sites for the commercial center and government zone which lay adjacent to each other. Unlike many of the other plans, this design made no attempt to create strong physical separation between the government and commercial functions of the city.

Extending westward away from the central zones would be the neighborhood sectors. The plan created three types of residential zones. Zone One would consist of rectangular superblocks containing single-family houses sited along cul-de-sac streets. Extending through the center of each superblock would be a band of parkland con-

34. "Resumo das apreciações do júri," p. 15. 35. Ibid.

36. In addition to the principal planners, the scheme involved the collaboration of architects Heitor Ferreira de Souza, Julio Roberto Katinsky, Mario Alfredo Reginato, and Ubirajara Gilioli. The following specialists were also consulted: Catulo Branco, assistant engineer, Department of Water and Electrical Energy, State of São Paulo; Dirceu Lino de Mattos, professor of economic geography, University of São Paulo; Flavio Motta, professor of architecture, University of São Paulo; José Calil, technical advisor to the Coordinating Council of the President of the Republic; Lauro Müller Bueno, professor of law, University of São Paulo; Maria José Garcia Werebe, docent of educational administration and comparative education, University of São Paulo; Odair Pacheco Pedroso, professor of hospital administration, University of São Paulo; Octacílio Pousa Sene, professor of sanitation, University of São Paulo; Rodolfo dos Santos Mascarenhas, professor of public health, University of São Paulo. Illustrations of the plan are published in *Módulo* 8 (July 1957): 74–79.

taining schools and other community facilities. The population of the neighborhood unit would be 12,000. In Zone Two, widely spaced high-rise apartments, designed to a maximum of ten stories, would create neighborhood units of 29,000. Zone Three was to consist largely of relatively low-cost housing in the vicinity of the industrial district. Each of these neighborhoods would have a population of 14,000 people housed in apartments. As the urban population was projected, 348,000 would live in single-family houses, 145,000 in the Zone Two apartments, and 42,000 in the working-class buildings.

The circulation pattern of the city was given a terminology similar to that used by Le Corbusier in his Seven V system. In this case the V stood for *via,* rather than *voie.* The V1 represented the major interurban highway. The V2 signified through traffic within the city, and the V3 local motor traffic. Pedestrian paths were designated as V4.[37]

The jury considered the plan to be well presented, clear, and decisive, and it praised the proposals for the development of the rural economy. Within the physical plan itself, however, they criticized the residential zones as too uniform and considered the circulation patterns from the housing zones to the government and commercial center to be inadequately planned. It was noted that no provision had been included for the siting of embassies and consulates, and the failure of the government center to be in any way oriented toward the lake was considered a fault. The jurors also objected to the extensive built-up area and the excessively low population density of twenty persons per acre.

The Construtécnica Plan

Sharing fifth place was a design produced by a group calling itself Construtécnica and working under the direction of the architect Milton Ghiraldini (figs. 140, 141).[38] The planning report submitted by this group contained a long introduction summarizing much generally accepted philosophy of urban design, and including reference to Patrick Geddes, Clarence Perry, Le Corbusier, Ebenezer Howard, Clarence Stein, Gaston Bardet, Patrick Abercrombie, and others. Planning principles were drawn from the Garden City Movement, the Radburn Idea, the Neighborhood Unit, and the Greenbelt Towns, as well as from the Charter of Athens and the slogans of

37. Le Corbusier developed his Seven V system in the 1940s, first applying it to a project for Marseilles. The street classification was as follows: The V1 represented a regional road, the V2 a major urban artery, and the V3 a motor road surrounding residential sectors. The V4 would form a shopping street, while the V5 and V6 streets would provide access to individual dwellings. The V7, sited within parkland, would give pedestrian circulation to schools, clubs, and sport grounds.

38. Associated with Ghiraldini were the architects Clovis Felippe Olga, Nestor Lindenberg, Manoel da S. Machado and Wilson Maia Fina. The engineers Milton A. Peixoto and Rubens Gennari also assisted in the development of the plan.

Le Corbusier. The ideal of regional planning was stressed, together with the need for planning to be oriented to human values.[39]

The plan began with a consideration of the rural region surrounding Brasília. This zone was to be divided into units of one hectare (2.5 acres) or less for country houses or small farms close to the city, units of one to ten hectares, and large farms of over ten hectares. The settlement pattern was also to include a series of "cooperative rural centers."

The design of the city itself was prefaced by the Charter of Athens version of urban functions: dwelling, working, recreation, and circulation. The overall intent was described as "an organic distribution of the zones of different activities; their precise definition and the plasticity of the composition are the principal objectives which determined our design."[40]

Four rectilinear residential sectors were grouped around a similarly defined central zone. The residential sectors were to be composed of neighborhood units, each a nearly square area 950 by 1,000 meters containing a population of 5,000 to 6,000. Each unit would have a central parkband containing schools and intersected by a series of green strips on which houses would face. Single-family housing was projected for the neighborhoods with population density at 44 persons per acre. Each neighborhood would have a kindergarten and primary school, a community center, a health center, church, and small commerce. Neighborhoods would be grouped in clusters of three, each cluster being provided with a secondary school, hospital, community center, and shopping facilities.

The central zone of the city was intended to house all nonresidential functions of the city and would contain the federal government buildings, a cultural center, and all major business and commerce. High-rise housing would also be accommodated here. Of all the entries, this plan seemed the least concerned with the monumental aspects of the city, and the government center was in no way differentiated in character from the commercial buildings.

As in all the schemes, a system of traffic division was incorporated, permitting the segregation of fast motor arteries from local streets, and the creation of separate pedestrian circulation. Considerable space in the report was devoted to the question of mass transit, with the preference given to trolleybuses.

The gradual development of the city was projected in five steps, beginning with construction of the center and a few adjacent residential neighborhoods. It was estimated that completion of the scheme would take fifty years.

39. The report of the Construtécnica team was published as a book, with the title *Brasília: Plano pilôto: Relatorio justificativo* (São Paulo, 1957). Information on the plan is also published as "Brasília—Plano pilôto para o novo capital do Brasil," *Habitat* 40–41 (March–April 1957): 12–18.

40. *Brasília: Plano pilôto: Relatorio justificativo.*

Although the jury admired the "charming model of the agricultural village," they considered that the city itself embodied a vast oversimplification of zones. It was noted that all major urban functions were placed in one central district, while the rest of the city consisted of identical superblocks with the same type of low-density housing. They objected, also, to the "enormous length of road in addition to the main grid,"[41] citing difficulty in the cross-connections in the center.

The Judgment

By and large, the Brasília competition designs produced little which was unexpected and were in many ways united by a similar employment of widely known urban-design devices. Almost all were based on the idea of functional zoning, with a sharp segregation of major urban activities. Systems of traffic separation were included, and the greenbelt was used extensively as an urban divider. All of the designs contained residential areas ordered by the superblock and neighborhood unit.

The discrete zoning of many of the plans tended to produce a fragmentation of urban form as well as an oversimplification of urban function. Most of the designs revealed a lack of intimacy with the site, a factor particularly noticeable with regard to the lake. Although this body of water served to define the setting of the city, none of the designs sought to incorporate the lake into the urban plan or to use the contours of its shoreline as a generator of urban form. Only the Levi scheme contained any orientation to the lake view. This is all the more remarkable when one considers the extraordinary influence of the shoreline on the development of Rio de Janeiro. In isolating the waterfront from urban development, the competition plans would have denied the future citizens of Brasília easy access to the principal natural beauty of the city.

The Brasília site is relatively flat, with a slight rise in elevation as the land slopes away from the lake. For the most part, the competition plans made no reference to the contours of the site, with the exception of the Construtécnica plan which placed the city center on the highest point in the city. Rather, the competition schemes tended to reflect that aspect of modern urban design which was obsessed with geometric "rational" ordering and opposed to any suspicion of romanticizing nature.

The Brasília plans were primarily generalized schemes, appearing somewhat like textbook diagrams illustrating theories of urban design, rather than plans based on applied knowledge of real Brazilian cities. None of the projects, even those which included elaborate demographic studies, seemed designed to include the range of population actually existing in most Brazilian cities. Brasília was conceived as a city without poor and free of the technical problems found elsewhere in Brazil.

41. "Resumo das apreciações do juri," p. 16.

In presentation, some plans put forth essentially physical designs while others attempted lengthy and detailed proposals for many aspects of urban and regional development in Brasília. Although the bulk of some of the reports was impressive, it need not be concluded that the entries accompanied by the most statistical data were necessarily superior to the others. In examining the competition reports one is led to conclude that just as the physical designs incorporated rather superficially the orthodox formulas of urban design, so the statistical studies appear to have been an unsubstantial gesture toward the idea of "scientific" planning.

Although it is true that many aspects of city planning involve statistical studies, such information is assembled with specific purpose. By contrast, the information accompanying some of the Brasília competition schemes appears to have been garnered more or less at random and was essentially irrelevant to the plans produced. In terms of design, all the plans were based on intuitive decisions.

Included in some of the reports were elaborate projections of population in terms of occupation. The Roberto report included such detailed data as a projection for the number of dressmakers and barber shops to be established in the Urban Zone of the Rural District. The lengthy report of the Cascaldi-Artigas group contained a complete analysis of projected economic activity for Brasília, including such information as the amount of capital investment, number of persons employed, and number of establishments per 50,000 and per 550,000 persons for agencies renting bicycles, establishments devoted to the repair of leather articles, and shops renting movie equipment. Similar data was provided for every type of contemplated activity, including hairdressers, which, for statistical purposes, were subdivided into hairdressers for men, hairdressers for women, and hairdressers for both men and women. If the compilation of such material had any effect on the design of the city, it is not evident from the plan submitted by this group.

The major concern of the Construtécnica report appears to have been the transportation system, and laborious studies were presented to justify the decision to employ trolleybuses in the city. Having devoted so much effort to this relatively minor decision, the planning group failed to develop effectively more important aspects of the plan.

It should be borne in mind, moreover, that in Brazil accurate statistical information is rare. The government itself had little information regarding the Federal District, and the competition entrants had neither adequate time nor the resources to conduct meaningful planning studies. The elaborate reports accompanying some of the designs were in substance little more than window dressing. The creation of the city would be a step in the dark. No one could say exactly how it would be built, how soon it would be populated, or how much it would cost. No one could foresee the effect of the city on the surrounding region.

Many of the plans attempted to establish incremental patterns of growth, foreseeing a long period of gradual development in the new capital. What was wanted, however, under the circumstances, was a city which could be built as completely as possible as soon as possible. Brasília needed to be virtually an instant capital if it was to be a capital at all.

Discussing the design competition, Oscar Niemeyer pointed out: "In the case of Brasília, there is one predominant objective of the contest: *a project for the capital of the country*. It does not concern, therefore, the projection of an ordinary city, but, benefiting from the achievements of contemporary urbanism, the attainment of a solution which will harmonize the locale and the program of the competition, with the atmosphere of culture, civilization and monumentality which a city of this nature requires."[42]

From their evaluations of the competition entries, it was clear the jury was seeking, above all, a monumental plan, a grand design which would definitively embody the conception of a major capital. There appeared an evident determination, in moving the government from Rio, to place the national administration within the sort of symbolic setting which, for all its natural beauty, the old capital had never provided. In spite of the proposals of the Agache plan to monumentalize Rio, the city had remained without ceremonial focus. Rio had never been a monumental city; Brasília was to be primarily a monument.

The jury stated that "a Federal Capital, to express the grandeur of a nation-wide desire, should differ from other cities of half a million inhabitants. . . . Its principal characteristic is the governmental function, and around this and converging upon it, all the other functions should be grouped."[43]

The desire for monumentality may be seen throughout the project evaluations. William Holford complained that the second-prize winner, the plan of Gonçalves, Milman and Rocha did not form "a complete capital city."[44] The elaborately developed plan of the Roberto firm was criticized by the jury as being "valid for any city on a flat site; it is not special to Brasília; it is not a plan for a national capital."[45] The Rino Levi scheme, with its audacious system of high-rise housing, produced objections that the government buildings were overshadowed by the apartment houses, while the design of Construtécnica was rejected as having "no capital city character."[46]

In awarding first prize to Lúcio Costa, the jury stated that they had been "seeking a well-knit project which would give the city grandeur through the clarity and proper ranking of its components; in the opinion of the members, the project which best

42. "O concurso para o plano pilôto de Brasília: declarações de membros do júri," *Módulo* 8 (July 1957): 28.

43. "Atas da Comissão Julgadora do Plano Pilôto de Brasília," *Módulo* 8 (July 1957): 17–21. Quotation from English supplement, p. 12.

44. "O concurso para o plano pilôto de Brasília," p. 25.

45. "Resumo das apreciações do júri," p. 15.

46. Ibid., p. 16.

integrates the monumental elements into the city's daily life as a Federal Capital, and which is presented as a rational, essentially urban composition—in fact a work of art—is number 22, submitted by Mr. Lúcio Costa."[47]

In comparison with the other schemes, Costa's design appeared "the only plan which is for an administrative capital for Brazil. The elements of the plan can be seen at once: It is clear, direct and fundamentally simple, as exemplified by Pompeii, Nancy, Wren's London, Louis XV's Paris."[48] Costa's plan had also been distinguished by its minimal presentation—five cards containing a few freehand sketches and a brief statement (fig. 142). He had begun with an apology, explaining that: "It was not my intention to enter the competition—nor in fact am I really doing so. I am merely liberating my mind from a possible solution which sprang to it as a complete picture, but one which I had not sought."[49]

Although to base a major urban plan on a sudden inspiration may seem a drastic violation of all currently accepted design tenets, such an intuitive approach has a certain appropriateness in Brazil. Extemporization seems to accord with the Brazilian temperament, and in a developing country, decisions in many areas must of necessity be made without recourse to elaborate information or preliminary study.

Aware of accusations that they had made their decision with undue haste, and of criticisms for having rejected many elaborate presentations in favor of a simple sketch, the jurors explained their judgment. William Holford made clear that "the conditions of the competition, in my understanding, concerned a contest of ideas and not of details. No architect, firm or company could develop, *in this phase,* a detailed operational plan, including social and economic data, and the exact cost. In the program, the conditions required only a pilot plan and a report to explain the ideas embodied. This was obligatory."[50] Other information might be presented, but was not essential to the plan.

> In judging the competition, the jury gave first priority to an idea which offered the best and most ingenious base for a city which could be constructed, and which could serve as a capital city. . . .
>
> A successful idea for a city must have unity. It cannot be simply a sum of little designs juxtaposed on a map. All great plans are fundamentally simple. They can be appreciated in a glance, not only by architects, but by all people. . . . It suffices to examine, for example, the piazza of St. Peters in Rome, the design of Michelangelo for the Campidoglio, or the plan of Rome of the epoch of Pope Sixtus V. Or, yet, observe the lineaments of central Washington, from the height of the

47. "Atas . . . ," p. 15.
48. "Resumo das apreciações do júri," p. 13.
49. "Pilot Plan for Brasília," *Módulo* 18 (June 1960). Costa's competition report has been widely published and appears in a number of English translations (see chap. 10, n. 1). The wording given here is from the report as published in *Módulo*.
50. "O concurso para o plano pilôto de Brasília," p. 24.

> monument, or the plan of Wren for London (1666); or, finally, the plan of Saint Dié by Le Corbusier. . . .
>
> An idea which cannot be communicated has no value; an idea which could unshackle others is of more value to civilization. It is this which the jury sought in the competition for the new capital. . . . When we see a beautiful woman or a lovely square we don't need much time to know we are pleased.[51]

The other jurors concurred. André Sive noted that in his years as consultant to the French Minister of Reconstruction and Housing, he had studied many plans, concluding, "my experience demonstrates that good projects are always those which one can understand at a glance."[52] According to Stamo Papadaki, "The plan of a new capital must present, above all, the essence of unity—we could even say, of a unique personality. It is this characteristic unity which must be easily recognized from above in an airplane, on the ground level, in the streets, from within and without, from the totality and from a fragment of the whole. In my opinion, the only project presented in the competition for the pilot plan for Brasília which has the seed of unity is that of Lúcio Costa."[53]

Far from objecting to the brevity of Costa's presentation, the jury concluded its verdict by observing: "One must proceed from the general to the particular, not vice versa. The general can be expressed simply and shortly: but it is easier to write a long letter than a short one. Here we have many projects which could be described as overstatements. Number 22 appears, by contrast, as an understatement, but in fact it explains all one needs to know at this state; and omits everything irrelevant."[54]

William Holford described the judgment as the result of a "choice between breadth and depth."[55] At the first reading of Costa's report

> one realized that here was a thinker, an urbanist, of the first order. On second reading one realized that there was not a single unnecessary word in the report, and not a single unnecessary line in the sketch plan or diagrams: yet everything essential was said. And on further reading this member of the jury, at least, became more and more convinced that the direction of advance for a great administrative capital had been indicated in a masterly way, and the fundamental problems of communication, urban residence, metropolitan character and richness of growth within a unity of artistic conception, had all been recognized and anticipated.[56]

51. Ibid.
52. Ibid., p. 23.
53. Ibid., p. 22.
54. "Resumo das apreciações do júri," p. 13.
55. "Brasília: A New Capital City for Brazil," p. 397.
56. Ibid., p. 398.

10. THE COSTA PLAN

In introducing his competition entry, Costa apologized for "the sketchy manner in which I am submitting the idea," pointing out that:

> I come forward, not as a properly equipped expert, since I do not even run an office of my own, but as a mere "maquisard" of town planning who does not even mean to continue working out the idea offered in this report, save as a consultant. And if I speak with such candour, it is because I base my reasoning on this simple assumption: if my idea has any validity, my data, although given apparently in such a sketchy manner, will prove quite sufficient, showing that despite its spontaneous origin, I subsequently gave it a great deal of thought before reaching this solution. And if the suggestion has no validity, then the Jury will find it easy to eliminate, and I shall not have wasted my time, nor that of anybody else.[1]

The simplicity of Costa's presentation, it has been seen, was no handicap to its judgment, and the accompanying report came to be regarded as a model of its kind. Costa submitted no statistical data, made no social projections, and attempted no suggestions for regional development. His report was restricted to a discussion of the elements of the urban design (fig. 143).

Costa noted that the city would be

> not the result of regional planning, but the cause; its foundation will be the starting point for the development of a regional plan. For this is a deliberate act of conquest, a gesture of pioneers acting in the spirit of their colonial traditions: and each competitor is, in effect, being asked how he conceives of such a city. It

1. "Pilot Plan for Brasília," the report accompanying Costa's competition entry. The wording given here is taken from the English translation appearing in *Módulo* 18 (June 1960). Other sources for English translations of the Costa report are the following: William Holford, "Brasília, A New Capital City for Brazil," *Architectural Review* 122 (December 1957): 394–402; Lúcio Costa, "Brasília Pilot Plan," *Arts and Architecture* 76 (November 1959): 21–23; *Brasília,* special issue of *Acropole* (São Paulo, 1960); Aloisio Magalhães and Eugene Feldman, *Doorway to Brasília* (Philadelphia, 1959); Willy Stäubli, *Brasília* (New York, 1965), pp. 12–16.

> should be conceived, I believe, not as a mere organic entity, able to function effortlessly and vitally like any modern town; not as an "urbs," therefore, but as a "civitas," having the virtues and attributes appropriate to a true capital city. To achieve this, the town planner must be imbued with a certain dignity and nobility of purpose, for it is from this basic attitude of his that must spring the sense of order, fitness and proportion which will confer real monumentality on his urban scheme.

In describing the origin of the design, he stated: "It was born of that initial gesture which anyone would make when pointing to a given place, or taking possession of it: the drawing of two axes crossing each other at right angles, in the sign of the Cross. This sign was then adapted to the topography, the natural drainage of the land, and the best possible orientation: the extremities of one axial line were curved so as to make the sign fit into the equilateral triangle which outlines the area to be urbanized."

In employing a cross-axial scheme, Costa was basing his plan on one of the oldest devices of urban design. What is believed to be the earliest symbolic representation of a city appears in an Egyptian hieroglyph consisting of a cross within a circle. The cross axis was embodied in ancient Roman town planning as well as in ritually derived traditional Indian plans. It provides a concentration of focus—a means of emphasizing a central point, together with directional expansiveness. Many traditional urban plans have contained the cross axis within an external, often rectilinear form defining the outer boundaries of the settlement. Costa let it determine the overall configuration of the city. The urban form thus became essentially linear and open, with visual implications of boundless extension.

The traffic system was of considerable importance to the plan. According to Costa:

> Finally, it was decided to apply the free principles of highway engineering together with the elimination of road junctions, to the technique of town planning. The curved axis, which corresponds to the natural approach road, was given the function of a through radial artery, with fast traffic lanes in the center and side lanes for local traffic. And the residential district of the city was largely located along this radial artery.
>
> As a result of this concentration of the city's housing, it seemed logical to dispose the other important centers along the transverse radial artery, which thus came to be regarded as the monumental radial artery.

This system seems, in fact, to have been the primary generator of the design. Familiar with Rio and the continual conflict there between the existing urban fabric and the growing needs of motor traffic, Costa might naturally have wished to forestall future difficulties by adapting the new capital to the circulation of automobiles. Costa believed that

> with the creation of three complete clover-leaves in each arm of the residential radial artery, and of an equal number of underpasses, car and bus traffic will flow unimpeded through the central and residential districts, and with no road intersections. An independent and secondary traffic system has been worked out for heavy vehicular traffic; it has crossings marked by traffic lights, but does not communicate with the first system except beyond the sports center. It has basement level access to buildings in the shopping center, and it skirts the civic center at lower than ground level, with approach galleries tunnelled through the terraced embankment.

Although the plan incorporated the principle of the separation of motor and pedestrian traffic, Costa felt that such a system "must not be taken to unnatural extremes, since it must not be forgotten that the car, today, is no longer Man's deadly enemy; it has been domesticated and is almost a member of the family. It only becomes 'dehumanized' and reassumes its hostile, threatening attitude, when it is reintegrated into the anonymous body of traffic. Then indeed, Man and Motor must be kept apart, although one must never lose sight of the fact that, under proper conditions and for mutual convenience, co-existence is essential."

The residential radial artery would pass over the monumental axis, and at this intersection there would be a multilevel traffic interchange accommodating the central bus terminal at a lower level. The interchange would be designed so that its upper level provided a broad platform serving as a site for the theater and entertainment district. Through traffic would be routed at lower levels. Adjacent to the intersection of the two urban axes, "but functioning essentially as part of the organization of the monumental radial artery," were to be the banking and financial center and the central business district.

The axis as it extended from the interchange eastward toward the lake would be devoted to the headquarters of the national government. Although the residential axis was dominated by a motor freeway, giving the city an immediate image of mechanization and modernity, the monumental government axis remained essentially a traditional Beaux-Arts composition. A long grass mall would be flanked by uniform rows of federal office buildings and terminated by a triangular plaza comprising the major government complex.

Describing his design for the monumental center, Costa observed that "the highlights in the outline plan of the city are the public buildings which house the fundamental powers. These are three, and they are autonomous: therefore the equilateral triangle associated with the very earliest architecture in the world—is the elementary frame best suited to express them. For this purpose, a triangular terraced embankment (terreplein) was designed: it will be supported on retaining walls of rough stone rising above the surrounding countryside." Costa believed that "to transfer to present-day usage the ancient technique of the terreplein lends a certain harmony to the monumental strength.

"At each angle of the triangular plaza—the Plaza of the Three Powers, as it might be called—stands one of the three buildings: the Government Palace and the Supreme Court at the base; the Congress Building at the tip." In a schematic indication of the architecture of this complex, the government buildings were shown as rectilinear low-rise blocks. The Congress building was similarly proportioned but was shown carrying a shallow dome and accompanied by a single high-rise slab. Ornamenting the plaza would be a grove of royal palms, similar to that proposed by Le Corbusier in 1936 for the Ministry of Education, which Costa included as a tribute to the French architect.

As the long mall would be developed, the sites adjacent to the Congress would be given to the ministries of foreign and home affairs. The war, sea, and air ministries would face a separate square, and all other ministries would line the mall, taking the form of identical slabs, with the narrow end of each facing the grass verge. The last in the row would be the Ministry of Education, which would be sited adjacent to a cultural center occupying the area between the ministries and the freeway interchange. This district would be treated as a park providing sites for museums, a library, a planetarium, academies, and institutes. Close by would be the university.

On the opposite side of the mall would be sited the cathedral, facing on its own plaza, "not so much for reasons of protocol, since in Brazil the church is separated from the state, but more because of the question of human scale and the need to give this building its monumental value."

The platform of the traffic interchange, which was to be developed as a theater and entertainment center, would have, as Costa hopefully expressed it, "something in it of Picadilly Circus, Times Square and the Champs Elysées." The front of the platform would be

> lined with cinemas and theaters, all with the same low height regulations, so that if viewed as a whole, they will make an uninterrupted architectural mass, with arcades, wide sidewalks, terraces and cafes. The façades of the buildings provide a fine field for illuminated advertisements. The theaters will be inter-connected by lanes barred to motor traffic, in the traditional manner of Rio's Ouvidor Street, Venetian alleys, or arcades which run into small patios where there will be bars and cafes. Behind the buildings, footways and lanes will lead to "loggias" overlooking the park. . . . The upper floors will be glassed-in on both sides, so that the restaurants, clubs, tearooms, etc., may look on to the lower esplanade on one

side, and on the other may have a view of the hilly park—an extension of the monumental radial artery on which the commercial and tourist hotels are located—and beyond this, of the imposing Radio-TV tower, which is treated as a plastic element in the composition of the urban mass.

The adjacent banking and business centers would be developed with a unified building plan characterized by "three high-rise blocks and four lower ones, all interconnected by a wide street-level area with the mezzanines, which will provide covered communication and ample space for branches of banks, business firms, restaurants, etc."

The monumental radial axis as it extended westward from the intersection would contain a central band of parkland punctuated by the television tower. As described by Costa:

> This tower is triangular and consists of a monumental base of unfaced reinforced concrete stretching up to a studio and office floor, and of a metal superstructure with a lookout section half way up. On one side it overlooks the stadium and its pavilions, with the botanical gardens behind them; on the other, it has a view of the racecourse, grandstands, stables and ancillary buildings and, adjacent to these, the zoological gardens. The two great green parks symmetrically laid out in relation to the monumental radial artery, are the "lungs" of the new city.

At the western terminus of the axis would be sited the municipal square containing the town hall, police headquarters, fire station, and public welfare building. Beyond this would be the barracks, railroad station, and a warehousing and industrial area. In describing his scheme, Costa wrote: "Now that we have travelled down the monumental radial artery from point to point, we can perceive that its flexibility and compactness of pattern from government plaza to municipal square, do not exclude variety; and that each part appears to be individually important, forming a living plastic organism in the overall planning scheme."

The residential district of the city was planned in a sequence of superblocks flanking the motor axis and containing apartment housing. Within these blocks, Costa stated, residential buildings could "be arranged in varying manners, though always in obedience to two general principles: uniform height regulations—perhaps a maximum of six stories above the pilotis—and segregation of motorized traffic and pedestrian transit, especially near the entrances to the primary school and the urban amenities located in each superblock." The schematic superblock which Costa included in his presentation showed apartment blocks in the form of slabs set at right angles to one another.

Each block was to be surrounded by a band of greenery planted with trees, and "each one will give pride of place to one species of tree; the ground will be carpeted with grass, and shrubs and foliage will screen the internal groupings of the superblock from the spectator, who will get a view of the layout through a haze of greenery. This will have the two-fold advantage of guaranteeing orderly planning, even when the density, category, pattern or architectural standard of individual buildings are of a different quality."

Short streets at right angles to the radial artery were intended as sites for local commerce, with neighborhood facilities designed to be shared by groups of four superblocks. Although the housing of the city was designed to reflect relatively uniform standards, Costa believed that the social structure of the residential zone could be graded by setting a greater value on specified superblocks, such as the rows adjoining the diplomatic quarter. He maintained, however, that the four-by-four grouping of the superblocks would

> while favoring co-existence of social groups, avoid any undue and undesirable stratification of society. And, in any case, variations in the standard of living from one superblock to another will be offset by the organization of the urban scheme itself, and will not be of such a nature as to affect that degree of comfort to which all members of society have a right. Any differences in standard will spring from a greater or lesser density, a larger or smaller living space allocated to each individual or family, or from the quality of building materials selected and the degree of finish which these receive. And since such problems are being raised, the growth of slums, whether on the city outskirts or in the surrounding countryside, should at all costs be prevented. The Development Company should, within the scope of the proposed outline plan, make provision for decent and economical accommodation for the entire population.

In addition to the apartment housing, two districts near the lake were set aside for large detached houses, although in subsequent modifications of the plan, such single-family housing would be restricted to the peninsulas and the far shore of the lake. By and large, the land along the lakefront was to be left as natural parkland, providing sites for sport clubs, restaurants, and playing fields.

According to Costa:

> It is easy to grasp the criteria used in this plan for a capital city, since its characteristics are the simplicity and clarity of the original pattern. As has been shown, these factors do not exclude variety in treatment of the individual parts, each of which is conceived according to the special nature of its respective function. The result of such treatment should be harmony, despite requirements which are apparently contradictory. Thus, although the city is monumental, it is also convenient, efficient, welcoming and intimate. At one and the same time it is spread

> out and compact, rural and urban, lyrical and functional. The automobile traffic rolls along swiftly, unhampered by road junctions, yet the ground is given back in a fair measure to the pedestrian. And since the structure of the city is so clearly outlined, its construction will be easy: it is based on the crossing of two axes, on two terraced embankments or terrepleins, a platform, two arteries going in one direction and one in another.

Costa concluded that Brasília would be the "capital of the airplane and the highway, city and park" (figs. 145–53).

Although many of the competition plans might be said to have been influenced by Le Corbusier, Costa's scheme represented the most complete realization of the French architect's visionary urban designs. Like Le Corbusier, Costa sought to provide a way to have one's cake and eat it—to enjoy the benefits of a technically advanced, mechanized environment and at the same time have the salubrious advantages of suburban living.

Le Corbusier had viewed the modern city as a symbol of man's technical control of his environment, once defining the city as "the grip of man upon nature. . . . a human operation directed against nature."[2] In similar spirit was Costa's observation that Brasília was "a deliberate act of conquest." However one might prefer the charming irregularities of a city representing the accumulated growth of centuries, there was no point, Costa believed, in trying to make Brasília appear to be other than what it was —a deliberately planned, man-made creation.

Regarding the speed of construction, Costa once remarked, "We have to finish in five years or the forest will come back."[3] The forest was figurative, but the sense of threat was real. It is against a wilderness which still bears almost no imprint of human occupation that the image of Brasília must be seen. Although parkland is included within the city, Costa's design, like those of the other contestants, was essentially a formal diagram bearing little relation to the site. There is little in the conception of Brasília which indicates a desire to harmonize the works of man with those of nature. But Brazil is a country where nature has long been dominant; thus the symbolic image of the city is enhanced through its ostentatious display of mechanization and technical mastery.

Brasília reflects a somewhat dated glorification of the machine; yet, because Brazil is a relatively unindustrialized country, the façade of modern technology retains an appeal it may have lost elsewhere. The automobile in Brazil is not a commonplace possession, and the romance of the machine has not yet ceased to thrill. Anyone familiar with Rio, who has witnessed the eagerness of the Cariocas to sacrifice urban amenities, including the world's most beautiful waterfront, to the rapid flow of motor

2. Le Corbusier, *City of Tomorrow* (London, 1947), pp. xxi–xxii.

3. Quoted in Douglass Haskell, "Brasília: A New Type of National City," *Architectural Forum* 113 (November 1960): 127.

traffic, would not be surprised to find the new Brazilian capital having as a dominant feature a wide motor freeway. Brazilians exhibit no desire to restrict urban traffic or render the automobile inconspicuous, and to have built an entire city to the scale of the motor is a source of pride.

In addition to its mechanized aspect, Brasília shares with Le Corbusier's early schemes a similar conception of the residential superblock, comprising uniform-height apartment buildings raised on pilotis and set amid open space and greenery. Common to Le Corbusier's designs and the Costa plan is a simplified conception of urban content which includes the reduction of building types to a few relatively standardized designs.

The Costa plan set up the outline of a controlled environment in which the city was conceived as a single unified work of art. Within the overall scheme, a hierarchy of form was established, relating all parts to the whole and permitting the permanent dominance of the monumental sector. It was in part this aspect of the plan which motivated the jury to accept Costa's scheme in preference to others.

From the sketches which were submitted for the competition, Costa developed a working plan in which the city was sited somewhat closer to the lake, with the peninsula areas plotted for single-family housing (fig. 143). Beyond the revision of the plan, however, Costa took little direct part in the creation of the city. Once the development of Brasília was under way, Costa did not visit the site, freeing himself from the day-to-day vicissitudes of construction and the temptation to make changes which might vitiate the purity of the design.

Although the design provided a beginning for Brasília, it did not provide guidelines for expansion, and it would be inevitable that some modifications in the plan as well as a number of additions would be necessary. The major weakness of the Costa plan lay in its relatively static quality, and although the overall conception had merit, it is increasingly evident that a more comprehensive and flexible scheme was needed. As Brasília continues to grow, it becomes clear that no city plan can be said to be complete, and that the planning of a city is a continuing, not a finite, process. The Costa plan provided what was desired at a given moment; what has been needed in the years since its inception is a skillful, thoughtful, and sensitive planning effort which could maintain the essence of the pilot plan, while adapting it to the changing needs of the city. Moreover, because of the failure to develop a sufficiently farseeing plan for the Federal District, the "purity" of the pilot plan has come to be surrounded by a relatively haphazard fringe development (fig. 144).

Although the creation and selection of the Costa plan may be seen as an understandable reflection of a given moment in time and a given set of circumstances, it was foreseeable that the design conception it embodied would subsequently be subject to criticism. Brasília, with its rigid zoning of activities, its massive motorways, and standardized building patterns, is not unique, but rather a thoroughgoing embodiment of a type of environment becoming, in more fragmentary form, a common experience.

Inevitably, as the imperfections of planned perfection have evidenced themselves, some theorists have rejected the ideal of the totally ordered city for a determined advocacy of variety, spontaneity, and flexibility. The desire for functional zoning has been replaced by a tendency to regard close physical juxtaposition of housing, commerce, and institutions as essential to liveliness and convenience within the city. Geometric, modular design and repetitive forms are frequently derided as sterile and monotonous, and to a generation prizing formal and functional complexity, Brasília may exemplify what Lewis Mumford has termed "yesterday's city and tomorrow."[5] Because of its resemblance to the simplistic schemes of the 1920s and 1930s, Brasília, in the short time of its existence, has come to embody a somewhat outmoded conception of modernity.

In *The Death and Life of Great American Cities,* Jane Jacobs stressed that *"A city cannot be a work of art. . . .* To approach a city, or even a city neighborhood, as if it were a larger architectural problem, capable of being given order by converting it into a disciplined work of art, is to make the mistake of attempting to substitute art for life."[4] Taking this statement at face value would, of course, involve a total rejection of such urban designs as the Costa plan. It is perhaps more accurate to say that a city is in part a work of art and has been appropriately regarded as such for most of human history. The special circumstances under which Brasília was created made the conception of the city as architecture essential to the city's existence. Costa was well aware that his plan would bring about no miracles. It proposed no new philosophy of life and intended neither revolution nor social reform. It outlined a physical framework which would enable the government to move to the interior of Brazil. No more. Brasília was a stage set for which the future would provide the actors and the drama.

4. Jane Jacobs, *The Death and Life of Great American Cities* (New York, 1961), pp. 372–73.
5. Leur's Mumford, "Yesterday's City of Tomorrow," *Architectural Record,* 132 (November 1962): 141.

11. THE REALIZATION OF A CITY

Pressures of time were such that work progressed in Brasília even before the master plan had been selected. On 2 October 1956, Kubitschek began his first stay at the Brasília site, making his headquarters in a small wooden house which came to be called "Catetinho" (little Catete), in reference to the President's Rio headquarters, the Catete Palace.

On 1 November, Israel Pinheiro and Oscar Niemeyer arrived to begin studies for the first buildings of the city. Independent of any master plan, sites had already been selected for the President's Palace and a hotel, both to be placed near the lake. These buildings, together with the major government buildings of Brasília were to be designed by Niemeyer who, as director of the Department of Architecture of NOVACAP, would supervise the architectural development of the city. Meanwhile, NOVACAP had established an office in the nearby town of Luziâna.

Brasília, 584 air miles from Rio, was at this time 78 miles from the nearest railroad, 400 miles from the nearest paved highway, and 120 miles from the nearest airport. Among the first tasks of the city builders, therefore, was to start linking the site with the outside world. On 9 October 1956, a road was initiated between Brasília and the nearby town of Anapolis, with projections for outside rail connections commencing a month later. The Brasília airport was begun on 2 December to be inaugurated on 2 April 1957, its 3,300 meter runway making it the largest in Brazil. By the following month, the engineer Bernardo Sayao Carvalho Araújo had begun the initial studies for a new national highway extending 1300 miles between Belém, at the mouth of the Amazon, and Brasília. The development of a system of interior highways paralleled the construction of Brasília, and, two months before the dedication of the city, a "Caravan of National Integration" traveled simultaneously by road from Belém, Cuiaba, Rio de Janeiro, and Porto Alegre, meeting in Brasília on 2 February 1960. Intended to encourage the economic development of the interior, the new highway system was to prove a generator of urban development, attracting a series of new settlements along its length.

An American once described the construction of Brasília by stating: "It was as if the opening of the West had been delayed a hundred years and then done with bulldozers."[1] Simultaneously, and at a feverish pace, roads were built; apartments, houses, and government buildings designed and erected; water mains, sewers, and electrical installations prepared. As the land was graded and excavated, the dry red soil of the city hung over the site in a perpetual thick cloud, which one visitor noted, "soon dries the lips, clogs the nostrils, invades the ears and hair."[2]

The dedication date for the city had been set for 21 April 1960, and during the preceding year construction activity continued around the clock, with work proceeding at night under floodlights. The creation of Brasília represented a triumph of administration in a country never noted for efficient administration; it represented adherence to a time schedule in a society where schedules are seldom met; and it represented continuous hard work from a people reputedly reluctant to work either hard or continuously. Henrique Mindlin once observed of Brasília that "the spirit in which it was launched, a spirit which in many respects can only be compared to that which prevails in defensive war, when the instinct to survive comes before any practical consideration, can be seen now as the only spirit that would spark the collective will to the effective and immediate action necessary."[3]

The comparison with a wartime mentality might also be applied to the financing of the city, in which the achievement of a desired goal overrode monetary caution. Cost figures given for Brasília tend to vary, reflecting both a lack of detailed information and prejudice either for or against the city. William Holford once declared:

> Nobody knows, least of all I think the New Town Corporation (NOVACAP), what this new town has cost. When I asked Dr. Pinheiro, the President of NOVACAP, whether he was bothered by accountants over capital expenditure, or by capital accounts committees and things of that kind, he said, "No, no, no." I said, "Do tell me the secret. How is it that you survive?" He said, "It is quite simple. We have fixed a D-Day—April 21, 1960. The town must be ready then. I have said to Parliament, 'If you criticize me, you do not get your town.' "[4]

A similar experience was reported by the British architect Max Lock, who observed: "I had the privilege of meeting Niemeyer, and I asked him how much his palace cost. He shrugged his shoulders, as I would like to be able to do, and said 'I do not know. How should I know?' "[5]

The total cost of Brasília from the initiation of construction to the dedication of

1. Douglass Haskell, "Brasília: A New Type of National City," *Architectural Forum* 113 (November 1960): 126.
2. "The 'Folly' is a City," *Newsweek*, 7 September 1959, p. 45.
3. Henrique E. Mindlin, *Brazilian Architecture* (Rome, 1961), p. 48.
4. William Holford, "Brasília," *Journal of the Royal Institute of British Architects* 67 (March 1960): 158.
5. Ibid., p. 157.

the city has been calculated as $600 million, with estimates of additional expenditures up to 1966 of $1 billion.[6] The infrastructure and major government buildings were financed through NOVACAP, which received direct congressional appropriations in addition to an initial endowment of Cr $500 million. The residential construction of the city, however, was largely undertaken by government pension institutes.[7] Also involved in the construction of housing in Brasília was the government savings bank (the Caixa Economica Federal) and the Foundation of People's Housing (Fundação da Casa Popular), together with the National Bank of Brazil.

On 20 September 1957, the United States Import-Export Bank granted Brazil $10 millon to provide steel for the eleven government ministries of Brasília.

Part of the cost of the city was offset by the sale of land to private owners, and during the initial years of construction, NOVACAP—which had set up offices in Rio, São Paulo, Curitiba, Porto Alegre, Recife, Anapolis, Belo Horizonte, and Goiânia, as well as in Brasília—offered a total of 18,018 lots for sale. By 1960 it was reported that 13,769 had been sold at a value of Cr $4,755,803.[8]

Confidence in the new city was such as to inspire considerable speculation in the vicinity of Brasília, and many enterprising land agents were reported to be selling plots in outlying areas of the Federal District to unsuspecting buyers who were led to believe that their land lay within the pilot plan area. Inspired by the anticipated development of the whole region, a private company acquired a large tract of land

6. These figures were provided in August 1966 to the Subcommittee for Appropriations of the U.S. House of Representatives by Lincoln Gordon, undersecretary of state and former ambassador to Brazil. The figures were based on Brazilian sources, having been compiled by a member of the Brazilian Treasury Delegation. A Brazilian journalist, Maurício Vaitsman, published a book purporting to disprove this estimate, *Quanto custou Brasília* (Rio de Janeiro, 1968). Vaitsman provides an exaggerated transposition of Gordon's dollar figures into cruzeiros. It is always difficult to make such conversions because of the rapid inflation of the cruzeiro. At the commencement of Brasília (December 1956), the cruzeiro was valued at 65 per dollar. At the time of the dedication of Brasília (June 1960), the rate of exchange was 187 per dollar. By 1966, when Gordon made his report, the rate was 2,220 per dollar. Vaitsman converted Gordon's estimate (which covered the period from 1956 to 1966) at the 1966 rate, producing a total of 3 trillion, 536 billion cruzeiros. Vaitsman's financial estimates are based on the results of a Brazilian parliamentary commission which assembled reports from all government agencies participating in the Brasília project. The total for construction costs up to December 1961 is given (p. 88) as 81 billion, 805 million, 827 thousand, 191 cruzeiros (Cr $81,805,827,191). These figures cover a period when the cruzeiro ranged in value from 65 (December 1956) to 318 (December 1961) per dollar. If one were to use 200 as an average conversion rate for this period, the figure in dollars would be approximately $400 mililon ($409,029,140). The figure of $600 million for the initial construction period is given by Mindlin in *Brazilian Architecture,* p. 46. Mindlin at that time (1961) estimated subsequent completion costs for the city as $1 million.

7. In Brazil the national government sponsors workers' foundations which combine some of the aspects of labor unions and a social security system. Each foundation receives salary deductions from employees and provides pensions and sometimes medical services and cooperative housing. Having large amounts of accumulated capital at their disposal, these organizations were induced to invest heavily in the new city. Among the foundations constructing housing in Brasília were the Commercial Employees Pension and Retirement Institute (IAPETC), the State Employees Pension and Retirement Institute (IPASE), the Industrial Workers Pension and Retirement Institute (IAPI), the Railway and Public Service Workers Pension and Retirement Institute (IAPFESP), and the Bank Employees Pension and Retirement Institute (IAPB).

8. Because of the steady devaluation of the cruzeiro, it is difficult to make an accurate conversion of this cruzeiro figure into dollars. From December 1956 and December 1960 the rate of exchange went from 65 per dollar to 205 per dollar.

just outside the Federal District, with the intention of sponsoring farming settlement together with the creation of a new city of 200,000 to be called Cidade Marina. Oscar Niemeyer was engaged to prepare an urban plan which exhibited a schematic similarity to Le Corbusier's Ville Radieuse plan of 1930. The design embodied a civic center isolated above the main body of the city. Below this would be high-rise housing and residential superblocks of low-rise houses. An industrial zone would extend along the lower edge. Like many ambitious projects in Brazil, this new town never achieved realization.

To the opponents of Brasília, the high cost of the city would remain one of the principal objections to its establishment, and an ex-minister of finance in Brazil once proclaimed that "construction of a new capital in a poor country . . . is a crime against the country's economy."[9] The years of Brasília's construction coincided with a sharp increase in inflation, and opponents of the city have cited the project as having had a disastrous effect on an already shaky economic development. A pessimistic American businessman once predicted, "Brazilians will have to decide between Brazil and Brasília."[10]

To the proponents of Brasília, the long-term benefits of the city would far outweigh the initial government investment, and it was argued that, "a work of such magnitude cannot be measured by an annual budget, or even by a five-year plan: it is measured in terms of centuries!"[11]

In June 1958, Oscar Niemeyer set up permanent headquarters in Brasília to direct more efficiently the construction of the city. Living conditions at this time were far from comfortable. Heavy rains turned the ground to mud, food was poor, and there was neither electricity nor hot water. Niemeyer assembled a staff of fifteen, all friends, and motivated by a high enthusiasm for the project. In spite of the loneliness and isolation from family and familiar surroundings, morale was high, and after the day's work, the architects would customarily meet for long, spirited discussions.

Recalling the problems of this period, Niemeyer observed:

> We soon found out that we were not merely up against the technical, economic and like problems—huge enough in themselves—that the construction of a city poses. Others arose or were worsened by a lack of understanding or by the systematic campaign that the enemies of the Government waged against Brasília. At first they pursued this campaign rather listlessly, feeling it was unnecessary; but when they saw that the work was really going ahead, they broadened the range of their attacks and brought them out into the open in a vain attempt, successfully frustrated, to wreck the entire undertaking. The unfairness of the purely negative criticism levelled at us was a constant source of irritation; we

9. "Brazil Builds a New Capital," *Fortune* 59 (April 1959): 109.
10. "Brazil Lavishes Money, Hopes on Dream City," *Business Week,* 12 September 1959, p. 133.
11. J. O. de Meira Penna, *Brasília* (Rio de Janeiro [196?]).

> were specially hurt by the lack of generosity shown in evaluating the immense effort and sacrifice involved. But the repulsion that all this aroused in us had a positive effect, driving us to work with greater determination and an accrued sense of responsibility.[12]

In Brasília Niemeyer maintained his preference for a relatively small office and an informal work atmosphere. A North American visiting him in 1960 observed that Niemeyer

> has a drafting table in a construction shack, a telephone, and apparently no secretary. There are perhaps two dozen draftsmen in an adjoining room. One of his chores is the making of hundreds of on-the-spot decisions in the course of a day. "They are always asking Oscar what to do," said one of his assistants. "Don't you have people who could help?" I asked. Outside there were some 45,000 workmen who were doing, in effect, what Niemeyer had told them to do. "Oscar isn't an organization type," he replied. Suddenly he laughed. "You know, if we had been organized we never could have done it."[13]

Although the construction was generally supervised by NOVACAP, the building of the city was by no means an exclusively government enterprise. Much of the building was carried out by large private contractors who provided their own engineering staff, specialized workers, and construction experience. On 30 August 1957, Israel Pinheiro conducted a meeting for leaders of Brazilian industry in which he justified the Brasília project as a stimulant to the economy in its employment of Brazilian materials and labor and in its extensive reliance on the local building industry.

Although such a large-scale project as Brasília could have been a proving ground for experimental building techniques and new materials, the construction of the city followed conventional usages. The most important factor governing building was the need for speed, and this, together with the large number of unskilled workers, prompted the employment of relatively simple designs and easily mastered techniques. With the exception of the Brasília Palace Hotel and the government ministries, which used steel frame construction, all large buildings were of reinforced concrete. Gravel and sand were obtained at distances of from six to 37 miles around Brasília, and bricks could be produced near the site. Other materials had to be brought over considerable distances. Timber came from the State of Parana, about 746 miles to the south, while steel had to be transported over 1000 miles. Although initially airplanes were used for some supply transport, almost all materials were brought to Brasília by truck. In the early phases of construction, tank trucks supplied

12. Oscar Niemeyer, "My Brasília Experience," *Módulo* 18 (June 1960): 23.

13. George Nelson, "Out of the Trackless Bush, a National Capital," *Saturday Review of Literature*, 43 (12 March 1960): 40.

water for both building and drinking purposes. Each building site had a diesel-powered generator to furnish current for machinery, workshops, and lodgings.

For the initial phase of construction, building activity was centered in the south axis of the city, the side nearest the highway approaches from Rio and São Paulo. It was hoped that, by the time of dedication, Brasília would be sufficiently completed to provide housing for 30,000 government employees.

A visitor arriving at the airport during the days of construction observed that the "waiting crowd of restless, sunburned men in blue jeans, broad-brimmed hats, and dusty boots suggests a television Western rather than an ultramodern capital."[14] Certain similarities between Brasília and the popular image of the wild west were noted by many North Americans. There was the same boom-town enterprise and optimism, the same picturesque mixture of population, the same freedom from constraints.

The sense of involvement in a common enterprise was such as to create among the builders of Brasília a sense of democracy far from common in Brazil. Niemeyer noted a sense of determination "striking a common denominator between chiefs and subordinates, workers and engineers, that brought us all to the same level, a natural and spontaneous affinity that the class differences still existing in our country make it difficult if not impossible to set up."[15]

It was in tribute to the pioneering workmen that the citizens of Brasília came to adopt a name for themselves—the *candangos.* Although the precise derivation of the term is not clear, it is believed to be of African origin and used during the colonial period to designate the rough and impoverished inhabitants of the countryside. Finding themselves pioneering an unsettled site, accustomed to dust and mud, and adopting the boots and informal dress of the backlands, the inhabitants of Brasília took pride in identifying themselves with the early pioneers of Brazil.

As building progressed, Brasília became a magnet for workers from all over Brazil. A pattern of migration from poverty-stricken rural areas which had already swollen the populations of most major cities was repeated in the new capital where the magnitude of the construction effort gave hopes for steady employment. Work camps, providing barracklike housing close to large building sites, accommodated some of the influx. In addition, outside the pilot plan area, a temporary settlement called Cidade Livre (Free Town) was established. Within this town, land was made available free, with the understanding that, once Brasília was completed, the town would be demolished.

Consisting largely of wooden shacklike buildings, Cidade Livre provided not only a place of residence, but the shopping, business, and entertainment center for the area. By 1958, this settlement contained about 340 business establishments, including

14. "The 'Folly' is a City," p. 45.

15. Niemeyer, "My Brasília Experience," p. 19.

thirteen hotels, five banking agencies, four churches, four airline offices, and various enterprises such as restaurants, butcher shops, bakeries, drugstores, sawmills, a movie house, and, as an inevitable accompaniment to a predominantly male population, an assortment of brothels.

Observing Cidade Livre, one visitor reported that "all sorts of riffraff and fugitives populate this wide-open shanty-town, . . . it is not safe to venture far from the car."[16] Another witness concurred, stating: "Everyone carries a gun or knife, and life is cheap as in a mountain mining town. Police are not in evidence except for traffic."[17] Others, however, were attracted to Cidade Livre, finding it a lively and colorful contrast to the grandiose but somewhat sterile city taking form nearby. In the opinion of one foreign observer, "The rip-roaring, blood-red life of the downtown Free City should have been placed bang in the centre of the main city right from the word 'go.' "[18]

Throughout the construction of Brasília, the president was much in evidence, providing encouragement and also supporting the city through a massive government program of publicity. Each step in development was accompanied by fanfare and ceremony, speeches, photographers, and Kubitschek. On 3 May 1957, the first Catholic mass on the Brasília site was performed by the Cardinal-Arch-Bishop of São Paulo. During the ceremonies, for which 15,000 people had been gathered, Kubitschek remarked that, "With the first mass, the spiritual seed of Brasília is planted."[19] The first school in Brasília, accomodating thirty children of engineers and construction workers, was ceremonially inaugurated by the Brazilian minister of education on 18 October 1957. The Brasília Palace Hotel designed by Niemeyer received its first guests on 2 May 1958, the president of Paraguay and his entourage. On 28 June of the same year, the first Catholic church within the pilot plan area was dedicated, Our Lady of Fatima, by Niemeyer. The first completed housing in Brasília, a project of 500 row houses built by the Foundation of People's Housing, was inaugurated by Kubitschek on 1 September 1958.

Almost any event, from the opening of the Brasília radio station in May 1958 to the inauguration of the first postal service in April 1959, provided an occasion for presidential rhetoric. During Kubitschek's first sojourn in Brasília, in October 1956, he had announced, "From this central tableland, from this solitary place which will be soon transformed into the brain center of the highest decisions, I cast my eyes once again on the tomorrow of my country, with unshakable faith and unlimited confi-

16. Wolf von Eckardt, "Brasília: Symbol in the Mud," *American Institute of Architects Journal* 36 (November 1961): 42.

17. Walter McQuade, "Brasília's Beginning," *Architectural Forum* 110 (April 1959): 98. He was quoting from a report by Chicago architect Alfred Shaw.

18. "Conversation in Brasília, between Robert Harbinson and George Balcombe," *Journal of the Royal Institute of British Architects* 68 (November 1961): 494.

19. "A historia da construção de Brasília," *Brasília* 40 (21 April 1960): 49.

dence in the greatness of its destiny."[20] This message formed the essence of many subsequent statements in which the president tirelessly reiterated his conviction that the creation of Brasília was inextricably bound to the future development of Brazil.

As the city took form, it received a constant stream of visitors—statesmen, architects, and critics, many of them under government sponsorship. Among those viewing the new capital during its construction were the president of Italy, Giovanni Gronchi, the prime minister of Cuba, Fidel Castro, President Sukarno of Indonesia, the president of Mexico, Adolfo López Mateos, and Craveiro Lopes, president of Portugal.

A group of United States senators and representatives visited Brasília on 1 August 1958, and on 6 August, Secretary of State John Foster Dulles ceremonially planted a magnolia tree on the grounds of the Presidential Palace. Two months before the official dedication of Brasília, President Dwight D. Eisenhower made a state visit, an occasion which Kubitschek celebrated as a "pre-inauguration" of the city.

Foreign architects viewing the burgeoning capital included Mies van der Rohe, Philip Johnson, Richard Neutra, Kenzo Tange, Eero Saarinen, and Frederick Kiesler. An international congress of art critics was convened in Brasília, Rio de Janeiro, and São Paulo in September 1959, having as its inevitable point of reference the new Brazilian capital. Opinions of all visitors were eagerly sought and disseminated, emphasizing to Brazilians that the project in which they were engaged was achieving international recognition and was contributing to the respect in which Brazil was held abroad.

Although not all observers were unanimous with regard to Brasília, most found themselves responsive to the spirit which seemed to motivate the new city. As J. M. Richards expressed it:

> The European visitor touring the site of the future city finds he readily catches the enthusiasm that is shown there. Initial doubts and indifference undergo a change, just as the attitude of many Brazilians towards the controversial project undergoes a change, when actually confronted with this city that is rising before their eyes. And why not? That power of decision which is prepared to act unhesitatingly upon a vision of the future is also capable of endowing the results with a degree of authoritativeness that makes theoretical points of city-planning relatively unimportant.[21]

In addition to the government-sponsored visits to the site, the new city was publicized through traveling exhibitions in Europe and the Americas. It was triumphantly reported that

> Brasília has had a sensational effect on public opinion in Europe, the USA and

20. Ibid., p. 46.
21. "Brasília as Seen by an Englishman," *Módulo* 14 (August 1959): 5.

> our South American neighbors. Latin Americans see in it a proof of Brazil's power. The Americans find it arouses a kind of longing attachment to their own pioneer history; they see Brazil using twentieth century techniques to build an immense modern city, and thereby doing what they themselves did in the nineteenth century (maybe they recall the building of Washington). And for the Europeans it is a double surprise. Just imagine this country which, in their ill informed minds, they till recently thought of as a vast virgin forest, populated by poisonous snakes and naked Indians, this country, that many thought was sunk in the lackadaisical inertia of the tropics, builds a capital city in but three years right in the heart of the jungle, raising delicate concrete structures where the crocodile and the leopard used to roam; this nation hurls its mighty tractors through the densest virgin forest in the world, to carve out gigantic highways; in short this nation provides western civilization with a foretaste of the renewal of its ancient culture on a more beautiful and more human foundation![22]

Although the Brazilian author of the foregoing seems to have been somewhat ill-informed himself as to the nature of the Brasília site, the tone of the statement reflects the nationalistic fervor which came to be felt by the proponents of Brasília.

Observing the Art Critics Congress of 1959, a Brazilian commentator concluded, "For us Brazilians, the results of the Congress could not be better. Our aims have been fully attained: Brasília is now in the limelight of foreign professional criticism."[23]

Meanwhile the work went on. The date which had been set for the formal inauguration of Brasília, 21 April 1960, was exactly three years, one month, and five days following the selection of the master plan, and as the time of dedication drew near, preparations reached a frantic pace. Israel Pinheiro, as Henrique Mindlin recalled, was to be seen "running madly from place to place on April 21st, shouting orders, terribly embarrassed and disappointed about so much not being thoroughly and completely finished, and saying all the time, in the most innocent good faith to whoever would listen: 'If I had only had another five days, another five days . . .' "[24] In a final frenzied cleanup, 60,000 workers carted off debris, planted palm trees and scrubbed the red dust from the monumental buildings. In one day 2,000 steel light poles were installed, while overnight 722 houses were painted white.

In addition to a sizable infrastructure, the completed work included the Presidential Palace, the Brasília Palace Hotel, and a government complex containing the Supreme Court, the Palace of the Planalto (the executive headquarters), and the National Congress. Eleven government ministry buildings bordered the monumental

22. J. O. de Meira Penna, "Brazilian Architecture Exhibitions," *Módulo* 12 (February 1959): 43.
23. Mario Pedrosa, "Lessons to be Drawn from the International Congress of Critics," *Módulo* 16 (December 1959): 12.
24. Mindlin, *Brazilian Architecture,* pp. 42–43.

axis, although all were not ready for occupancy. Completed housing within the superblocks included 94 apartment blocks, 500 one-story and 222 two-story houses, accompanied by schools and shopping facilities.

The dedication of Brasília was conducted with appropriate bravura. A reported 150,000 people converged on the site, placing overwhelming demands on the new city's meagre accommodations. Five thousand invited dignitaries competed for the 150 first-class rooms of the Brasília Palace Hotel, prompting a rule that no one below the rank of ambassador, cabinet minister, or full general might be housed there, while among the deputies it was reported that arms were drawn to assert the right to lodging space. The ceremonies, over which Kubitschek presided, included a special midnight mass, a joint session of congress, and a parade of 5,000 troops and 10,000 workers, all culminating in a display of 38 tons of fireworks. Although the city was still unfinished, Kubitschek's triumph was complete.

12. THE PLAN AND THE REALITY

Although Kubitschek had succeeded in his goal of establishing Brasília as the nominal capital of Brazil, the dedication of the city did not mark an immediate transfer of major government activity. Once the ceremonies were over, the results of the haste with which the city had been built became readily evident.

The air conditioning in the legislative halls failed to work, and most government offices were without adequate equipment and staff. Only four of the eleven ministry buildings were functioning. Both the Congress and Supreme Court recessed, and many officials returned to Rio, leaving token offices in the new capital. Although by the dedication date a reported 975 federal employees were working in Brasília, it appeared that the bulk of the government establishment would continue to function in Rio for an indefinite period.

The initial development of Brasília had been heavily dependent on the personal dedication and administrative support of Juscelino Kubitschek, and the loss of his leadership, following his departure from office in 1961, had an immediate effect on the morale of the planning staff. Niemeyer recalled: "With the departure of JK, from one day to the next, our life in Brasília changed completely. Gone was the old enthusiasm which surmounted everything, which permitted us to construct in so little time, which set us in the planalto with no other preoccupation except the work to be realized. From one day to the next, we became bureaucrats, given to useless discussions and barren disputes, enervated by the endless morass which engulfed us. . . . We felt, deeply, that our work in Brasília was paralyzed."[1]

Jânio Quadros, who held the presidency briefly in 1961, came into office giving verbal support to the new capital and declaring to Kubitschek, "You started Brasília; I shall complete it."[2] In practice, however, his major orientation was in the field of foreign policy, and he did little to promote the development of the city. President

1. Oscar Niemeyer, *Quase memorias: viagens, tempós de entusiasmo e revolta 1961–1966* (Rio de Janeiro, 1968), p. 14.
2. Quoted in Vladimir Reisky de Dubnic, *Political Trends in Brazil* (Washington, D.C., 1968), p. 109.

João Goulart, who remained in office from 1961 to 1964, was strongly concerned with internal social reform, and was less than enthusiastic about Brasília, which he tended to view as an extravagant and antisocial waste of resources. Meanwhile, Niemeyer left Brazil to begin execution of a number of commissions abroad. Thus, shortly after its dedication, the city lost both the strong political support of the president and the continuing presence of its chief designer.

The Goulart administration was overthrown by a military coup in 1964, following which General Castelo Branco assumed the presidency. With the new military regime, governmental support for Brasília revived. The reason may have involved a recognition that the government commitment to the city was too extensive to be withdrawn. It is likely, also, that Brasília, with its strong monumental emphasis, accorded well with the military fondness for ceremony and nationalist symbols. The new capital, with its orderly plan and architectural uniformity, may have appeared a wholly suitable setting from which to administer a new program of discipline and austerity.

During the Branco regime, Brasília underwent an administrative renovation, in which a newly reorganized municipal prefecture took over the major planning responsibility for the city. Although Brasília has never enjoyed any form of participatory local government, the dedication of the city in 1960 had been followed by the creation of a municipal administration, with Israel Pinheiro leaving NOVACAP to become the first prefect of the Federal District.

Although NOVACAP continued to function as a planning agency, the 1964 reorganization of government placed this office within the administrative structure of the municipality and subject to the authority of the Secretary of Transport and Works (Secretaria de Viaçâo e Obras)—equivalent to an office of public works. Also included under this agency were three other departments, the Coordination of Architecture and Urbanism (Coordenação de Arquitetura e Urbanismo), the Department of Roads (Departamento de Estradas de Rodagem), and the Coordination of Works and Services (Coordenação de Obras e Serviços). In addition to these agencies, the Society for Housing of Social Interest (Sociedade de Habitações de Interêsse Social), under the authority of the Secretary of Social Service (Secretaria de Serviços Socias), would direct a program of subsidized low-cost housing, primarily in outlying areas.

Another government agency with planning powers, and subject to direct federal authority, is CODEBRAS, the Coordination of the Development of Brasília (Coordenação do Desenvolvimento de Brasília). This organization, created in 1967, evolved from the Work Group (Groupo de Trabalho), an agency instituted in 1958 for the purpose of organizing the transfer of government employees to the new capital. Although the function of the Work Group had initially involved administration, rather than design, CODEBRAS began to include in its work the design and construction of housing.

Brazilian government organization tends to be somewhat confusing and is characterized by overlapping agencies and redundancy of function. Hence, the proliferation of planning agencies in Brasília is not surprising. The division of function among CODEBRAS, NOVACAP, and the Coordination of Architecture and Urbanism (CAU) is not altogether clear. The most powerful agency, however, appears to be the CAU, which attempts to coordinate the activities of all the agencies involved in the development of Brasília, and also to establish planning policy. NOVACAP, meanwhile, has become primarily an agency for the execution of urban works.

Although the progress of Brasília is dependent on political vagaries, and especially on presidential support, the idea of the city appears to have become politically acceptable. Castello Branco's successor, Costa e Silva, continued the support offered by the previous president, announcing as he took office in 1967 that he was determined to complete the transfer of the government to Brasília during his administration. The statement was by no means intended literally, but it did indicate a general policy of support for the new capital. Following the incapacitating illness of Costa e Silva, Emílio Garrastazu Médici took office in October 1969, repeating similar assurances of his intention to promote the development of Brasília, and he observed the tenth anniversary of the city with the decree that cabinet ministers conduct all subsequent business in the new capital.

Although in the ten years following its dedication Brasília received sufficient government support to assure its steady growth, no timetable was established for the completion of the city. While Kubitschek's successors appear generally to have accepted an obligation toward its development, the strong personal identification which Kubitschek felt for the city has been notably, and perhaps understandably, lacking in other presidents. Brasília has inevitably remained Kubitschek's monument. His massive sculpted head adorns the museum of the Plaza of the Three Powers, and his words incised in stone conspicuously embellish the wall surfaces of the monumental buildings. Kubitschek's successors may naturally have found themselves less than enthusiastic in furthering an enterprise so strongly associated with a previous regime.

The pressures for rapid construction which governed the initial phases of Brasília no longer exist, although many of its original engineers, architects, and planners remain associated with the project, and continue in their devoted enthusiasm for the city. The intensity of work has slowed, and the development of Brasília has reverted to a normal Brazilian pace. No one doubts the city will eventually be completed; it is all a matter of time. But in Brazil this can mean quite a lot of time.

In 1966, the Brazilian Foreign Office announced the intention to transfer its entire staff and activities to Brasília, providing impetus for the eventual transfer of all embassies, together with the diplomatic colony. The Itamarity Palace, headquarters of the Foreign Office, designed by Oscar Niemeyer, was officially dedicated in 1967, and new housing for agency staff was begun in the North Axis. The deadline for the move was set for April 1970, ten years after the dedication of Brasília. Foreign embassies were informed that, after 7 September 1972 (Brazilian Independence Day), diplomatic accreditation, immunities, and privileges would be granted only to those diplomats residing in Brasília.

Although in the years following the dedication of Brasília, Niemeyer developed an international practice necessitating intermittent residence outside Brazil, he continued as the designer of major buildings in Brasília and, together with Lúcio Costa, served as a permanent member of an advisory council directing planning policy for the city. Niemeyer's political activities were such that he would inevitably be regarded as a controversial figure by some members of the ruling military establishment. His unquestioned status as a leading architect, however, and his acknowledged responsibility in the creation of Brasília appeared sufficient to insure that his dissociation from the city for political reasons was not immediately attempted.

Niemeyer's work, however, has not always been immune to criticism, as shown in the case of the design for the international airport of Brasília. The initial but unconstructed design was produced by Sergio Bernardes in 1960. This scheme created a circular plan in which most of the terminal would be established underground. Passengers would move from plane stations directly to a subterranean concourse in which all transport connections would be located. The only structure extending aboveground would be a central high-rise hotel with the control tower on top. By organizing airport space vertically on the principle of the aircraft carrier, rather than horizontally, Bernardes sought to minimize distances to be traversed while freeing the ground for aircraft runways and servicing.

The scheme which Niemeyer developed in 1964 contained some of the elements of the Bernardes plan, including a circular terminal from which passengers would move to the aircraft through underground extensions. Expansion of the airport facilities would be made by the construction of additional circular terminals. Niemeyer claimed that the airport, which would provide "the principal entrance to the city," would be designed "fundamentally in the architectural spirit of Brasília."[3]

Niemeyer's plan was initially approved by the prefect and NOVACAP superintendent and by some military officials. The newly appointed director of engineering of the Ministry of Aeronautics, Brigadier General Castro Neves, disapproved, however, and the design soon became a matter of public controversy. It was claimed by opponents that the Niemeyer plan was nonfunctional and not as readily expandable as would be a linear plan. Inevitably, Niemeyer's political stance would become involved, and on one occasion the opposition informed the press, "The place for a Marxist architect is in Moscow."[4]

Niemeyer made energetic efforts to keep the dispute before the public, issuing

3. Niemeyer, *Quase memorias*, pp. 70–72.

4. Ibid., p. 73.

published statements in justification of his design and enlisting considerable professional support. He pointed out that his design had already met with official approval, and that Neves' campaign was not only unjustified, but violated legitimate administrative procedures. Neves continued his influential opposition, however, supervising the creation by his own agency of an alternate plan for the airport, which Lúcio Costa condemned as "unworthy of Brasília,"[5] but which was nevertheless put into effect. To Niemeyer, the opposition to his design indicated "an intolerance against national interests . . . marking a flagrant contrast between the enthusiasm which helped construct the capital, and the unscrupulousness of those who today contrive, deliberately, to discredit it."[6]

During the initial construction of Brasília, it was Niemeyer who had been responsible for the detailing of Costa's plan, and in doing so he had respected Costa's schematic indications for the major elements of the city. The government complex retained the essential character of the Costa scheme, and even the architectural development followed rather closely Costa's initial sketches. While the business and banking centers were redesigned, they maintained Costa's concept of architectural control and standardization of building form. Both areas were developed with a pattern of uniform-height, high-rise slabs.

Although the principal motor artery of the city is the central freeway axis, another through street, parallel to it, was designed to border the apartment superblocks to the west. This street was initially intended to serve as a service road for heavy vehicles, and the site of garages, workshops, and wholesale warehouses. As the city began to develop, however, the central business district was slow in being realized, and retail commerce, restaurants, banks, and theaters began to occupy this street, with the result that it became Brasília's downtown. This street was designated the W3, indicating its location as the third street west of the motor axis (the Eixo Rodoviario). The location along this street gave business establishments proximity to the first residential neighborhoods to be developed, as well as accessibility for automobile traffic. Commercial establishments were built only on the eastern side of the street, with the opposite side given over to single-family houses.

The plan had provided for neighborhood commerce along short streets running at right angles to the main motor axis. As originally planned, these streets would serve as rear service lanes for the shops, which were to be oriented inward toward the pedestrian areas of the superblocks. Because of the long-standing custom for shops to focus on the street, however, most of the shopkeepers have put their main entrances, show windows, and signs facing toward the street.

Notably missing in Brasília are the open-air food markets which characterize Rio and other Brazilian cities but were considered too old-fashioned for the new Brazilian

5. Ibid., p. 79.

6. Ibid., p. 81.

capital. As a result, food distribution within the new city has been restricted to the sterile confines of American-style supermarkets, and only in outlying settlements of the Federal District can one find the delight and colorful confusion of the traditional Brazilian market or *feira*.

The internal planning of the superblocks tended to follow Costa's initial schematic design in which long, narrow building slabs were sited at right angles to one another. In his competition report, Costa had stated, "I feel that the superblocks should not be subdivided, and suggest that not the land, but shares in the land, should be sold. The price of these shares would depend on the location and the height regulations. This would overcome any obstacles standing in the way of present planning and any possible future replanning of the internal arrangement in the superblocks."[7]

It has been the opinion of some planners that in new communities land ownership should be retained by the government to facilitate overall planning and forestall undesirable private development. In the case of Brasília, however, Israel Pinheiro favored the sale of land in order to gain immediate revenue, although the development of such privately owned land would be regulated by the planning office. This policy appears to have been largely successful in terms of maintaining controls.

The system of land sale was developed to permit acquisition of either an entire superblock or a projection of a building within a block. In the former instance, the internal design of the block could be devised by the owner, subject to the approval of the planning office. In the latter case, the superblock would be designed by the planning office, with indications of building sites. The purchaser would buy the right to construct on a designated site within the block. Landscape maintenance would remain the responsibility of the city, financed through a special tax.

In general, although superblocks varied somewhat in layout, all included open landscaped areas and play spaces for children, with primary schools sited within the blocks. Local automobile traffic was generally permitted to enter the superblock interiors, frequently slowed by means of dips. Parking facilities consisted of open, outdoor lots with occasional garage space. Residential densities were controlled by apartment size and also by the number of building—from eleven to eight—within a given superblock.

Costa had recommended in his initial report that, "Street numbering should be started from the intersection of the two axes—using the monumental radial artery as a point of reference to divide the city into two halves, North and South. The superblocks will be given numbers; the buildings inside each, letters; and finally each apartment will be numbered according to the usual practice. For instance, one address might be N–Q3–L apt. 201."[8] The recommendation was generally adhered to, with superblocks given numbers in the hundreds. Along the motor axis, blocks to the

7. Costa competition report, "Pilot Plan for Brasília," as published in *Módulo* 18 (June 1960).
8. Ibid.

west are numbered in the 100s and those to the east in the 200s. Blocks along the W3 carry 300 designations, while the double superblocks on the eastern edge of the residential axis are given 400 numbers. Since the numbering is duplicated on either side of the monumental axis, the directional designation of South or North is an essential part of an address.

The embassy district occupies an area in the South axis between the residential district and the lakefront. Here large individual plots have been made available free to foreign governments.

The peninsulas were developed as a district of large detached houses, with the plotting following in part a system suggested by Costa in his competition report. In his schematic design, private house plots were to be oriented toward bands of common parkland, with access from cul-de-sac streets. The demand for land near Brasília soon became such that the entire perimeter of the lake opposite the city was parceled out in private lots.

Housing throughout the capital was standardized to four basic types. Six-story apartment blocks were to account for 90 percent of the housing in the pilot plan area, with three-story apartments used for lower-cost units. The district opposite the W3 was given over to single-family row houses of either one or two stories. The row houses were designed to focus toward bands of greenery, with the rear of the houses having automobile access from service lanes.

In the early stages of development, housing in Brasília was made available at minimal cost, in order to provide an incentive for employees to transfer to the new city. Costs and methods of allocating housing differed somewhat because of the varied institutional ownership of the housing facilities. Later, however, government housing was made available for tenant purchase at prices generally equivalent to the cost of construction. The disposition of government land was placed under the direction of the Division of Real Estate Operations (Divisão de Operações Imobiliárias), operating under the Economic Department of NOVACAP.

Free grants of land are made to educational, sport, and religious institutions. To obtain such grants, the organization must submit building plans for approval and furnish evidence of the ability to build. Construction must begin within two months of the grant and be completed within two years. The area within the pilot plan which has been given over primarily to institutional use is a district of large plots on the western edge of the residential axis, adjacent to the area of single-family houses. Included in the conditions of grant is a provision that 10 percent of the vacancies in educational institutions and clubs be reserved for the disposition of the prefecture of the Federal District. All other land—whether for housing, commercial, or industrial use—is sold, subject to planning regulations. Generally a purchaser must provide 20 percent of the total price as a down payment and pay the rest in fifty equal, consecutive monthly installments. For government employees required to reside in Brasília, however, one hundred monthly payments are permitted.

Sample prices authorized in 1964 would require, for a typical building projection in a superblock, a payment calculated on the basis of $2.50 per square meter of total projected floor-space, excluding the ground area of the pilotis. The price for a similar projection on one of the double superblocks near the lake would be $5.00 per square meter of floor-space. Typical plots for single-family row houses cost $1,500, while in the suburban lakefront district a house plot would be about $2,000.

Within the central business district, building projections were sold on the basis of $12.50 per square meter of total projected floor-space, while within the banking district, similar plots were sold at the basis of $10 per square meter.[9] For institute-sponsored apartment units, typical purchase prices given for 1965–1967 ranged between $1,956 and $20,000, depending on size and location.[10] In general, prices of housing in Brasília, in terms of unit size, are considerably lower than in Rio. Food, however, costs more, and because of the virtual necessity of owning an automobile, living in the new capital is far from cheap.

The only government land in the urban vicinity which is leased is that used for gas stations, depots for combustible liquids, and some roadside commerce. Large tracts in the rural zone, however, may be leased.

The development of Brasília tends to emphasize a major weakness of the Costa plan—its failure to make long-range provision for the orderly growth and for the planned development of the Federal District. The evolution of the city has been such that, although the pristine order of the pilot plan has been carefully maintained, the surrounding districts have been subject to an accretive patchwork of development. Although the pilot plan residential areas were planned to achieve a suitable relationship of housing, schools, and commercial facilities, large tracts of suburban lots have been laid out without any attempt at creating neighborhoods or at providing these districts with necessary community facilities.

The area between the city and the lake increasingly has been parceled out into separate plots for hotels and private clubs. Although Costa had intended this area for public recreational use, no long-range plan for the development of this area was devised, and it has been subject to piecemeal distribution. In general, the city has little relation to the lake, and there is no comprehensive scheme for shoreline development. The borders of the lake are easily accessible only to the members of clubs which have developed their own shoreline property.

The area west of the city provides a logical area for expansion, and has tended to become a repository for numerous urban functions not provided for in the initial

9. Because of the continual devaluation of the cruzeiro, it is difficult to make accurate conversions of cruzeiros to dollars. The prices given here are calculated on the basis of 1,200 cruzeiros per dollar, the rate for June 1964. The prices were included in a table provided by the administrative council of the Companhia Urbanizadora, and published in *Anuario de Brasília* (Brasília, 1967), pp. 116–17.

10. These prices are based on tables provided by several pension institutes and published in *Anuario de Brasília*, pp. 167–69. Although published in 1967, the prices appear to be based on 1965 figures, and the conversion rate is calculated at the June 1965 rate of Cr $1,850 per dollar.

projection of the city. The western terminus of the government axis is formed by the municipal plaza flanked on either side by the prefecture and the courts. Included in this western district is a center for printing firms, together with the headquarters of the national press. A sizable tract has been allotted to a military enclave, with another large area given over to the national observatory. Near the rail terminal is a district of low-cost housing serving the industrial district along the tracks. Also included in the western district are several hospitals, a prison, a water treatment station, and the municipal garages. Directly adjacent to the edge of the city, large plots have been laid out for institutional use, primarily intended for schools, religious organizations, and clubs. Although this western portion of the city is becoming increasingly urbanized, it lacks any visible scheme of urban order, and has neither a unified and ordered pattern of land use, nor a logical road system.

The plan of Brasília appears today as a peculiar juxtaposition of strict symmetrical design and loose, virtually planless layout. Although the Costa plan may have comprised a satisfactory outline for the initiation of the city, it is clear that the scheme required careful elaboration to provide for the necessary range of urban functions and the orderly use of urban land. At present, an exaggerated sense of respect for the Costa plan seems to have produced a sense of paralysis among the Brasília planning staff. Although the need for long-range detailed planning seems increasingly evident, all decisions since the creation of the pilot plan appear to have been made without any governing discipline or large-scale conception of urban design. The quality which most recommended the Costa plan to the competition jury was its overall monumental unity—its conception of the city as a single coherent entity. Because of the failure to extend such a design sense to later developments, much of the impact of the monumental pilot plan may one day be vitiated, and it is not impossible to imagine the Brasília of a future date appearing as a small island of planned urbanity surrounded by disordered urban sprawl.

As the city develops, certain functional problems may also increase. Costa based his plan on the idea of automobile circulation, and, in its use of freeway and cloverleaf together with the elimination of traffic lights, the scheme was publicized as a solution to urban traffic problems. In fact, the system of traffic circulation lacks both sophistication and thoroughness, and even in the presently incomplete state of settlement, traffic in Brasília does not always flow smoothly.

Although the central motor axis provides extensive road surface, there is ample evidence of the ability of automobiles to render any freeway inadequate. As the city expands, an increasing traffic burden will be placed on this single artery, with the inevitable creation of severe bottlenecks. Connections between the peninsulas and the center of the city are particularly awkward and have already prompted the construction of a bridge connecting the southern peninsula with the main urban area.

The detailed design of the roads themselves has sometimes been slovenly, and the radii of the cloverleaves was calculated so small that motor traffic is slowed almost to a halt in negotiating the turns. Although, as a matter of principle, Brasília was to have no traffic lights, policemen serve to regulate the flow and are especially necessary along the congested W3 street. The W3, which runs parallel to the main motor axis, provides an alternative for through traffic along the residential axis, but the relative narrowness of this street, together with its proximity to housing and commerce, creates frequent interruptions to the traffic.

In Brasília, just as in Le Corbusier's early urban designs, the romantic image of the automobile in motion was not countered by a realistic assessment of what would happen when the vehicle reached its destination. Neither the commercial districts nor the government center were designed with adequate parking facilities, and as these areas continue to develop the situation will worsen.

It was natural that the creation of the new capital should be accompanied by attempts at improvement in civic facilities, and perhaps also natural that not all hopes would be realized. It was initially intended that Brasília would incorporate an improved school system which would replace the half-time operation common to most Brazilian schools. Under the proposed plan, elementary school pupils would attend the usual half-day sessions in their local schools. Then, for the rest of the day, they would attend classes in a School Park, an educational complex with facilities for art, music, athletics, crafts, and other special activities. Each grouping of four superblocks was to have had such a facility. Only one School Park was built, however, before the idea was abandoned as too expensive (fig. 198).

A plan to provide a unified system of hospital construction also failed to be put into effect, and medical facilities remain in an uncoordinated pattern of independent foundation-sponsored establishments.

Another problem arose in development of the University of Brasília. The university, as it was organized during the administration of João Goulart, contained a number of innovations in curriculum and academic structure. Consciously modeled on the open American system rather than the European system of rigidly separated faculties, or schools, students were to spend their first two years in a program of broad general education before deciding on a specialization. An attempt was made to create a close rapport between the students and faculty, who, in contrast to many Brazilian academicians elsewhere, were devoting full-time effort to teaching. The esprit was such that the university attracted an unusually distinguished teaching staff, some of whom left positions abroad to serve in the new program.

Following the military coup of 1964, however, the university, with its experimental focus and openly left-wing activity, was subject to governmental interference. In the fall of 1965, disputes over faculty dismissals produced large-scale resignations and student demonstrations. These were followed in turn by military occupation and a temporary closing of the university.

The Satellites

Among the faults which may be found in the planning and development of Brasília, the aspect which has been most disturbing to many visitors is the social segregation within the Federal District. It may be recalled that Costa, in his competition report, implied that the full range of urban population would be accommodated within the city, and, familiar with the favelas of Rio, he stressed that the "growth of slums, whether on the city outskirts or in the surrounding countryside, should at all costs be prevented. The Development Company should, within the scope of the proposed outline plan, make provision for decent and economical accommodation for the entire population."[11] The achievement of such a goal would have made Brasília unique among Brazilian cities, none of which has successfully solved the problem of housing for the poor.

During the initial period of construction, the founders of Brasília were engaged in an intense and single-minded effort to give the city physical reality within a short time. The city's opponents confidently prophesied its failure, and at the time it was easier to predict that the isolated settlement would never attract population, than to foresee the great numbers of people who would converge on the site.

Brasília had never had a coordinated plan of housing governing the size and types of units to be built and which would relate to a projected population. In general, the constructed housing tended to be middle class, partly because the capital was conceived as a city of white-collar civil servants, but also because its builders were reluctant to lower housing standards in what they envisaged as a model city. Brasília would have failed to achieve its image of an ideal modern environment if it had not embodied a high standard of living. The city's housing thus tended to reflect idealized standards, rather than those common to Brazil. Some of the dwellings initially conceived as low cost were sufficiently commodious to be claimed immediately by people of the professional ranks.

Although some relatively low priced units, in the form of three-story apartments, were constructed within the city, the volume was small and by no means sufficient to accommodate the number of people needing such housing. The growing demand for land in Brasília tended to keep property values high in and around the city, and in this competitive situation, it was inevitable that the poor would be the losers.

When Kubitschek made his first inspection of work camps in November 1956, there were a total of 232 workers on the site. By January 1957 the number had risen to 2,500 and continued increasing rapidly. By 1959 the resident population of the Federal District was given as 64,314. Of these, 28,020 were living in work camps on the city site, 11,565 were in Cidade Livre, and 6,196 in another temporary settlement. Outlying towns contained 6,277 while 12,256 resided in the rural zone.

11. "Pilot Plan for Brasília."

Initially obsessed with urgent problems of construction, planners tended to regard the large working-class populace as a temporary phenomenon. Only gradually, as the city achieved realization, did they recognize that the large numbers of workers drawn to the Federal District were not likely to leave and would require permanent accommodation. In order to retain the existing character of Brasília, it was decided to create housing for low-income people through the establishment of outlying so-called satellite towns (fig. 154). The siting of these communities related not to any overall plan for the expansion of the Brasília pilot plan area, but to the rural development of the Federal District.

In an effort to create local sources of food supply, the Federal District had been planned with a series of rural centers (Núcleos Rurais), each consisting of a group of small family farms ranging from 60 to 150 acres in size. These farms, leased on a homestead system, were plotted as narrow strips extending from stream beds. Land laid out in this manner gave each farm part of the narrow forest belt lying on the valley bottoms and a larger area extending up the slope. Since it was projected that these rural settlements would eventually acquire small town centers for local commerce, schools, and cooperatives, planners considered it convenient to expand the rural centers into satellite towns for low-cost housing. For this reason, the Brasília satellites are frequently surrounded by farmsteads.

The town of Taguatinga was founded in 1958, with Sobradinho and Gama following in 1960. In 1961 Cidade Livre, which had originally been intended as a temporary settlement, was made into a permanent satellite town and rechristened Núcleo Bandierante (Pioneer Center). Planaltina, the oldest existing town in the Federal District, founded around 1859, was declared a satellite in 1967. Among the more recent satellites are Guará, established in 1969, and Jardim. In addition, the existing settlements of Paranoá and Brazlândia have been given satellite status.

The administration of the satellites was established during the 1964 governmental reorganization in which the Federal District was divided into eight regions. Brasília and Núcleo Bandierante are contained within one region, while the other satellite towns constitute the remaining seven regions.

The conception of a satellite grouping of communities derives from Ebenezer Howard's Garden City theory, in which the system would comprise a group of economically self-sufficient towns which might depend on a larger center for certain services. The Brasília satellites, however, are not true satellites, but essentially dormitory towns for workers in Brasília, and most of the residents are subjected to an inconvenient and expensive regimen of bus commuting. Neither Costa nor Niemeyer wished to associate himself with the design of the satellite towns, plans of which were produced by the NOVACAP staff.

The largest of the satellites is Taguatinga (figs. 159–62), occupying an area of 16 square kilometers and sited at a distance of 25 kilometers from Brasília. The first settlers were 4,000 people who had been removed in 1958 from favela settlements within the urban area of Brasília; by 1970 the population had reached 109,584. The plan of Taguatinga has been expanded from time to time to accommodate new residential plots. The street layout consists of narrow blocks containing small building plots, with commerce primarily concentrated in small shops bordering a central avenue.

Sobradinho (figs. 165, 166), located 22 kilometers from Brasília along the Brasília-Forteleza highway, had a population in 1970 of 42,782. The plan developed for this satellite incorporates a neighborhood-unit system. Within the superblocks, narrow rows of house plots are separated alternately by access roads and park strips. Commercial and community facilities are to be distributed throughout the neighborhoods.

The town of Gama, situated 38 kilometers southeast of Brasília, had a population in 1970 of 75,947. The plan of the town is based on a series of rectangular and hexagonal sectors within which communal facilities are distributed on a neighborhood basis. The planning provided for the initial development of the town to take place on the periphery, with central open tracts left for future development, including a large industrial area. Gama has been termed the "largest proletarian center"[12] of the Federal District, with its population drawn largely from former favelados.

While the plans of the satellites indicate what would appear an ample distribution of community facilities, in terms of actual development, urban amenities in these towns are decidedly inferior to those provided the inhabitants of Brasília. Schools are few, and medical facilities scarce, parks are absent, streets are generally unpaved, and utilities are unreliable and unevenly distributed. While some small commerce exists in the satellites, it is far more limited than the plans show, and although some districts have been designated for industry, employment opportunities in these settlements are few.

By and large, the satellites present the appearance of ordinary, unprosperous country towns, with housing ranging from wooden shacks to relatively comfortable brick bungalows. Because urban amenities are so primitive, however, and so many of the houses little more than huts, some visitors tend to confuse the satellites with favelas. Although the satellites were initially created for small private householders, government agencies have begun constructing housing for their employees in these towns. Sobradinho, for example, contains housing projects for employees of NOVACAP and the Federal Savings Bank of Brazil (Caixa Econômica).

It may be recalled that the initial intention with regard to Cidade Livre was that its population would be moved into Brasília when the city was completed, and the shack town would be destroyed. In 1960, a partial effort was made to accomplish such

12. Instituto Brasileiro de Geografia et Estatística (IBGE), *Brasília* (Coleção de Monografias, no. 325, 2nd ed.), p. 75.

a move, and low-cost plots were made available in the section of the North Axis west of the W3. Wooden construction was permitted, with the understanding that the owners would eventually replace such structures with brick. However, the number of these lots made available was not sufficient to provide for all the inhabitants of Cidade Livre, nor, it later proved, were all those who moved to the North Zone of Brasília able to finance the expensive brick construction required by regulations. This part of Brasília remains partially unsettled and partially built in wooden buildings, with occasional brick structures (figs. 194, 195). Because of the slow pace of development in the North Axis, the inhabitants of this district seem to have been left temporarily undisturbed. As pressures on land use increase, however, it is likely that a forced clearance of the wooden building will be effected.

In spite of the amount of unbuilt land it contains, Brasília has become virtually the only city in Brazil that appears largely free of internal favelas. The many squatter districts that developed during the initial period of construction were removed, and an energetic program of control serves to eliminate promptly any new illegal settlers, forcing them into the outlying areas.

When Cidade Livre was reorganized as the satellite Núcleo Bandierante, it received a town plan of regular house blocks and streets, retaining the essential outlines already established, but incorporating new school sites, shopping areas, and a town center indicating a plaza, two cinemas, an auditorium, and an open-air theater. In terms of observable change, however, the achievement of satellite status has had relatively little effect on this settlement. Although inhabitants now have permanent ownership of their plots, most of the buildings are still small wooden shacks indistinguishable from nearby favela houses. Shopping facilities still consist of small booths and outdoor market stalls, and although one street is paved and a school has been built, the community facilities indicated on the plan are yet unrealized (figs. 155–58).

Because Planaltina was already an existing town at the time it was designated a satellite, planners had to take into account the problem of preservation. Planaltina had played host to both the Cruls and Coelho commissions during their search for a capital site and had received the symbolic cornerstone of the new city from President Epitacio Pessôa in 1922. Although no direct government action followed this event, the town had experienced a modest boom in which electricity was installed and land values increased. Nevertheless, Planaltina had remained an essentially quiet and sleepy village, in many ways resembling a town of the colonial period (fig. 167).

In developing Planaltina, it was considered desirable to maintain the traditional qualities of the existing town, with its pleasant palm-shaded plaza and tile-roofed, pastel-tinted houses. A scheme for urban extension was devised by the NOVACAP planner Paulo Magalães, beginning in 1964, in which the existing town would be preserved in its visual aspects while receiving street paving and upgraded utilities. A new settlement would be constructed, slightly separated from the old town. Between the two areas would be a common civic center containing secondary schools, municipal offices, and shopping and entertainment facilities, providing a place of meeting for the two communities.

Also included in Planaltina would be a settlement for recent migrants to the urban area—people still rural in habits and without the financial resources for urban housing. For this area, Magalães developed an experimental transitional house which, in part, could be built by the occupant (fig. 168). The method of construction involved the casting of panels using cement, sand, and a local vegetable fiber or bamboo for reinforcing. Such houses, although intended as temporary, could last, it was estimated, as long as twenty years. In addition to its cheapness and relative ease of fabrication, this type of construction bore some resemblances to a frequently used traditional local building technique, similar to wattle and daub. It employs a light basket frame of flexible wooden members, which is packed with mud, then plastered and painted. Many of the existing houses of Planaltina have been built by this method.

Although land costs in the satellites are low compared with Brasília, there are many people for whom lots even in these towns are prohibitively expensive. In order to meet the need for minimal-cost housing, the Federal District pursues a program of subsidized housing similar to that operated by COHAB in Guanabara. The agency which organizes this program in the Brasília area is SHIS (Sociedade de Habitações de Interêsse Social). The work of this agency, organized in 1962, has centered primarily on the construction of tracts of small brick houses designed for enlargement by purchasers (figs. 163, 164). By 1967, SHIS was reported to have either completed or to be in the process of completing 1,620 houses in Taguatinga, 1,332 in Gama, and 600 in Sobradinho, in addition to 168 low-cost apartment units in the North Zone of Brasília. Contemplated was additional apartment housing for Brasília and a large development including both houses and apartments near the industrial district of the city.

Although the houses, like those constructed by COHAB in Rio, are extremely small, especially for the sizable families of the poor, the shortage of housing produces a reported average of five applicants for each unit. Selection of purchasers is made on the basis of number of dependents, amount of time employed in Brasília, and evidence of ability to make payments. An official indicated that houses tend to be granted to those applicants "with the saddest story to tell."[13] The price of a SHIS house in 1967 averaged $855, which could be met through payments over a period of fifteen years. Low-cost apartments in the North Axis of Brasília were priced at $900 for a two-bedroom unit, and $1,260 for a three-bedroom apartment, to be paid in five installments.[14]

The rate of growth for the satellites has been rapid, and the combined population of these outlying districts has tended to exceed that of Brasília itself. In 1964, the

13. E. d'Almeida Vitor, *A SHIS e o problema habitacional de Brasília* (Brasília, 1967).
14. Prices provided in Vitor, *SHIS*. Conversion based on the rate of $ Cr 2,200 per dollar.

population of the Federal District was estimated as 268,315, of which 89,231 inhabited the Pilot Plan area. By 1970, ten years after the founding of the new capital, the population of the Federal District had reached 538,351. Of this number, 236,477 were living in the Pilot Plan area, and the remainder occupied the satellite communities.[15]

The division of social classes between Brasília and its satellites reflects a pattern of class distinction characteristic of Brazilian communities. In Rio and many other Brazilian cities, the urban center tends to be occupied by the upper classes, while the suburbs are generally given over to low-income groups, a settlement pattern the reverse of many North American cities. The burden of commuting in Brazil is thus thrust on the people least able to afford it. Whatever inconveniences middle-class commuters in the United States may suffer are minimal compared with the daily hardships of lower-class Brazilians subjected to lengthy and costly journeys in slow, antiquated, dangerously overcrowded, and inconveniently scheduled buses and trains. In Brasília, satellites continue to be projected, even though transport facilities are not yet adequate to serve them.

The physical segregation of rich and poor in Brasília, although embodying an overall pattern of dwelling common to other cities, represents a much more clear-cut and thoroughgoing separation than is seen elsewhere. In Rio, by contrast, there is a wider range of income and social class within the central city. The squatter favelas, moreover, place colonies of the very poorest inhabitants cheek by jowl with some of the most expensive housing. Although this physical juxtaposition does not imply social mixture, the poor of Rio are at least highly visible and difficult to ignore.

Although the exclusion of the poor continues to impress some as a highly discordant element in a city which serves as a focus of Brazilian national pride, to the planners of Brasília, it apparently seemed an inevitable reflection of prevailing social conditions. Even to Oscar Niemeyer, social segregation seemed understandable within the circumstances of Brasília. Writing a memoir of his experiences in 1960, he noted:

> We were constrained by the conviction that it would be unfeasible to insure the workers the standard of living assigned them by the Pilot Plan, which situated them, as would have been only fair, within the collective housing areas so as to allow their children to grow up with the other children of Brasília in a friendly, impartial association . . . We realized to our regret that the social con-

15. Information on the 1964 population is obtained from IBGE, *Brasília,* monograph no. 325 (Rio de Janeiro, 1966), pp. 11–12. The satellite populations are given as follows: Taguatinga, 68,947; Gama, 27,524; Núcleo Bandierante, 22,772; Sobradinho, 19,205. The remainder of the Federal District population was distributed throughout the rural zone and a few in a few small settlements. Population figures for 1970 are obtained from IBGE *Sinopse preliminar do censo demográfico* (Rio de Janeiro, July 1971), p. 244. The 1970 satellite populations are as follows: Guará, 24,392; Núcleo Bandierante, 11,133; Gama, 75,947; Taguatinga, 109,584; Brazlândia, 11,521; Sobradinho, 42,782; Planaltina, 21,932; Paranoá, 2,237; Jardim, 2,346.

ditions in force conflicted at this point with the spirit of the Pilot Plan, creating problems it was impossible to solve on the drawing board and even demanding—as some of the more ingenuous suggested—a social architecture that would lead us nowhere without a socialist basis.

Reiterating his view that architects should seek social change by action outside, rather than within the profession, he concluded, "Once again it was brought home to us that all we could do was to support the progressive movements that envisage a better and a happier world."[16]

Although Niemeyer seemed to express a measure of resignation regarding the social pattern of Brasília, he assumed, at a later date, a more disapproving attitude. On the occasion of his being awarded the Lenin Peace Prize in 1963, Niemeyer addressed a meeting of celebration held at the University of Brasília by calling attention to the social inequalities of the city.

What has been done for our brothers, the workers who aided in its construction? Who, like us, even more than us, suffered for it, and struggled humbly for it? . . . This is what I ask the deputies and senators, the men of government who meet to discuss Brasília. And I remind them . . . that these comrades have been a long time in the capital they have constructed, and the houses that they built, the schools, nurseries, clubs and palaces, all of which they created, in truth have no relation to them. . . . And consider conditions in the satellite towns to which they are relegated; what is it like in these incredible dormitory towns, this heap of favelas, where the poor are in a perpetual cry of revolt? But I remind you also that our comrades are tired of this abandonment which so abases them, conscious that the hour will come to control their own destiny, . . . And they will honestly show how the plan of Lúcio Costa has been distorted. How the residential superblocks, closed to those most needy, were destined for all the inhabitants of Brasília, . . . They will show—if they wish—how a discriminatory spirit dominates all the Federal District, . . . And they may finally ask, what is going to be done to correct such injustice.[17]

The quality of life which Brasília will eventually possess is difficult to predict at present. Superficially, compared with Rio, with its lively commercial activity, its abundant recreational facilities, its dramatic setting, and ebullient populace, Brasília will doubtless for a long time strike many as antiseptic and dull. Administrative capitals have seldom been among the most exhilarating of cities, and such planned bureaucratic centers as Canberra, New Delhi, and Washington, D. C., have often been derided for their lack of stimulation.

During the initial years of development, however, Brasília was anything but dull. Imbued with the excitement of the frontier, its citizens were buoyed up through par-

16. Niemeyer, "My Brasília Experience," p. 26.

17. Niemeyer, *Quase memorias,* pp. 28–29.

ticipation in a common adventure. A visitor to the city in 1959 observed, "I have never seen happier people—I mean naturally happy. They seem to have a definite purpose."[18] For the builders, the city represented a challenge, and the architects, engineers, planners, and construction workers viewing the visible progress of the city can still find satisfaction in a positive achievement. Even today, some of the old excitement remains; new buildings rise, there are more people, and every day Brasília achieves more complete realization. For those who came in the beginning and have remained, to have participated in the creation of Brasília can provide the sense of a lifetime well spent.

It had been hoped at one time that a similar spirit might underly the whole government operation in Brasília, and that the giant, torpid bureaucracy which had hampered so much government effort in Rio, would in the new capital be replaced by a small, efficient, hard-working core of civil servants dedicated to national welfare. The more the government becomes centered in Brasília, however, the more evident it becomes that the new capital will create no administrative miracles. Offices in Brasília, as in Rio, tend to operate only part-time, and in the new soil, the old inefficiency flowers. Brasília is still Brazil, and those anticipating a drastic alteration in the pace of bureaucratic activity will inevitably be disappointed.

An American journalist in Brasília observed in 1967 that, "The city is not only extraordinarily homogeneous in respect of class and income; it is also, as befits 'the most modern city in the world,' a city of young people."[19] Older government employees, with seniority in their positions, and with homes firmly established in Rio, have naturally been less amenable to moving than have younger workers, for whom the transfer usually meant faster promotions and also housing superior to what they could afford in Rio. It was opined that "Brasília is, above all, a family town . . . overwhelmingly 'young married.' "[20] The superblocks, with their primary schools, lawns, and playgrounds seem clearly intended for the raising of small children, and the residential portions of the city exhibit much the same atmosphere as many North American suburbs.

In time to come, Brasília will doubtless provide tempting ground for social investigation. There is already a study by José Pastore published as *Brasília: a cidade e o homem,* which is based on a 1966 survey of 653 male householders residing in both the pilot plan and satellite areas. Pastore was concerned with illuminating the factors determining satisfaction and dissatisfaction experienced by immigrants to the new capital. The study indicated generally favorable reactions, among all social strata, to life in Brasília, although the reasons varied. It was noted that, "in general, migrants of high status, living in the most developed sectors of Brasília, tend to present a basis for response the opposite to that of the inhabitants of the satellite towns, poorer and

18. Ludwig Bemelmans, "Brasília: the Capital and the Cardiogram," *Holiday* 25 (March 1959): 52.
19. Gladys Delmas, "Brasília Comes of Age," *The Reporter* 36 (23 February 1967): 32.
20. Ibid.

of relatively inferior status. For the migrants of high status, non-material realizations seem more important than material gain in determining their level of satisfaction in Brasília. For the residents of the satellite towns, on the other hand, conditions of work and economic stability form the most important variables in explaining satisfaction."[21]

While the provision of urban amenity in the pilot plan area was notably superior to that in the satellites, it was observed that "individuals of the highest status, with the best standard of living and education, inhabiting sectors containing a relatively large number of institutional facilities, feel themselves more deprived than people of the lowest status, inhabiting the poorest areas."[22] To those accustomed to the variety and comfort of upper-class living in Rio and São Paulo, Brasília presented a Spartan contrast, while to poorer immigrants, even the minimal facilities of the satellites often embodied an improvement over their previous existence. Although residents of the pilot plan area complained of a lack of leisure facilities and poor schools, the relatively inferior provisions for leisure and education in the satellites were often cited as a source of satisfaction.

Many of the satellite dwellers expressed a distaste for the urban ambient of the pilot plan area, and Pastore reported such comments as, "It is horrible to live in a place which on weekends reminds you of the emptiness of outer space," and "a city without corners is good for traffic but bad for people." One respondent declared, "I find myself lost in the middle of those big spaces."[23] The inhabitants of the pilot plan area were often ambivalent in their reactions to Brasília, and one resident reported, "My wife and I don't know what we want in life anymore: we are anxious to go to Rio or São Paulo, but when we get there, we want nothing else but to return to Brasília." Included in the comments of those interviewed were such statements as, "We deeply miss the beaches we left behind us, but at the same time, we can't dispense with the calm life which Brasília affords us." "The schools are horrible here, but the climate is excellent for our children." "The city is sad, but life is serene."[24]

While the residents of the satellites found satisfaction in material improvement, the more affluent citizens of the pilot plan area seemed to find their greatest satisfaction in the intangible aspects of professional life. Pastore reported that, "We frequently observed individuals who felt themselves compensated for the change simply by feeling themselves responsible for important decisions in the federal government; others obtain satisfaction merely by being nearer to 'key men.' "[25]

Socially as well as physically, Brasília is a city of fundamentals. It offers a place to work, a place to raise a family, and a street by which to get from one to the other. The complexities, it is assumed, will come in their own time.

21. José Pastore, *Brasília: a cidade e o homem* (São Paulo, 1969), pp. 117–18.

22. Ibid., p. 118.

23. Ibid., p. 49.

24. Ibid., p. 122.

25. Ibid.

13. THE ARCHITECTURE OF BRASÍLIA

Brasília became known to the world primarily as an architectural image. Comprehensively embodying one of the major trends in postwar design, the city could initially have been viewed as the apotheosis of the glass box, with the symmetrical clarity of the plan reflected in a pristine regimentation of building form. Because of the speed with which the city was designed, its building pattern still tends to reflect a single moment in the history of architecture.

In its adherence to many of the visual qualities of the International Style, Brasília maintained characteristics commonly associated with Brazilian modern architecture. What was notably uncharacteristic of Brazil, however, was the architectural control of the city. In Brasília, the freely expressive variety of forms typical of Brazilian design was replaced by strict discipline. Brasília had been conceived as a unified design, and the plan of the city was inextricably bound to its architectural realization. In Brasília, there were to be no architectural accidents. Rather, although it avoids extremes of bad taste, the ambient is bland and, in the view of some, cold and monotonous. Defending the maintenance of aesthetic controls in Brasília, Oscar Niemeyer once observed:

> I am not in accord with a permanent censorship in any city, but anyone who is familiar with the level of Brazilian architecture, especially its incomprehensible capacity for debasement, will understand and accept the purpose which it served in the new capital as an educative and disciplinary measure to impede the aberrations which are lamentably spread all over the country under the pretext of revolutionary or modern architecture. I remember, for example, a project for a church which we rejected in Brasília, representing an enormous fish, and also an apartment house which adopted the columns of the Alvorada Palace (a project which has established an unfortunate precedent for imitation) in a way im-

> proper and ridiculous in its reference to the architecture of the government buildings. It is evident that in our urban sectors a certain restriction is indispensable in order to maintain the equilibrium and harmony required by the master plan. One cannot accept that a new planned city should present the same mistakes, the same urbanistic and architectural confusion as existing cities, which expand without control, where each building is treated as an isolated building, without relation to those surrounding it, or to the harmony of the group, which a conscientious architect would know how to preserve.[1]

Throughout Brasília, building has been dominated by a few standardized types. A single design sufficed for all of the government ministries bordering the central mall. Office buildings in the central business district were designed within a prescribed envelope of controlled height and orientation. Neighborhood shops adhere to a uniform two-story scheme, while those along the W3 maintain a consistent three-story pattern. The designs of individual private buildings such as clubs, schools, churches, and even foreign embassies are subject to regulation and approval by the planning agency.

Housing

The layouts of the neighborhood superblocks have generally tended to follow Lúcio Costa's initial projections, with rectilinear apartment slabs placed at right angles to one another. The buildings, adhering to a six-story height limitation, combined with the requirement of an open ground level, resemble, because of their exposed ground floor columns, the prototypical apartments of Le Corbusier's early visionary schemes.

The six-story apartments were intended to provide the predominant housing of the city, with additional housing types consisting of low-income, three-story apartments, and row houses of one or two stories. Individually designed detached houses were to be restricted to the peninsulas and border areas of the lake, which provided the upper-class residential districts (figs. 169–78, 183–92).

Although Oscar Niemeyer was primarily engaged in overall supervision of construction in Brasília and in the design of major buildings, he also produced a few housing designs for the city. He developed, for the National Savings Bank (Caixa Econômica), a two-story row house employing a crisp geometric outline and white plastered surface. The glass of the living room was partially shaded by an overhanging upper floor, while the second-floor windows carried sliding shutters as a sun protection. The device of the overhanging second story was subsequently adapted in many of the row house designs.

Niemeyer also designed a small single-story row house for the Foundation of

1. Oscar Niemeyer, quoted in *Inquérito Nacional de Arquitetura* (Belo Horizonte, 1963), pp. 115–16.

People's Housing (Fundação da Casa Popular), in which a screen of horizontal wooden slats was used to shield the bedroom windows on the main façade. It may be recalled that all row houses in Brasília were designed to face linear parkbands, with front access from pedestrian walkways. The rear of the houses was to be oriented toward service lanes upon which the garages and maids' rooms would face. In addition to the prototypical row houses, Niemeyer designed a three-story, low-cost apartment house for the Foundation of People's Housing, a rather spartan block without pilotis, and a group of six-story apartments sponsored by the Pension Institute for Bank Employees (IAPB).

The housing pattern of Brasília was developed to provide for separate groupings of identical housing types, rather than for building mixtures. An exception to this prevailing pattern occurred, however, in an enclave developed by the Bank of Brazil for its own employees. To achieve planning control, the bank purchased five blocks in the South Zone in the district set aside for row houses. Here, architects Ney Fontes Gonçalves and João Henrique Rocha created a grouping of single-story row houses and apartment blocks of two stories above the pilotis. Because of the relatively low height of the apartment units, the mixture of houses and apartments was essentially harmonious, and an overall sensitivity of design with regard to both architecture and landscaping made this ensemble one of the most pleasing housing projects in Brasília.

In general, interior layouts for both houses and apartments throughout Brasília were relatively conventional, and implied no alterations in living pattern. Middle-class housing in Brazil is similar to that in Europe and the United States, except that, as servants are still commonplace in Latin America, accommodation for them is always included. Separate service circulation of both stairways and elevators is considered essential, and each apartment has its own service area containing the kitchen, servants' rooms, and a service balcony where washing is done and laundry hung to dry.

The open placement of apartment blocks in Brasília, with all façades equally exposed to view, created a problem of concealment for the service areas. In most Brazilian cities, where buildings front on the street, the service balconies open onto concealed interior courts, and have seldom been of architectural concern. In Brasília, however, the architects were faced with the task of making the necessary service areas visually unobtrusive. The problem was generally solved by giving each apartment block in Brasília what might be termed an "open" and a "closed" façade. On one side the building would carry the main living areas often illuminated by large windows. The other side would be primarily given over to the service areas with their balconies shielded by various screening devices. Panels of open brickwork or concrete screens were frequently used for this purpose. Because of the abundant use of glass in the walls of the living areas, it was suggested that buildings be placed so that the apartment windows overlook the service façade of the next building, to prevent occupants from looking directly into their neighbors' windows. However, this has not been adhered to consistently.

Those who had hoped to find in Brasília some evidence of a new democratic way of living were highly disappointed to find there the traditional social inequalities. A Brazilian sociologist reported a criticism that the servants' rooms in the new capital were "little better than prison cells."[2] Such rooms were, however, no worse than servants' quarters elsewhere in Brazil, where maids' rooms are usually minimal, often windowless, and with little furnishing beyond a narrow cot. It had been clear from the beginning that, although Brasília might provide improvements in living standards for some, the city as a whole embodied no social revolution.

The climate of Brasília seems to have had little or no influence on the design of housing or of other building types within the city. This may be partially because, compared with many other places in Brazil, the new capital has an undemanding climate. There is relatively little temperature variation throughout the year; the sun is frequently hot, but the air is dry and breezy, and the nights are usually cool. Presented with no extraordinary challenges, the architects of Brasília appear to have been largely unconcerned with climatic adaptation. The major problem in this regard has been the internal heat and glare inevitably accompanying the extensive use of glass. No apparent efforts have been made within the city to orient buildings with regard to sun, and many of the ubiquitous glass façades receive massive doses of sunlight throughout the day. On some buildings, external sunbreakers have been employed, but in most, only curtains and blinds are available to control the penetration of the sun. In addition to the failure to consider the effects of sunlight, many buildings in Brasília are woefully lacking in natural ventilation, a circumstance which would be excusable if there were adequate air conditioning. This is used sparingly, however, and only in a few major buildings.

Although the mildness of the climate might encourage a degree of outdoor living, housing in Brasília generally does not afford private open space. In the apartment blocks, building regulations maintain a uniform contour by prohibiting balconies or other projections beyond the building line. The heavily screened, inset service balconies thus provide the only apartment space open to the air. The design of row housing provides for orientation toward common greenery but fails to include private gardens or patios, except for small service courts at the rear.

Although the predominant architectural image of Brasília is one of relative uniformity, the expansion of the city into the North Axis has produced variations in superblock design and building treatment. Some of Brasília's more recent housing designs have abandoned the use of extensive glass façades for an increased employ-

2. Gilberto Freyre, "A Brazilian's Critique of Brasília," *The Reporter* 22 (31 March 1960): 32.

ment of brick and concrete and a more restricted pattern of fenestration (figs. 179, 180). A major departure from what had been the prevailing style of Brasília apartments became visible in the housing for Foreign Office employees begun in 1966 (figs. 181, 182). The customary superblock layout of narrow slabs was replaced by an ensemble which included both slabs and six-story point blocks. The external design reflected not the International Style aesthetic of smooth finishes, but another trend in contemporary design, employing a surface treatment of exposed concrete, with windows shielded on the exterior by narrowly spaced vertical concrete sunbreakers. Although the creation of Brasília was dominated by a single architectural vision, it is reasonable to assume that, as the city grows, it will, like other cities, reflect a degree of evolution in building style.

By and large, the capital's architecture reveals neither technical nor formal innovations. The conditions under which the city was constructed, including extreme pressures of time and a relatively untrained labor force, necessitated the use of generally conventional methods of building. Much of the construction of apartments and offices consisted of poured-in-place concrete structural framing with brick infilling panels, although limited use of precast concrete elements was to be found in some apartment construction. Surface finishes, for the most part, were those common elsewhere in Brazil, consisting frequently of painted plaster surfaces and tile.

In view of the scale of the Brasília project, however, it was natural to see the city as a logical site for industrialized methods. With this in mind, Oscar Niemeyer projected some experimental schemes for prefabricated housing in Brasília. Included was a design for a seven-story apartment block of prefabricated columns, wall panels, and 26 by 20 foot floor slabs. The building was to be organized with the fifth floor used as a nursery. Access to apartments would be by staircases leading to each pair of apartments, "thus doing away with the corridors that are so destructive of intimacy."[3] An external freestanding elevator would provide access to the fifth floor so that it would not be necessary for tenants to climb more than two flights of stairs.

Like many modern architects, Niemeyer was convinced that modern housing problems could only be met through apartments, stressing that: "Collective housing is the solution of modern times and arises inevitably therefrom. For Brasília, it is a necessity for major reasons, inasmuch as the very planning of the city is based upon collective housing."[4] He felt, however, that in the satellite towns, a mixed solution would be possible and attempted to develop a low-cost prefabricated unit which would be adaptable to use both as a single-family house and as part of an apartment complex. This would take the form of a single boxlike unit which could be placed on the ground to serve as a small house, or be hoisted by a crane to compose apartment build-

3. Niemeyer, "Habitaçao pre-fabricada em Brasília," *Módulo* 27 (March 1962): 28.
4. Ibid., p. 35.

ings of two, three, or four floors. In developing the apartment scheme, Niemeyer projected an assemblage of units in which each apartment would have next to it an open space usable as a private terrace.

Except for housing, the only buildings placed directly within the residential superblocks of Brasília are elementary schools and kindergartens. These buildings are generally of one story and are usually unobtrusively scaled. Most embody interior courtyards including covered outdoor play spaces (figs. 196, 197).

Adjacent to the superblocks are the neighborhood shopping streets (figs. 199–201). The shops are designed in architecturally unified rows, differing slightly from street to street, but all following a similar two-story scheme with the flat roof plane extending to provide a shaded walkway. Plot sizes were designed to provide a minimum building unit 11½ feet wide and 33 feet deep, although owners of large establishments could acquire more than one plot. Many shops have a double façade, with entrances and show windows on both the pedestrian walkways of the superblocks and on the street side. (It may be recalled that initially the street was to have functioned essentially as a service lane, with the main orientation toward the pedestrian ways of the superblocks.)

The neighborhood shopping streets were not designed as through arteries, and they are periodically extended on axis, not by roadway, but by bands of parkland intended to contain community facilities such as churches, clubs, sport facilities, and the like. Terminating a shopping street and set within such a parkband is the first church built within the pilot plan area of Brasília, the Chapel of Our Lady of Fatima by Oscar Niemeyer. Although small, this church is visually distinguished by a highly sculptural form. The plan is horseshoe shaped, with the entrance at the narrow end, and the exterior surface is faced with blue and white ceramic tiles. Over this a heavy, swooping, tentlike, triangular concrete roof extends well beyond the body of the chapel to be met at its outer corners by tapering concrete supports. In its use of unconventional forms and its employment of the traditional device of tiles, this chapel is somewhat reminiscent of the equally unorthodox church Niemeyer had designed previously for Pampulha.

Although Niemeyer favored architectural controls as a means of disciplining the excesses of other achitects working in Brasília, he awarded himself complete creative freedom in those structures which he designed.

The Commercial Center

Inherent in the architectural control of Brasília was the maintenance of a visual hierarchy between the monumental architecture and the more utilitarian buildings of the city. The housing was disciplined in form so that, although it covered a large area, it would still be visually subordinate to the center of the city.

In modern cities, it is frequently the commercial buildings which, through their size and assertiveness, often tend to achieve visual dominance. Even though Brasília was conceived as a government city, the plan acknowledged the necessity for an extensive commercial district of high-rise building. The commercial center was kept separate from the monumentally scaled government complex, however, so that each could maintain a distinct character. Although the commercial buildings would be greater in scale than many of the government office buildings, their controlled placement and design would, it was anticipated, render them noncompetitive with the government center (fig. 202).

As initially projected by Costa, the business, hotel, and banking centers would be sited adjacent to the intersection of the major urban axes; the commercial and hotel district would be symmetrically disposed on either side of the government axis to the west of the interchange and the banking center similarly disposed to the east. In Costa's competition scheme, the banking district had been based on a grouping of "three high-rise blocks and four lower ones, all interconnected by a wide street-level extension which will provide covered communication and ample space for branches of banks, business firms, restaurants etc."[5] The central business district would contain a single row of buildings followed by one larger building, all of uniform height and connected at ground level by a low-rise structure containing shops and arcades.

As replanned by Oscar Niemeyer, both of these areas were expanded and modified somewhat. Because of the lay of the land, which sloped away from the level of the motor axis, the banking center was designed with a plaza level even with the road, but raised above the surrounding terrain. The area below the plaza was given over to service functions, such as power plants, security areas for banks, and underground parking. Although the buildings of the district are similar in that they are all rectilinear slabs, they differ somewhat in surface treatment and height. Centrally sited and dominating the complex is the Bank of Brazil, a twenty-four-story building faced with bright blue panels. The lobby floor extends beyond the building line, its roof providing an extensive overhanging shelter at plaza level. The adjacent twenty-story buildings provide variations on the theme of the curtain wall. The Seguradoras Building, containing headquarters for insurance organizations, exhibits a lightly framed glass façade, while the National Bank for Economic Development in Brazil employs a surface of glass and light infilling panels framed with slender metal mullions. The Credit Bank of the Amazon attempts to shield its glass surface areas with a system of movable external shades of green slats (figs. 203–07, 237).

The central business district, across the motor axis, although similar architecturally, does not exhibit the same spacious layout and somewhat monumental siting as the banking center. The commercial buildings, fifteen stories in height, are closely

5. "Pilot Plan for Brasília," *Módulo* 18 (June 1960).

sited in a partial row formation. As in the banking center, construction employs concrete framing, with external wall surfaces of light infilling, including extensive use of glass. Although the commercial district bordering the main motor axis is restricted to uniform high-rise building, smaller buildings of seven to eight stories are permitted in the portion of the district extending toward the W3 street (figs. 208–11).

Adjacent to the business district is the hotel center which stretches along the government axis to the west. In order to provide for a wide range of accommodation, a variety of building types was included, ranging from such luxury establishments as the twelve-story Hotel National to more modest two-story hotels along the W3.

One of the earliest buildings of Brasília was the Brasília Palace Hotel designed by Oscar Niemeyer in 1956 and completed in 1958. This hotel was begun before the city plan was made and bears no relation to the existing hotel district. It was sited near the lakefront, in the general vicinity of the Presidential Palace. The hotel consists of a slab 667 feet long and 40 feet wide supported on exposed steel columns. The plan was simple, with the entrance at the center of the building, and rooms placed on the east accessible from corridors running the length of the west side. The east façade was walled in glass, and the west side with a concrete screen perforated by numerous small, round glass windows. Auxiliary functions were housed in ground floor extensions.

As the Brasília Palace Hotel was one of the first buildings of Brasília, it served as an introduction to the architecture of the new city, and received considerable critical comment from some of Brasília's early visitors. The lobby areas were confusing, Niemeyer's favored stairways without railings were deemed hazardous, sound insulation seemed lacking, and one visitor trudging the apparently endless hallway noted that, "the sun that shone through the round peepholes had warmed the narrow corridor to a degree that made me wonder if the little apertures contained magnifying glass."[6]

The Government Axis

In its architectural realization, Brasília reinforced the master plan in underlining the symbolic role of the capitol. It was in the creation of this ensemble that Oscar Niemeyer concentrated his major efforts in Brasília. Just as the urban design had represented the first application of the principles of the Modern Movement to the creation of a major capital city, the government center represented a notable opportunity for the application of modern architecture to a monumental complex.

The government axis reflects a conventional Beaux-Arts composition in its employment of a long, symmetrical mall terminated by a cluster of major buildings. Although the plan of the government center was traditionally oriented, the architec-

6. Emily Hahn, "Man Decides Where," *The New Yorker* 36 (12 March 1960): 170.

tural accompaniment is contemporary in style, thus combining in a single ensemble both references to the past and adherence to the present.

As the master plan of the city embodies a hierarchy of function, so the government axis is designed to contain its own symbolic hierarchy. The long open mall gives an emphatic focus to the National Legislature and the Plaza of the Three Powers lying beyond. The buildings of lesser symbolic importance, the bureaucratic headquarters of the government ministries, are architecturally identical and simple in outline, flanking the mall on either side, defining the approach, and providing the preamble to the more dramatically styled monumental buildings. Individually restrained in design, the government ministries achieve architectural importance primarily through their relation to the adjacent mall and in their cumulative visual impact (figs. 212–14).

In designing the ministry buildings, Niemeyer chose to create a single building type, standardized externally and containing undifferentiated interior space applicable to general office use. This decision may have been motivated by a desire to establish visual unity and a symbolic equality among the ministries. It was doubtless also influenced by the need for speed in the design and construction of the capital.

Initially, eleven ministries were constructed, five on the north side of the mall and six on the south side. Sites for four additional ministries were projected on the north side, and it was foreseen that future needs for expansion could be accommodated by extending the government sector both north and south away from the mall. The building type developed for the ministries was a simple ten-story rectilinear slab framed in steel imported from the United States, with the principal façades sheathed in glass and the end walls faced in ceramic tile. Each building is 336 feet long, 58 feet wide, and 125 feet high. The basic plan provided for a double-height entrance hall on the ground floor, with the remaining space containing a mezzanine story. Above this level, all floors were initially planned to provide open unpartitioned space of approximately 19,375 square feet. As eventually partitioned, the interior offices were divided by plywood panels. Floors are of parquet and lighting is provided by fluorescent tubes. The glass walls were designed so that only small sections at top and bottom could be opened, and poor ventilation, combined with glare and solar heat, produced notably uncomfortable offices. In an attempt to shade the interiors, movable vertical plastic louvers were subsequently installed inside the glass. The unrelenting heat of the sun, however, made the plastic brittle, and the louvers have tended to break off.

Although most of the building along the mall consists of repetitive government ministries, a few individually designed buildings are also sited in this area. On the north side of the mall, adjacent to the central traffic interchange, the National Theater was constructed, accessible from both the level of the mall and the elevated platform of the interchange (figs. 215, 216). The theater plan involved the establishment of two halls, the larger seating 2,000 and the smaller 500. As ultimately developed, Niemeyer's design combined the stage areas of the two theaters in the center of the building, with the larger hall placed on the west side facing the interchange platform, and the smaller hall opposite. The central stage area was designed for variations in staging, including the possibility of opening the whole interior so that both seating areas and the central stage could become a single unified space.

The exterior of the theater creates a heavy wedge-shaped concrete mass, with the sloping east and west walls carrying a fan-shaped configuration of projecting concrete ribs. The side walls were designed to carry a series of decorative projections creating a dramatic pattern of light and shadow and enhancing still more the already emphatic sculptural presence of the building. Although most of the buildings of the government complex are delicately framed, appearing to rest but lightly on the ground, the theater is emphatically rooted in the earth, evoking the solidity of a primitive earth mound, massive and eternal.

Even more dramatic in sculptural form is the cathedral which Niemeyer designed for a site on the south side of the mall just west of the row of ministries (figs. 217, 218). The architect sought a compact solution which could present the same purity of form seen from any point of view, an intention which resulted in a circular plan 200 feet in diameter. From a concrete ring defining the perimeter of the building, sixteen curving ribs of hollow concrete sweep upward and inward, joining at a point 85 feet above the ground. Here they curve outward to provide a crownlike projection extending 16 feet above the roof line. The floor of the interior was planned ten feet below ground level, with entrance by means of a shallow ramp. Although many churches employing circular plans are designed to accommodate a central altar surrounded on all sides by the congregation, Niemeyer's cathedral was planned with the altar at one end and the congregation placed slightly to one side of the center and opposite the choir. Because the cathedral was designed solely to house religious services, two adjacent low-rise structures were projected to accommodate auxiliary church functions. One was designed to contain a salon and auditorium. The other, a long L-shaped building, would contain the archbishop's curia, a choir residence, and a sisters' residence.

Although construction of the cathedral was begun during the early phases of the city, a continuing lack of funds tended to delay completion. The refracting glass, intended to fill the spaces between the ribs, was slow to be installed, and the cathedral long remained an unused, but compelling piece of outdoor sculpture.

Discussing the architecture he was developing for the Brazilian capital, Niemeyer claimed:

> works in progress in Brasília . . . mark a new stage in my professional activities. This step is characterized by a constant seeking for conciseness and purity, as

> well as greater attention to basic architectural problems. . . . I have become interested in compact solutions, simple and geometric: the fitness of unity and harmony amongst the buildings, and, further, that these no longer be expressed through their secondary elements, but rather through the structure itself, duly integrated within the original plastic conception.[7]

Although such an intent may have influenced the rectilinear plans and essentially classical partie of many of Niemeyer's government buildings, his long-lived fondness for decorative curving shapes was also much in evidence.

Summarizing his design philosophy at the time of Brasília's dedication, Niemeyer reaffirmed his adherence to the formal liberty which had so long characterized his work, insisting that, "I am in favor of an almost unlimited plastic freedom, a freedom that is not slavishly subordinate to technical determinants or to functionalism, but which makes an appeal to the imagination, to things that are new and beautiful, capable of arousing surprise and emotion by their very newness and creativeness; a freedom that provides scope—when desirable—for moods of ecstasy, reverie and poetry."[8]

The tenets of the functionalists, he felt, were "unsound when it is a question of special jobs where the problem of outlay is secondary. Thereupon they adduce social reasons which they deem to require simple, economic projects, as if this argument were not long out-dated, at any rate for whoever is really interested in the social problem and knows that its solution evades the attributions of architects and architecture, and demands, outside of professional activities, a coherent attitude in support of progressive movements."[9] Firmly endorsing a "freer and more creative" approach to design, Niemeyer declared: "To this end, I accept any device, any compromise, convinced that architecture is not just a matter of engineering, but an exteriorization of mind, . . ."[10] Such creative liberty was not to be granted universally, however, and Niemeyer warned that:

> Of course, this freedom cannot be used freely. In urban localities, for instance, I am, on the contrary, all for restricting it, or rather, for preserving the unity and harmony of the overall plan by avoiding solutions that do not wholly fit into it, however inspired they may be and however high their architectural level. And with this end in view, in Brasília, . . . regulations are set up to cover volumes, free spaces, heights, facing materials, etc., in order to prevent the city from proliferating, like other modern cities, in a regime of disharmony and confusion.[11]

The creation of Brasília coincided with a period in Niemeyer's career in which he

7. Niemeyer, "Testimony," *Módulo* 9 (February 1958): 3–5.
8. Niemeyer, "Form and Function in Architecture," *Módulo* 21 (December 1960): 3.
9. Ibid.
10. Ibid., p. 5.
11. Ibid., p. 3.

had stated an intention to devote increasing time and care to individual projects. The short deadline for the construction of the new city, however, compelled him to rely once more on his demonstrated talent for rapid improvisation. He claimed that each of the major government buildings of Brasília consumed no more than fifteen days design time, but, making a virtue of necessity, insisted that time pressures could be seen as a favorable element in architecture. Lacking the chance for lengthy modifications, Niemeyer had been able to realize his initial design concepts without loss of purity or spontaneity.

The monumental complex of the city as developed by Niemeyer followed the general layout of the Costa plan. The Plaza of the Three Powers, which terminated the ceremonial mall lined with government ministries, was based on a triangular plan with the National Legislature building marking the apex toward the mall. Beyond this, the Supreme Court building and the Palace of the Planalto (housing the presidential staff) face each other across a wide paved plaza. Of the three, the most arresting visually is the National Legislature, which provides the dominant focus of the government axis (figs. 219–24).

In developing his design for this building, Niemeyer sought a scheme which would not completely close the end of the mall, but which would invite a visual penetration past the Legislature toward the space beyond. He pointed out: "Had the Palace been designed in the academic spirit, . . . we should have had a tall structure, blocking the view that now stretches out in depth, away and beyond the building, over the esplanade, between the domes, embracing the Plaza of the Three Powers. . . .[12]

The design of the National Legislature combined an attempt to maintain the visual openness of the mall with a desire to emphasize the symbolically important legislative chambers. The main portion of the building was designed in the form of a low, horizontal platform carrying on its roof the upper extensions of the two assembly halls. The Senate chamber was defined by a shallow dome, and the larger Hall of Deputies by a saucerlike inverted dome. The utilitarian functions of the building were thus contained in a large, but unobtrusive block serving to provide a base for the sculpturally dominant legislative chambers.[13]

The intent was further emphasized by incorporating the building into the slope of the terrain, excavating the land so that on the side facing the mall the lower portion of the National Legislature is contained in a shallow depression. The roadways passing on either side are at roof level, and from a distance the sculptural shells of the

12. Niemeyer, "Form and Function in Architecture," p. 6.

13. It may be noted that there is a schematic similarity between Niemeyer's legislative assembly in Brasília and an unbuilt project which the Polish architect Matthew Nowicki produced in 1950 for the provincial assembly of Punjab in Chandigarh, India. Nowicki had sought to give visual dominance to the assembly chamber by placing it on the roof of a flat, platform-like building. The use of a long approach ramp leading to the roof may also be seen in Nowicki's scheme. For details of Nowicki's design, see Norma Evenson, *Chandigarh* (Berkeley, 1966).

legislative chambers appear to be resting directly on the ground from which, in the architect's words, "their forms sprout like a symbol of the legislative power."[14] The wide, flat roof of the National Legislature serves as a marble-paved promenade accessible by means of a long sloping ramp at the front of the building.

The main block of the National Legislature building is 656 feet by 262 feet, and 49 feet high, containing two stories plus a basement. The basement level contains a garage, public waiting room, service machinery, and offices. The middle level provides a hall for deputies and senators, committee rooms, offices, and general service functions. The upper floor, in addition to press rooms, lounges, and offices, contains the floor level of the assembly chambers. The Hall of Deputies provides 528 seats for members and places for 120 guests, while the Senate contains 115 seats and accommodations for 150 guests. The parabolic dome of the Senate is 128 feet in diameter, while the bowl-shaped enclosure of the Hall of Deputies is 203 feet in diameter and rises 33 feet above the surface of the roof.

Construction of the Congress building was directed by the engineer Joaquim Cardoso, who on many previous occasions had assumed the challenging task of giving physical realization to Oscar Niemeyer's sculptural concepts. In the case of the large, bowl-shaped Deputies chamber, the roof was designed in the form of a shallow cupola 69 feet in diameter, built within the convex outer frame. From this roof, a horizontal ceiling was hung.

Directly adjacent to the Congress, the administrative offices rise in the form of twenty-five-story twin slabs of reinforced concrete sheathed in glass. Sited with the narrow end of the slab toward the mall, these buildings extend partially into a shallow ornamental pool in the Plaza of the Three Powers. Linked to the main Legislature building by a covered passageway, these towers are also connected to each other at the eleventh, twelfth and thirteenth floors. The office blocks, while dominant in height, do not detract from, but serve as an effective foil for the smaller, but sculpturally assertive legislative chambers. In their central placement within the government complex, the office towers serve somewhat like an obelisk in forming a visual pivot for the surrounding composition.

Although the power of the Brazilian national legislature may be questionable, Niemeyer's legislative complex in Brasília provided the new capital with a highly photogenic symbol. In summarizing his overall intent, he once stated:

> My aim has been to determine the plastic elements according to function, giving them the relative importance required by treating them, in their ensemble, as pure and balanced forms. Thus the horizontal line of the composition is asserted in the immense esplanade and stands in contrast to the two blocks for the administration and for Congressmen's offices; thus also the halls for plenary sessions

14. Oscar Niemeyer quoted in Willy Stäubli, *Brasília* (New York, 1965), p. 80.

stand out, creating—together with the other elements—that play of forms which is the very essence of architecture and which Le Corbusier defines so well: "Architecture is the erudite, correct and magnificent play of forms under light."[15]

The Plaza of the Three Powers

Referring to the Plaza of the Three Powers, Niemeyer once observed that "unity was my great preoccupation."[16] To this purpose, he sought to imbue the architecture of the complex with a similarity of form, decorative devices, and materials. The stylistic imagery which harmonized the major government buildings was initially developed in the presidential residence, called the Palace of the Dawn (Alvorada Palace). This building was the first permanent structure completed in Brasília, and Niemeyer had begun his design in September 1956, before the selection of the master plan (fig. 225). Describing his scheme, Niemeyer noted:

> In finding a solution for the Brasília Presidential Palace we sought to apply the principles of simplicity and purity which characterized great architectural works in the past. To this end, we avoided choppy solutions rich in shapes and constructive elements (marquees, balconies, protective items, colors, materials, etc.) and chose instead a compact and simple solution whose beauty derives from its proportions and from the structure itself.
>
> This caused us to give a great deal of attention to the pillars, and we made a careful study as to their spacing, shape and proportions in relation to technical needs and the plastic effects we wished to achieve. The pillars in turn led us to a rhythmic, flowing solution, which gives the building lightness and elegance and makes it appear merely to touch the ground.[17]

In Niemeyer's preliminary scheme for the palace, the building was conceived as a rectilinear block, with two main floors and a ground level service area. The enclosed portion of the ground level was recessed beneath the upper floors, permitting a covered area with freestanding columns, while a ramp led from ground level directly to the first floor. The roof was to be used as a promenade, and carried a freeform shelter. In this early scheme, the main floors were framed by a row of decorative curving columns placed just beyond the glass. In outline, these columns rose from a narrow base at ground level, curving outward to mark the first-floor level, then tapering inward to a narrow point at the top.

In its final form, the Palace of the Dawn was built with its main floors lower to the

15. Niemeyer, untitled article in Aloisio Magalhães and Eugene Feldman, *Doorway to Brasília* (Philadelphia, 1959).
16. Ibid.
17. "Palacio residencial de Brasília," *Módulo* 7 (February 1957): 21. Quotation from English supplement.

ground than in the initial studies, with the ground floor replaced by an excavated basement. The rooftop promenade was abandoned, together with its freeform structure, giving the building a simple, rectilinear outline. Consisting essentially of a 362 by 100 foot two-story glass-walled pavilion, the palace seems to hover slightly above the ground, resting lightly on the points of the tapering columns.

The interior was planned to provide large reception areas on the first floor and private apartments on the second. Although the overall form of the Palace of the Dawn was relatively austere, an effect of luxury was obtained through the use of fine materials. The external columns were faced with white marble and the veranda paved in black granite. Interior wall surfaces were embellished with gold tiles, mirrors, tapestries, and paneling of jacaranda, a dark satiny wood used also for much of the flooring.

On the south, the palace was connected at basement level with a low service building, while on the other side was built a small chapel, also connected to the basement by a covered passageway. The chapel, at its upper level is contained by two freestanding, semicircular walls faced in white marble and designed to produce a spiral effect. The unbroken interior is faced in wooden panels.

In developing his definitive scheme for the Palace of the Dawn, Niemeyer moved the outer columns well beyond the building block, framing an 18½-foot-wide veranda on each long façade. A similar screen of freestanding curving columns was to be employed subsequently in the major buildings of the Plaza of the Three Powers. Niemeyer considered the withdrawal of the columns from the main body of the building desirable in "enabling visitors approaching them to walk around them, thereby appreciating their true scale and the space that surrounds them—separating them from the building proper—in all their variety of form. I have avoided solutions where the columns are brought into such close connection with the main body of the building as to prevent this essential multiplicity of aspect."[18] The screen of decorative tapering columns was intended to add a delicate sculptural plasticity to basically simple boxlike building forms. To a spectator moving around the government buildings, the columns would present a continuously changing perspective, "as though they were not just things, inert and static."[19]

Niemeyer also felt that the use of decorative curving forms allied his monumental buildings to the baroque tradition, forging "a link with the old architecture of colonial Brazil, not by the obvious use of the elements common to those days, but by expressing the same plastic intention, the same love of curves and richly refined forms that is so telling a characteristic of the colonial style."[20]

The Supreme Court and the Palace of the Planalto, which houses the executive headquarters, face each other across the 300-meter expanse of the Plaza of the Three

18. Niemeyer, "Imagination in Architecture," *Módulo* 15 (October 1959): 11.
19. Niemeyer, "Form and Function in Architecture," p. 7.
20. Ibid.

Powers. Of the two, the Palace of the Planalto is the larger and is sited with its long side facing the plaza. Passing directly between the building and the plaza is a roadway leading from the mall toward the Palace of the Dawn. The rear façade of the Planalto faces a landscaped garden (figs. 226–28).

Entrance into the Palace of the Planalto is customarily made at ground level, which contains the main lobby, and below which is a basement service area. The entrance lobby is recessed behind the upper floors, exposing a row of supporting columns. The upper floors, in turn, extend slightly beyond the supporting columns, enabling the building to be sheathed in a glass curtain wall of aluminum-framed glass panels. Surrounding the building block, a row of flat decorative columns extends from the widely projecting roof to the ground, presenting a narrow edge toward the plaza, and curving inward to join the main structure at the level of the second floor.

Above the ground floor lobby, the Palace of the Planalto has three floors. The first of these provides the official reception area, with a two-story high marble-paneled reception room facing the plaza, and a banquet hall. A ceremonial entrance to the area is provided by a sloping ramp leading from plaza level. In addition, a freestanding outdoor speaker's rostrum is connected to this floor by an open bridge. On the next floor, there is additional reception area, with access provided by Niemeyer in the form of an open curving ramp. This floor also contains the office of the president and his personal staff. On the top floor are the offices of the executive staff, including the heads of military and civilian departments.

The Supreme Court is sited with its narrow end toward the plaza and has a row of columns extending down the long sides (figs. 229–31). In contrast to the Palace of the Planalto, where emphasis is given to the second floor and the building appears to be lifted high off the ground, the Supreme Court, like the Palace of the Dawn, seems to hover close to the ground, having a wide veranda, elevated only four feet above the plaza, which is approached by a broad, shallow ramp. The columns, however, are similar in design to those of the Planalto, slender and brittle, with the thin edge leading outward and a wide taper inward to the edge of the veranda. The use of materials is similar to that of the Planalto Palace; the columns are sheathed in marble and the building carries a curtain wall of glass set in aluminum frames. The Supreme Court comprises an underground basement and three upper floors, with the court chamber in the center of the building rising two stories in height.

In addition to providing a site for the Palace of the Planalto and the Supreme Court, the Plaza of the Three Powers contains a small "museum," designed to commemorate the founding of the city. This structure consists of a single boxlike enclosure supported by two reinforced concrete beams, 115 feet long, elevated and supported near the midpoint by two slablike pillars. Entrance into the museum chamber is made by means of a stairway placed between the two pillars (fig. 233).

The museum was initially intended to contain plans, documents, photographs, models, and other exhibits relating to the founding of Brasília. However, permanent exhibits have never been installed, and the interior carries only statements by the founders of Brasília incised in the marble wall surfaces. Externally, the museum appears to be primarily a monument to Juscelino Kubitschek. His sculpted head projects from one of the pillars accompanied by a dedicatory inscription, and the cantilevered museum block is embellished by an excerpt from one of his speeches.[21]

Other sculptural elements in the plaza include a statue of Justice by Alfredo Ceschiatti, placed outside the Supreme Court, and two abstract figures by Bruno Giorgi, titled "The Warriors," located near the Planalto. Near the outer edge of the plaza rises a tall concrete dovecote, somewhat suggestive in form of a giant clothespin (fig. 232).

Although the government buildings of the Plaza of the Three Powers were unified by the employment of external marble facing to mask the concrete surfaces, Niemeyer chose to leave the concrete exposed on the exterior of the Brazilian Foreign Office, the Itamarity Palace, dedicated in 1967. This building is located near the Legislative Assembly, adjacent to the row of ministries on the south side of the mall. Although most of the government ministries were housed in identical structures, indicating an equality of rank, the sites nearest the Legislature were set aside for two ministries of notable prestige and importance: the Foreign Office and, on the opposite side of the mall, the National Treasury.[22]

The Itamarity Palace itself was designed to contain the office of the minister of foreign affairs and to provide facilities for banquets, ceremonies, and diplomatic receptions (figs. 234–36). The more utilitarian administrative functions of the foreign office would be housed in an eight-story office slab directly adjacent.

As designed by Niemeyer, the Itamarity Palace, which adopted the name of the old Foreign Office Building in Rio, took the form of a square pavilion set within a frame of landscaped pools. The device of surrounding a glass-walled building block with a screen of columns was maintained, although the form of the columns abandoned the fluid curves seen in the older buildings for a brittle and disciplined row of thin, slablike concrete columns rising directly from the ornamental pools and joined by arches beneath the level of the overhanging roof.

The use of exposed concrete, in which the marks of the formwork are exploited in creating a rough surface texture is characteristic of much contemporary architecture.

21. The inscription accompanying the sculpted head reads in translation: "To President Juscelino Kubitschek de Oliveira, who tamed the wilderness and raised Brasília with audacity, energy and confidence, the homage of the pioneers who helped in the great adventure." The statement by Kubitschek which appears on the side of the museum was made in October 1956, during his initial stay in Brasília. In translation the statement reads: "From this central tableland, from this solitary place which will be soon transformed into the brain center of the highest decisions, I cast my eyes once again on the tomorrow of my country, with unshakable faith and unlimited confidence in the greatness of its destiny."

22. In order to preserve the symmetry of the government complex, the National Treasury was designed to mirror the Itamarity Palace, combining an almost identical forebuilding with an adjacent office slab.

Frequently accompanying this use of material is a conception of building form which is weighty and heavily sculptural. In the Itamarity Palace, however, the overall effect is far from brutalist, and the building as a whole conveys a sense of precision and refinement. On the exterior, the dull surface of the concrete arcade provides an effective foil for the smooth dark glass of the curtain walls and the reflective surface of the pools.

Although all the major government buildings of Brasília reveal a striving for fineness of effect, those which were produced during the initial development of the city show some evidences of hasty construction, carelessness in detailing, and economy in materials. The Itamarity Palace, however, conveys an effect of thoroughgoing opulence, surrounding its occupants in a luxurious ambient of smooth polished marble, mirrors, deep carpets, tapestries, and fine furnishings. In addition to a basement containing service areas and meeting rooms, the palace contains two main floors, with the central areas given over to large reception halls. The top floor contains a large landscaped terrace roofed by a pergola. Roberto Burle-Marx, Brazil's most noted landscape designer, was charged with the creation of the roof garden, as well as an indoor garden in the ground floor reception room. He was also responsible for the exterior planting in the ornamental pools.[23]

One of the notable aspects of the Itamarity Palace, as well as Niemeyer's other government buildings for Brasília, is the employment of relatively low, horizontal spaces for the major reception areas. In more traditional monumental design, important interiors have customarily been endowed with lofty proportions. Niemeyer's buildings may thus be seen to embody a uniquely contemporary conception of monumental space, making no concessions to the visual associations of the past. To those still responsive to the attributes of traditional architecture, the interiors of Niemeyer's buildings in Brasília seem spatially meagre, lacking the sense of nobility, awesomeness, and exultation customarily associated with ceremonial spaces. The shallow curving ramps, without balustrades, which provide vertical circulation in major reception areas, seem in some respects a witty parody of the idea of a monumental staircase.

The architectural drama of Brasília tends to be primarily external—in the relationship of building to site and in the establishment of large-scale composition. One foreign critic observed, at the time the city was dedicated: "The town is all exterior, from the viewpoint of interest; for Brazil, with far more than its share of brilliant architects, planners, and landscape architects, has not yet produced an interior designer of stature. As a result many of the most important buildings, inside, look as if nobody quite knew what to do with what the architect left behind him."[24]

23. In spite of his preeminence in his field, Burle-Marx had not participated in the initial landscape planning of Brasília because of personal differences with Kubitschek.

24. George Nelson, "Out of the Trackless Bush, a National Capital," *Saturday Review of Literature* 43 (12 March 1960): 67.

The Monumental Concept

In creating the monumental complex of Brasília, Niemeyer was entering a realm of design which has been subject to considerable debate in the field of modern architecture. Throughout most of history, it has been customary for important human institutions to be symbolized architecturally. Since communal ideals could endure in a way that individuals could not, permanent monuments representing the collective strength of civic, religious, and cultural institutions have been designed to communicate to men unborn. The survival of such monuments reflects the collective survival of a society and the continuance of a cultural heritage. Thus the Greeks built their houses of mud and their temples of stone. It is not accidental that our architectural legacy from the past has been largely in the form of institutional monuments. Our ancestors meant such buildings to last.

Monumental architecture presupposes the existence of viable institutions which can be appropriately embodied in architectural form, and it assumes also a general responsiveness to the symbolism of monumental building. In the view of many, neither of these conditions is representative of the modern age. To some, the rapid social change of our time has rendered the traditional institutional base of society obsolete. Many see modern society as essentially fragmented, without strong civic focuses or need for collective symbols. Moreover, the directed communal effort which produced the monuments of the past can be seen as anachronistic and imbued with antidemocratic authoritarianism. It is not difficult, in fact, to interpret every monumental achievement of the past, from the Parthenon to Chartres Cathedral, from the Campidoglio to the United States Capitol, as a symbol of tyrannical power and antisocial waste. One can argue quite convincingly that the modern democratic state has no need of institutional monuments.

Among those who have expressed this view is John Summerson, who once stated:

> We must accept, willingly and without self-pity, the fact that architecture today cannot be monumental. . . . Today, to endeavor to be monumental is to be untrue to our own times. . . . At the town hall, where, if we go at all, we usually go to complain about something, . . . we do not really care to be reminded by the grand staircase of the majesty and greatness of Mr. Mayor. Of course, some of us may think that these things are nice. Perhaps they are. But they are no longer of the slightest importance. . . . All those things which suggested and supported monumentality are in dissolution. . . . Monumentality in architecture is a form of affirmation; and affirmations are usually made by the few to impress the many. . . . Architecture is no longer required to give symbolic cohesion to society. Cohesion is now maintained by new methods of communication.[25]

25. John Summerson, *Heavenly Mansions* (London: Cresset Press, 1949; reissue, New York: Norton, 1963), pp. 203–09. Additional discussion of the role of monumentality in modern architecture may be found in a symposium, "In Search of a New Monumentality," *Architectural Review* 104 (September 1948): 117–27, which

Such arguments were especially prevalent at the time when the International Style was dominant. Traditionally, monumental design had embodied a building type which was massive, plastically powerful, and evocative of the strength, permanence, and dignity of the institutions it represented. In its customary imagery, a monument could be perceived almost as a living thing, firmly rooted and drawing its sustenance from the soil, belonging to a given place as its creators felt themselves to belong. Architecture thus could be both an actual and a symbolic means of possessing the earth, evoking the human presence, and providing the assurance of a continuing presence.

With a modern architecture—freed from the constraints of masonry construction, embodying an imagery of volume rather than mass, and characterized by smoothness of surface, lightness of framing, and a visual suggestion of transience—it was natural to regard the concept of modernity as incompatible with the physical qualities of traditional monumental building. Those who still felt aesthetically drawn to the qualities of sculptural massiveness were sometimes advised to consider grain elevators, factories, dams, and power plants as contemporary equivalents of the monuments of the past. Such a view disregarded the question of symbolic significance entirely, assuming that any large, solid, seemingly permanent construction could properly be deemed monumental. Walter Gropius once observed that "the grain silos, the coal bunkers of the leading railroads, the newest workhalls of the industrial trusts, can bear comparison, in their overwhelming monumental power, with the buildings of ancient Egypt."[26]

Although modern architects were vehement in their condemnation of traditional styles, the failure of the International Style to provide what seemed an acceptable set of symbols for monumental projects resulted in a continuation of revivalism in major government building. The Ministry of Education and Health, begun in Rio in 1936, provided an isolated example of modern design applied to government building, and

---

included contributions by Henry-Russell Hitchcock, Gregor Paulsson, William Holford, Sigfried Giedion, Walter Gropius, Lúcio Costa, and Alfred Roth. Typical of the sentiment expressed was the statement by Gregor Paulsson that, "monumentality can arise only from dictatorship. . . . The democratic society in conformity with its nature is anti-monumental. Intimacy, not monumentality, should be the emotional goal, even in cities, as far as this is possible." According to Alfred Roth, the editor of *Werk,* "Our buildings are no longer symbols of transcendental power. . . . Representational duties no longer chain them. . . . What is unacceptable to anyone convinced of the ideology of modern architecture is to accept any attempt made by men with a historical bias to divide buildings into non-monumental (i.e. every day) and monumental." The generally antimonumental bias expressed by most of the participants was reflective of the immediate postwar temper and may be considered in part a reaction against the discredited monumental building programs of recently deposed dictators. Basic agreement as to the questionable validity of monumental building in our time may also be found in more recent commentary, however. In this context could be cited an article by Robert Venturi titled, "A Significance for A & P Parking Lots, or Learning from Las Vegas," *Architectural Forum* 128 (March 1968): 36–43 ff. Venturi considers the "big low space" of the Las Vegas casino to be the "archetype for all public interior spaces whose heights are diminished for reasons of budget and air conditioning." To Venturi, low spaces are prompted not only by economics and technology, but "a changing attitude to monumentality in our environment." Like many others he questions the validity of a search for monumentality in our time, claiming that "we rarely achieve architectural monumentality when we try; our money and skill do not go into the traditional monumentality which expressed cohesion of the community through great scale, unified, symbolic architectural elements."

26. Walter Gropius, "The Development of Modern Industrial Architecture," *Yearbook of the German Werkbund,* 1913.

although highly praised by critics, it had no observable influence on the conservative trend of the 1930s. During this era such diverse patrons as the Roosevelt administration in Washington, the Hitler regime in Berlin, and the Stalinist rule in Moscow supported massive building programs characterized by classical style. Apparently, when appropriate symbols were needed to express the vigor of a capitalist democracy, the Aryan supremacy of the Reich which was to last 1000 years, and the proletarian triumphs of a socialist state, masonry walls, classical pediments, and Doric columns were still the most satisfying solution.

It was not until the 1950s that the modern style would be extensively applied to monumental projects, the two most notable achievements of this period being Le Corbusier's government complex in Chandigarh, the planned capital of the Indian province of Punjab, and Niemeyer's work in Brasília.

Le Corbusier's work in Chandigarh provided the outstanding realization of his postwar idiom. Abandoning the stylistic imagery of the International Style, Le Corbusier turned, during this period, to a heavily sculptural, emotionally expressive form, exploiting the rough massiveness of exposed concrete. The capitol complex in Chandigarh, which Le Corbusier began developing in 1951, included a large paved plaza on which were sited the provincial High Court, Legislative Assembly, and Secretariat. As the buildings of this ensemble were realized, it was evident that Le Corbusier had achieved a remarkable fusion of innovative form and traditional qualities of monumentality.

In the weighty massing of their concrete exteriors, in the dignity of their solemn porticos, and the exultation of their lofty interior spaces, the capitol buildings of Chandigarh evoke an imagery long associated with civic architecture. Le Corbusier, whose early work had been timely, consciously reflecting his view of contemporary life, seemed, in Chandigarh, to reach outside of time, seeking an embodiment of the most enduring human values and achieving an expression of almost primordial strength. Like the monuments of the past, the government buildings of Chandigarh convey a sense of permanence defiant of time and destruction.

At the time Chandigarh was built, India was celebrating her new independence; self-government had been hard won, and it was appropriate that governmental functions be surrounded with dignity and drama. As a resurgent nationalism began to make itself felt throughout much of the postwar world, and as new nations achieved political identity, it became clear that the desire for institutional symbols was by no means dead. With the appearance of Chandigarh, it was also evident that the achievement of monumental building was well within the scope of modern design which, with its new richness of form, could encompass a wide range of imagery. Contemporary, yet respectful of the associations of the past, Le Corbusier's buildings in Chandigarh may be said to have revitalized the modern concept of monumental architecture.

When Oscar Niemeyer began his work in Brasília, Chandigarh was taking form, and Le Corbusier's postwar idiom had already begun to influence a number of contemporary architects. This influence seems to have been notably lacking in Brasília, however. Although Chandigarh provided a magnificent example of contemporary monumentality, the relation of Le Corbusier's work to the development of the Brazilian capital appears to have been largely through the precedent of his early visionary urban designs, rather than through his postwar architecture. In the years following Le Corbusier's initial impact in Brazil, Brazilian architecture had developed its own momentum as a national art form reflecting local sensibilities. While Niemeyer had been notably influenced by Le Corbusier at the beginning of his career, by the time he assumed direction of the Brasília project, he was sufficiently mature and confident to formulate the design problem in his own terms.

Describing his intention in developing the monumental complex, Niemeyer reported:

> My special concern was to find—without functional limitations—a beautiful clear-cut structure that would define the characteristics of the main buildings—the palaces, strictly so-called—within the indispensable criterion of simplicity and nobility. . . . I called to mind the Piazza San Marco in Venice, the Palace of the Doges and the Cathedral of Chartres, . . . Plastic beauty alone is the guiding, dominating spirit, with its permanent message of grace and poetry."[27]
>
> Yet, when thinking out the forms for those Palaces, I also bore in mind the kind of mood they would impart to the Plaza of the Three Powers. It should not seem, as I saw it, cold and technical, ruled by the classical, hard and already obvious purity of straight lines. On the contrary, I visualized it with a richness of forms, dreams and poetry, like the mysterious paintings by Carzou, new forms, startling visitors by their lightness and creative liberty; forms that were not anchored to the earth rigidly and statically, but uplifted the Palaces as though to suspend them, white and ethereal, in the endless nights of the highlands; surprising and breathtaking forms that would lift the visitor, if only for a few brief instants, above the difficult and at times overwhelming problems which life poses for all of us.[28]

The drama which Niemeyer sought to create in the government complex of Brasília embodied an imagery which was not only a departure from traditional monumentality but was in a sense antimonumental. Lifted from the ground, sheathed in glass and a glistening veneer of white marble, the symbolic buildings of Brasília display variations on a theme of lightness and fragility. As implied in Niemeyer's description, the government ensemble does frequently convey an atmosphere of dreamlike unreality. For much of the year, the sky is filled with scudding clouds bathing

27. Niemeyer, "My Brasília Experience," pp. 19–20.
28. Niemeyer, "Form and Function in Architecture," p. 7.

the site in shifting light and shadow, the floating formations of vapor often sustaining the illusion of greater substance than the man-made structures below. Appearing to rest but lightly on the tips of tapering supports, the buildings seem to have been placed by a magician's hand, rather than constructed by patient human labor, creating an apparition which strikes the vision with hallucinatory clarity. There is no emphatic and secure sense of possessing the site, of somehow marking it forever for human occupation. There is a poignant awareness of the ephemeral, a melancholy and sophisticated perception of how tenuous is man's grasp of the earth and how transient are his works.

The ceremonial plaza marks an edge of settlement, defined by a retaining wall above a stretch of rough open land. It is here that one becomes most conscious of the expansiveness of the site and the enormity of the wilderness which seems waiting without to engulf the city. The insubstantiality of the architecture is accentuated against the image of the surrounding wasteland, and one senses what an act of daring the creation of Brasília was. The entire city reflects the bravado of a frontier town, and the gleam of marble and glass in the decorative elegance of Niemeyer's designs defies the wilderness just as gilt and plush once brought a breath of gentility and civilization to our own western wilds.

In a sense, the lightly framed pavilions of the ceremonial complex may not be altogether inappropriate as symbols of Brazilian governmental institutions. A Brazilian scholar, Aleu Amoroso Lima, once observed that, "Brazil has no organic political structure, no political institutions which are characteristically Brazilian and participate in the native Brazilian humanism. . . . in matters of politics, Brazilians are conformistic. They are not partisan-minded, or even very strongly public minded."[29] It is possible to see in Niemeyer's buildings a certain unconscious evocation of the very insecurity and shallowness of Brazilian political institutions.

It is possible also to see a certain underlying falseness in the symbolic placement of the major government buildings. It may be recalled that Costa introduced his plan for the complex by stating that "the highlights in the outline plan of the city are the public buildings which house the fundamental powers." He continued, "These are three, and they are autonomous: therefore the equilateral triangle."[30] In practice, there is not such a balance of power in Brazilian government. Authority is largely vested in the president who frequently writes his own constitution and to whom legislative and judicial functions tend to be subordinate. A more symbolically accurate architectural ensemble might well have focused on the executive building, as Lutyens' government complex in New Delhi focused on the viceroy's palace. The visual dominance given to the legislature in Brasília may be considered essentially a gesture to the ideal of parliamentary democracy.

29. Aleu Amoroso Lima, "Men, Ideas and Institutions," *Atlantic Monthly* 197 (February 1956): 118.
30. Costa, "Pilot Plan for Brasília."

Although Niemeyer's government complex was intended to provide a ceremonial focus to which the rest of the city would be architecturally subordinate, the visual impact of Brasília lies in the whole, rather than in a single grouping of buildings. From the beginning the city was meant to represent a single, unified work of art, planned as a totality and controlled in execution.

In this respect, Brasília provides a notable contrast with Chandigarh. In the Punjab capital, the distinction between the monumental complex and the overall fabric of the city is sharply defined, giving the effect of two separate Chandigarhs: that of Le Corbusier, consisting of monumental building, and that of the other architects, consisting of low-rise government housing. In Brasília, although an architectural hierarchy gives emphasis to the government complex, there is an essential unity of architectural style and scale throughout the city. Chandigarh is a city containing monuments; in Brasília, the city is a monument.

As might be expected, critical opinion has been divided regarding the architecture of Brasília. To some, the antiseptic modernity and regimentation of the city are repellent. Many consider the overall design quality to be mechanical and unimaginative, while others have been quick to observe slovenliness in workmanship and maintenance. Those who had opposed the creation of the capital naturally tended to be critical of its architecture, and those who favored the project more generous in overlooking defects. To many of Brasília's supporters, the establishment of the new capital in the midst of a wilderness was an achievement of such magnitude as to render insignificant the details of its architectural design. The importance of Brasília lay not in how it was built, but in the fact of its having been built at all. Learning to live with continuing criticism during the difficult years in which Brasília took form, Niemeyer pointed out, "it is easy enough to find something wrong with any work of architecture." He was well aware that certain foreign visitors "adopted a professorial attitude, flaunting a supercilious superiority scarcely justifiable by their own work, often enough of very mediocre quality. None of this," he claimed, "worried us."[31]

With their novel forms and visual drama, Niemeyer's government buildings tended to attract most of the critical attention. Some observers praised what seemed a refreshing and audacious departure from monumental orthodoxy, while others disapproved of such marked disregard for conservative usage. Robert Moses, for example, considered Niemeyer's design to be too exhibitionistic for a national capital, remarking that he might "feel favorable toward these fresh and novel conceptions if they had been designed for, let us say, a world's fair." He was of the opinion that "these clever architectural conceptions are too bizarre and too ephemeral in character to last in the roles in which they have been cast. They are dramatic and, as such, they undoubtedly appeal to young practitioners of architecture and the arts; but . . . The

31. Niemeyer, "My Brasília Experience," p. 23.

business of government is serious and requires for its protection a conservative physical environment."[32]

Many viewers, however, were more tolerant of Niemeyer's "innocent, lyrical and dance-like"[33] forms, and one critic elected to withhold judgment, suggesting that we "leave these palaces 'resting lightly on the ground,' as Niemeyer wanted them, until we gain perspective. And let us hope that this particular iconoclasm is the beginning of a searching development rather than of a fashion. For few imitators will be able to muster Niemeyer's sure sense of scale and proportion."[34]

Whether Niemeyer's capitol buildings are to be considered as essentially innovative or as fundamentally related to older architectural tradition depends somewhat on the sensibilities of the critic and the qualities he chooses to associate with traditional building. If one regards classical architecture primarily as a pristine and geometric reflection of human rationality set against the opposing forms and forces of nature, it is possible to see Niemeyer's work as maintaining the spirit of this tradition. A British architect once noted that "perhaps the most exciting of all these buildings' visual qualities is a reference back to Classical Greece! Niemeyer's buildings stand white, clear and abrupt in the landscape, exactly as Greek temples do."[35] A similar observation was made by André Malraux, who proclaimed "this Brasília on its great plateau is a bit like the Acropolis on its rock," adding that, "the forms of art destined to remain in the memory of men are invented forms."[36] One may perceive that, just as the Acropolis lifted an intense and vivid image of man against the sky of Athens, so the less reassuringly rooted structures of Brasília may be seen to create, in their own way, an equally uncompromising affirmation of the human presence.

While it may be assumed that nothing is preordained, once achieved, events tend to acquire an air of inevitability and rightness. Brasília was a city of buildings before it was a city of people. It was architecture which gave Brasília its existence, and architects who made a reality of the founders' dreams. Although the city is a conscious creation, and could have been conceived otherwise, the reality of Brasília now obliterates alternatives. The idea of the new capital is now inseparable from its realization.

32. Robert Moses, Letter to the Editor, *The Reporter* 22 (28 April 1960): 10–11.

33. A quotation from an unspecified writer included by Wolf von Eckardt in "Brasília: Symbol in the Mud," *American Institute of Architects Journal* 36 (November 1961): 39.

34. Ibid., p. 40.

35. George Balcombe, "Conversation in Brasília, between Robert Harbinson and George Balcombe," *Journal of the Royal Institute of British Architects* 68 (November 1961): 493.

36. André Malraux, *Brasília na palavra de Andre Malraux* (Rio de Janeiro, 1959), p. 10.

14. CITIES AND SYMBOLS

Although it was once fashionable to consider the origin and growth of cities in primarily economic terms, more recently, historians have tended to emphasize the importance of human institutions as the generating factor in urban development. The city may be seen, therefore, not merely as an agglomeration of people drawn together for economic advantage, but also as a human organization involved, both consciously and unconsciously, in the evolution and perpetuation of a common culture. The city is more than an accumulation of buildings, streets, and utilities; it is a physical ordering directed by the human will and subject to human sensibilities.

To a degree, the city has been not solely the home of man, but of his gods as well, and the form of the city has sometimes reflected both the earthly needs of men, and the greater ordering of the cosmos as perceived by men. While the laying out of cities may no longer involve blood sacrifices and augury, priestly incantations, and the ploughing of sacred furrows, the city may still embody certain mystical and intangible attributes, fully as important as its utilitarian aspects, which give to its inhabitants a sense of participating in the deepest aspects of communal life.

A capital city by definition is not self-contained, rather it provides a focus of power and control for a larger society. A national capital belongs not only to its inhabitants, but also symbolically to the nation. It does not merely house government functions, it celebrates them, becoming the seat of national, secular shrines. A Brazilian scholar, discussing Brasília, observed that "the founding of a new capital is endowed with certain sacramental qualities, as if the act involved the participation of hidden powers or was, indeed, to mark a solemn moment of creation, the birth of a new era."[1]

Although the term "capital" refers primarily to the center of government, it may also be broadly applied to the focus of other functions. Many of the major cities of the world are multifunctional capitals, serving not only as the headquarters of a national government, but as the leading commercial, financial, and cultural center.

1. J. O. de Meira Penna, *Brasília* (Rio de Janeiro, 1960).

London, Paris, Buenos Aires, Tokyo, and Moscow are all multiform capitals, each embodying in a single city the central focus for many aspects of national life. Although cuch cities provide a richness of urban content, it is possible to deplore their excessive centralization and their tendency to draw into themselves an ever-increasing share of major urban functions.

If one were to consider the national capital to be that city which is most typical of a nation, and which seems most comprehensively to reflect national temperament and character, the purely political administrative center would not always qualify. In the United States, for example, it is New York which, with its intense commercial activity, its financial power, its energetic, contentious, heterogeneous population, summarizes, exaggerates, and elaborates those qualities generally accepted as American. The concentrated skyscrapers provide the visible nerve center for a highly organized industrialized society and, together with the stock exchange, make the city the symbolic and functional capital of capitalism. The mythical New Yorker, the ambitious, hard-driving, efficient organizer and entrepreneur, may be seen as the legendary modern American.

It is the very qualities which make New York a characteristically American city which might make the city unsuitable, in the eyes of many, for a national capital. The establishment of the government headquarters in a separate urban enclave reflects less the requirements of administrative efficiency than a desire to place the institutions of government in a setting symbolically detached from competing and conflicting social forces. In Washington, the functions of government are exhibited in a serene ambient, physically removed from the fleshpots and commercial frenzy of more typical cities. A monumental intent clearly dominated the initial planning of the city in which the grandeur of baroque axes, wide avenues, and classical building reflected the confidence of a new republic. Architecturally, the city has been controlled to subordinate its more utilitarian aspects to its function as a seat of national monuments.

Although some may find it difficult to equate either the ideals or the realities of the United States with the calm beauty of marble colonnades, and others may question the validity of monumental imagery in a modern democratically oriented society, there is ample evidence that, for many, the monumentality of the city is a wholly appropriate embodiment of its capital function. Few of those for whom Washington is a place of pilgrimage would wish to discover there an ordinary American city.

In Brazil, Rio is the city which most typifies the nation. Unlike São Paulo, which is unique in its industrialized prosperity, Rio encompasses qualities characteristic of both the North and South, appearing in many ways as a microcosm of Brazil. The physical qualities of the site create a pervasive consciousness of the power of nature, a visual reminder of the vast and unconquered green empire beyond. The man-made aspects of the city reflect both the Brazilian past and the somewhat precarious and uneven modernization of the country. The people of Rio reveal the racial and ethnic mixture of Brazil as well as its economic and political imbalance. Perhaps most importantly, Rio symbolizes the Brazilian way of living, with the Carioca personality providing a summation of the Brazilian temperament. The legendary inhabitant of Rio, pleasure-loving, amiable, emotional, and easygoing, has become the legendary Brazilian.

To some of the proponents of Brasília, it was those characteristically Brazilian attributes which tended to make Rio unsuitable as a national capital. Just as a North American might uneasily view New York as epitomizing greed, violence, and irresponsible power, so the Carioca mentality could be seen to represent indolence, inefficiency, and corruption. Rio, with its beach resort atmosphere, might be deemed a lovable embodiment of precisely those qualities which had hampered national advancement, while Brasília could symbolize a new Brazil—dynamic, progressive, and pioneering. For this reason, the development of Brasília may be regarded not as an effort to recreate a typical Brazilian city, but rather to represent new ideals, attitudes, and images.

There were many, however, who would have found Brasília more palatable if it had transplanted some of the qualities of Rio into the hinterland. The sociologist Gilberto Freyre, for example, considered the image of efficiency and austerity to be not only thoroughly un-Brazilian, but reflective of qualities perhaps no longer needed in the modern world. Freyre opined that, with increasing automation, the habits of work dominant in industrialized societies would become obsolete, and the Carioca temperament, far from needing reform, would become the ideal modern mentality. In the coming age of leisure, the Brazilians, "who have always been criticized by foreigners for their disdain of systematic work and an exaggerated fondness for dance, music and idleness," would become the model for the world. Brazil would no longer be the recipient of teams of foreign technical experts; on the contrary, men of the technically advanced nations "will have to learn how to use their free time from people like the . . . neo-Iberians of tropical America who have developed pure leisure (or unproductive idleness) almost to a form of art. . . . That might be a mission for Brasília: to be an ultramodern city where leisure would be the dominant note in the social atmosphere. . . . Instead, the seemingly extravagant abundance of space in Brasília has been used in a conventional, cramped, old-fashioned way."[2]

Freyre objected to Brasília as "a city of architectural sculpture, with its creation ordered exclusively by architects—however illustrious—as by a caste of high-priests, all-powerful and omniscient."[3] The result, he felt, was not a truly Brazilian city, drawing its inspiration from the wellsprings of indigenous culture, but a monumental abstraction—a type of environment which he felt already characteristic of the

2. Gilberto Freyre, "A Brazilian's Critique of Brasília," *The Reporter* 22 (31 March 1960): 32.
3. Gilberto Freyre, *Brasis, Brasil, Brasília* (Lisbon: Edição Livros do Brasil, 1960), p. 154.

"ingenuous bourgeois of the United States and the simplistic dictators of the Soviet Union."[4]

Yet the task of creating a specifically "Brazilian" city would not have been easy to define. It might be noted that Rio was never at any time consciously designed to accord with a local cultural tradition. Much of the urban planning as well as the architecture was based on foreign models. With the arrival, early in the nineteenth century, of Grandjean de Montigny and his colleagues, Rio was extensively redeveloped according to the prevailing tenets of French classicism. The renovations of the early twentieth century under Pereira Passos were inspired by Haussmann's work in Paris and architecturally reflected a belated Second Empire mode. In the 1920s the Beaux-Arts master plan of Alfred Agache emphasized the continuance of outside influences, while in the 1950s and 1960s, an acceptance of foreign planning techniques may be seen in the employment of Doxiadis and in the technical assistance given by the United States. Although beginning in the 1930s, Brazilian architecture evidenced remarkable creativity, the work of foreigners, especially Le Corbusier, provided strong inspiration. Rio is a Brazilian city not through the intent of its planners, but because its inhabitants have made it so.

It may be borne in mind that a capital city embodies the face which a nation turns to the world and the place where representatives of other nations are officially received. The planning of such cities may thus emphasize the cosmopolitan nature of the capital, rather than an emphatic provincialism. Peter the Great intended St. Petersburg to be a European, rather than a typically Russian city, and Washington, D. C., was designed to reflect an international classical ideal rather than any specifically American image. A series of design efforts sought to give Rio the image of a world capital—a city which with its broad avenues and landscaped promenades reflected internationally recognized attributes of urban design. Although the assertive commercial structure of the city, together with the dominant natural setting, tended to overshadow Rio's monumental aspects, such plans as that of Agache clearly intended to enhance the city's image as a symbolic capital.

While it may be tempting, in comparing Rio and Brasília, to consider Rio as a "real" city and Brasília as "artificial," both are equally man-made creations (figs. 238, 239). Rio, however, encompasses the results of a complex piecemeal building and planning process extending over many years and accommodating a variety of commercial, industrial, residential, and governmental functions. In Brasília, the civic design represents a single moment in time, while the civic functions have been simplified to focus on the administration of the national government. The product of both long-term preparation and impulsive action, Brasília provided the nation, for better or worse, with a wholly monumental capital.

4. Ibid., p. 156.

The symbolism of Brasília rests on many levels, embracing both the reasons for the city's existence and the nature of its design. As a political concept, the idea of an inland capital is as old as the Brazilian nation itself, initially symbolizing Brazilian independence and remaining the symbolic focus of a desired political unity. For many years the idea of Brasília was embedded in the prevailing political rhetoric of Brazil, with its continuing dream of national greatness. Associated with the long-standing aim of populating the interior, the new capital, through the placement of institutional monuments on previously unsettled land, creates a symbolic possession anticipating actual development.

The removal of the national administration from its previous juxtaposition with the varied activity of Rio focuses attention as never before on the government establishment. The move inland could be seen to symbolize the freeing of government from conflicting interests and as an effort to direct official concern to the welfare of the nation as a whole. At the same time, the city could be viewed as an ostentatious power symbol of the elite ruling class and as an effort to avoid association with the visible aspects of national problems. Although Brasília symbolizes government institutions, it is possible to question the degree to which these institutions themselves symbolize the nation.

Conceived as a national monument, Brasília in its physical realization embodies an interworking of symbolic images, reflective more of aspiration than reality. The motorized scale of the city, with its visual emphasis on freeways and traffic interchanges must be seen against the prevailing lack of technical advancement in Brazil as a whole. Brasília visually symbolizes a degree of mechanization which Brazil has not achieved, but seeks as a national goal.

The architecture of Brasília presents no real innovations. At the outset, it reflected many of the visual qualities of the International Style, which, rapidly adopted in the 1930s, was an easily acquired and recognizable symbol of modernity and persists in the new capital to reinforce the industrialized imagery of the city. With its wide motor roads and the glossy up-to-dateness of its building, Brasília presents a façade which even the most unsophisticated can proudly identify as "modern."

Just as the mechanized image of Brasília represents a yet unachieved degree of industrialization, the residential districts within the pilot plan area present a vision of prosperous middle-class living which is far above that enjoyed by most Brazilians. The fact that, to preserve intact this vision of an atypical way of life, the poor were banished from the city, has, of course, disturbed many visitors. For those who can overlook the social segregation inherent in the city, however, the housing of Brasília may effectively represent the achievement of an ideal environment.

It has been previously noted that in the Plaza of the Three Powers the symbolic placement of the major buildings provides a somewhat misleading representation of governmental authority. The relatively powerless National Congress provides the compositional focus, while the dominant executive authority appears visually balanced by the Supreme Court. Just how many Brazilians ponder this discrepancy, however, is open to speculation. The government complex photographs effectively and is not without its own sense of poetic drama. The National Legislature building, easily recognizable and frequently reproduced photographically throughout the country, has provided Brazil with its first truly national architectural symbol.

William Holford once observed of Brasília, "For the poor and illiterate this town building is a symbol which they can see and understand."[5] It is not only the unsophisticated who have responded to the city, however. For all its controversial aspects, Brasília has increasingly become a focus of legitimate national pride. While to its opponents, it remains a ruinous extravagance, an act of political bravado irrelevant to practical problems, Brasília actually represents more than a dictator's whim and owes its existence to a genuinely enthusiastic common effort. It may be remembered that the achievements which throughout human history have inspired the most dedication have seldom been utilitarian, but more frequently those with strong symbolic meaning. The Acropolis was a civic extravagance, and the cathedrals of the Middle Ages were similarly wasteful of resources. Behind Brasília may be seen an impulse akin to the irrational optimism which once prompted a group of thirteen bankrupt former British colonies to establish a capital so grandiose in its outlines as to provoke derisive comment for at least fifty years after its founding.

If Brasília is a folly, it is in the grand tradition of human folly. Although one may regard Rio as an essentially nineteenth-century conception of a city, and Brasília as representing the twentieth century, both are in many ways old-fashioned. The city of Brasília, like Rio, is conceived as a permanent, relatively stable, ordered human environment. The static quality of the Brasília plan, together with its visual hierarchy, reflects the maintenance of traditional images and values. It is perhaps significant that Brasília is not the creation of a wealthy, powerful, industrialized, technically advanced nation. Perhaps only a rather old-fashioned society could take Brasília seriously.

Throughout history, men have built walls, plotted axes, dedicated shrines, laid out streets. They have been impelled by complex, not always noble motives, and the physical mark of the human presence on earth does not always move us to pride. Yet if the building of cities has been bound to power and ambition, to waste and extravagance and symbols of worldly vanity, it has also embodied the highest and most enduring ideals of collective life. As our urban inheritance reminds us of the lives and hopes and follies of our ancestors, so Brasília takes its place as a visible witness to the flawed, aspiring human spirit.

5. William Holford, "Brasília," *Journal of the Royal Institute of British Architects* 67 (March 1960): 154.

BIBLIOGRAPHY

1. General Works on Brazil

The scholarly literature dealing with Brazil is vast and includes many areas of specialized study. Listed below are some relatively recent books available in English which provide a good introduction to various aspects of Brazilian society.

Azvedo, Fernando de. *Brazilian Culture*. New York: Macmillan, 1950.
Bello, José Maria. *A History of Modern Brazil 1889–1964*. Stanford: Stanford University Press, 1966.
Burns, E. Bradford. *Nationalism in Brazil: A Historical Survey*. New York: Praeger, 1968.
Camacho, José Abel. *Brazil: An Interim Assessment*. 2nd ed. London and New York: Royal Institute of International Affairs, 1954.
Deland, Robert T. *Brazilian Planning: Development, Politics and Administration*. Chapel Hill: University of North Carolina Press, 1967.
De Dubnic, Vladimir Reisky. *Political Trends in Brazil*. Washington, D.C.: Public Affairs Press, 1968.
Fernandes, Florestan. *The Negro in Brazilian Society*. New York: Columbia University Press, 1969.
Freyre, Gilberto. *Brazil: An Interpretation*. New York: Knopf, 1945.
———. *The Mansions and the Shanties*. New York: Knopf, 1966.
———. *The Masters and the Slaves*. New York: Knopf, 1956.
———. *New World in the Tropics*. New York: Knopf, 1959.
———. *Order and Progress: Brazil from Monarchy to Republic*. New York: Knopf, 1970.
Furtado, Celso. *The Economic Growth of Brazil: A Survey from Colonial to Modern Times*. Berkeley: University of California Press, 1963.
Harris, Marvin. *Town and Country in Brazil*. New York: Columbia University Press, 1956.
Momsen, Richard. *Brazil: A Giant Stirs*. Princeton: Van Nostrand, 1968.
Moog, Clodomir Vianna. *Bandierantes and Pioneers*. New York: Braziller, 1964.
Oliveira Lima, Manuel de. *The Evolution of Brazil Compared with That of Spanish and Anglo-Saxon America*. New York: Russell and Russell, 1966.

Prado, Caio. *The Colonial Background of Modern Brazil.* Berkeley: University of California Press, 1967.

Putnam, Samuel. *Marvelous Journey: A Survey of Four Centuries of Brazilian Writing.* New York: Knopf, 1931.

Rodriques, José Honorio. *The Brazilians: Their Character and Aspirations.* Austin: University of Texas Press, 1967.

Smith, Thomas. *Brazil: People and Institutions.* Baton Rouge: Louisiana State University Press, 1963.

Wagley, Charles. *An Introduction to Brazil.* New York: Columbia University Press, 1966.

2. *General Historical and Descriptive Works on Rio de Janeiro*

Although this book has considered Rio primarily in terms of its modern planning, the following books may be useful in pursuing a more intensive study of the history of the city. A large body of literature, almost all of it in Portuguese, deals with the historical development of Rio.

Berger, Paulo and Eneida. *Copacabana.* Rio de Janeiro: Departamento de História e Documentação da Prefeitura do Distrito Federal, 1959.

Callcott, Maria (Dundes) Graham. *Journal of a Voyage to Brazil, and Residence There during Part of the Years 1821, 1822, and 1823.* London: Longman, 1824.

Coaracy, Vivaldo. *Memórias da cidade do Rio de Janeiro.* Rio de Janeiro: José Olympio, 1965.

Costa, Cássio. *Gávea.* Rio de Janeiro: Departamento de História e Documentação do Estado da Guanabara, 1959.

Costa, Luiz Edmundo da. *A côrte de D. João do Rio de Janeiro.* 2nd ed. 3 vols. Rio de Janeiro: Conquista, 1957.

———. *O Rio de Janeiro o meu tempo.* 2nd ed. 5 vols. Rio de Janeiro: Conquista, 1957.

———. *Rio in the Time of the Viceroys.* Rio de Janeiro: J. R. de Oliveira, 1936.

Cruls, Gastão Luis. *Aparência do Rio de Janeiro.* 2 vols. Rio de Janeiro: José Olympio, 1965.

Debret, Jean Baptiste. *Viagem pitoresca e histórica ao Brasil.* New York: Continental News, 1965.

Drummond, Victor. *Rio de Janeiro, Capital do Brasil.* Rio de Janeiro: Estado de Guanabara, Secretaria Geral de Educação e Cultura, 1962.

Dunlop, Charles. *Album do Rio Antigo.* Rio de Janeiro: Editôra Rio Antigo, 1965.

———. *Apontamentos para a história dos bondes no Rio de Janeiro.* 2 vols. Rio de Janeiro: Gráf. Laemmert, 1953–55.

———. *O Rio Antigo.* 4 vols. Rio de Janeiro: Gráf. Laemmert, 1955.

Ferreira da Rosa, Francisco. *Memorial de Rio de Janeiro.* Rio de Janeiro: Redação e Administração, 1951.

Ferrez, Gilberto. *Aquarelas de Richard Bate o Rio de Janeiro de 1808–1848.* Rio de Janeiro: Editado pela Galeria Brasiliana, 1965.

———. *O Velho Rio de Janeiro através das gravuras de Thomas Ender.* São Paulo: Edições Melhoramentos, 1956.

Fontainha, Afonso. *História dos monumentos do Rio de Janeiro.* Rio de Janeiro: Estado da Guanabara, 1963.

Gerson, Brasil. *História das ruas do Rio.* Rio de Janeiro: Livraria Brasiliana, 1965.

Gibson, Hugh. *Rio.* Garden City, N.Y.: Doubleday, Doran, 1937.

Mariano Filho, José. *O passeio publico.* Rio de Janeiro: Est. de artes Gráfica, 1943.

Mauricio, Augusto. *Algo do meu velho Rio.* Rio de Janeiro: Editôra Brasiliana, 1966.

Maurois, André. *Rio de Janeiro.* Paris: F. Nathan, 1951.

Morales do Los Rios Filho, Adolfo. *Grandjean de Montigny e a evolução da arte brasileira.* Rio de Janeiro: Editôra a Noite, 1941.

———. *Rio de Janeiro imperial.* Rio de Janeiro: Editôra a Noite, 1946.

Noronha Santos, Francisco Angenor. *Meios de transporte no Rio de Janeiro.* 2 vols. Rio de Janeiro: Jornal do Commercio, 1934.

Sá, Victor de. *Terra carioca.* Rio de Janeiro: Editôra Alba, 1960.

Ribeiro Lamego, Alberto. *O homen e a Guanabara.* Rio de Janeiro: Serviço Gráfico do Instituto Brasileira de Geografica e Estatística, 1948.

Tourinho, Eduardo. *Revelações do Rio de Janeiro.* Rio de Janeiro: Editôra Civilização Brasileira, 1964.

In addition to numerous books on the development of Rio, a source of articles relating to the city may be found in the *Revista do instituto histórico e geographico Brasileiro,* Rio de Janeiro: Imprensa Nacional.

3. Modern Planning in Rio de Janeiro

Agache, Alfred. *Cidade do Rio de Janeiro: Remodelaçao, extensão, e embelezamento.* Paris: Foyer Brésilien, 1930. Portions of the Agache report were printed in the *Revista de diretoria de engenharia* published in Rio by the Secretaria Geral de Viação e Obras. They appeared in the following issues: July 1933, pp. 76–82; September 1933, pp. 34–45; November 1933, pp. 34–43; January 1934, pp. 64–85; March 1934, pp. 55–59.

Athayde, Raymundo. *Pereira Passos: O reformador do Rio de Janeiro.* Rio de Janeiro: Editôra a Noite, 1944.

Cidade Universitaria da Universidade do Brasil. Rio de Janeiro: Ministério de Educação e Cultura, 1953.

Comissão Executiva Para o Desenvolvimento Urbano (CEDUG)–Doxiadis Associates. *Guanabara—A Plan for Urban Development.* Rio de Janeiro: The State of Guanabara, Document Dox-Bra-A6, 20 November 1965.

Ferrez, Marc. *Avenida Central.* Paris: Erhard, 1906.

Goulart, José Alipio. *Favelas do Distrito Federal.* Rio de Janeiro: Ministério da Agricultura, 1957.

Grupo de Trabalho Criado em 5/2/65. *A Ponte Rio-Niterói.* Rio de Janeiro: Departamento de Estradas de Rodagem, 1966.

Nascimento Silva, Fernando, ed. *Rio de Janeiro em seus quattrocentos anos.* Rio de Janeiro and São Paulo: Distribuidora Record, 1965.

Szilard, Adalberto, and Reis, José de Oliveira. *Urbanismo no Rio de Janeiro.* Rio de Janeiro: Editôra o Constructor, 1950.

A highly valuable and continuous source of information on the planning and development of Rio de Janeiro is the *Revista de Engenharia do Estado da Guanabara* published in Rio by the Secretaria de Obras Públicas. This official periodical provides detailed articles on all phases of government public works, including tunnels, roads, public transport, filling operations, parks, and urban redevelopment. The *Revista de Engenharia* has replaced the *Revista Municipal de Engenharia* published previously by the Prefeitura do Distrito Federal. Between July 1932 and September 1937 this periodical was known as the *Revista da Diretoria de Engenharia* and was published by the Secretaria Geral de Viação e Obras. Another source of articles relevant to the planning of Rio is the *Revista do Clube de Engenharia* published in Rio by the Clube de Engenharia.

A source of statistical information about Guanabara is the *Anuário estatistico do Estado da Guanabara* published by the Documents Department of the State of Guanabara. Statistical information may also be obtained from the *Revista brasileira de estatística* published annually in Rio de Janeiro by the Instituto Brasileiro de Geografia e Estatística (IBGE).

4. The Modern Movement in Brazilian Architecture

Although Brazilian architecture is to an extent represented in the international architectural press, the best periodical sources are Brazilian journals. These include the architectural magazines *Acrópole* and *Bem estar,* and the art and architecture magazine, *Habitat,* published in São Paulo. An excellent source is *Módulo,* a review of architecture and the visual arts published in Rio de Janeiro. Also of interest is *Arquitetura e Engenharia,* published in Belo Horizonte, and *Cadernos de Estudos* published by the Faculty of Architecture, University of Rio Grande do Sul in Pôrto Alegre.

The most comprehensive architectural surveys in book form are Philip Goodwin, *Brazil Builds* (New York: Museum of Modern Art, 1943) and Henrique Mindlin, *Modern Architecture in Brazil* (New York: Reinhold, 1956). Also of interest are the works listed below.

Architecture d'Aujourd'hui 90 (June–July 1960). Issue devoted to Brazil.

Boase, Arthur J. "Brazilian Concrete Building Design Compared with United States Practice." *Engineering News–Record* 902 (28 June 1945): 80–88.

———. "Building Codes Explain the Slenderness of South American Structures." *Engineering News–Record* 564 (19 April 1945): 68–77.

Boavista, Paulo T. "Modern Architecture." *London Studio* 26 (October 1943): 121–29.

"Brazil Builds a New City: Cidade dos Motores, Brazil." *Progressive Architecture* 27 (September 1946): 52–74.

"Brazil Builds on Tradition and Today." *Art News* 41 (February 1943): 14–19 ff.

"Brazil's Leadership." *Carnegie Magazine* 17 (May 1943): 51–53.

Castedo, Leopoldo. *The Baroque Prevalence in Brazilian Art.* New York: C. Frank, 1964.

Goodwin, Philip. "Brazil Builds for the New World." *California Arts and Architecture* 60 (February 1943): 21–23.

Hitchcock, Henry-Russell. *Latin American Architecture Since 1945.* New York: Museum of Modern Art, 1955.

Inquérito Nacional de Arquitetura. Belo Horizonte: Escola de Arquitetura da Universidade de Minas Gerais, 1963.

Mindlin, Henrique. *Brazilian Architecture.* Lethaby Lectures, Royal College of Art, 1961. Rome: Brazilian Embassy, 1961.

Mock, Elizabeth. "Building for Tomorrow." *Travel* 81 (June 1943): 26–32.

Penna, J. O. de Meira. "Brazilian Architecture Exhibitions." *Módulo* 12 (February 1959): 38–43.

"Report on Brazil." *Architectural Review* 116 (October 1954): 235–50.

Sitwell, Sacheverell. "The Brazilian Style." *Architectural Review* 95 (March 1944): 64–68 ff.

Smith, Carleton Sprague. "Architecture of Brazil." *Architectural Record* 119 (April 1956): 187–94.

Smith, G. E. Kidder. "Architects and the Modern Scene." *Architectural Review* 95 (March 1944): 78–84.

"The United States of Brazil." *Architectural Forum* 87 (November 1947): 65–112.

5. *Works by Lúcio Costa on Modern Architecture*

"Architecture and Contemporary Society." *Arts and Architecture* 71 (October 1954): 14–15 ff.

Arquitetura brasileira. Rio de Janeiro: Ministério da Educação e Saúde, Serviço de Documentação, 1952.

"Arquitetura contemporânea." In *Rio em Seus quatrocentos anos,* edited by Fernando Nascimento Silva. Rio de Janeiro and São Paulo: Distribuidora Record, 1965, pp. 242–57.

"Art and Education." *Módulo* 17 (December 1959): 29–28.

Consideracões sôbre arte contemporânea. Rio de Janeiro: Ministério da Educação e Saúde, Serviço de Documentação, 1952.

"In Search of a New Monumentality." *Architectural Review* 104 (September 1948): 117–27. Article includes statements by several contributors; Costa's statement appears on page 127.

Sôbre arquitetura. Porto Alegre: Centro dos Estudantes de Arquitetura, 1962.

"Testimony of a Carioca Architect." *Atlantic Monthly* 197 (February 1956): 137–39.

6. *Works by and about Oscar Niemeyer*

A wide range of Niemeyer's design, together with English text, may be found in the following books by Stamo Papadaki: *The Work of Oscar Niemeyer* (New York: Reinhold, 1950), *Oscar Niemeyer: Works in Progress* (New York: Reinhold, 1956), and *Oscar Niemeyer* (New York: Braziller, 1960). His work is also included in general studies of Brazilian architecture and in architectural periodicals. The following writings by Niemeyer are helpful in illuminating some of his ideas.

"Considerações sôbre a arquitetura Brasileira." *Módulo* 7 (February 1957): 5–10. English translation included.
"Contradição na arquiteture." *Módulo* 31 (December 1962): 17–20. English translation included.
"Form and Function in Architecture." *Módulo* 21 (December 1960): 3–7.
"Imagination in Architecture." *Módulo* 15 (October 1959): 6–13.
Letter from Oscar Niemeyer to Le Corbusier published in Le Corbusier's *Oeuvre complète 1938–1946* (Zurich: Girsberger, 1946), p. 90.
Minha experiência em Brasília. Rio de Janeiro: Editôra Vitoria, 1961. French translation, *Mon expérience à Brasilia.* Paris: Forces Vives, 1963.
"My Brasília Experience." *Módulo* 18 (June 1960): 18–24.
"Palacio residential de Brasília." *Módulo* 7 (February 1957): 20–27. English translation included.
Quase memorias: viagens, tempós de entusiasmo e revolta 1961–1966. Rio de Janeiro: Editôra Civilização Brasileira, 1968.
"Testimony." *Módulo* 9 (February 1958): 3–6.
Textes et dessins pour Brasília. Paris: Forces Vives, 1965.

7. *Le Corbusier in Brazil*

Le Corbusier's description of his first visit to Rio appears in *Précisions sur un état présent de l'architecture et de l'urbanisme* (Paris: Editions Crès et Cie, 1930; reprint, Paris: Editions Vincent, Fréal et Cie, 1960). Illustrations of his design projects in Rio are published in his books *Oeuvre complète 1934–1938* (Zurich: Girsberger, 1939; reprint, New York: Wittenborn, 1964) and *Oeuvre complète 1938–1946* (Zurich: Girsberger, 1946; reprint, New York: Wittenborn, 1964). Le Corbusier's early urban design concepts were presented in his book *City of Tomorrow* (London: Architectural Press, 1947), first published in France as *Urbanisme* (Paris: Editions Crès et Cie, 1925). His next major book on city planning was *The Radiant City* (New York: Grossman, Orion Press, 1967), first published in France as *La Ville Radieuse* (Boulogne [Seine]: Editions de l'Architecture d'Aujourd'hui, 1935). A concise summary of Le Corbusier's urban concepts may be found in Norma Evenson, *Le Corbusier: The Machine and the Grand Design* (New York: Braziller, 1969).

8. *Brasília and Its Background*

Brasília has received considerable attention in the architectural and popular press, especially during the phase of development leading up to the dedication of the city. Among architectural periodicals, the largest concentration of material may be found in the Brazilian magazines *Módulo* and *Habitat.* Of particular interest are volumes 8 (July 1957) and 18 (June 1960), both of which are devoted entirely to Brasília. Articles in *Módulo* are frequently accompanied by translations into other languages. Also consistently useful is *Brasilia,* the journal of the Companhia Urbanizadora da Nova Capital do Brasília (NOVACAP). As an official journal, its purpose is essentially propagandistic, but it provides a continuous source of articles and photographs tracing the development of Brasília from its inception.

The following works deal with broad aspects of Brasília, with the historical background of the project, with its geographic and nationalistic implications, and with the selection of the site.

Arnau, Frank. *Brasília: Phantasie und Wirklichkeit.* Munich: Prestel-Verlag, 1960.

Banco Regional de Brasília. *Brasília Conteúdo e Continente.* Brasília: Publicação do Banco Regional de Brasília S.A. e da Secretaria do Governo do D.F., 1967. Série Documentos e Estudos No. 1.

Barbosa, Raul de Sá. "Brasília, evolução, História de una ideia." *Módulo* 18 (June 1960): 28–42. English translation included.

Castro, Henrique Luttgardes Cardoso de. *Brasília e o desenvolvimento nacional.* Rio de Janeiro: D.A.S.P. Service de Documentação, 1960.

Comissão de Estudos para localização da Nova Capital do Brasil. *Relatório técnico.* Rio de Janeiro, 1948.

Corbusier, Roland. *Brasília e o desenvolvimento nacional.* Rio de Janeiro: ISEB, 1960.

Crease, David. "Brasília Becomes a Capital City." *Geographical Magazine* 41 (March 1969): 419–28.

———. "Brasília: Brazil Looks West." *Geographical Magazine* 36 (March 1964): 633–48.

———. "Joining the Brazils." *Geographical Magazine* 37 (July 1964): 184–97.

Cruls, Luiz. *Relatorio da Comissão Explorada do Planalto Central do Brasil.* Rio de Janeiro: Companhia Editora Nacional, 1947.

Giovate, Moises. *Brasília: Uma realização em marcha.* São Paulo: Edicôes Melhoramentos, 1959.

Kent, Hollister. "Vera Cruz: Brazil's New Federal Capital." Ph.D. dissertation, Cornell University, 1956. Available through University Microfilms, Ann Arbor, Michigan. Publication no. 20,046, 1957. Library of Congress card (microfilm) 57–2218.

Ludwig, Armin K. "The Planning and Creation of Brasília: Toward a New and Unique Regional Environment?" in *New Perspectives of Brazil,* ed. Eric N. Baklanoff. Nashville: Vanderbilt University Press, 1966, pp. 179–204.

Orico, Oswaldo. *Brasil, capital Brasília.* Rio de Janeiro: Serviço Gráfico do IBGE, 1958. Revised edition, Rio de Janeiro: Distribuidora Record, 1961.

Penna, J. O. de Meira. *Brasília.* Rio de Janeiro: Divisão Cultural, Ministério das Relações Exteriores, 196?.

———. *Brazil Builds Brasília.* Rio de Janeiro, 1960.

———. "Brazil Builds a New Capital." *Landscape* 5 (Spring 1956): 17–22.

Pinheiro, Israel. "Uma realidade: Brasília." *Módulo* 8 (June 1957): 3–8. English translation included.

Presidência da República. *Brasília e a opinião mundial.* Rio de Janeiro: Imprensa Oficial, 1958–59.

Silveira, José Peixoto da. *A nova capital: para que, para onde e como mudar a nova capital.* Rio de Janeiro: Editôra Pongetti, 1960.

Snyder, D. E. "Alternate Perspectives on Brasília." *Economic Geography* 40 (January 1964): 34–45.

Stephenson, Glenn V. "Two Newly Created Capitals: Islamabad and Brasília." *Town Planning Review* 41 (October 1970): 317–32.

9. The Design Competition for Brasília

Brasília. Material relating to the competition may be found in nos. 3, 4, and 6 (March, April, and June 1957).

Construtécnica. *Brasília: Plano pilôto: Relatorio justificativo.* São Paulo: Habitat Editôra, 1957.

Habitat 40–41 (March–April 1957). This issue devoted to the Brasília competition contains an account of the competition judgment. The Levi plan and the Construtécnica scheme are illustrated, together with Portuguese texts, pp. 4–18.

Habitat 42 (May–July 1957). The MMM Roberto plan is published with a Portuguese text, pp. 2–24.

Holford, William. "Brasília: A New Capital City for Brazil." *Architectural Review* 122 (December 1957): 394–402.

Módulo 8 (July 1957). Issue devoted to the Brasília competition. Articles include the minutes of the committee for judging the pilot plan, the program of the competition, the jury's comments on the finalists' designs, and statements by individual jurors regarding the judgment. Costa's competition report is reproduced in full. Illustrations of all the prize-winning entries are included. The text is in Portuguese, with a German translation. An English translation is included only for the committee minutes and the Costa report.

10. The Design of Brasília: Description and Commentary

Included in the works listed below are descriptions of the construction of Brasília, pictorial representations, discussion of the architecture and urban design, and critical commentary regarding the design. The number of items appearing in periodicals relating to Brasília is extensive, and the articles included in the list below represent a somewhat arbitrary selection. In addition to the works listed here, abundant illustrative material dealing with Brasília may be found in the Brazilian journals *Brasília, Módulo,* and *Habitat.*

"Architects and Critics Speak About Brasília." *Módulo* 16 (December 1959): 29–31.

Brasília. Special issue of *Acrópole.* São Paulo: M. Grunewald, 1960.

Brasília. Special issue of *Arquitetura e Engenharia,* combining nos. 61–63 (July–December 1961).

"Brasília." *Architecture d'Aujourd'hui* 33 (April 1962): 22–37.

Bemelmans, Ludwig. "Brasília: the Capital and the Cardiogram." *Holiday* 25 (March 1959): 46 ff.

Buchanan, Colin. "The Moon's Backside." *Journal of the Royal Institute of British Architects* 74 (April 1967): 159.

Choay, Françoise. "Une Capitale prefabriquée." *L'Oeil,* November 1959, pp. 76–83.

"Conversation in Brasília, between Robert Harbinson and George Balcombe." *Journal of the Royal Institute of British Architects* 68 (November 1961): 490–94.

Crease, David. "Progress in Brasilia." *Architectural Review* 131 (April 1962): 256–62.

Delmas, Gladys. "Brasilia Comes of Age." *The Reporter* 36 (23 February 1967): 25–33.

Eckardt, Wolf von. "Brasilia: Symbol in the Mud." *American Institute of Architects Journal* 36 (November 1961): 37–42.

Evenson, Norma. "The Symbolism of Brasilia." *Landscape* 18 (Winter 1969): 18–28.

Freyre, Gilberto. "A Brazilian's Critique of Brasilia." *The Reporter* 22 (31 March 1960): 31–32.

Gautherot, Marcel. *Brasília.* New York: Doubleday, 1966.

Hahn, Emily. "Man Decides Where." *The New Yorker* 36 (12 March 1960): 163–70 ff.

Haskell, Douglass. "Brasília: A New Type of National City." *Architectural Forum* 113 (November 1960): 126–33.

"A história da construção de Brasília." *Brasília* 40 (21 April 1960): 44–53.

Holford, William. "Brasília." *Journal of the Royal Institute of British Architects* 67 (March 1960): 154–59.

———. "Problemas e perspectivas de Brasília." *Módulo* 17 (April 1960): 2–3. English version included.

McQuade, Walter. "Brasília's Beginning." *Architectural Forum* 110 (April 1959): 97–99.

Magalhães, Aloisio, and Feldman, Eugene. *Doorway to Brasília.* Philadelphia: Falcon Press, 1959.

Malraux, André. *Brasília na palavra de André Malraux.* Rio de Janeiro: Presidencia da República, Servico de Documentação, 1959.

"Metropolis Made to Order." *National Geographic Magazine* 117 (May 1960): 704–24.

Moholy-Nagy, Sibyl. "Brasilia: Majestic Concept or Autocratic Monument." *Progressive Architecture* 40 (October 1959): 88–89.

Nelson, George. "Out of the Trackless Bush, a National Capital." *Saturday Review of Literature* 43 (12 March 1960): 39 ff.

"Opiniões sôbre Brasília." *Habitat* 58 (January–February 1960).

Penna, J. O. de Meira. "The Special International Congress of Art Critics." *Módulo* 16 (December 1959): 26–29.

Richards, J. M. "Brasilia." *Architectural Review* 125 (February 1959): 94–104.

Roche, M. "Symposium sur Brasília: exposé introductif." *Caravelle* 3 (1964): 369–85.

Stäubli, Willy. *Brasília.* New York: Universe Books, 1965.

University of Brasília. Plano orientador da Universidade de Brasília. Brasília: Editôra Universidade de Brasília, 1962.

Vitor, E. d'Almeida. *A SHIS e o problema habitacional de Brasília.* Brasília: Souvenir Publicadade, 1967.

11. Sources of Statistical Information for Brasília

Anuario de Brasília. Brasília: Souvenir Publicadade, 1967.

Companhia Urbanizadora da Nova Capital do Brasil. *NOVACAP Relatório 1966.* Brasília: NOVACAP, 1967.

Instituto Brasileiro de Geografia e Estatística (IBGE). *Brasília.* Inspetoria Regional de Estatística Municipal em Goiás, 1958.

———. *Brasília.* Coleção de Monografias, no. 325, 2nd ed. Rio de Janeiro, 1966.

———. *Censo experimental de Brasília.* Rio de Janeiro, 1959.

Prefeitura do Distrito Federal. *Censo escolar do Distrito Federal.* Brasília, 1964.

Vaitsman, Maurício. *Quanto custou Brasília.* Rio de Janeiro: Editôra Pôsto de Serviço, Coleção Livro-Verdade, 1968.

Statistical information on Brasília may also be found, together with national census data, in the *Revista brasileira de estatística* published annually in Rio de Janeiro by the Instituto Brasileira de Geografia e Estatística (IBGE).

12. Sociological Surveys of Brasília

Fundação do Serviço Social, Federal District. "Aspectos demográficos e sócio-econômicos da invasão do IAPI." Brasília, June 1965.

———. "Aspectos demográficos e sócio-econômicos das invasões do Plano Pilôto de Brasília." Brasília, May 1965.

———. "Aspectos demográficos e sócio-econômicos do Núcleo Bandierante, 5ª Avenida." Brasília, July 1965.

———. "Aspectos demográficos e sócio-econômicos do setor 'D' (Vila Matias) do núcleo satélite de Taguatinga." Brasília, May 1965.

———. "Aspectos demográficos e sócio-econômicos do setor 'E' (Vila Dimas) do núcleo satélite de Taguatinga." Brasília, January 1965.

———. *Catálogo de recursos sociais do Distrito Federal.* Brasília: Prefecture of the Federal District, 1966.

Pastore, José. *Brasília: a cidade e o homem.* São Paulo: Editôra Nacional e Editôra da Universidade de São Paulo, 1969.

INDEX

ILLUSTRATIONS

1a. Rio de Janeiro is contained within the small state of Guanabara, formerly the Federal District of Brazil. Bounded in part by the Atlantic Ocean and Guanabara Bay, the urbanized area is divided into North and South Zones by a mountain barrier.

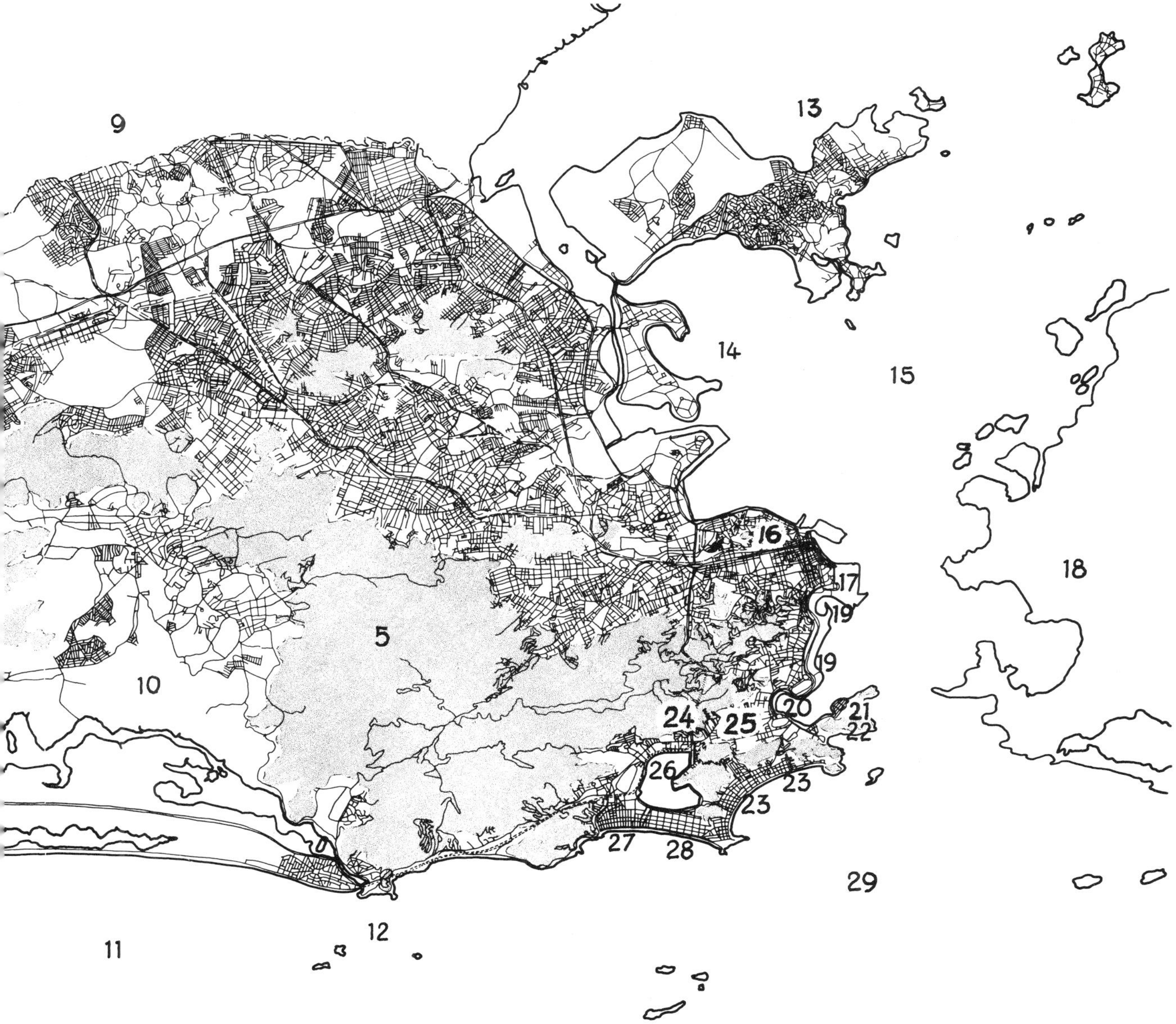

1. Santa Cruz
2. Sepetiba
3. Sepetiba Bay
4. Campo Grande
5. Mountains
6. Vila Kennedy
7. Vila Aliança
8. Bangú
9. North Zone
10. Cidade de Deus
11. South Zone
12. Barra da Tijuca
13. Ilha do Governador
14. University
15. Guanabara Bay
16. Central business district
17. Airport
18. Niteroi
19. Glória-Flamengo Park
20. Botafogo Bay
21. Urca
22. Sugarloaf
23. Copacabana
24. Corcovado
25. Botafogo
26. Lagôa Rodrigo de Freitas
27. Leblon
28. Ipanema
29. Atlantic Ocean

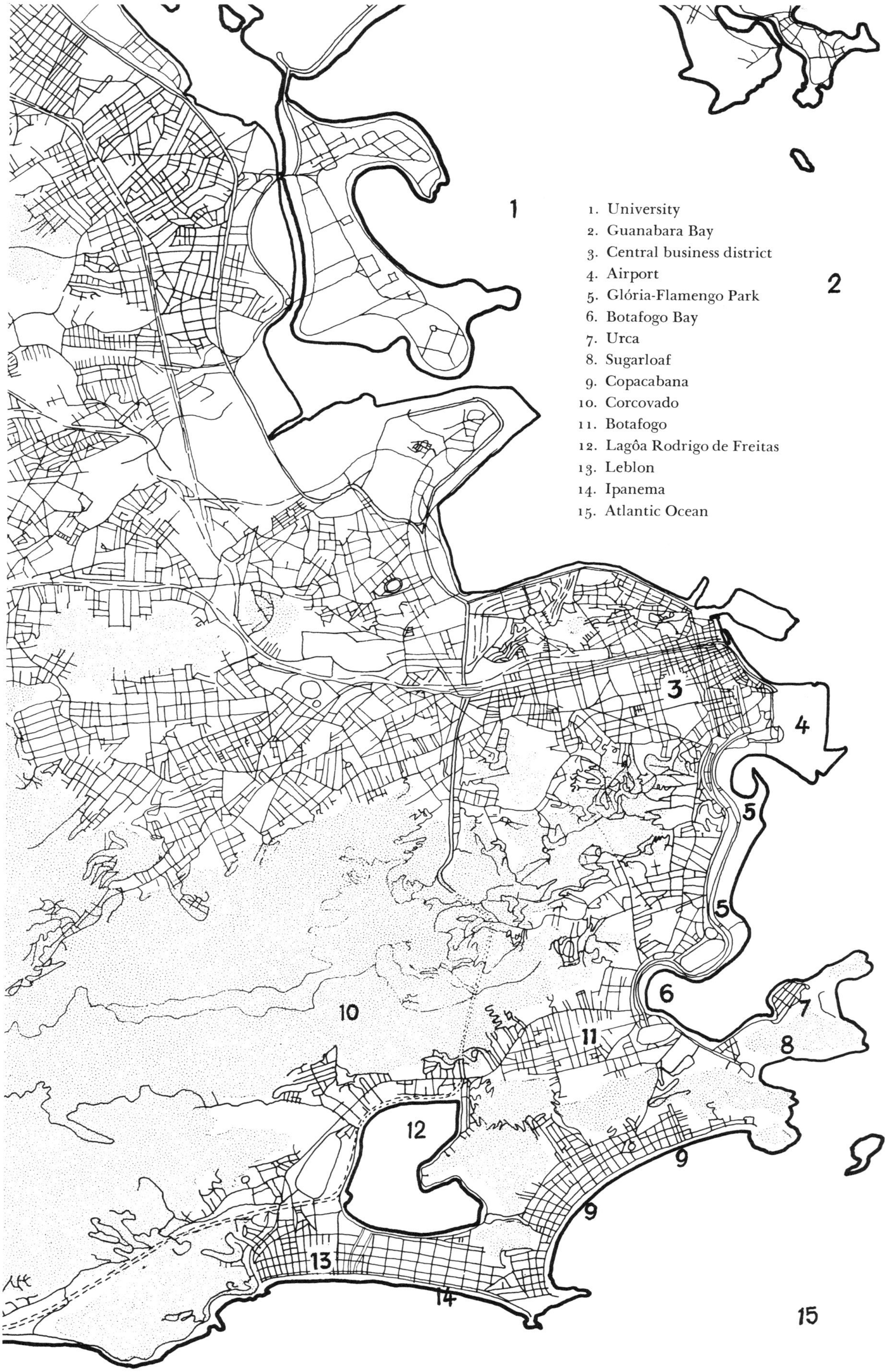
1. University
2. Guanabara Bay
3. Central business district
4. Airport
5. Glória-Flamengo Park
6. Botafogo Bay
7. Urca
8. Sugarloaf
9. Copacabana
10. Corcovado
11. Botafogo
12. Lagôa Rodrigo de Freitas
13. Leblon
14. Ipanema
15. Atlantic Ocean
1
2
3
4
5
5
6
7
8
9
9
10
11
12
13
14
15

1b. Central Rio de Janeiro.

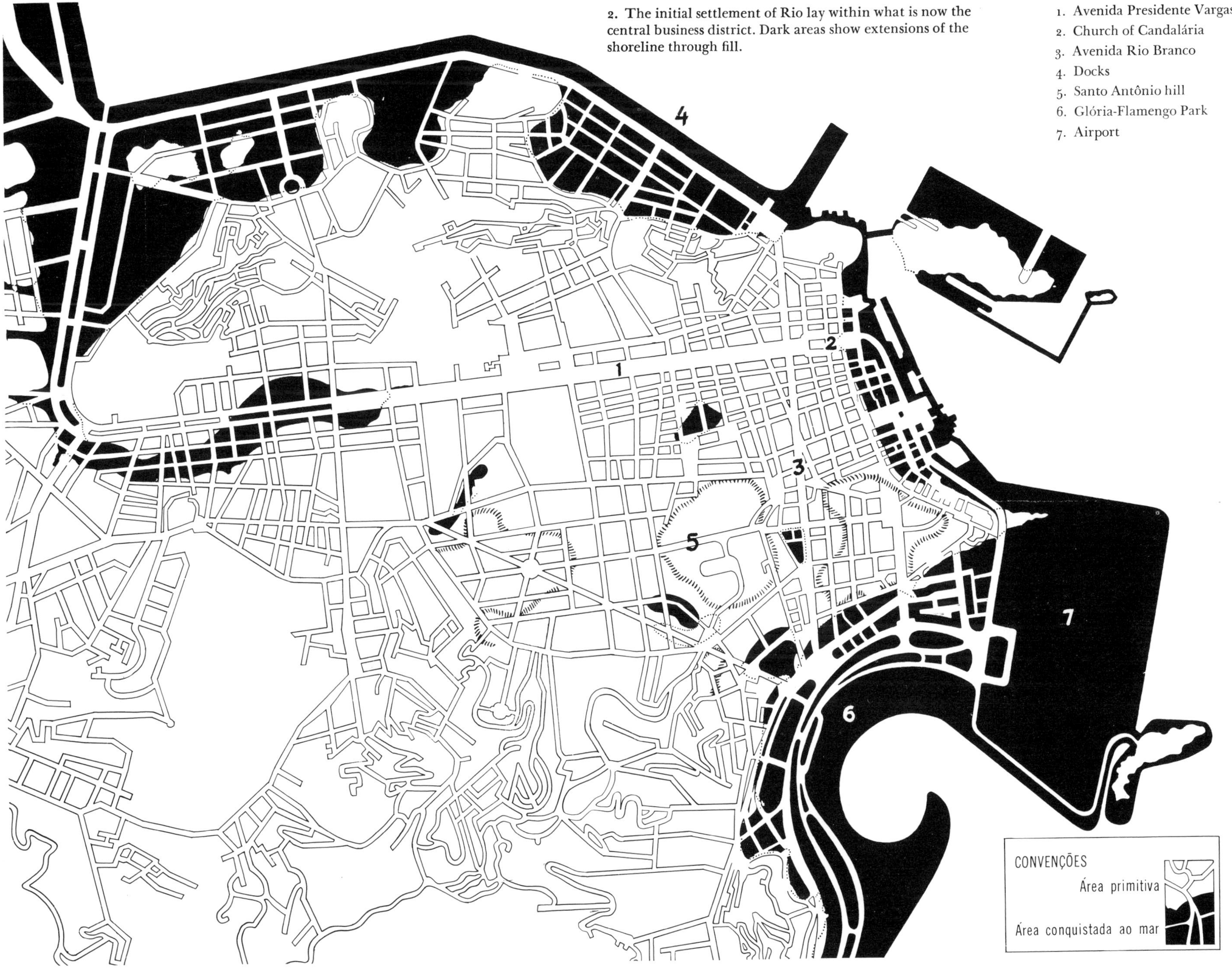

2. The initial settlement of Rio lay within what is now the central business district. Dark areas show extensions of the shoreline through fill.

1. Avenida Presidente Vargas
2. Church of Candalária
3. Avenida Rio Branco
4. Docks
5. Santo Antônio hill
6. Glória-Flamengo Park
7. Airport

3. Rio is not a city of bricks and mortar alone, but a harmonious interweaving of the works of man and nature. Looking from Sugarloaf toward Botafogo.

4. Sugarloaf and the bay of Botafogo seen from Mirante Donna Marta.

5. Looking from Sugarloaf toward Flamengo. Urca is seen at the base of Sugarloaf.

6. The central business district and airport viewed from Sugarloaf.

7. The North Zone.

8. Lagôa seen from Corcovado. Ipanema and Leblon occupy a narrow isthmus between the lake and the ocean.

9. Building patterns tend to follow the valleys and the shoreline. View from Santa Teresa.

10. The mountains are always close at hand. A street in Catete.

11. Hillside housing in Santa Teresa.

12. Houses on the hills of the North Zone.

13. Rio Comprido.

14. A house undermined by a landslide in Santa Teresa. The house was subsequently demolished.

15. An eighteenth-century aqueduct leads from the mountainous ridge of Santa Teresa to the central business district.

16. Rail lines lead outward from the central business district through the North Zone.

17. Mosaic sidewalk.

18. Narrow streets in Rio's central business district given over to pedestrians.

19. The North Zone. A street continues up a hillside without paving.

20. Outlying districts in the North Zone become semirural in character.

21. Copacabana seen from Sugarloaf. Copacabana occupies a crescent-shaped oceanfront area separated from Botafogo by a ridge of mountains.

22. High-rise building in Copacabana began along the beachfront and now crowds the slopes of the surrounding hills.

23. Copacabana beach.

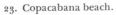

24. Avenida Atlantica bordering Copacabana beach. Street has since been widened.

25. Avenida Copacabana.

26. New building overshadows the old urban scale of Copacabana.

27. View from a rear window. Land coverage is high, especially along the beachfront.

28. Grocery shopping in Rio usually takes place at periodic street markets.

29. Ipanema provides a beachfront residential district just beyond Copacabana.

30. Apartment buildings bordering Lagôa. The Panorama Palace Hotel straddles the hillside at right.

31. The Barra da Tijuca beach area provides a site for further urbanization. New tunnels have recently increased accessibility of this district to central Rio.

32. Niteroi lies across the bay from Rio, in the state of Rio de Janeiro. As in Copacabana, the beachfront is lined with high-rise buildings.

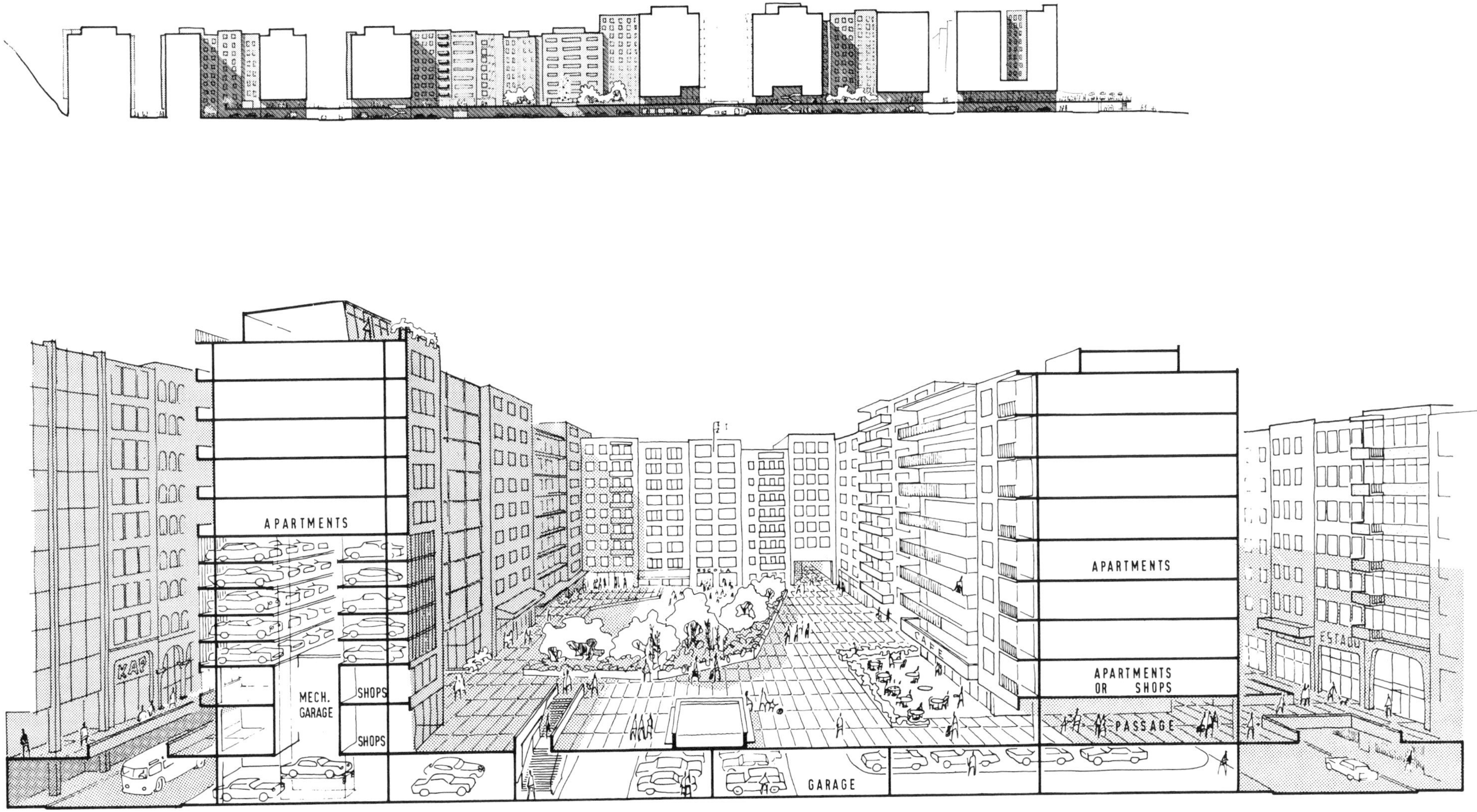

33. Proposal by Doxiadis for the renovation of Copacabana: cross-section and cutaway perspective view of typical block interior. Pedestrian circulation, together with the entrance level of buildings, would be raised one story above ground, leaving the ground level for motor traffic and parking.

34. Favela in Santa Teresa.

35. Favela occupying a hill slope along the shores of Lagôa.

36. Favela along the bayshore near the university.

37, 38. Favela near Lagôa.

39, 40. Salgueiro favela in the North Zone.

41. Salgueiro house under construction.

42. Nova Holanda project in the North Zone.

43. Public housing in Leblon.

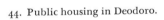

44. Public housing in Deodoro.

45. Pedregulho housing project by Affonso Reidy.

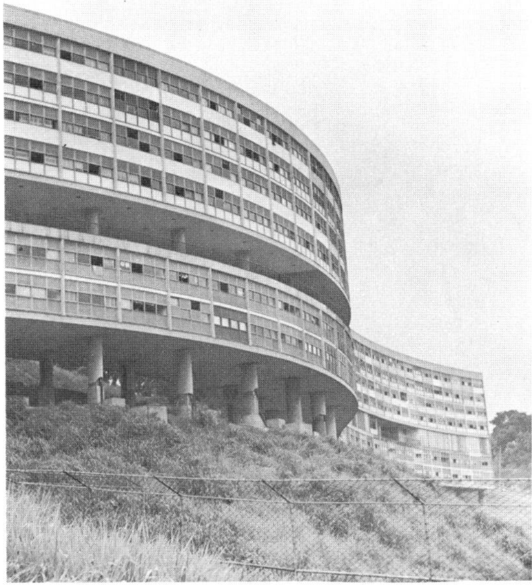

46. COHAB (Companhia de Habitaçao Popular) project Vila Kennedy. View of main square.

47. Vila Kennedy. Houses are designed to permit expansion by owners. In some cases a second story can be added.

48–50. Vila Kennedy.

48

49

50

51, 52. COHAB project Cidade de Deus.

53. The Avenida Beira-Mar bordering the bayfront, shown as new filling operations began during the 1950s on Glória-Flamengo Park.

54, 55. Avenida Rio Branco. Little of the original scale remains.

56. Academy of Fine Arts and National Gallery of Art.

57, 58. National Library.

59. Monroe Palace, built to house the National Senate.

60. Municipal Theater.

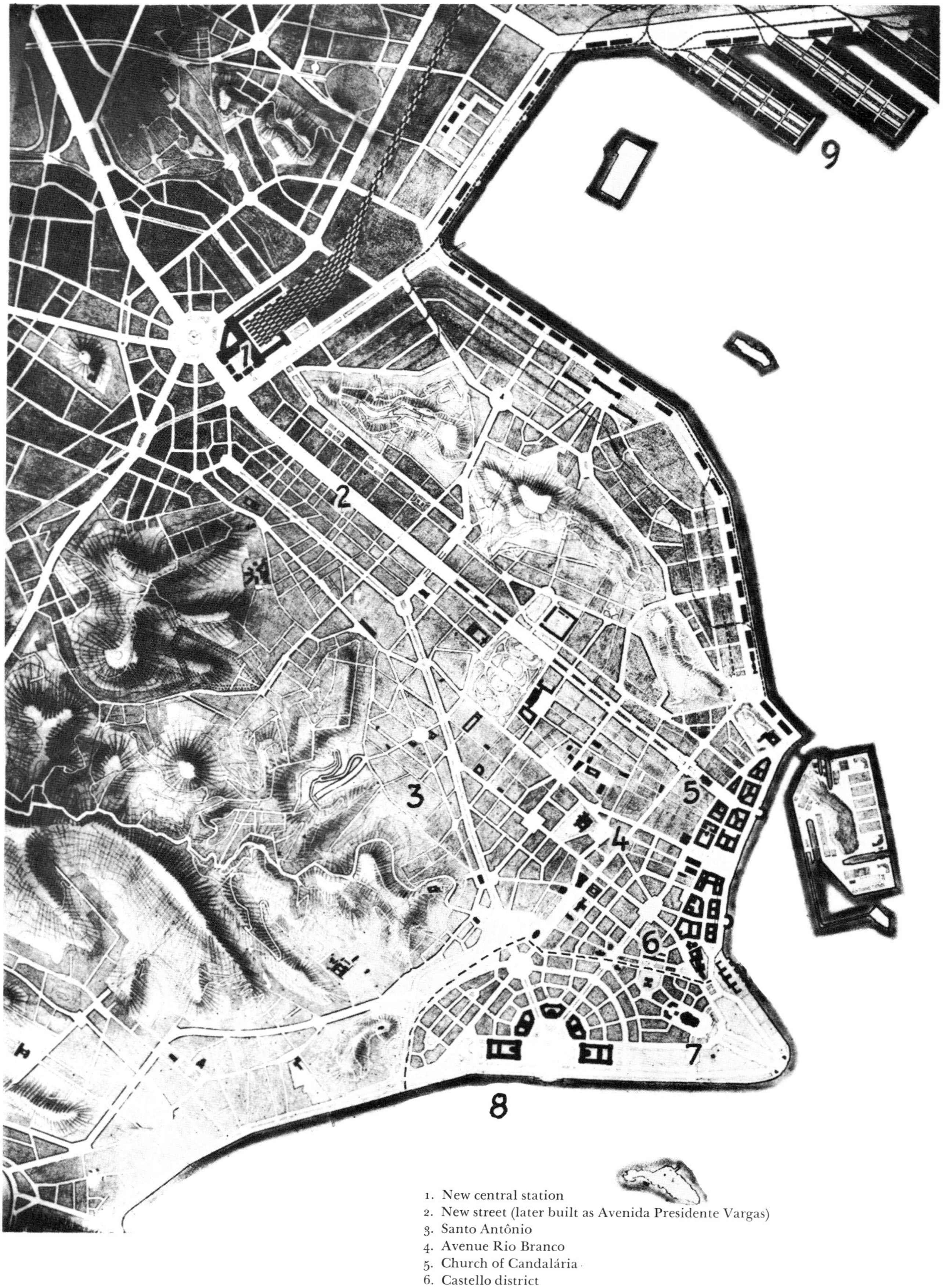

1. New central station
2. New street (later built as Avenida Presidente Vargas)
3. Santo Antônio
4. Avenue Rio Branco
5. Church of Candalária
6. Castello district
7. Pantheon
8. Gateway to Rio
9. Port facilities

61. Central Rio, showing streets projected by Agache.

——— Fill from Santo Antônio

62, 63. Agache projected a new monumental center to be constructed on fill land taken from Santo Antônio hill. The waterfront complex was to serve as a ceremonial gateway to Rio.

64. Waterfront development projected by Agache. In addition to the monumental "gateway" complex, the shoreline was to contain a "Pantheon."

1. Santo Antônio hill redevelopment
2. Municipal Theater
3. Avenida Rio Branco
4. Academy of Fine Arts and National Gallery of Art
5. National Library
6. Monroe Palace
7. Avenida Beira Mar
8. Castello district
9. Auditorium
10. Senate
11. Palace of Fine Arts
12. Hall of Deputies
13. Palace of Commerce and Industry
14. Gateway to Rio
15. Pantheon

——— Fill from Santo Antônio

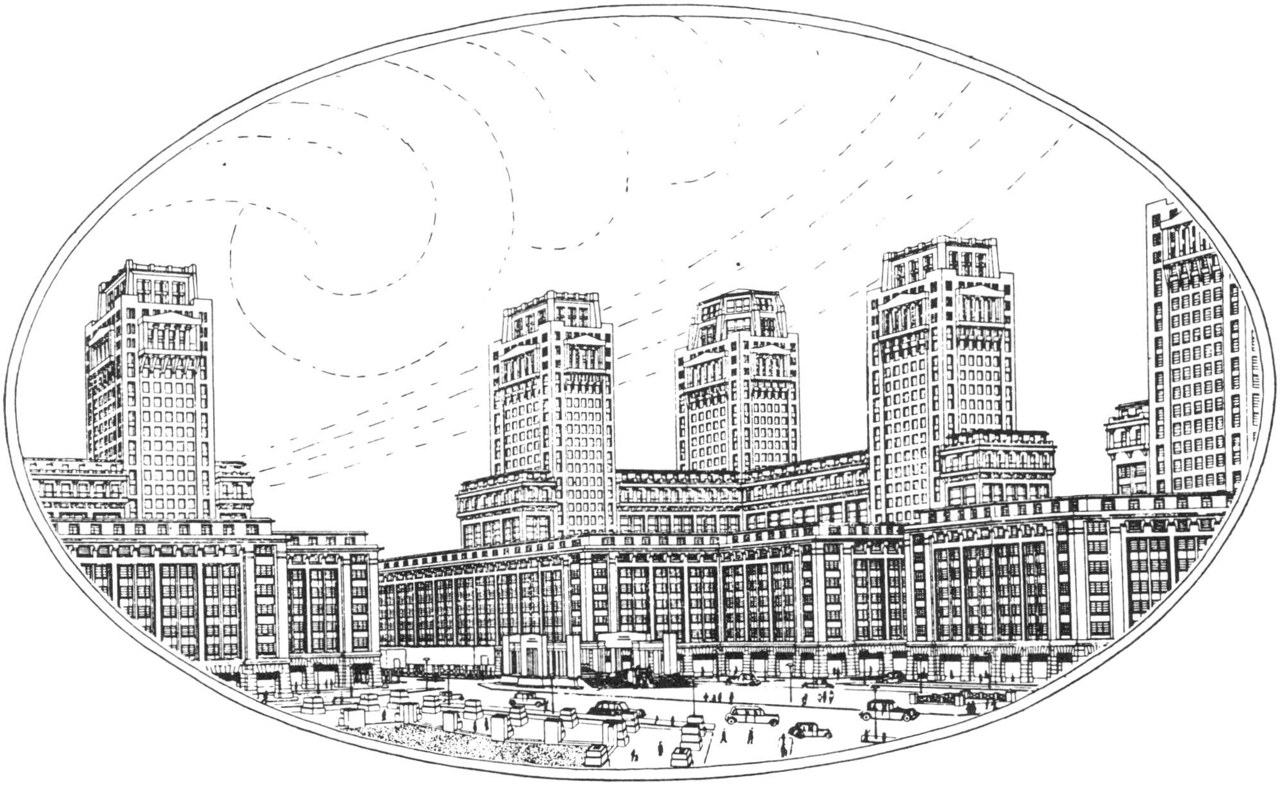

65. Projected buildings for the new Castello district.

66. Proposed building type for the central business district. Agache favored consolidating small plots to create larger office complexes. The ground floor would incorporate shopping arcades and pedestrian passageways.

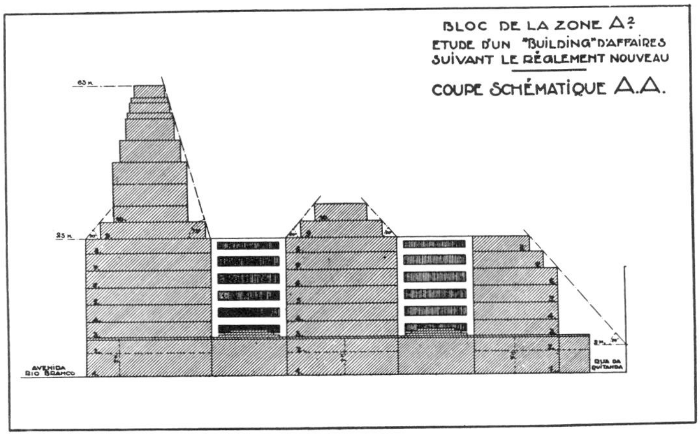

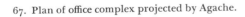

67. Plan of office complex projected by Agache.

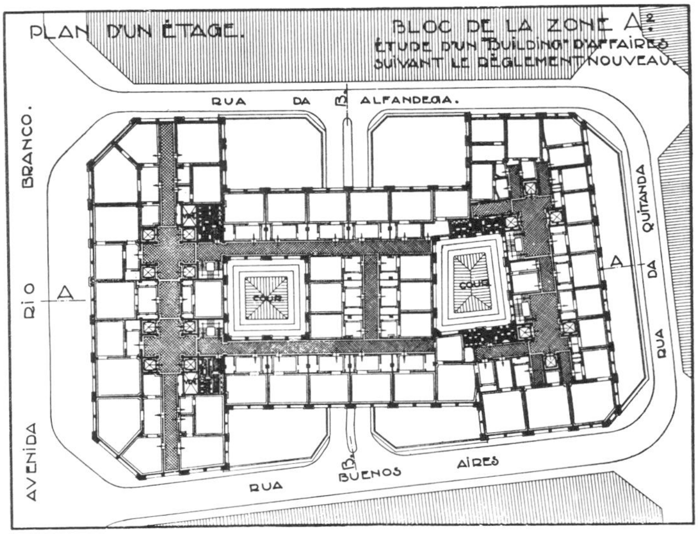

68. Avenida Presidente Vargas embodies a realization of one of the new streets projected by Agache. Originally intended to carry a central parkband, the street has been adapted to the demands for automobile parking.

69. Avenida Presidente Vargas, looking toward the church of Candalária.

70. The church of Candalária marks the intersection of Avenida Rio Branco and Avenida Presidente Vargas.

71. Le Corbusier's 1929 plan. An elevated motor freeway carrying housing below the roadway would extend through the city and connect with a bridge to Niteroi.

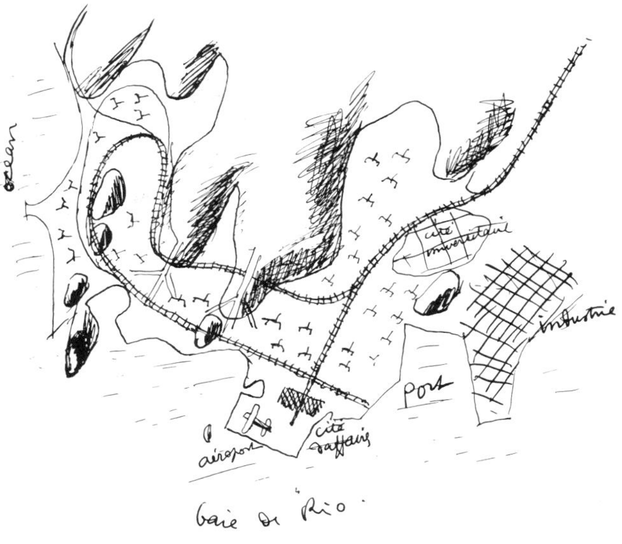

72. Le Corbusier modified his scheme on a subsequent visit in 1936. The central portion of the city would be rebuilt to provide for widely separated high-rise building. The elevated freeway now extends into the North Zone as well as along the shoreline.

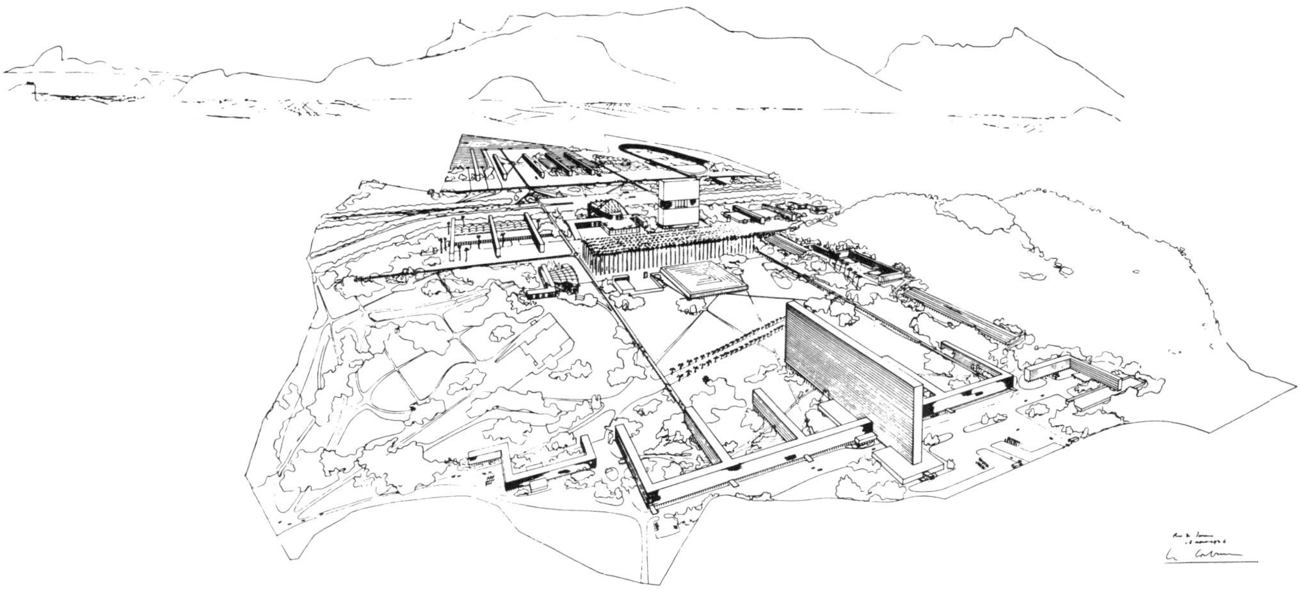

73, 74. Project by Le Corbusier for the University of Brazil.

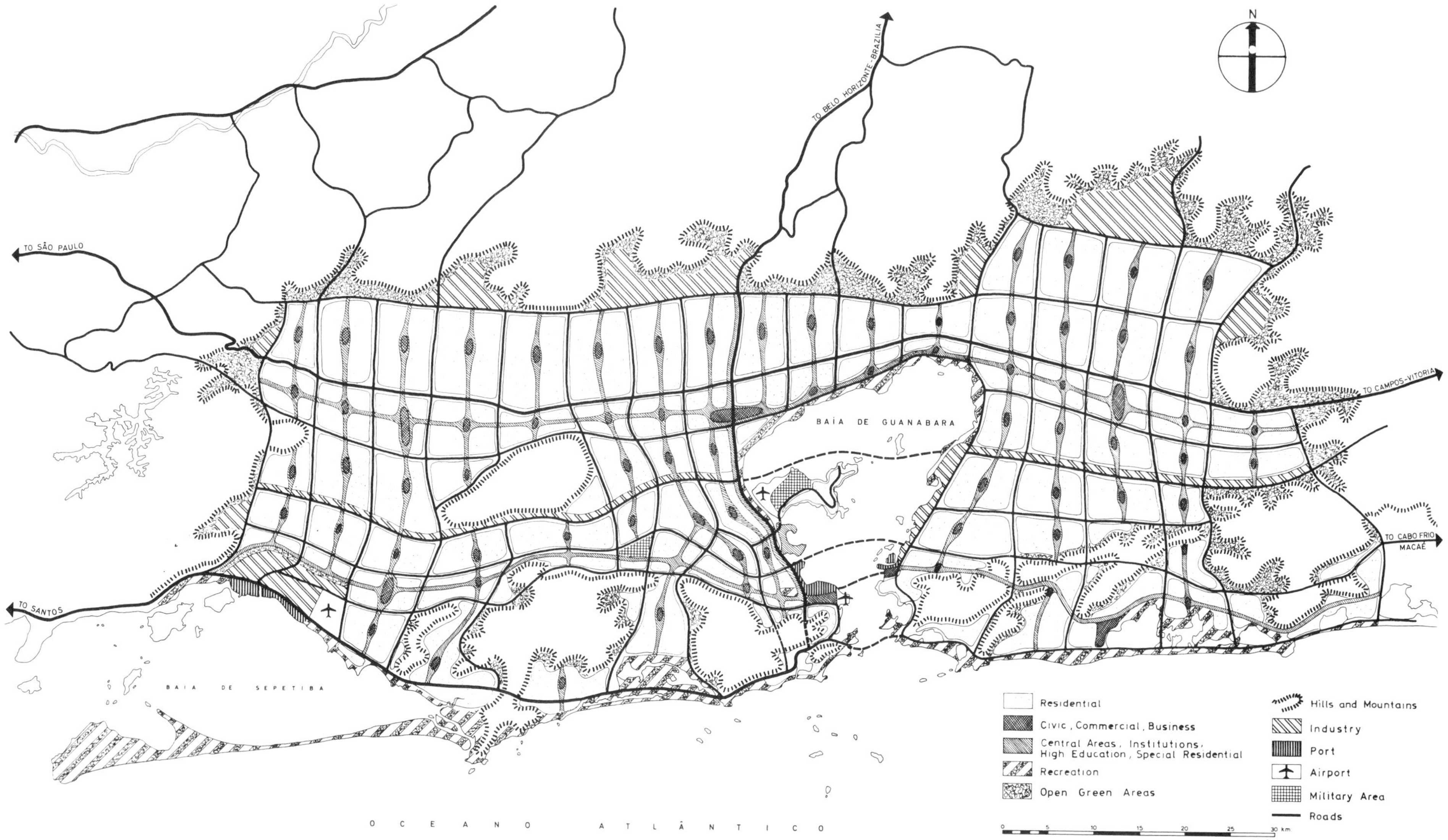

75. Master plan of Guanabara. Settlement patterns are projected in the form of a large-scale grid, with the port of Sepetiba intended as a second center of major urban concentration.

76. Projected linear development along transportation lines.

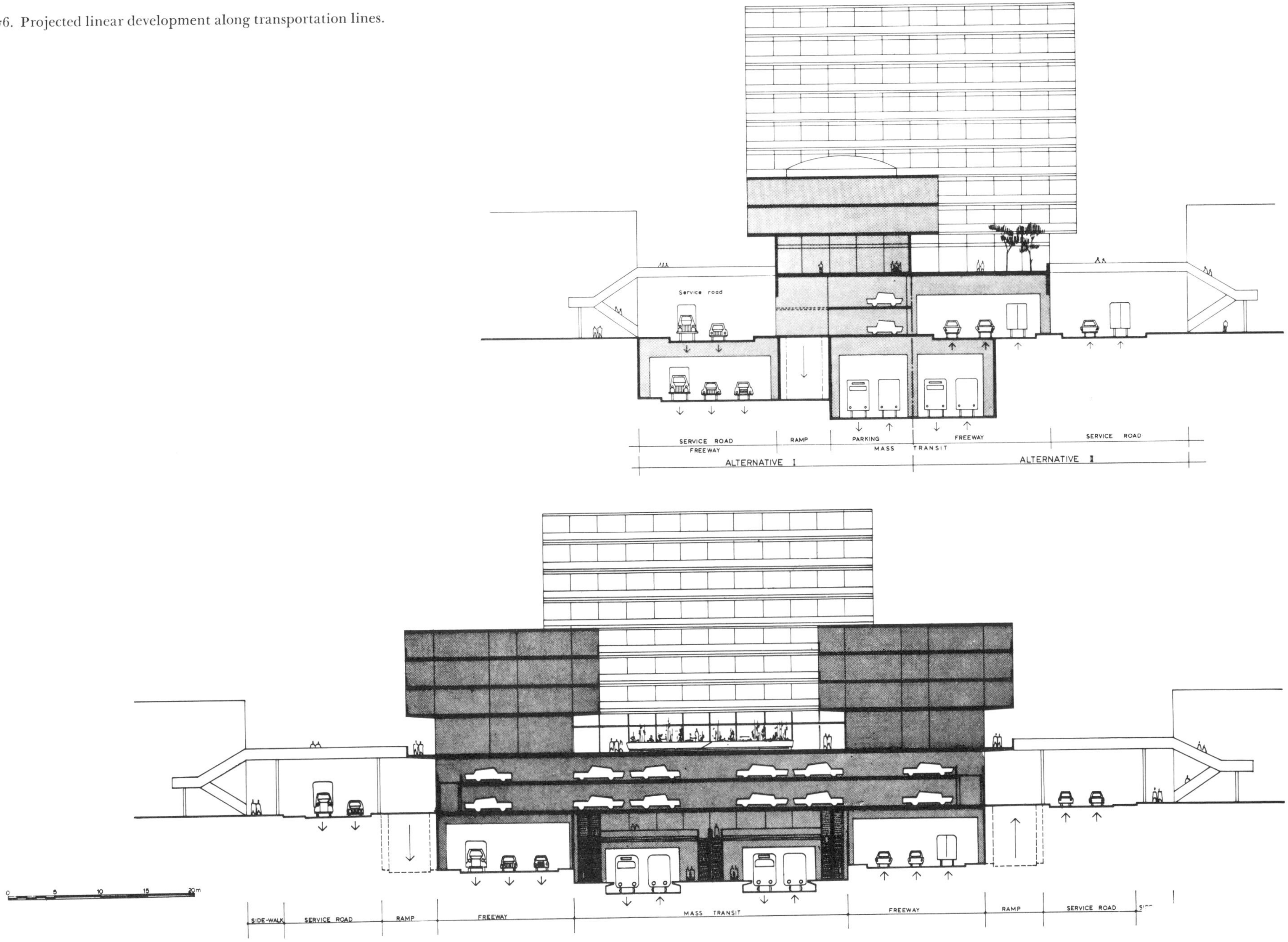

77, 78. Mangue. This district of Rio was intensively analyzed by Doxiadis as a center for urban renewal. It has subsequently been subject to demolition and reconstruction.

79. The entrance to the Rebouças tunnel connecting the Lagôa district with the North Zone, shown during construction.

80. Central business district viewed from Santa Teresa. Excavated area of Santo Antônio hill is at left.

81. Glória-Flamengo Park, constructed on fill taken from Santo Antônio hill.

82. Glória-Flamengo Park, World War II memorial.

83. Central business district seen from the plaza of the World War II memorial.

84. The house of Auguste Victor Grandjean de Montigny, who arrived in Rio in 1816 as part of a French delegation to direct the artistic life of the city.

85. University building near Urca.

86. Palácio Guanabara.

87. Domestic classicism in Santa Teresa.

88–92. Houses in Tijuca. Carioca interpretations of Second Empire and Art Nouveau reflect a taste for exuberant decor.

93

94

95

93–95. Gothic revival in Santa Teresa.

96. Building entrance in Flamengo.

97. Façade of an office building on Avenida Rio Branco.

98

98–100. Houses in Botafogo. Rio vernacular building developed a house type in which the main living area was raised one story above ground, with the lower level used as a service area. The entrance stairway is at the side of the house.

99

100

101. Cul-de-sac street in Botafogo.

102. Largo do Boticáro in Cosme Velho. An evocation of the colonial period.

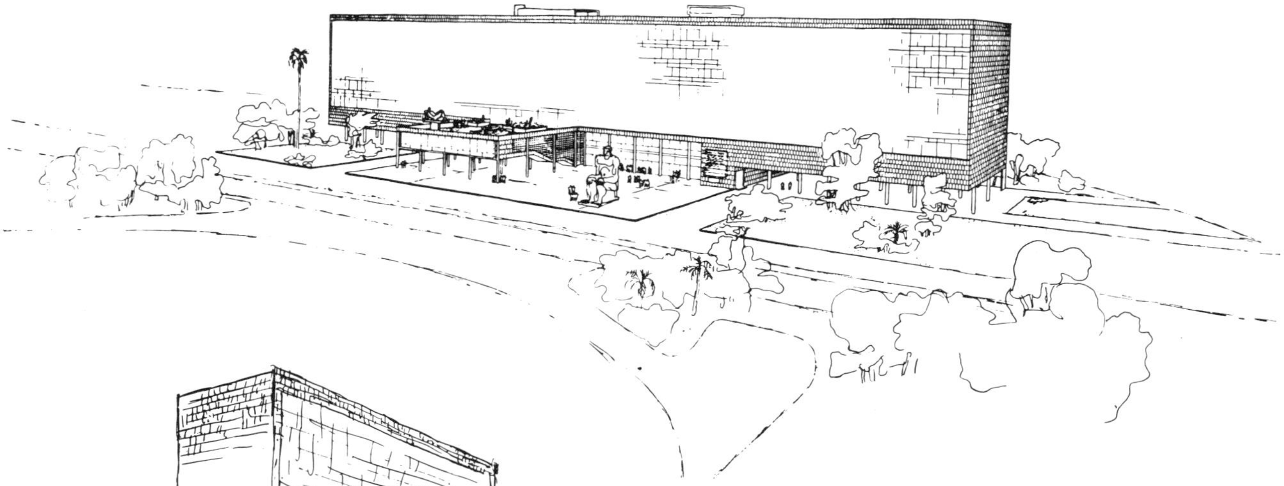

103. Initial project for the Ministry of Education and Health building by Le Corbusier, 1936.

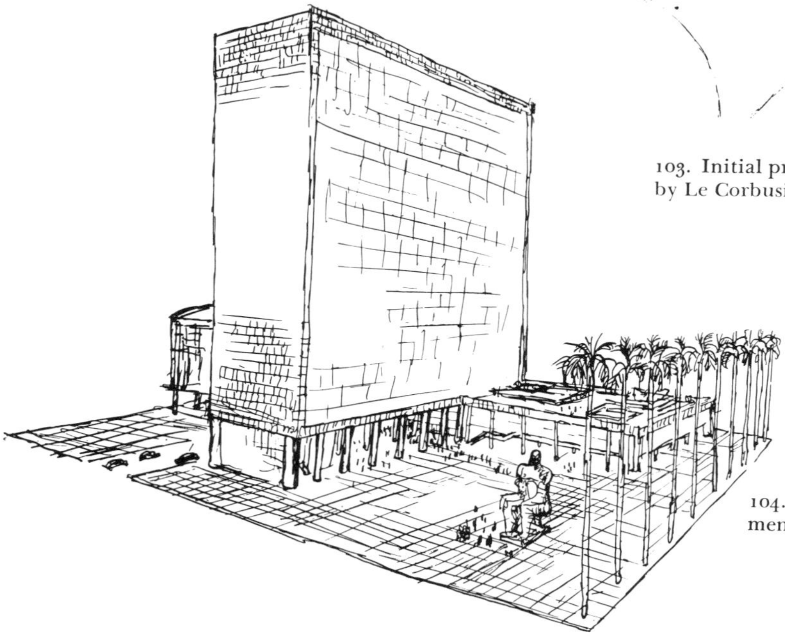

104. Sketch by Le Corbusier showing the definitive development of the Ministry of Education and Health building.

105. Ministry of Education and Health building, north façade, 1937–43.

106. Ministry of Education and Health building, south façade.

107. Ministry of Education and Health building and surrounding buildings.

108. Plaza of the Ministry of Education and Health building with the Barão de Mauá building by Oscar Niemeyer and Sabino Barroso.

109. The church of Candalária and the Banco do Commercio e Industria de São Paulo.

110. Apartments in Flamengo.

111. The ABI building and the National Library.

112. The ABI building, headquarters of the Brazilian Press Association, designed by MMM Roberto.

113. The old urban scale of the central business district is increasingly overshadowed by the new.

114. The Avenida Central building by Henrique Mindlin.

115, 116. Apartment buildings by Lúcio Costa in Eduardo Guinle Park, 1948–54.

117. Apartment building, Eduardo Guinle Park.

118. Apartments in Flamengo.

119. Panorama Palace Hotel in Ipanema, under construction, 1967.

120. Museum of Modern Art in Glória-Flamengo Park by Affonso Reidy, begun in 1954.

121. Residence of Oscar Niemeyer, 1953.

122. Brasília viewed from across a man-made lake.

123. The South Axis of Brasília seen from the television tower.

124. The monumental axis seen from the television tower.

125. The television tower.

126. Second prize was awarded to a collaborative scheme by Ney Gonçalves, Baruch Milman, and João Henrique Rocha.

1. Sport center
2. Transport center
3. Residential district for government employees
4. Government center
5. Housing for officials
6. Commercial center
7. Residential district for commercial and industrial employees
8. Industrial district
9. Military center and air base
10. University

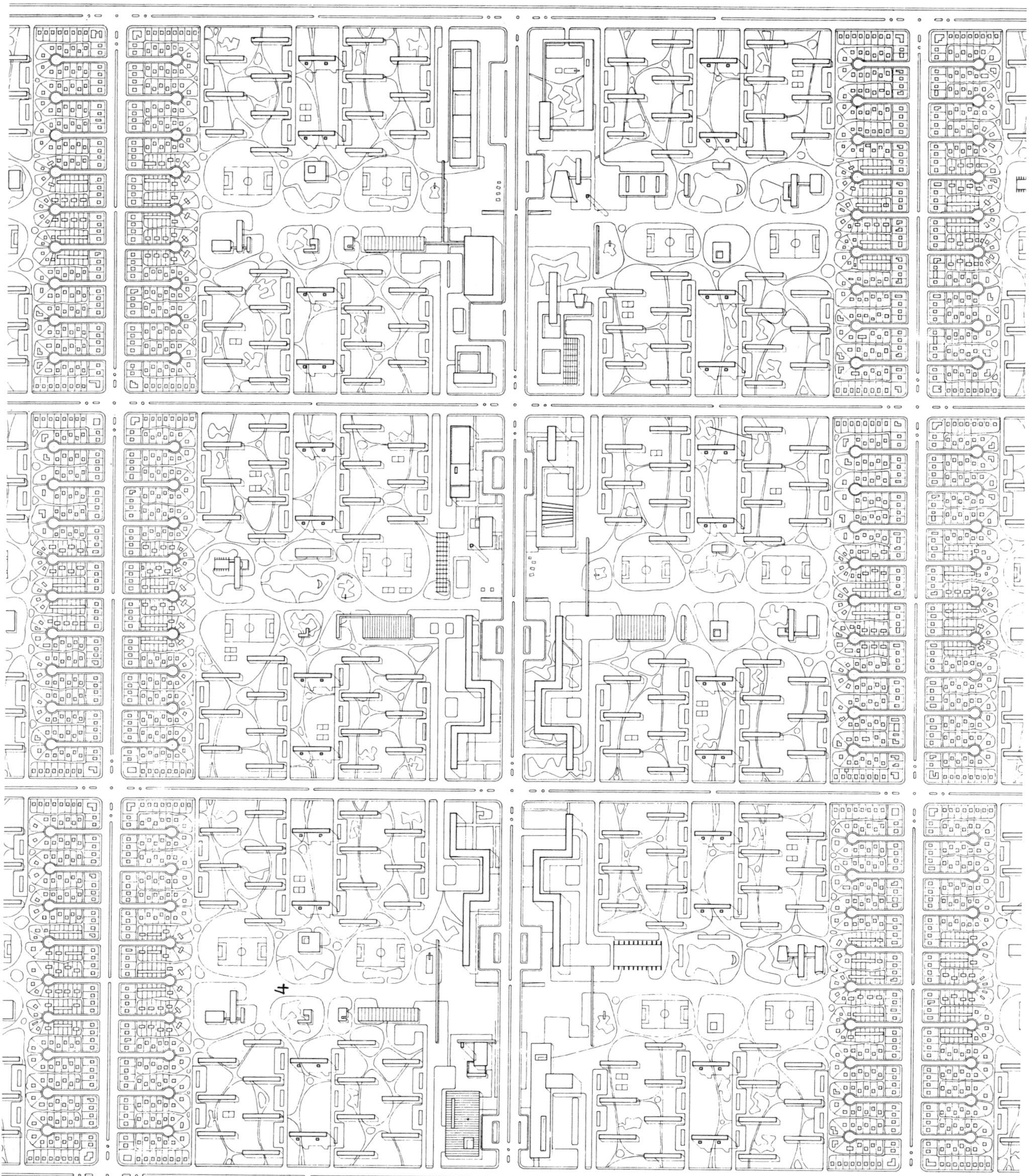

127. Gonçalves, Milman, and Rocha. Residential superblock.

1. Single-family houses
2. Three-story apartments
3. Twelve-story apartments, commercial facilities
4. Schools

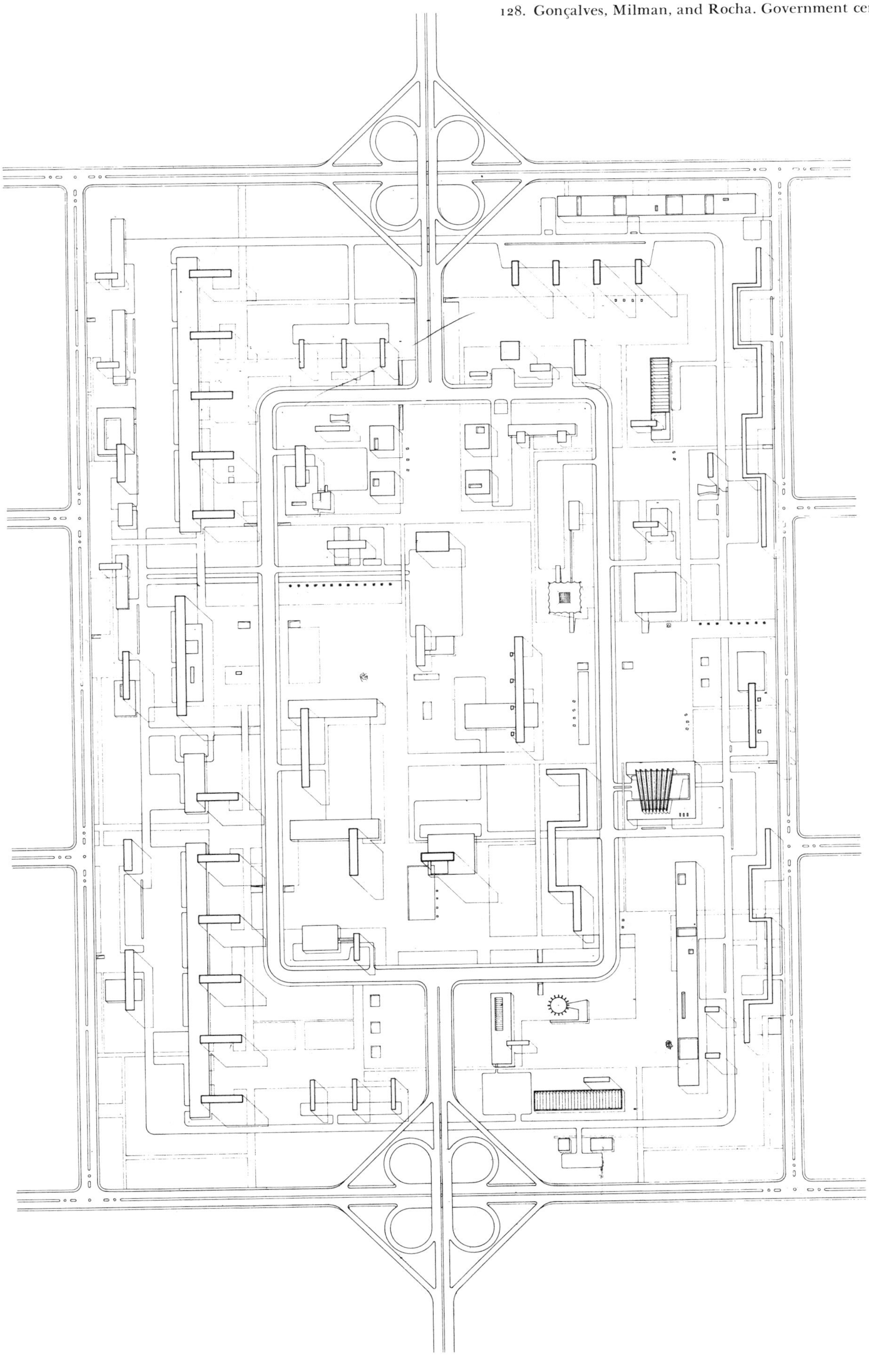

128. Gonçalves, Milman, and Rocha. Government center.

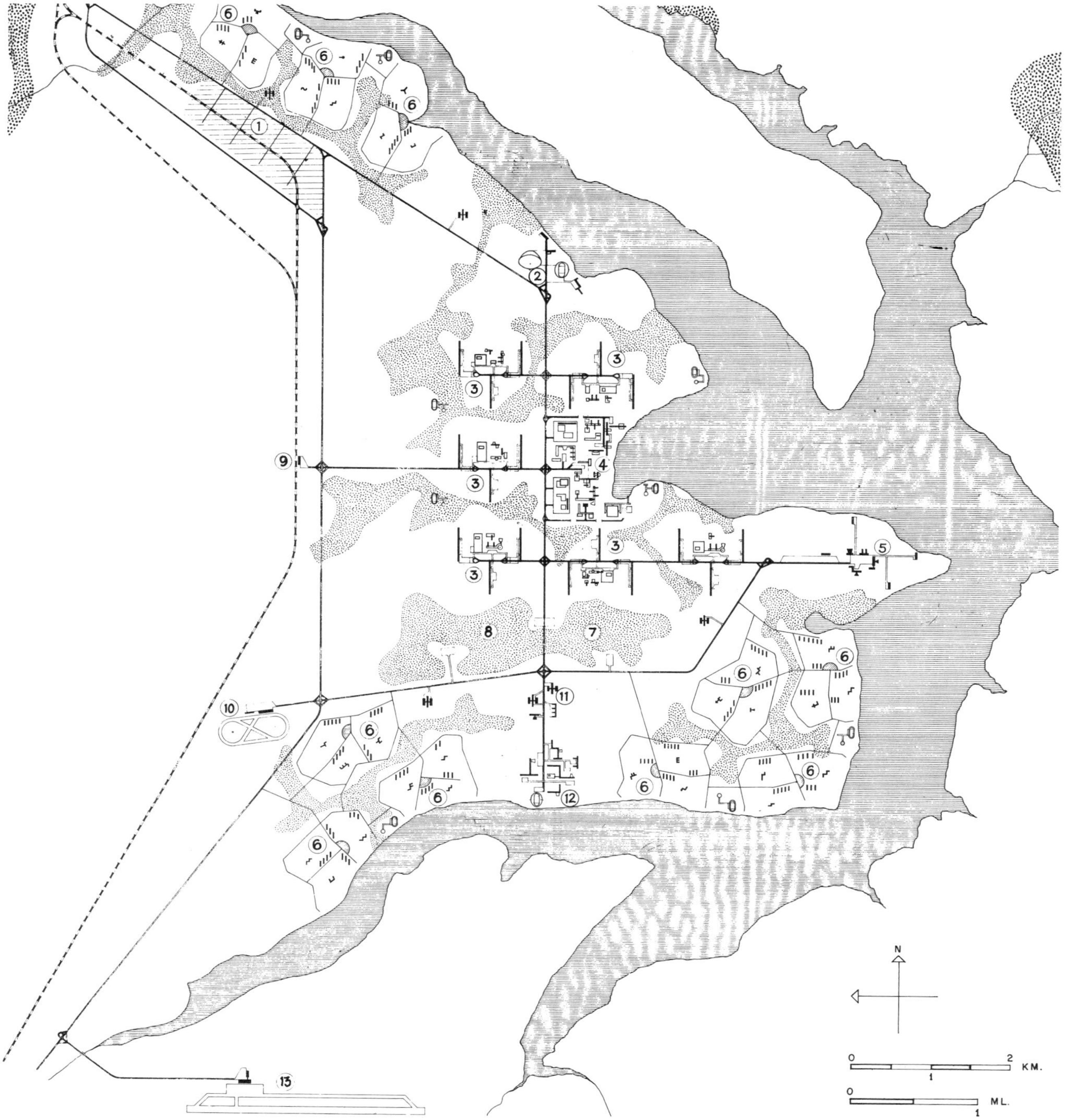

129. A combined third and fourth prize was divided between two entries, one of which was produced by the firm of Rino Levi. Master plan.

1. Industries
2. Sports center
3. Intensive housing
4. City center
5. Federal center (site of the executive, legislative, and judicial powers)
6. Extensive and semi-intensive housing
7. Zoo
8. Botanical garden
9. Railroad station
10. Racetrack
11. Medical center
12. University
13. Airport

130. Firm of Rino Levi. Neighborhood unit. Housing would be in 300-meter high apartment complexes, with neighborhood facilities in an adjacent low-rise center.

131. Firm of Rino Levi. Elevation of apartment housing complex.

A-A Mechanical floor
B-B Internal street
C-C Apartments
D-D Ground floor
E-E Underground parking garage

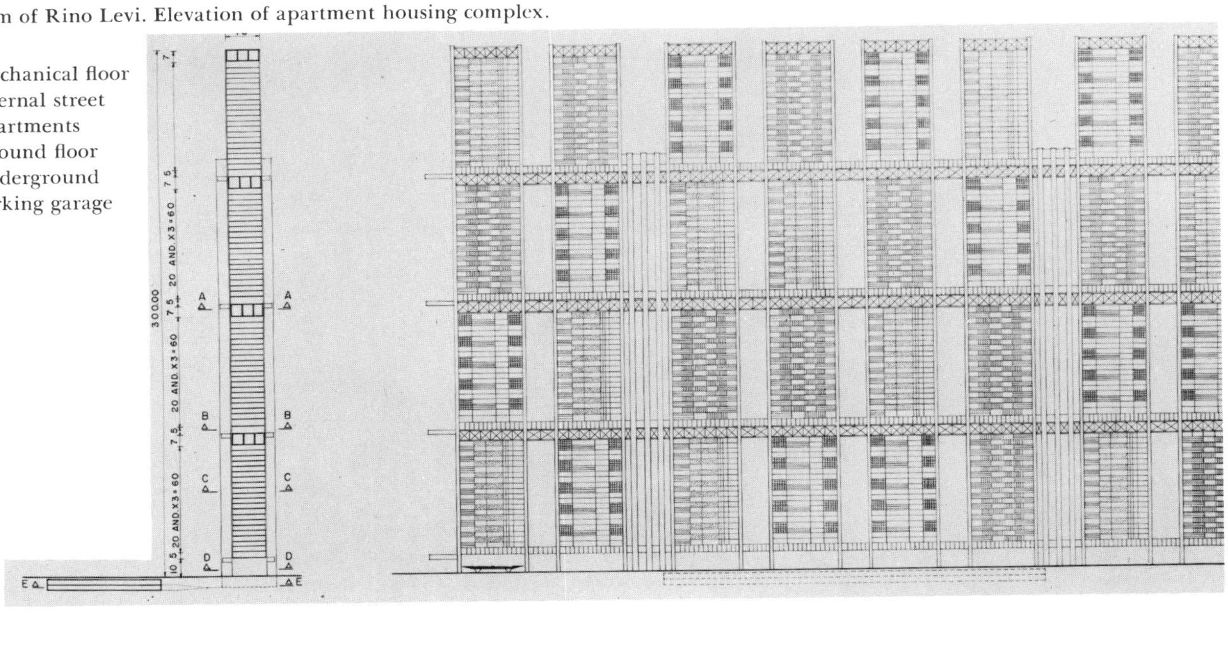

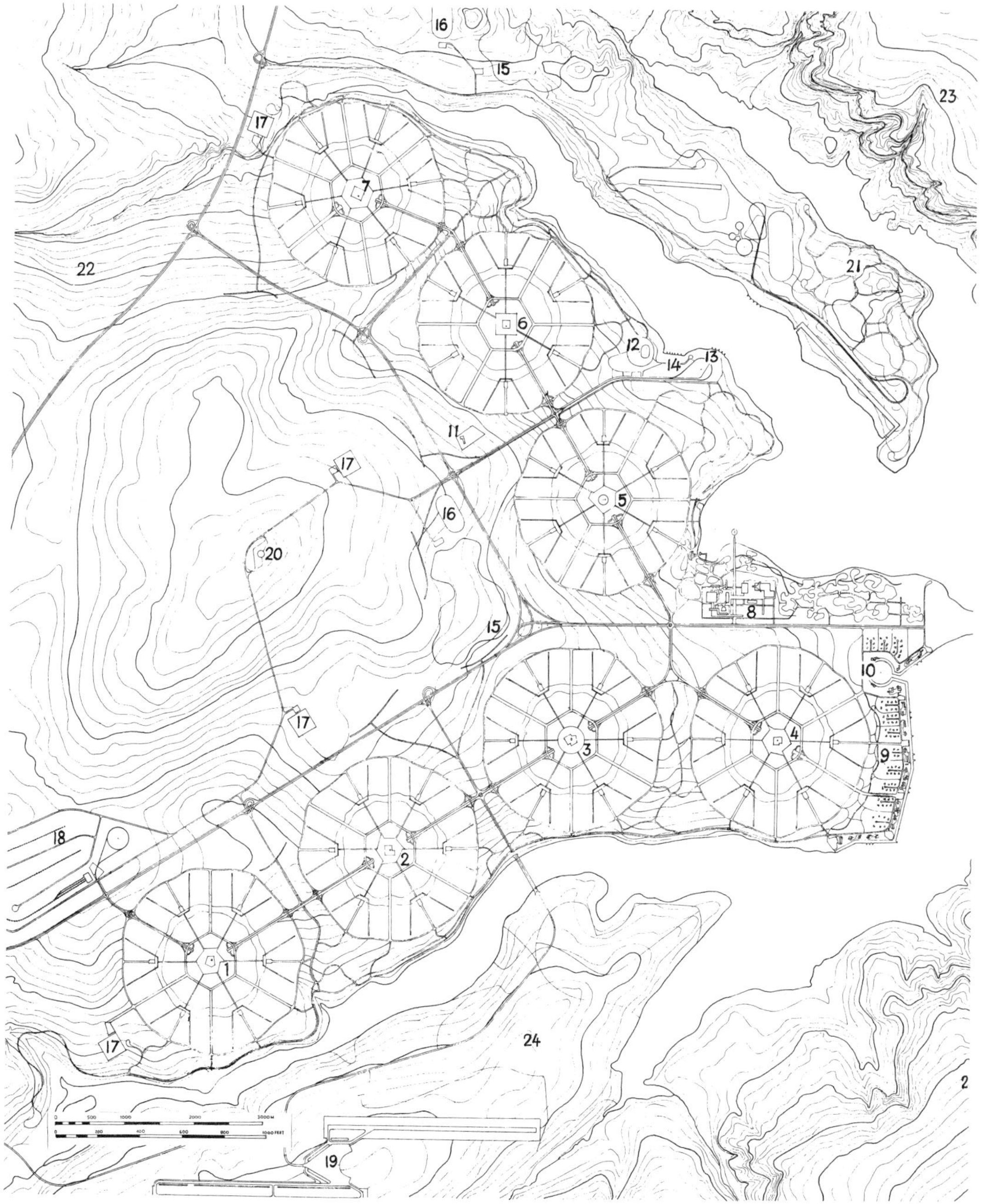

132. Combined third-fourth prize. The master plan submitted by the MMM Roberto firm embodied a division of the city into separate Urban Units containing both housing and employment.

1. Federal District administration
2. Communications
3. Finance
4. The arts
5. Letters and science
6. Social welfare
7. Agriculture and industry
8. Federal Park
9. Embassies, hotels, mansions
10. Yacht clubs
11. Federal hospital
12. Stadium
13. Ferry boat terminal
14. Rowing clubs
15. Golf course
16. Riding academy, polo grounds
17. Cemetery
18. Railroad and highway terminal, freight yards, warehouses, cold storage plants, construction materials storage areas, fuel tanks, grain elevators and mills, sawmill, stockyards, ready-mixed and precast concrete plants
19. Airport
20. Belvedere (highest elevation): restaurant, radio and television transmitters
21. Peninsula park (racetrack, amusement park, arena, exhibition halls, flying club, zoo and botanical garden, boat-racing course)
22. Parks, reserved areas
23. Forests
24. Croplands

133. Firm of MMM Roberto. Government center.

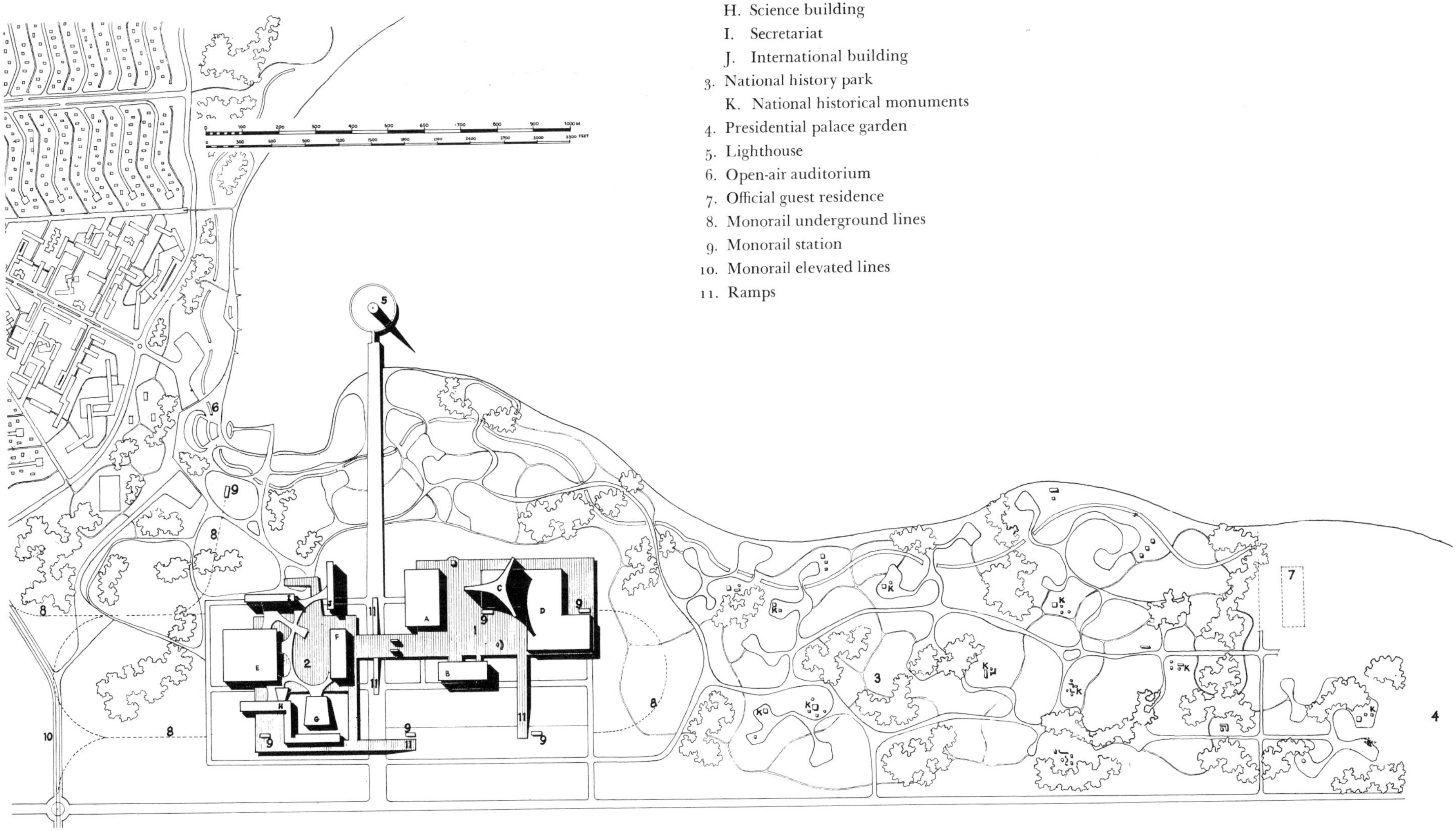

1. Government square
   - A. Legislative building
   - B. Judiciary building
   - C. Executive building
   - D. Economy, labor, and defense buildings
2. Culture square
   - E. National gallery and museum
   - F. Library
   - G. Theater
   - H. Science building
   - I. Secretariat
   - J. International building
3. National history park
   - K. National historical monuments
4. Presidential palace garden
5. Lighthouse
6. Open-air auditorium
7. Official guest residence
8. Monorail underground lines
9. Monorail station
10. Monorail elevated lines
11. Ramps

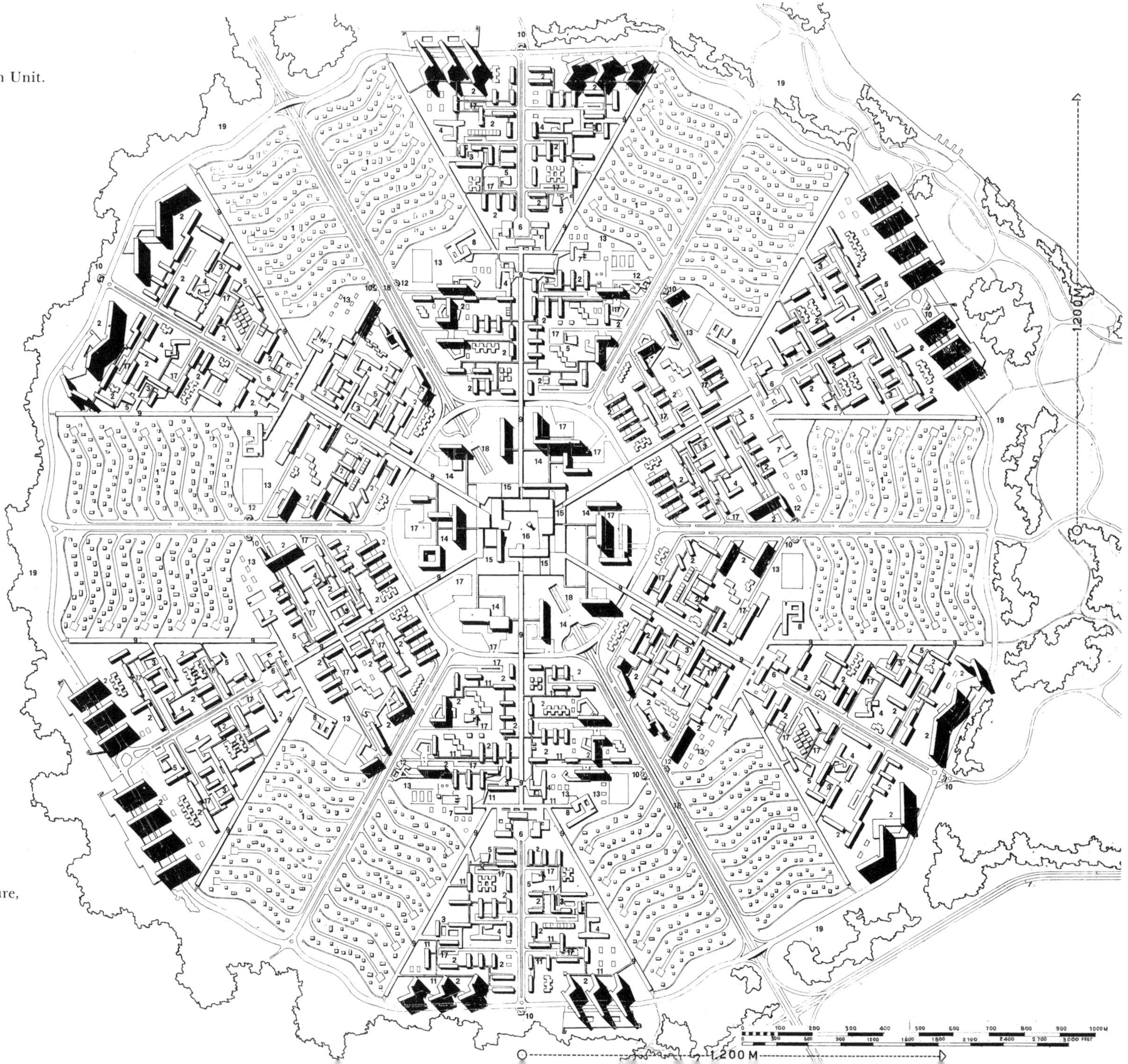

134. Firm of MMM Roberto. Urban Unit.

1. Single houses
2. Apartments
3. Neighborhood center
4. Primary school
5. Church
6. Sector center
7. Club
8. Secondary school
9. Covered way and conveyer
10. Gas station
11. Covered way
12. Auto repair shop and gas station
13. Playing fields and playgrounds
14. Administration, professions, culture, assistance, services
15. Shopping and amusement
16. Unit square
17. Parking area
18. Rapid transit
19. Park and woods

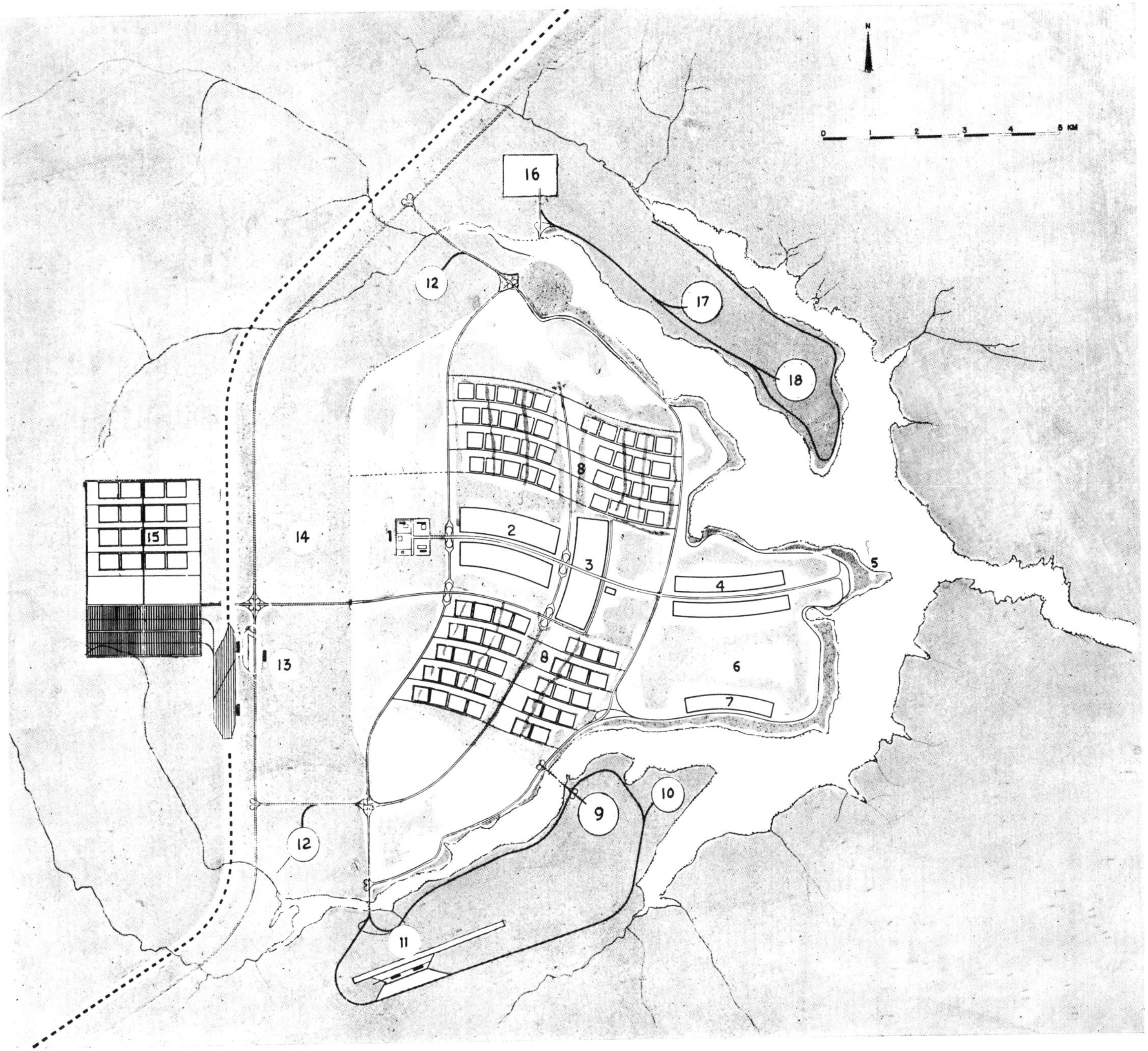

135. Three fifth prizes were awarded, one of them to the scheme of Henrique Mindlin and Giancarlo Palanti.

1. Government center
2. Ministries
3. Civic and commercial center
4. Embassies and legations
5. Presidential palace
6. Park, botanical garden, zoo
7. Large residences
8. Residential zone
9. Sport center
10. Water sports
11. Airport
12. Cemetery
13. Bus and railroad station
14. Forest reserve
15. Industrial zone
16. Military zone
17. University
18. Hospital zone

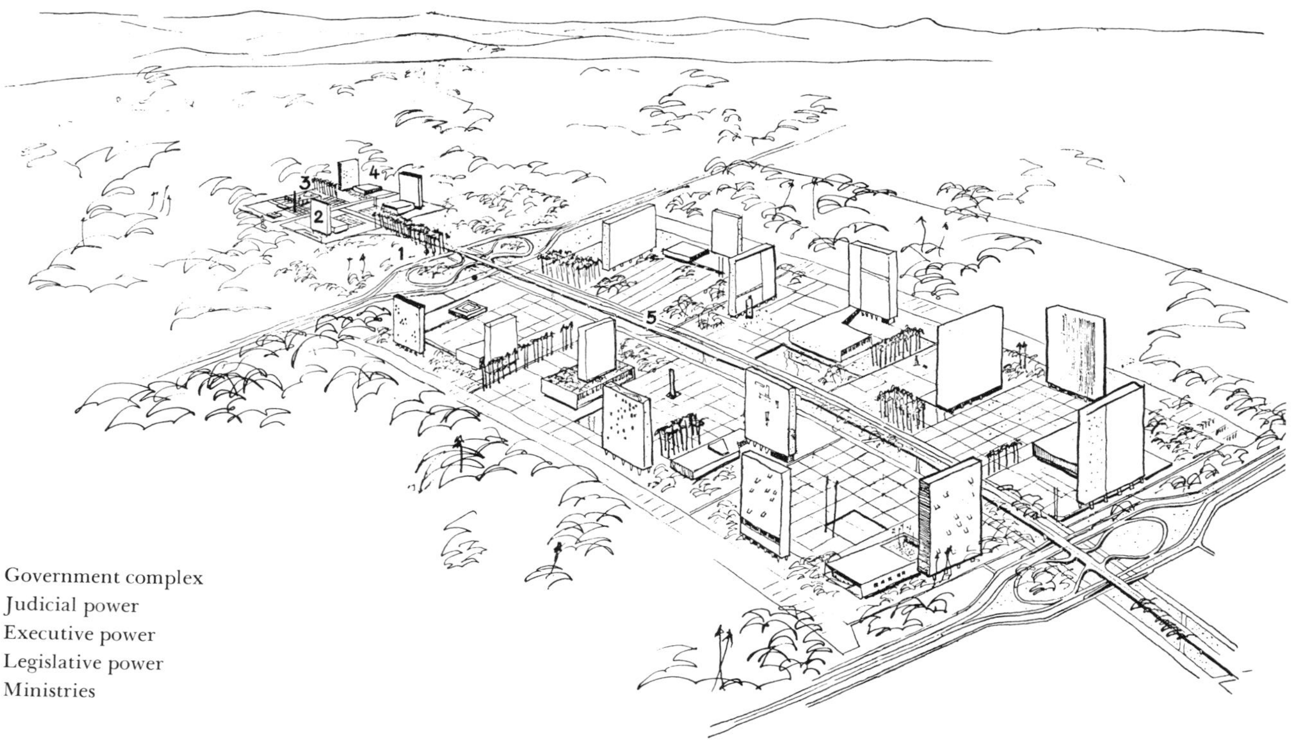

1. Government complex
2. Judicial power
3. Executive power
4. Legislative power
5. Ministries

136. **Mindlin and Palanti.** Government center.

137, 138. **Mindlin and Palanti.** Central business district.

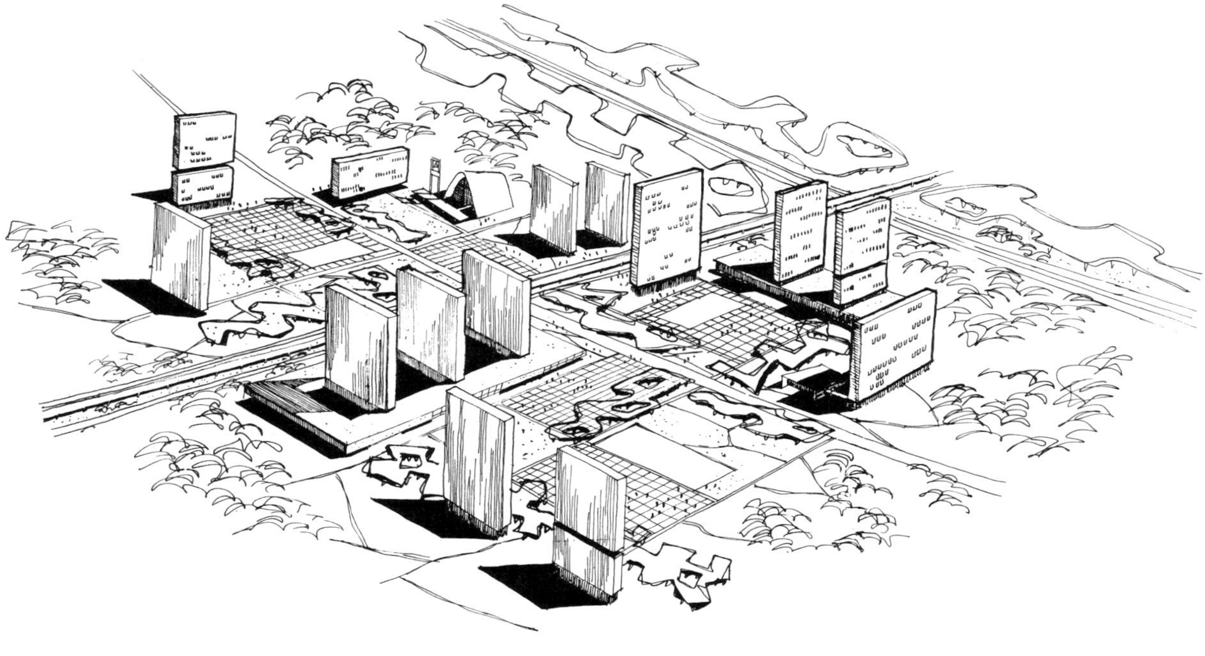

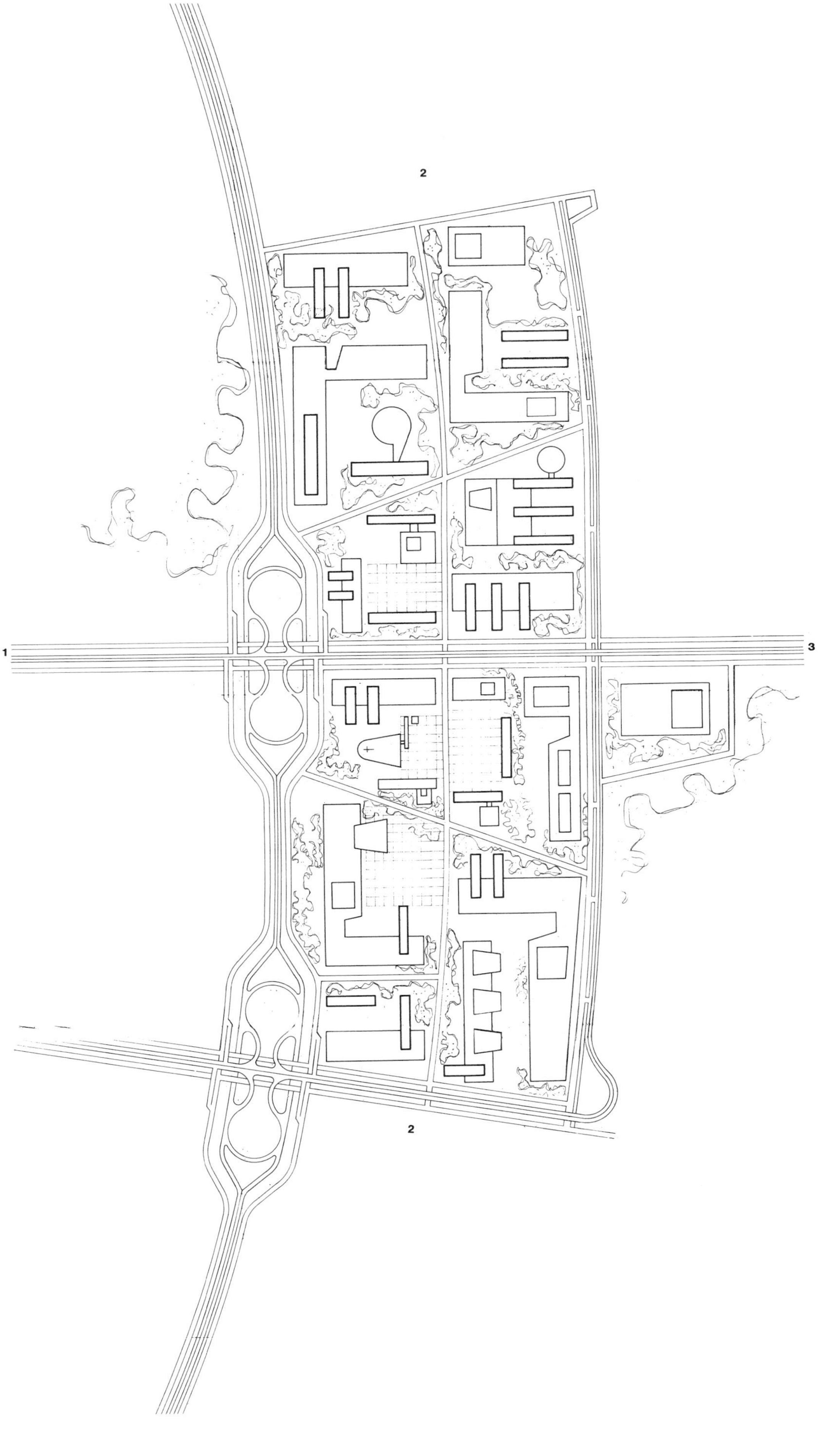

1. Ministries
2. Residential zone
3. Embassies

1. Apartment housing
2. Industrial zone housing
3. Industrial district
4. Residential superblocks (low-rise)
5. Government center
6. Commercial center
7. University
8. National park
9. Agricultural warehouses

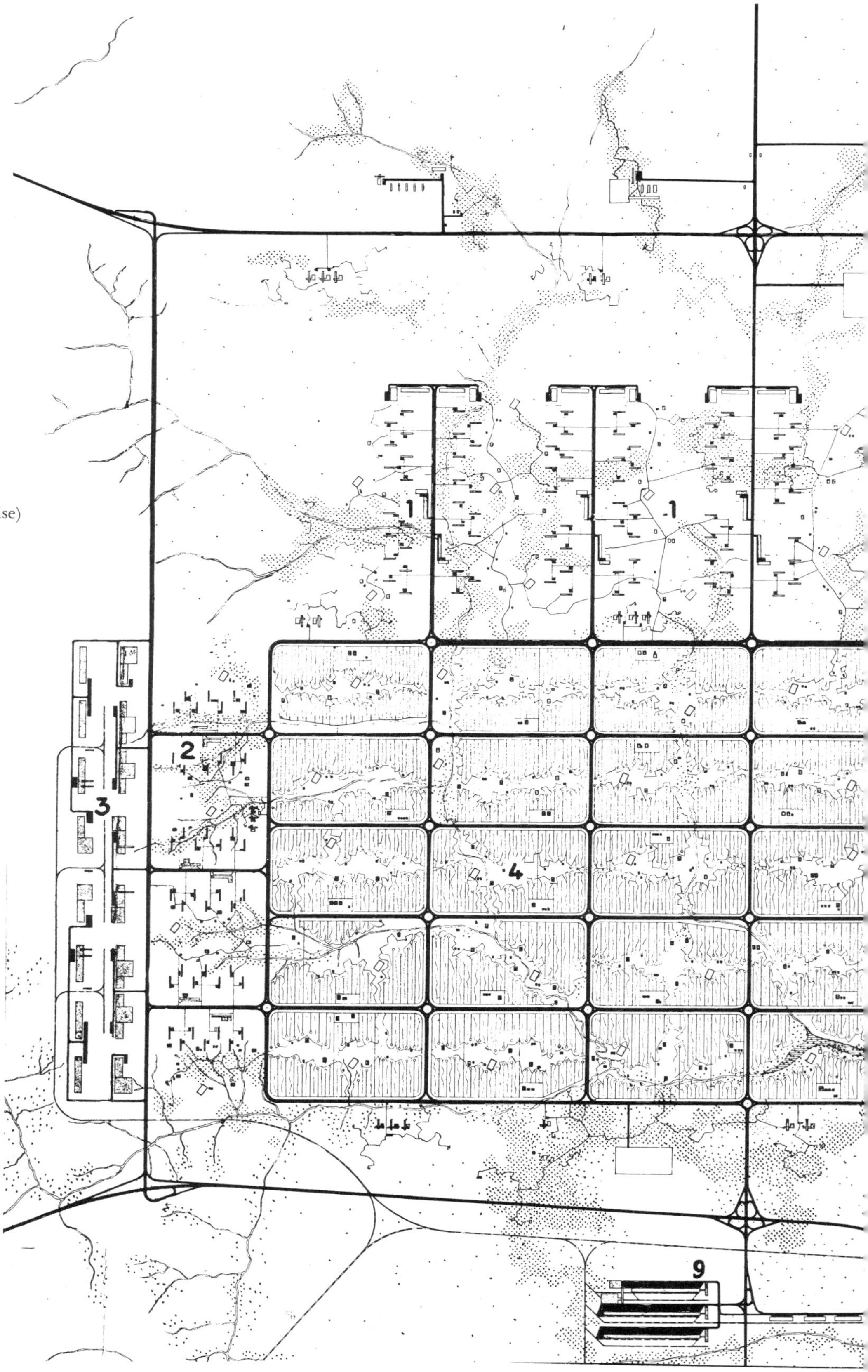

139. Fifth prize. Master plan produced by Carlos Cascaldi, João Villanova Artigas, Mario Wagner Vieira da Cunha, and Paulo de Camargo e Almeida.

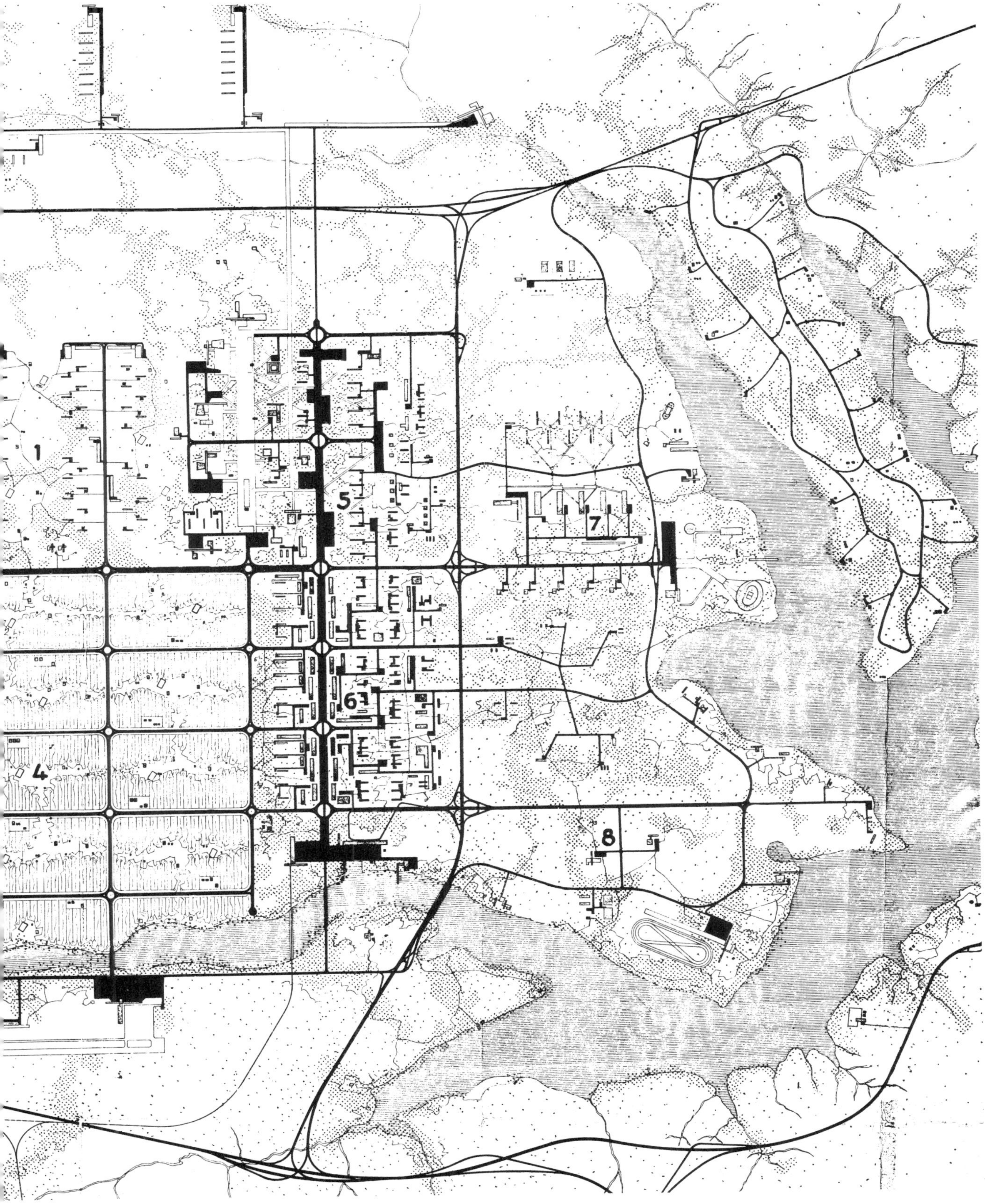
1
5
7
6
4
8

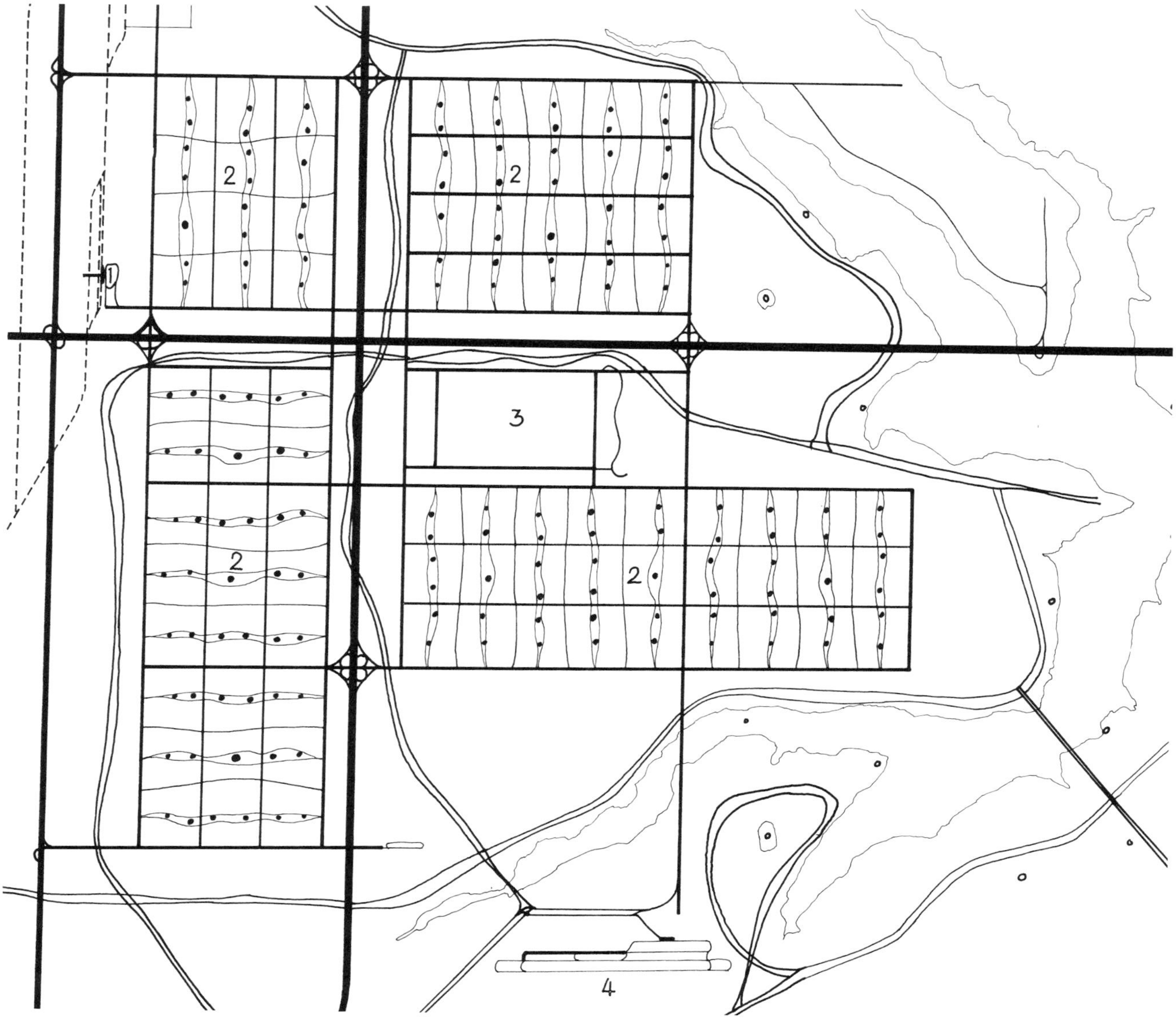

140. Fifth prize. Master plan produced by the Construtécnica group.

1. Railroad station
2. Residential superblocks
3. Civic and commercial center
4. Airport

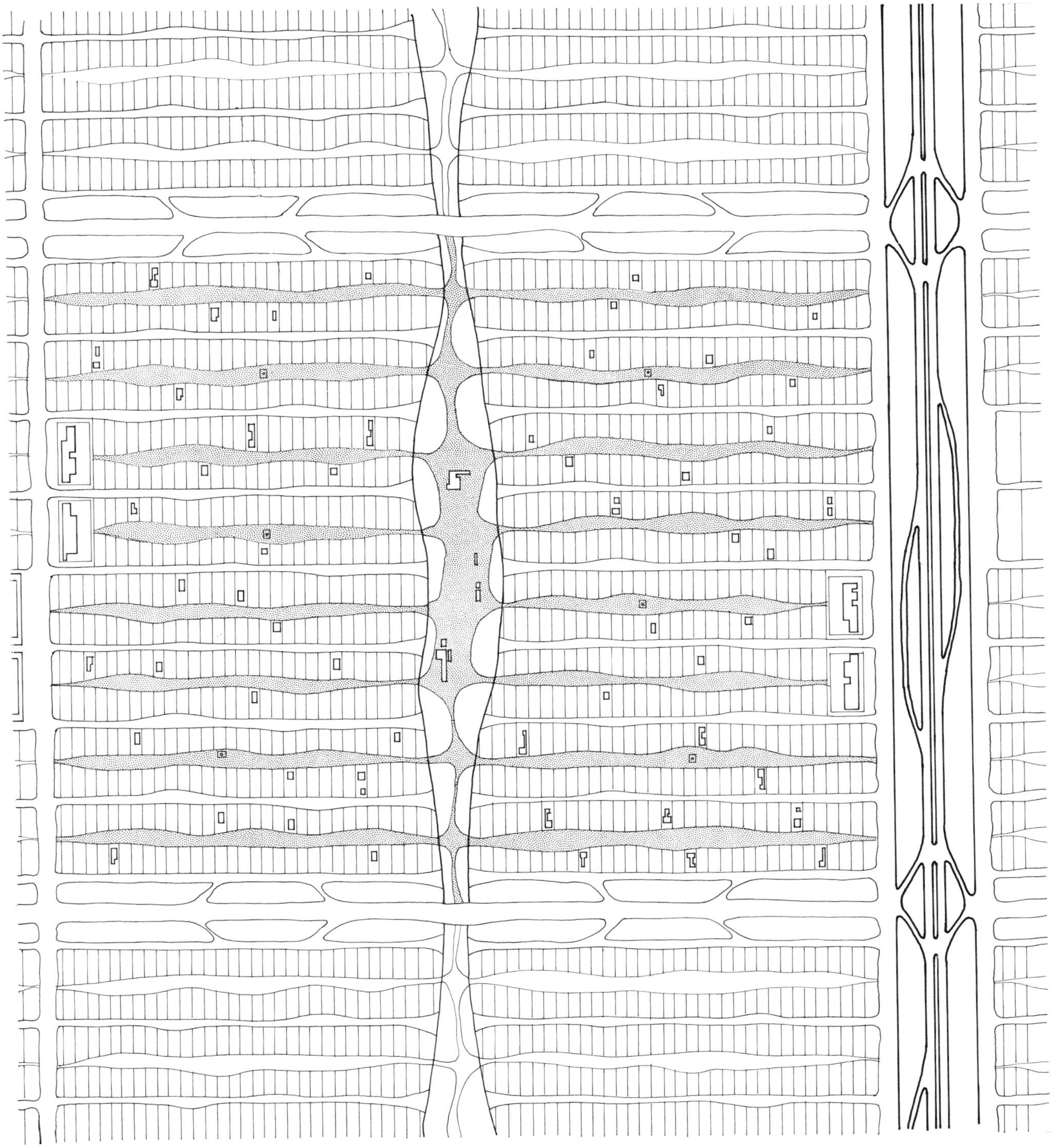

141. Construtécnica group. Residential superblocks.

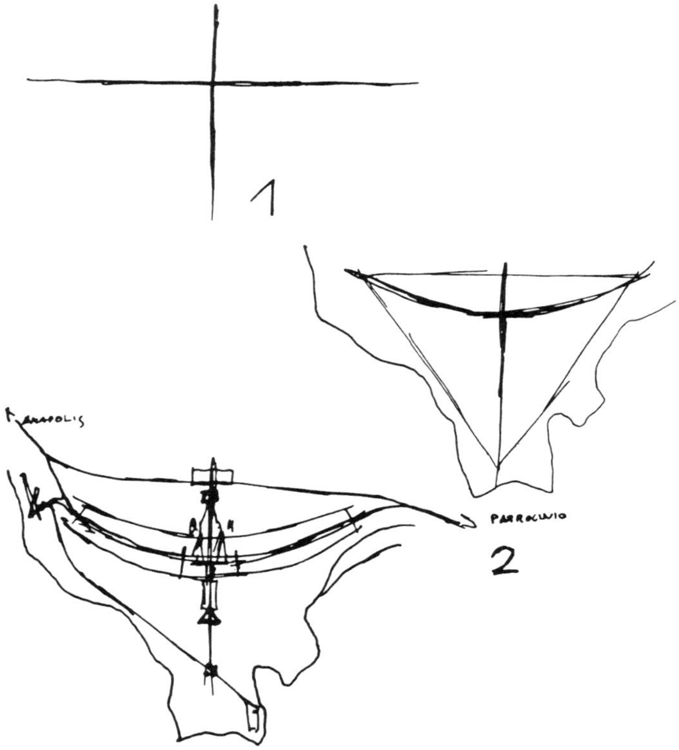

142. Competition sketches submitted by Lúcio Costa in 1956. The city was conceived in terms of two intersecting axes, one a motor freeway lined with residential superblocks, the other a monumental axis carrying the major government buildings.

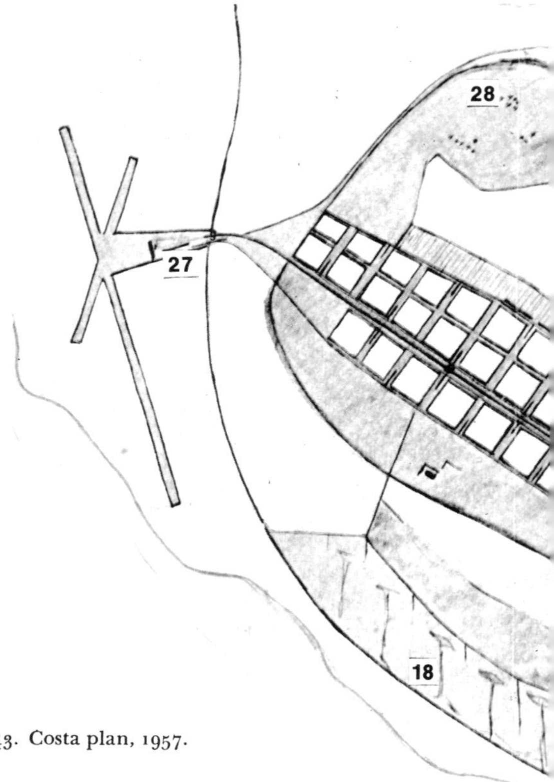

143. Costa plan, 1957.

1. Plaza of the Three Powers
2. Ministries
3. Cathedral
4. Cultural district
5. Amusement center
6. Banking center
7. Business district
8. Hotels
9. Television tower
10. Sports center
11. Municipal square
12. Barracks
13. Railroad station
14. Assembly plants and light industry
15. University
16. Embassies and legations
17. Residential zone
18. Single-family housing
19. Horticulture, floriculture, tree nursery
20. Botanical garden
21. Zoo
22. Golf club
23. Yacht club
24. Presidential residence
25. Jockey club
26. Area zoned for fairs, circuses, etc.
27. Airport
28. Cemetery

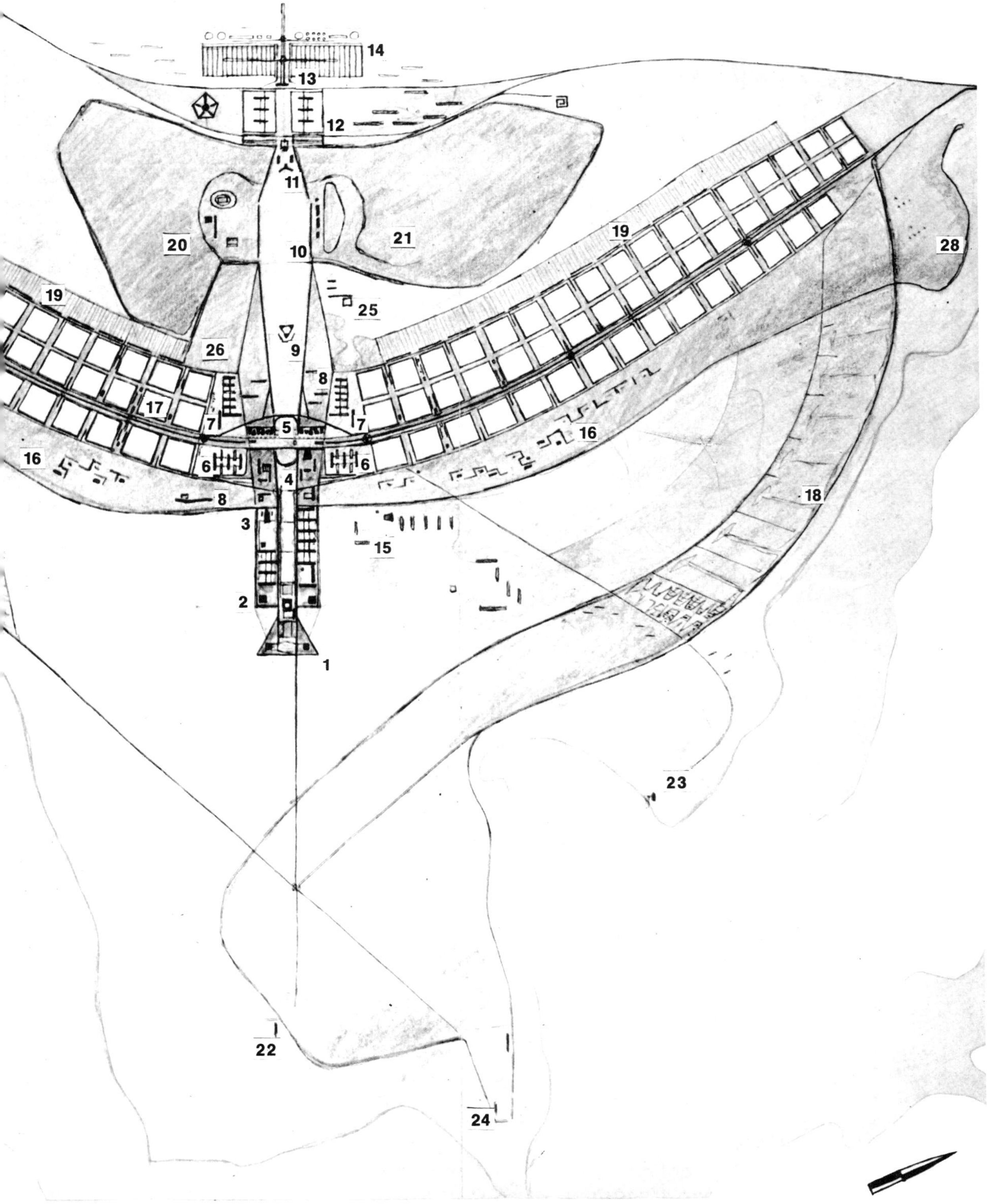
14
13
12
11
10
20
21
19
25
26
9
8
17
7
7
5
16
6
6
16
4
8
3
15
18
28
2
1
23
22
24

144. Plan of Brasília showing pilot plan area and immediate surroundings as projected in 1967.

1. Suburban lots
2. Núcleo Bandierante (Pioneer Center)
3. Airport
4. Motor axis (Eixo Rodoviário)
5. Residential superblocks
6. Row houses
7. Institutional use
8. Cemetery
9. Industrial district
10. Railroad station
11. Warehouses
12. Low-cost housing
13. Military center
14. Meteorological observatory
15. National press
16. Sports center
17. Hall of Justice
18. Municipal square
19. Municipal prefecture
20. Water treatment station
21. Jockey club
22. Television tower
23. Military college
24. Business district
25. Hotels
26. Banking center
27. Veterinary hospital
28. Isolation hospital
29. Penitentiary
30. Embassies
31. Ministries
32. Plaza of the Three Powers
33. Clubs
34. Hotel
35. Alvorada Palace (presidential residence)
36. Brasília Palace Hotel
37. Hilton Hotel
38. House lots
39. University
40. Sports and clubs
41. House plots
42. Large single-family houses
43. Monastery
44. Paranôa dam

9
10
11
12
13
27
28
29
8
14
8
6
7
15
17
19
20
18
6
7
4
16
21
4
6
23
6
22
5
5
25
24
40
30
26
39
38
31
41
32
42
37
33
36
34
41
35
41
43
44

145. Freeway axis (Eixo Rodoviário).

146, 147. City for Three Million designed by Le Corbusier in 1922. The urban image of Brasília, with its uniform-height apartment blocks and wide motor axis, is reminiscent of Le Corbusier's early visionary schemes.

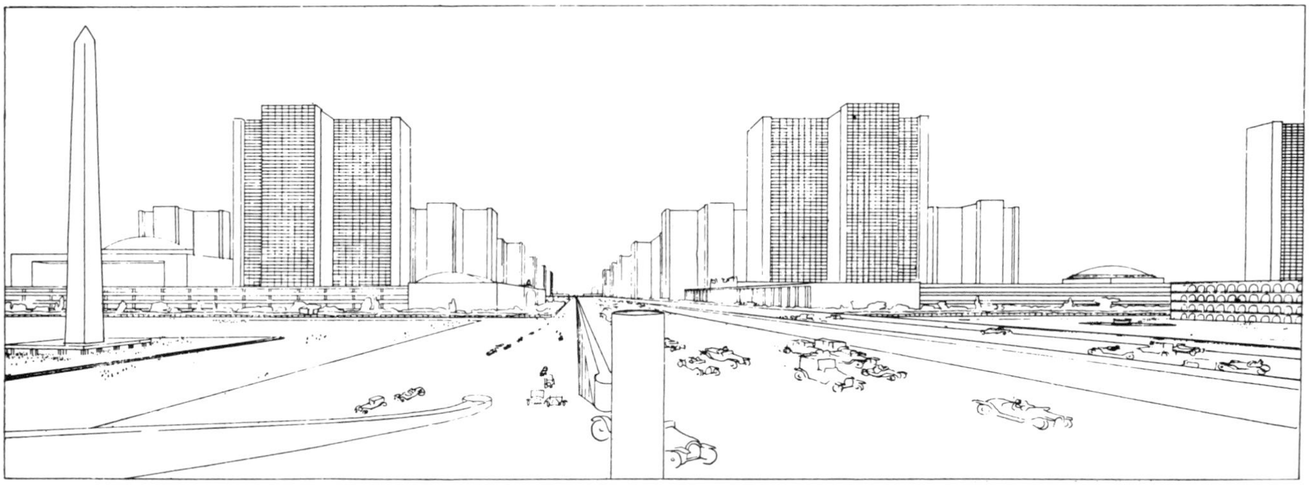

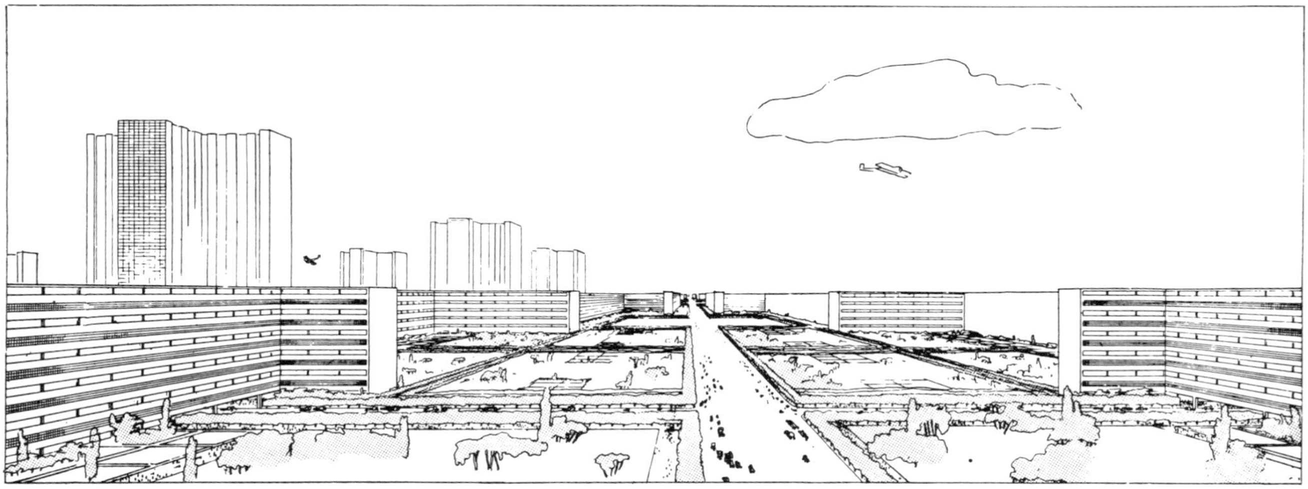

148. Neighborhood shopping street at point of intersection with freeway axis.

149. Traffic interchange marking the intersection of the major axes of Brasília.

150. Traffic center with National Theater.

151. Bus terminal on lower level of traffic center.

152. Looking toward the North Axis from the top of the interchange platform.

153. The W-3 street paralleling the main motor axis. Row houses at left. Commercial building at right.

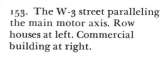

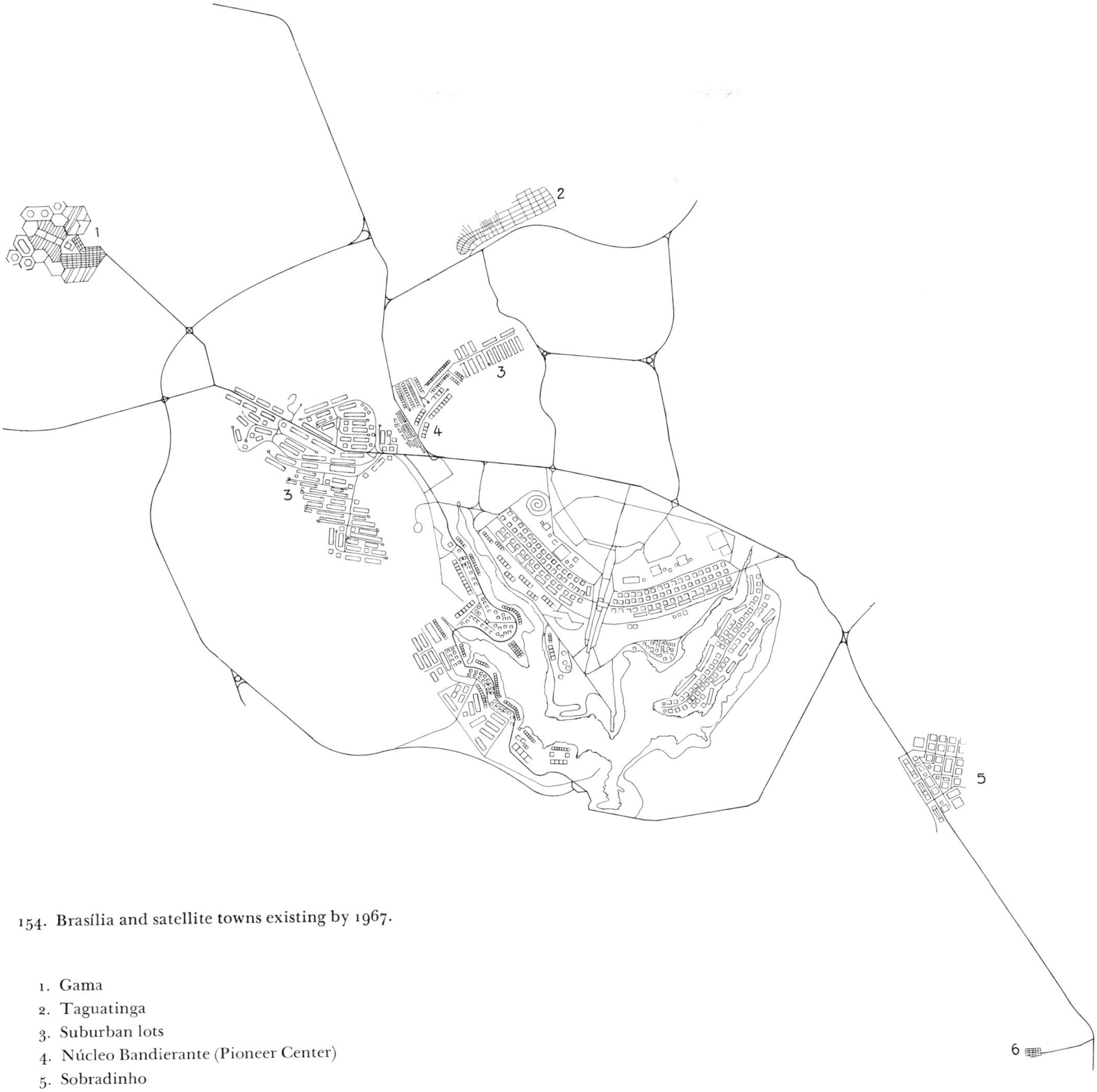

154. Brasília and satellite towns existing by 1967.

1. Gama
2. Taguatinga
3. Suburban lots
4. Núcleo Bandierante (Pioneer Center)
5. Sobradinho
6. Planaltina

155–58. Núcleo Bandierante (Pioneer Center). Initially called Cidade Livre (Free Town), this settlement was rechristened and made a permanent satellite in 1961.

159–62. Taguatinga, the largest of the Brasília satellites, was founded in 1958.

163, 164. Low-cost housing constructed outside Taguatinga by SHIS (Sociedade de Habitações de Interesse Sócial).

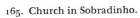

165. Church in Sobradinho.

166. Open-air market in Sobradinho.

167. Planaltina, an already existing town near Brasília, is being redeveloped as a satellite.

168. House in Planaltina.

169. Plan of a portion of the residential axis.

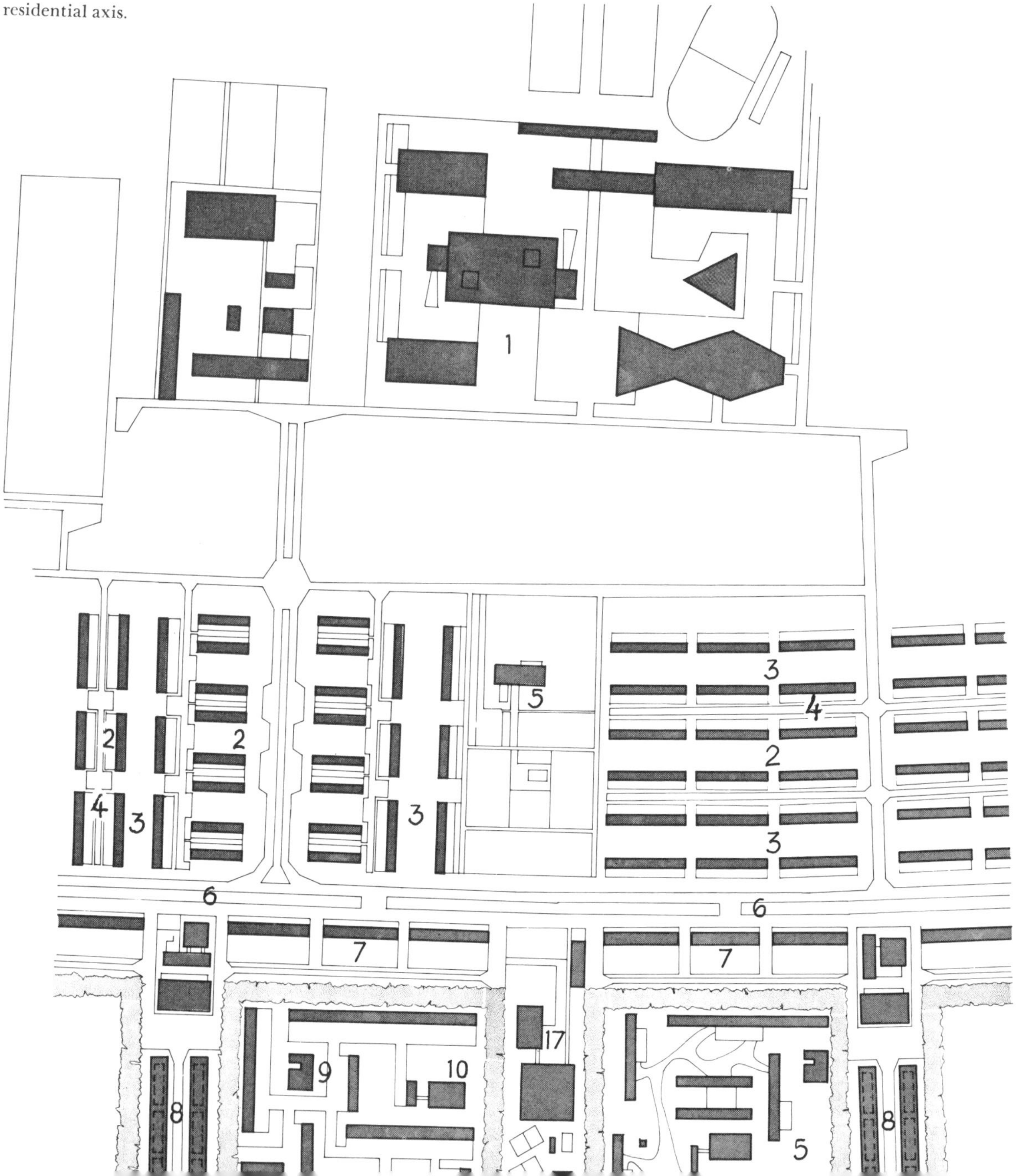

1. Institutional use
2. Row houses
3. Park
4. Service lane
5. School
6. W-3 Street
7. Commerce
8. Shops
9. Nursery school
10. Elementary school
11. Six-story apartments
12. Church
13. Cinema
14. Motor axis
15. Superblock
16. Three-story apartments
17. School park

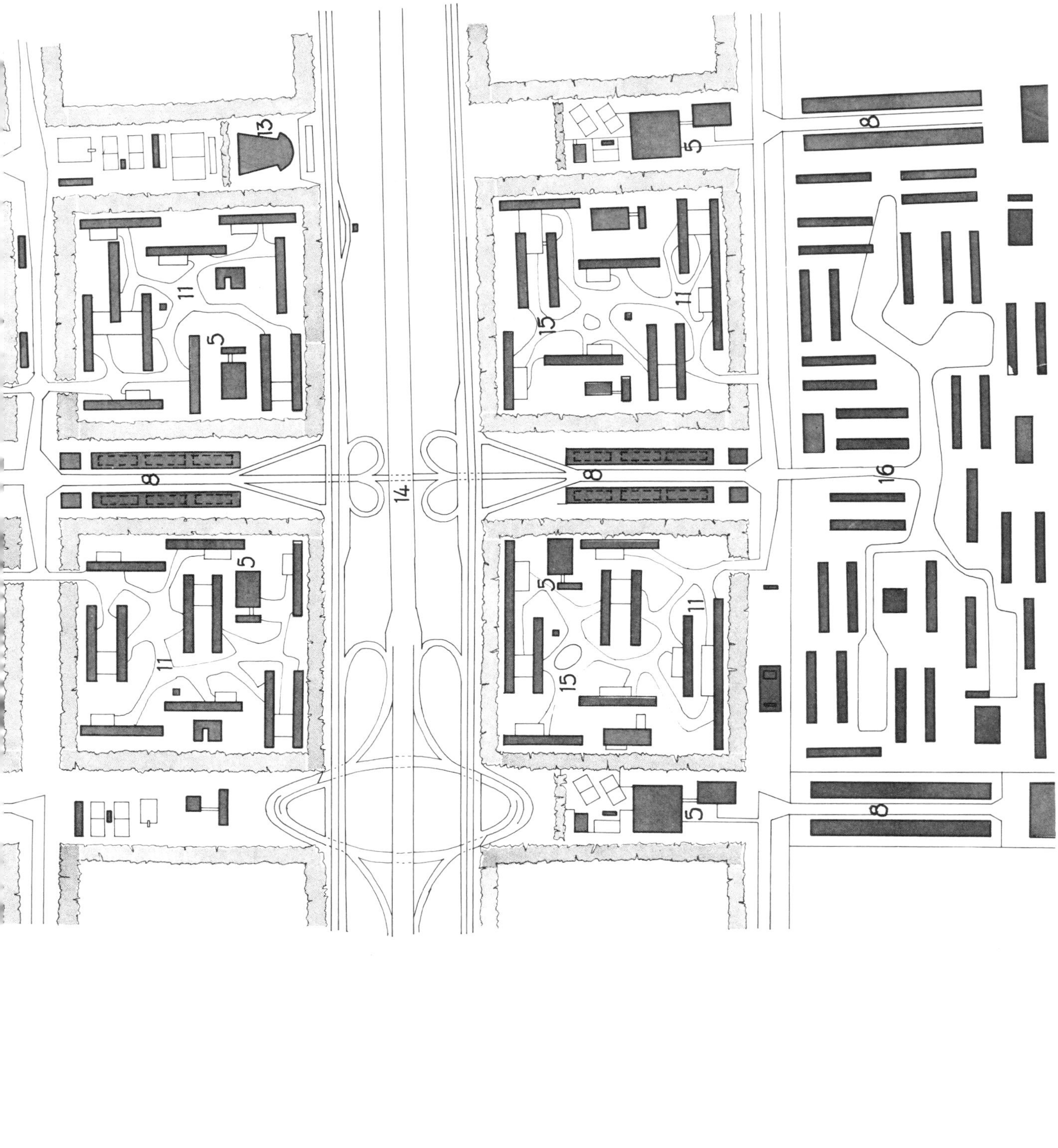
13
8
5
11
15
14
16

170. Residential superblocks.

171. Apartment blocks seen from the motor freeway.

172

173

174

175

172–78. Residential superblocks.

176

177

178

179, 180. Although much of the earlier housing of Brasília reflects the aesthetic of the International Style, some variation in the architectural pattern appears in more recent housing in the North Axis.

181, 182. Apartments for employees of the Brazilian Foreign Office in the North Axis, under construction.

183–85. Three-story blocks contain relatively low-cost apartments in Brasília.

186. Row houses designed by Oscar Niemeyer for the National Savings Bank. Such houses are designed to face bands of parkland, with automobile access by means of rear service lanes.

187

188

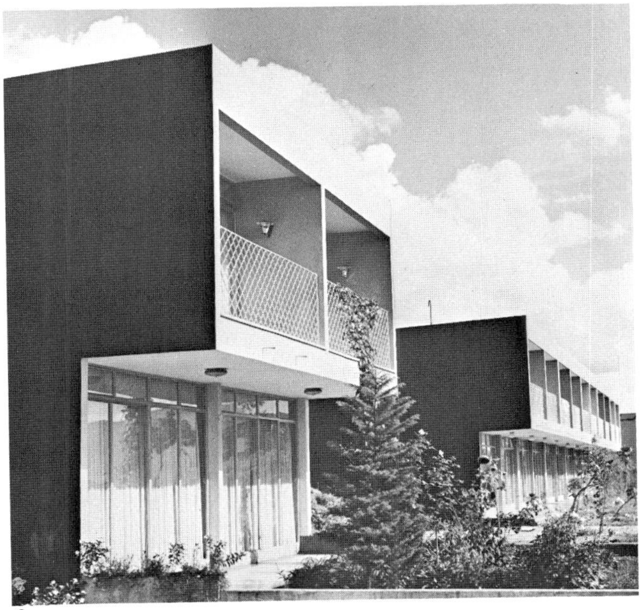

189

190

187–91. Row houses.

192. House in the peninsula district.

191

193. Low-cost housing in the industrial area of Brasília.

194, 195. Wooden buildings in the North Axis.

196, 197. Primary schools within the superblock areas.

198. School park designed to accommodate special studies for primary pupils.

199. Shop on the W-3.

200. Neighborhood shops.

201. Pushcart peddlers.

202. Central business district seen from the television tower. Hotels and W-3 in foreground.

203. Banking center. Bank of Brazil at right. Credit Bank of the Amazon at left.

204. Banking center. Seguradores Building and National Bank of Economic Development.

205, 206. Bank of Brazil.

207. Banking center, looking toward the central business district.

208

209

208–10. Central business district.

210

211. Commercial building on W-3. Banking center and government axis in distance.

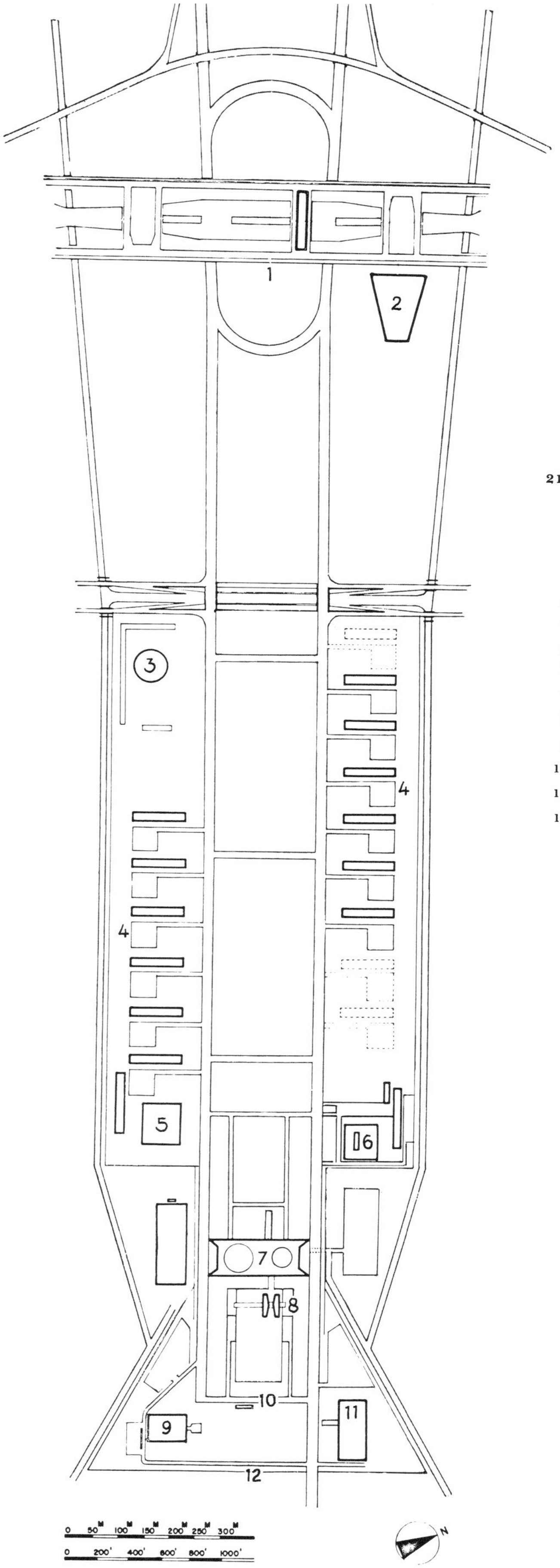

212. Plan of the monumental axis.

1. Interchange
2. National Theater
3. Cathedral
4. Ministries
5. Itamarity Palace (Foreign Office)
6. Treasury
7. National Legislature
8. Secretariat
9. Supreme Court
10. Museum
11. Palace of the Planalto
12. Plaza of the Three Powers

213. The mall.

214. Government ministries.

215, 216. The National Theater, under construction.

217, 218. The cathedral, under construction.

219–22. The visual focus of the monumental axis is provided by the National Legislature and its adjacent high-rise Secretariat. The Senate chamber and Hall of Deputies are expressed sculpturally through the forms of a shallow dome and a bowllike inverted dome.

223. Secretariat and dome of the Senate.

224. Secretariat and Plaza of the Three Powers. Supreme Court at left.

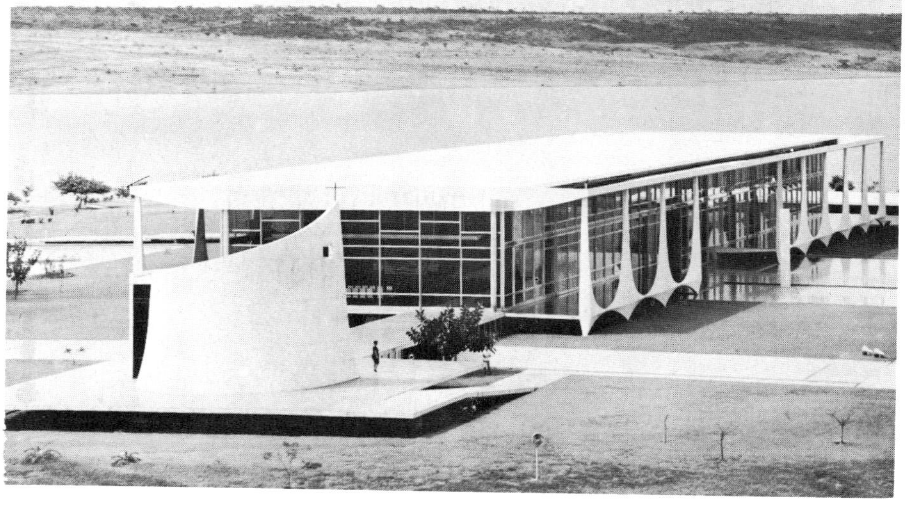

225. Alvorada Palace (Palace of the Dawn), the presidential residence.

226. Plaza of the Three Powers. Sculpture of "The Warriors" seen against the Palace of the Planalto housing the executive offices.

227. Palace of the Planalto, entrance façade.

228. Palace of the Planalto, garden façade.

229. Supreme Court.

230. Supreme Court and statue of Justice.

231. Secretariat seen from the Supreme Court.

232. Plaza of the Three Powers. Dovecote in foreground. Museum of Brasília and Secretariat in distance.

233. Museum of Brasília with sculpted head of Juscelino Kubitschek.

234–36. The Itamarity Palace, housing the Brazilian Foreign Office and dedicated in 1967, provides a variation on the architectural theme established by Niemeyer's earlier monumental building.

237. Banking center seen from the monumental axis.

238. Rio viewed from Corcovado.

239. Brasília. Monumental axis seen from the base of the television tower.